Lecture Notes in Computer Sci

Commenced Publication in 1973
Founding and Former Series Editors:
Gerhard Goos, Juris Hartmanis, and Jan van Leeuwen

Editorial Board

Sebastian Maneth (Ed.)

Implementation and Application of Automata

14th International Conference, CIAA 2009
Sydney, Australia, July 14-17, 2009
Proceedings

 Springer

Volume Editor

Sebastian Maneth
NICTA and University of New South Wales
Sydney, Australia
E-mail: sebastian.maneth@nicta.com.au

Library of Congress Control Number: Applied for

CR Subject Classification (1998): F.1, F.4, F.2, D.2

LNCS Sublibrary: SL 1 – Theoretical Computer Science and General Issues

ISSN 0302-9743

ISBN 978-3-642-02978-3 Springer Berlin Heidelberg New York

springer.com

© Springer-Verlag Berlin Heidelberg 2009

Typesetting: Camera-ready by author, data conversion by Scientific Publishing Services, Chennai, India
Printed on acid-free paper   SPIN: 12715176   06/3180   5 4 3 2 1 0

Preface

The 14th International Conference on Implementation and Application of Automata (CIAA 2009) was held in NICTA's Neville Roach Laboratory at the University of New South Wales, Sydney, Australia during July 14–17, 2009.

This volume of *Lecture Notes in Computer Science* contains the papers that were presented at CIAA 2009, as well as abstracts of the posters and short papers that were presented at the conference. The volume also includes papers or extended abstracts of the three invited talks presented by *Gonzalo Navarro* on Implementation and Application of Automata in String Processing, by *Christoph Koch* on Applications of Automata in XML Processing, and by *Helmut Seidl* on Program Analysis Through Finite Tree Automata.

The 23 regular papers were selected from 42 submissions covering various fields in the application, implementation, and theory of automata and related structures. This year, six additional papers were selected as "short papers"; at the conference these were allocated the same presentation length as regular papers. Each paper was reviewed by at least three Program Committee members, with the assistance of external referees. Papers were submitted by authors from the following countries: Australia, Austria, Belgium, Brazil, Canada, China, Czech Republic, Finland, France, Germany, India, Italy, Republic of Korea, Japan, Latvia, The Netherlands, Portugal, Russian Federation, Spain, South Africa, Turkey, United Arab Emirates, and the USA.

I wish to thank all who made this conference possible: the authors for submitting their papers, the Program Committee members and external referees (listed on the next pages) for giving their valuable opinions and writing reports about the submitted papers, and the three invited speakers for giving presentations related to the implementation and application of automata. Finally, I would like to express my gratitude to the sponsors (listed on the next pages), local organizers, and to the editors of *Lecture Notes in Computer Science*, in particular to Alfred Hofmann, for their help in publishing this volume in a timely manner.

July 2009   Sebastian Maneth

Organization

CIAA 2009 was organized in cooperation with NICTA, Australia's ICT Research Center of Excellence. It was held in NICTA's Neville Roach Laboratory at the University of New South Wales, Sydney, Australia.

Program Committee

Mikołaj Bojańczyk	Warsaw University, Poland
Ahmed Bouajjani	Université Paris Diderot, France
Cristian S. Calude	University of Auckland, New Zealand
Jean-Marc Champarnaud	Université de Rouen, France
Hubert Comon-Lundh	École Normale Supérieure de Cachan, France
Maxime Crochemore	Université Paris-Est Marne-la-Vallée, France
Michael Domaratzki	University of Manitoba, Canada
Frank Drewes	Umeå University, Sweden
Jan Holub	Czech Technical University in Prague, Czech Republic
Hendrik Jan Hoogeboom	Universiteit Leiden, The Netherlands
Juraj Hromkovic	ETH Zürich, Switzerland
Oscar H. Ibarra	University of California, Santa Barbara, USA
Lucian Ilie	University of Western Ontario, Canada
Masami Ito	Kyoto Sangyo University, Japan
Juhani Karhumäki	University of Turku, Finland
Markus Lohrey	Universität Leipzig, Germany
Sebastian Maneth (Chair)	NICTA and University of New South Wales, Australia
Denis Maurel	Université François Rabelais de Tours, France
Filippo Mignosi	Università Degli Studi - L'Aquila, Italy
Mehryar Mohri	Courant Institute of Mathematical Sciences, USA
Anca Muscholl	Université Bordeaux 1, France
Joachim Niehren	INRIA Lille - Nord Europe, France
Dirk Nowotka	Universität Stuttgart, Germany
Bala Ravikumar	Sonoma State University, USA
Wojciech Rytter	Warsaw University, Poland
Kai Salomaa	Queen's University, Canada
Thomas Schwentick	Technische Universität Dortmund, Germany
Stefan Schwoon	Technische Universität München, Germany
Colin Stirling	University of Edinburgh, UK
Hsu-Chun Yen	National Taiwan University, Taiwan
Sheng Yu	University of Western Ontario, Canada

Steering Committee

Jean-Marc Champarnaud	Université de Rouen, France
Oscar H. Ibarra	University of California, Santa Barbara, USA
Denis Maurel	Université François Rabelais de Tours, France
Kai Salomaa	Queen's University, Canada
Sheng Yu (Chair)	University of Western Ontario, Canada

External Referees

Cyril Allauzen
Pavlos Antoniou
Miroslav Balík
Hans-Joachim Böckenhauer
Iovka Boneva
Béatrice Bouchou
Arnaud Carayol
Giusi Castiglione
Loek Cleophas
Maxime Crochemore
Ömer Egecioglu
Yuan Gao
Stefan Göller
Giovanna Guaiana
Peter Habermehl
Mika Hirvensalo
Benjamin Hoffmann
Johanna Högberg
Jan Janoušek
Jarkko Kari
Dennis Komm
Jörg Kreiker
Manfred Kufleitner
Yoshiyuki Kunimochi
Dietrich Kuske

Alessio Langiu
Jürn Laun
Aurélien Lemay
Peter Leupold
Christof Löding
Alexander Meduna
Tobias Mömke
Marius Nagy
Cyril Nicaud
Alexander Okhotin
Paweł Parys
Andrei Păun
Narad Rampersad
Antonia Restivo
Giuseppina Rindone
Adam Rogalewicz
Jacques Sakarovitch
Sven Schewe
Olivier Serre
Fabien Torre
Szymon Toruńczyk
Nicholas Tran
Stavros Tripakis
Tomás Vojnar
Bruce Watson

Local Organization

Jane Gillis	NICTA
Sebastian Maneth	NICTA and University of New South Wales

Sponsors

National ICT Australia Limited (NICTA)
The University of New South Wales, Sydney, Australia
Yahoo! Research Latin America, Santiago, Chile

Table of Contents

Short Papers and Poster Abstracts

Implementation and Application of Automata in String Processing*

Gonzalo Navarro

Department of Computer Science
Univiversity of Chile
gnavarro@dcc.uchile.cl

Automata have been enormously successful in matching different types of complex patterns on sequences, with applications in many areas, from text retrieval to bioinformatics, from multimedia databases to signal processing. In general terms, the process to match a complex pattern is (1) design a NFA that recognizes the pattern; (2) slightly modify it to recognize any string ending with the pattern; (3) convert it into a DFA; (4) feed it with the sequence, signaling the endpoints of a pattern occurrence each time the DFA reaches a final state. Alternatively one can omit step (2) and backtrack with the DFA on the suffix tree of the sequence, which leads to sublinear-time complex pattern matching in many relevant cases. This process, as it is well-known, has a potential problem in stage (3), because the DFA can be of exponential size. Rather than being a theoretical reservation, the problem does arise in a number of real-life situations.

Bit-parallelism is a technique that helps circumvent this problem in many practical cases. It allows carrying out several operations in parallel on the bits of a computer word. By mapping NFA states to bits, bit-parallelism allows one to simulate the NFA behavior efficiently without converting it to deterministic. We show how bit-parallelism can be applied in many problems where the NFA has a regular structure, which allows us simulating it using typical processor instructions on machine words. Moreover, we show that even on general regular expressions, without any particular structure, bit-parallelism allows one to reduce the space requirement of the DFA. In general, the bit-parallel algorithm on the NFA is simpler to program and more space and time efficient than the one based on the DFA.

We show the use of bit-parallelism for exact pattern matching, for allowing optional and repeatable characters, classes of characters and bounded-length gaps, and for general regular expressions. The paradigm is flexible enough to permit combining any of those searches with approximate matching, where the occurrence can be at a limited edit distance to a string of the language denoted by the automaton. We then show applications of these ideas to natural language processing, where the text is seen as a sequence of words, and bit-parallelism allows flexibility in the matching at the word level, for example allowing missing or spurious words.

---

* Partially funded by the Millennium Institute for Cell Dynamics and Biotechnology (ICDB), Grant ICM P05-001-F, Mideplan, Chile.

Applications of Automata in XML Processing

Christoph Koch

Cornell University
Ithaca, NY, USA
koch@cs.cornell.edu

XML is at once a document format and a semistructed data model, and has become a de-facto standard for exchanging data on the Internet. XML documents can alternatively be viewed as labeled trees, and tree automata are natural mechanisms for a wide range of processing tasks on XML documents. In this talk, I survey applications of automata in XML processing with an emphasis on those directions of work that so far have had the greatest practical impact. The talk will consist of three parts. In the first, I will discuss XML validation. The standard schema formalisms for XML, Document Type Definitions and XML Schema, are regular tree grammars at their core. These official standards of the World Wide Web Consortium are well-founded in automata theory and formal language theory, and are designed to incorporate special restrictions to facilitate the creation of automata for document validation. The second part will cover XML stream processing techniques and XML publish-subscribe systems, an area in which a number of exciting automata-based systems have been built. The third and final part covers XML query processing using automata, and applications in Web information extraction.

S. Maneth (Ed.): CIAA 2009, LNCS 5642, p. 2, 2009.

Program Analysis through Finite Tree Automata

Helmut Seidl

Lehrstuhl für Informatik II, Technische Universität München
Boltzmannstraße 3, D-85748 Garching b. München, Germany
seidl@in.tum.de

Dynamic Pushdown Networks (dpn's) have recently been introduced as a convenient abstraction of systems which provide recursive procedure calls and spawning of concurrent tasks such as Java programs [1, 4–6]. We show how the executions of dpn's can naturally be represented through ranked trees. The configuration reached by a program execution then can be read off from the sequence of leaves of this execution tree. This observation allows us to reduce decision problems such as reachability of configurations within a regular set for dpn's to standard decision problems for finite tree automata.

Our reduction does not only shed fresh light onto dpn's but also provides us with new efficient algorithms which can be implemented through standard libraries for finite tree automata. Finite tree automata on the other hand, can be nicely represented by specific *Horn clauses*. In the presentation, we therefore indicate how these algorithms can be realized by means of generic solvers for a particular decidable class of Horn clauses [2, 3].

Bibliography

[1] Bouajjani, A., Müller-Olm, M., Touili, T.: Regular Symbolic Analysis of Dynamic Networks of Pushdown Systems. In: Abadi, M., de Alfaro, L. (eds.) CONCUR 2005, vol. 3653, pp. 473–487. Springer, Heidelberg (2005)
[2] Nielson, F., Nielson, H.R., Seidl, H.: Normalizable Horn Clauses, Strongly Recognizable Relations and Spi. In: Hermenegildo, M.V., Puebla, G. (eds.) SAS 2002, vol. 2477, pp. 20–35. Springer, Heidelberg (2002)
[3] Goubault-Larrecq, J.: Deciding $\mathcal{H}_1$ by Resolution. Information Processing Letters 95(3), 401–408 (2005)
[4] Lammich, P., Müller-Olm, M.: Precise Fixpoint-Based Analysis of Programs with Thread-Creation and Procedures. In: Caires, L., Vasconcelos, V.T. (eds.) CONCUR 2007. LNCS, vol. 4703, pp. 287–302. Springer, Heidelberg (2007)
[5] Lammich, P., Müller-Olm, M.: Conflict Analysis of Programs with Procedures, Dynamic Thread Creation, and Monitors. In: Alpuente, M., Vidal, G. (eds.) SAS 2008. P. Lammich, M. Müller-Olm, vol. 5079, pp. 205–220. Springer, Heidelberg (2008)
[6] Lammich, P., Müller-Olm, M., Wenner, A.: Predecessor Sets of Dynamic Pushdown Networks with Tree-Regular Constraints. In: Int. Conf. on Computer-Aided Verification (CAV). LNCS. Springer, Heidelberg (to appear, 2009)

S. Maneth (Ed.): CIAA 2009, LNCS 5642, p. 3, 2009.
© Springer-Verlag Berlin Heidelberg 2009

An $n \log n$ Algorithm for Hyper-minimizing States in a (Minimized) Deterministic Automaton

Markus Holzer[1],[*] and Andreas Maletti[2],[**]

[1] Institut für Informatik, Universität Giessen
Arndtstr. 2, 35392 Giessen, Germany
holzer@informatik.uni-giessen.de
[2] Departament de Filologies Romàniques, Universitat Rovira i Virgili
Av. Catalunya 35, 43002 Tarragona, Spain
andreas.maletti@urv.cat

Abstract. We improve a recent result [A. BADR: Hyper-Minimization in $O(n^2)$. In *Proc. CIAA*, LNCS 5148, 2008] for hyper-minimized finite automata. Namely, we present an $O(n \log n)$ algorithm that computes for a given finite deterministic automaton (dfa) an almost equivalent dfa that is as small as possible—such an automaton is called hyper-minimal. Here two finite automata are almost equivalent if and only if the symmetric difference of their languages is finite. In other words, two almost-equivalent automata disagree on acceptance on finitely many inputs. In this way, we solve an open problem stated in [A. BADR, V. GEFFERT, I. SHIPMAN: Hyper-minimizing minimized deterministic finite state automata. *RAIRO Theor. Inf. Appl.* 43(1), 2009] and by BADR. Moreover, we show that minimization linearly reduces to hyper-minimization, which shows that the time-bound $O(n \log n)$ is optimal for hyper-minimization.

1 Introduction

Early studies in automata theory revealed that nondeterministic and deterministic finite automata are equivalent [1]. However, nondeterministic automata can be exponentially more succinct w.r.t. the number of states [2,3]. In fact, finite automata are probably best known for being equivalent to right-linear context-free grammars and, thus, for capturing the lowest level of the CHOMSKY-hierarchy, which is the family of regular languages. Over the last 50 years, a vast literature documenting the importance of finite automata as an enormously valuable concept has been developed. Although, there are a lot of similarities between nondeterministic and deterministic finite automata, one important difference is that of the minimization problem. The study of this problem also dates back to the early beginnings of automata theory. It is of practical relevance because regular languages are used in many applications, and one may like to represent the languages succinctly. While for nondeterministic automata the computation of an equivalent minimal automaton is PSPACE-complete [4] and thus highly

---

[*] Part of the work was done while the author was at Institut für Informatik, Technische Universität München, Boltzmannstraße 3, D-85748 Garching bei München, Germany.
[**] Supported by the *Ministerio de Educación y Ciencia* (MEC) grant JDCI-2007-760.

S. Maneth (Ed.): CIAA 2009, LNCS 5642, pp. 4–13, 2009.

intractable, the corresponding problem for deterministic automata is known to be effectively solvable in polynomial time [5]. An automaton is minimal if every other automaton with fewer states disagrees on acceptance for at *least one* input.

Minimizing deterministic finite automata (dfa) is based on computing an equivalence relation on the states of the machine and collapsing states that are equivalent. Here two states $p, q \in Q$, where Q is the set of states of the automaton under consideration, are equivalent, if the automaton starting its computation in state p accepts the same language as the automaton if q is taken as a start state. Minimization of two equivalent dfa leads to minimal dfa that are isomorphic up to the renaming of states. Hence, minimal dfa are unique. This allows one to give a nice characterization: A dfa M is *minimal* if and only if in M: (i) there are no unreachable states and (ii) there is no pair of different but equivalent states.

The computation of this equivalence can be implemented in a straightforward fashion by repeatedly refining the relation starting with a partition that groups accepting and rejecting states together yielding a polynomial time algorithm of $O(n^2)$; compare with [5]. HOPCROFT's algorithm [6] for minimization slightly improves the naive implementation to a running time of $O(m \log n)$ where $m = |Q \times \Sigma|$ and $n = |Q|$, where Σ is alphabet of input symbols of the finite automaton, and is up to now the best known minimization algorithm. Recent developments have shown that this bound is tight for HOPCROFT's algorithm [7,8]. Thus, minimization can be seen as a form of lossless compression that can be done effectively while preserving the accepted language exactly.

Recently, a new form of minimization, namely hyper-minimization was studied in the literature [9,10]. There the minimization or compression is done while giving up the preservation of the semantics of finite automata, i.e., the accepted language. It is clear that the semantics cannot vary arbitrarily. A related minimization method based on cover automata is presented in [11,12]. Hyperminimization [9,10] allows the accepted language to differ in acceptance on a *finite number* of inputs, which is called *almost-equivalence*. Thus, hyper-minimization aims to find an almost-equivalent dfa that is as small as possible. Here an automaton is *hyper-minimal* if every other automaton with fewer states disagrees on acceptance for an *infinite* number of inputs. In [9] basic properties of hyper-minimization and hyper-minimal dfa are investigated. Most importantly, a characterization of hyper-minimal dfa is given, which is similar to the characterization of minimal dfa mentioned above. Namely, a dfa M is *hyper-minimal* if and only if in M: (i) there are no unreachable states, (ii) there is no pair of different but equivalent states, and (iii) there is no pair of different but almost-equivalent states, such that at least one of them is a preamble state. Here a state is called a *preamble state* if it is reachable from the start state by a *finite* number of inputs, only; otherwise the state is called a *kernel state*. These properties allow a structural characterization of hyper-minimal dfa. Roughly speaking, the kernels (all states that are kernel states) of two almost-equivalent hyper-minimized automata are isomorphic in the standard sense, and their preambles are also isomorphic, except for acceptance values. Thus, it turns out that hyper-minimal dfa are not necessarily unique. Nevertheless, it was shown in [9] that hyper-minimization can be done in time $O(m \cdot n^3)$, where

$m = |\Sigma|$ and $n = |Q|$; for constant alphabet size this gives an $O(n^3)$ algorithm. Later, the bound was improved to $O(n^2)$ in [10]. In this paper we improve this upper bound further to $O(n \log n)$, and argue that it is reasonably well because any upper bound $t(n) = \Omega(n)$ for hyper-minimization implies that minimization can be done within $t(n)$. To this end, we linearly reduce minimization to hyper-minimization.

2   Preliminaries

Let S and T be sets. Their symmetric difference $S \ominus T$ is $(S \setminus T) \cup (T \setminus S)$. The sets S and T are almost-equal if $S \ominus T$ is finite. A finite set Σ is an alphabet. By Σ^* we denote the set of all strings over Σ. The empty string is denoted by ε. Concatenation of strings is denoted by juxtaposition and $|w|$ denotes the length of the word $w \in \Sigma^*$. A deterministic finite automaton (dfa) is a tuple $M = (Q, \Sigma, q_0, \delta, F)$ where Q is a finite set of states, Σ is an alphabet of input symbols, $q_0 \in Q$ is the initial state, $\delta \colon Q \times \Sigma \to Q$ is a transition function, and $F \subseteq Q$ is a set of final states. The transition function δ extends to $\delta \colon Q \times \Sigma^* \to Q$ as follows: $\delta(q, \varepsilon) = q$ and $\delta(q, \sigma w) = \delta(\delta(q, \sigma), w)$ for every $q \in Q$, $\sigma \in \Sigma$, and $w \in \Sigma^*$. The dfa M recognizes the language $L(M) = \{\, w \in \Sigma^* \mid \delta(q_0, w) \in F \,\}$.

Two states $p, q \in Q$ are equivalent, denoted by $p \equiv q$, if $\delta(p, w) \in F$ if and only if $\delta(q, w) \in F$ for every $w \in \Sigma^*$. The dfa M is minimal if it does not have equivalent states. The name 'minimal' stems from the fact that no dfa with less states also recognizes $L(M)$ if M is minimal. It is known that for M an equivalent minimal dfa can efficiently be computed using HOPCROFT's algorithm [6], which runs in time $O(m \log n)$ where $m = |Q \times \Sigma|$ and $n = |Q|$.

In the following, let $M = (Q, \Sigma, q_0, \delta, F)$ be a minimal dfa. Let us recall some notions from [9]. A state $q \in Q$ is a kernel state if $q = \delta(q_0, w)$ for infinitely many $w \in \Sigma^*$. Otherwise q is a preamble state. We denote the set of kernel states by $\mathrm{Ker}(M)$ and the set of preamble states by $\mathrm{Pre}(M)$. For states $p, q \in Q$ we write $p \to q$ if there exists $w \in \Sigma^+$ such that $\delta(p, w) = q$. The states p and q are strongly connected, denoted by $p \leftrightarrow q$, if $p \to q$ and $q \to p$. Note that strongly connected states are also a kernel states since both are reachable by the minimality of M. Finally, $q \in Q$ is a center state if $q \leftrightarrow q$.

3   Hyper-minimization

As already remarked, minimization yields an equivalent dfa that is as small as possible. It can thus be considered a form of lossless compression. Sometimes the compression rate is more important than the preservation of the semantics. This leads to the area of lossy compression where the goal is to compress even further at the expense of errors (typically with respect to some error profile). Our error profile is very simple: We allow a finite number of errors. Consequently, we call two dfa M_1 and M_2 almost-equivalent if $L(M_1)$ and $L(M_2)$ are almost-equal. A dfa that admits no smaller almost-equivalent dfa is called hyper-minimal. Hyper-minimization [9,10] aims to find an almost-equivalent hyper-minimal dfa.

Algorithm 1. Overall structure of the hyper-minimization algorithm

---

Require: a dfa M

    $M \leftarrow$ MINIMIZE(M) // HOPCROFT's algorithm; $O(m \log n)$
2: $K \leftarrow$ COMPUTEKERNEL(M) // compute the kernel states; see Section 3.1
    $\sim \leftarrow$ AEQUIVALENTSTATES(M) // compute almost-equivalence; see Section 3.2
4: $M \leftarrow$ MERGESTATES$(M, K, \sim)$ // merge almost-equivalent states; $O(m)$
    return M

The contributions [9,10] report hyper-minimization algorithms for M that run in time $O(n^3)$ and $O(n^2)$, respectively. Note that $|\Sigma|$ is assumed to be constant in those contributions. Our aim here is to develop a hyper-minimization algorithm that runs in time $O(n \log n)$ under the same assumptions.

Roughly speaking, minimization aims to identify equivalent states and hyper-minimization aims to identify almost-equivalent states, which we define next. Recall that $M = (Q, \Sigma, q_0, \delta, F)$ is a minimal dfa. Let $m = |Q \times \Sigma|$ and $n = |Q|$.

Definition 1 (cf. [9, Definition 2.2]). *For all states $p, q \in Q$, we say that p and q are* almost-equivalent, *denoted by $p \sim q$, if there exists $k \geq 0$ such that $\delta(p, w) = \delta(q, w)$ for every $w \in \Sigma^*$ with $|w| \geq k$.*

Let us present the overall structure of the hyper-minimization algorithm of [10] in Algorithm 1. Note that compared to [10], we exchanged lines 2 and 3. MINIMIZE refers to classical minimization. HOPCROFT's algorithm implements it and runs in time $O(m \log n)$ [6]. The procedure MERGESTATES is described in [9,10], where it is also proved that it runs in time $O(m)$. To make the paper self-contained, we present their algorithm (see Algorithm 2) and the corresponding results next. Note that merging a state p into another state q denotes the usual procedure of redirecting (in M) all incoming transitions of p to q. If p was the initial state, then q is the new initial state. Clearly, the state p can be deleted.

Theorem 1 ([9, Section 4]). *If the requirements of Algorithm 2 are met, then it returns in time $O(m)$ a hyper-minimal dfa that is almost-equivalent to M.*

Consequently, if we can implement: (i) COMPUTEKERNEL and (ii) AEQUIVALENTSTATES in time $O(m \log n)$, then we obtain a hyper-minimization algorithm that runs in time $O(m \log n)$. The next two sections will show suitable implementations for both procedures.

3.1 Identify Kernel States

As we have seen in Algorithm 2, kernel states play a special role because we never merge two kernel states. It was already shown in [9,10], how to identify the kernel states in time $O(mn)$. It turns out that the kernel states can easily be computed using a well-known algorithm due to TARJAN [13] (see Algorithm 3).

Theorem 2. $\mathrm{Ker}(M)$ *can be computed in time $O(m)$.*

Algorithm 2. Merging almost-equivalent states
___
Require: a minimal dfa M, its kernel states K, and its almost-equivalent states $\sim$

    for all $B \in (Q/\sim)$ **do**

2:      $S \leftarrow B \cap K$ // S contains the kernel states of the block B

      if $S \neq \emptyset$ **then**

4:         select $q \in S$ // select an arbitrary kernel state q from B

      else

6:         select $q \in B$ // if no such kernel state exists, pick any state q of B

      for all $p \in B \setminus S$ **do**

8:         merge p into q // merge all preamble states of the block into q

    return M

Proof. Using TARJAN's algorithm [13] (or the algorithms by GABOW [14,15] or KOSARAJU [16,17]) we can identify the strongly connected components in time $O(m + n)$. Algorithm 3 presents a simplified formulation because all states of M are reachable from q_0. The initial call is TARJAN(M, q_0). Thus, we identified states q such that $q \rightarrow q$ because such a state is part of a strongly connected component of at least two states or has a self-loop (i.e., $\delta(q, \sigma) = q$ for some $\sigma \in \Sigma$). Another depth-first search can then mark all states q such that $p \rightarrow p \rightarrow q$ for some state p in time $O(m)$. Clearly, such a marked state is a kernel state and each kernel state is marked because for each $q \in \mathrm{Ker}(M)$ there exists a state $p \in Q$ such that $p \rightarrow p \rightarrow q$ by [9, Lemma 2.12].   □

3.2 Identify Almost-Equivalent States

The identification of almost-equivalent states will be slightly more difficult. We improve the strategy of [9], which runs in time $O(mn^2)$, by avoiding pairwise comparisons, which yields a factor n, and by merging states with a specific strategy, which reduces a factor n to $\log n$. Since M is a minimal dfa, the relation $\sim$ coincides with the relation defined in [9, Definition 2.2]. Thus, we know that $\sim$ is a congruence relation by [9, Facts 2.5–2.7].

Let us attempt to explain the algorithm. The vector $(\delta(q, \sigma) \mid \sigma \in \Sigma)$ is called the *follow-vector* of q. The algorithm keeps a set I of states that need to be processed and a set P of states that are still useful. Both sets are initially Q and the hash map h is initially empty. The algorithm then iteratively processes states of I and computes their follow-vector. Since h is initially empty, the first follow-vector will simply be stored in h. The algorithm proceeds in this fashion until it finds a state, whose follow-vector is already stored in h. It then extracts the state with the same vector from h and compares the sizes of the blocks in π that the two states belong to. Suppose that p is the state that belongs to the smaller block and q is the state that belongs to the larger block. Then we merge p into q and remove p from P because it is now useless. In addition, we update the block of q to include the block of p and add all states that have transitions leading to p to I because their follow-vectors have changed due to the merge. The algorithm repeats this process until the set I is empty.

Algorithm 3. TARJAN's algorithm TARJAN(M, q) computing the strongly connected components of M

Require: a dfa $M = (Q, \Sigma, q_0, \delta, F)$ and a state $q \in Q$
    Global: index, low: $Q \to \mathbb{N}$ initially undefined, $i \in \mathbb{N}$ initially 0, S stack of states initially empty

2: index$(q) \leftarrow i$ // set index of q to i; q is thus explored
    low$(q) \leftarrow i$ // set lowest index (of a state) reachable from q to the index of q
4: $i \leftarrow i + 1$ // increase current index
    PUSH(S, q) // push state q to the stack S
6: **for all** $\sigma \in \Sigma$ **do**
    if index$(\delta(q, \sigma))$ is undefined **then**
8:       TARJAN$(M, \delta(q, \sigma))$ // if successor not yet explored, then explore it
      low$(q) \leftarrow \min(\text{low}(q), \text{low}(\delta(q, \sigma)))$ // update lowest reachable index for q
10:   **else**
      if $\delta(q, \sigma) \in S$ **then**
12:         low$(q) \leftarrow \min(\text{low}(q), \text{index}(\delta(q, \sigma)))$ // update lowest reachable index
    if low$(q) = $ index(q) **then**
14:   **repeat**
      $p \leftarrow$ POP(S) // found component; remove all states of it from stack S
16:     ...   // store strongly connected components
    until $p = q$

Example 1. Consider the minimal dfa of Figure 1(left) (see [9, Figure 2]). Let us show the run of Algorithm 4 on it. We present a protocol (for line 10) in Table 1. At then end of the algorithm the hash map contains the following entries:

$$\binom{B}{C} \to A \qquad \binom{F}{D} \to B \qquad \binom{H}{G} \to C \qquad \binom{I}{H} \to D \qquad \binom{I}{F} \to E$$

$$\binom{J}{E} \to F \qquad \binom{L}{H} \to G \qquad \binom{M}{I} \to H \qquad \binom{L}{J} \to I \qquad \binom{M}{J} \to J$$

$$\binom{P}{M} \to L \qquad \binom{Q}{M} \to M \qquad \binom{P}{R} \to P \qquad \binom{R}{R} \to R \qquad \binom{L}{I} \to I$$

$$\binom{I}{E} \to F \qquad \binom{I}{I} \to C \qquad \binom{I}{G} \to E \qquad \binom{F}{C} \to B \ .$$

From Table 1 we obtain the partition induced by $\sim$, which is

$$\{\{A\}, \{B\}, \{C, D\}, \{E\}, \{F\}, \{G, H, I, J\}, \{L, M\}, \{P, Q\}, \{R\}\} \ .$$

This coincides with the partition obtained in [9, Figure 2]. Since $E, F, I, J, L, M, P, Q,$ and R are kernel states, we can only merge C into D and merge G and H into I. The result of those merges is shown in Figure 1(right). The obtained dfa coincides with the one of [9, Figure 3].

Next, let us look at the time complexity before we turn to correctness. In this respect, line 14 is particularly interesting because it might add to the set I, which controls the loop. Our strategy that determines which states to merge will realize the reduction of a factor n to just $\log n$. To simplify the argument,

---

Algorithm 4. Algorithm computing $\sim$

Require: minimal dfa $M = (Q, \Sigma, q_0, \delta, F)$

    for all $q \in Q$ **do**
2:    $\pi(q) \leftarrow \{q\}$ // initial block of q contains just q itself

    $h \leftarrow \emptyset$ // hash map of type $h\colon Q^{|\Sigma|} \to Q$
4:   $I \leftarrow Q$ // states that need to be considered

    $P \leftarrow Q$ // set of current states
6: **while** $I \neq \emptyset$ **do**
      $q \leftarrow \text{RemoveHead}(I)$ // remove state from I
8:     $\text{succ} \leftarrow (\delta(q, \sigma) \mid \sigma \in \Sigma)$ // compute vector of successors using current δ

      if $\text{HasValue}(h, \text{succ})$ **then**
10:      $p \leftarrow \text{Get}(h, \text{succ})$ // retrieve state in bucket succ of h

        if $|\pi(p)| \geq |\pi(q)|$ **then**
12:         $\text{Swap}(p, q)$ // exchange roles of p and q

        $P \leftarrow P \setminus \{p\}$ // state p will be merged into q
14:      $I \leftarrow (I \setminus \{p\}) \cup \{r \in P \mid \exists \sigma\colon \delta(r, \sigma) = p\}$ // add predecessors of p in P to I
        $\delta \leftarrow \text{MergeState}(\delta, p, q)$ // merge states p and q in δ; q survives
16:      $\pi(q) \leftarrow \pi(q) \cup \pi(p)$ // p and q are almost-equivalent
      $h \leftarrow \text{Put}(h, \text{succ}, q)$ // store q in h under key succ
18: **return** π

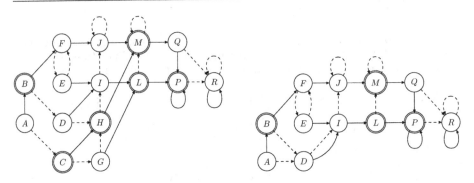

Fig. 1. An example automaton and the resulting hyper-minimal automaton with a-transitions (straight lines) and b-transitions (dashed lines). The initial state is A.

we will call $\delta(q, \sigma)$ a transition and we consider it the same transition even if the value of $\delta(q, \sigma)$ changes in the course of the algorithm.

Proposition 1. *The following properties of Algorithm 4 hold whenever line 7 is executed: (i) $I \subseteq P$ and (ii) $\{\pi(p) \mid p \in P\}$ is a partition of Q.*

Moreover, let us consider p and q after the execution of line 10. In essence, we would like to show that $p \neq q$. We thus need to show that $(\delta(q, \sigma) \mid \sigma \in \Sigma) \neq \alpha$ for every $\alpha \in h^{-1}(q)$ whenever line 8 is executed. Clearly, when line 8 is first executed with our particular q, then $h^{-1}(q) = \emptyset$ and thus the property trivially holds. Moreover, q is then no longer in I. It can be added to I in line 14, but only if $\delta(q, \sigma) \notin P$ for some $\sigma \in \Sigma$. Then it is changed in line 15 such that $\delta(q, \sigma) \in P$ after its execution. Thus, all stored values $h^{-1}(q)$ have at least one component that is not in P, whereas $\delta(q, \sigma) \in P$ for every $\sigma \in \Sigma$ after execution of line 15. Consequently, in line 10 the retrieved state p cannot be q itself.

Lemma 1. *For every $r \in Q$ and $\sigma \in \Sigma$, the transition $\delta(r, \sigma)$ is considered at most $(\log n)$ times in lines 14 and 15 during the full execution of Algorithm 4.*

Proof. Suppose that $p = \delta(r, \sigma)$ in line 14. Moreover, $|\pi(p)| < |\pi(q)|$ by lines 11–12. Then line 15 redirects the transition $\delta(r, \sigma)$ to q; i.e., $\delta(r, \sigma) = q$ after line 15. Moreover, $|\pi(q)| > 2 \cdot |\pi(p)|$ after the execution of line 16 because $p \neq q$ as already argued, and thus, $\pi(p) \cap \pi(q) = \emptyset$ by Proposition 1. Moreover, by the same proposition $|\pi(q)| \leq n$ for every $q \in Q$. Consequently, $\delta(r, \sigma)$ can be considered at most $(\log n)$ times in lines 14 and 15. □

Theorem 3. *Algorithm 4 can be implemented to run in time $O(m \log n)$.*

Proof. Clearly, we assume that all operations except for those in lines 14 and 15 to execute in constant time. Then lines 1–5 execute in time $O(n)$. Next we will prove that the loop in lines 6–17 executes at most $O(m \cdot \log n)$ times. By Proposition 1 we have $I \subseteq P$. Now let us consider a particular state $q \in Q$. Then $q \in I$ initially and it has $|\Sigma|$ outgoing transitions. By Lemma 1, every such transition is considered at most $(\log n)$ times in line 14, which yields that q is added to I. Consequently, the state q can be chosen in line 10 at most $(1 + |\Sigma| \cdot \log n)$ times. Summing over all states of Q, we obtain that the loop in lines 6-17 can be executed at most $(n + m \cdot \log n)$ times. Since all lines apart from lines 14 and 15 are assumed to execute in constant time, this proves the statement for all lines apart from 14 and 15. By Lemma 1 every transition is considered at most $(\log n)$ times in those two lines. Since there are m transitions in M and each consideration of a transition can be assumed to run in constant time, we obtain that lines 14 and 15 globally (i.e., including all executions of those lines) execute in time $O(m \log n)$, which proves the statement. □

Finally, we need to prove that Algorithm 4 is correct. By Proposition 1, $\{\pi(p) \mid p \in P\}$ is a partition of Q whenever line 7 is executed. Let $\simeq$ be the induced equivalence relation. Next we prove that $\simeq$ is a congruence.

Lemma 2. *Whenever line 7 is executed, π induces a congruence.*

This proves that we compute a congruence. Now we can use [9, Lemma 2.10] to prove that all states in a block of the returned partition are almost-equivalent.

Theorem 4. *The partition returned by Algorithm 4 induces $\sim$.*

Proof. Let $\simeq$ be the congruence (see Lemma 2) returned by Algorithm 4. For every $\sigma \in \Sigma$ and $p, q \in Q$ that are merged in line 15 we have $\delta(p, \sigma) \sim \delta(q, \sigma)$. Thus, $p \sim q$ by [9, Lemma 2.10], which proves $\simeq \subseteq \sim$. For the converse, let $p \sim q$. Clearly, δ is the transition function of $M/\simeq$ at the end of the algorithm. Denote

Table 1. Run of Algorithm 4 (at line 10) on the automaton of Figure 1(left)

I	$Q \setminus P$	q	p	π (singleton blocks not shown)
$\{B,\ldots,R\}$	$\emptyset$	A		
$\cdots$	$\emptyset$			
$\{R\}$	$\emptyset$	P	Q	
$\{M\}$	$\{Q\}$	R		$\{P,Q\}$
$\emptyset$	$\{Q\}$	M	L	$\{P,Q\}$
$\{H\}$	$\{M,Q\}$	J	I	$\{L,M\},\{P,Q\}$
$\{F,I\}$	$\{J,M,Q\}$	H		$\{I,J\},\{L,M\},\{P,Q\}$
$\{I\}$	$\{J,M,Q\}$	F		$\{I,J\},\{L,M\},\{P,Q\}$
$\{C,D,G\}$	$\{J,M,Q\}$	I	H	$\{I,J\},\{L,M\},\{P,Q\}$
$\{D,G\}$	$\{H,J,M,Q\}$	C		$\{H,I,J\},\{L,M\},\{P,Q\}$
$\{G\}$	$\{H,J,M,Q\}$	D	C	$\{H,I,J\},\{L,M\},\{P,Q\}$
$\{B\}$	$\{D,H,J,M,Q\}$	G	I	$\{C,D\},\{H,I,J\},\{L,M\},\{P,Q\}$
$\emptyset$	$\{D,G,H,J,M,Q\}$	B		$\{C,D\},\{G,H,I,J\},\{L,M\},\{P,Q\}$

the transition function of $M/\simeq$ by δ' and the original transition function of M by δ. Since $p \sim q$, there exists $k \geq 0$ such that $\delta(p,w) = \delta(q,w)$ for every $w \in \Sigma^*$ with $|w| \geq k$. Clearly, this yields that $\delta'([p],w) = \delta'([q],w)$ for every such w. This implies the existence of $B, D \in (Q/\simeq)$ such that $\delta'(B,\sigma) = \delta'(D,\sigma)$ for every $\sigma \in \Sigma$. However, an easy proof shows that the algorithm does not terminate as long as there are distinct states B and D such that $\delta'(B,\sigma) = \delta'(D,\sigma)$ for every $\sigma \in \Sigma$. Consequently, $p \simeq q$, which proves the statement. $\qquad\square$

Theorem 5. *For every dfa we can obtain a almost-equivalent, hyper-minimal dfa in time $O(m \log n)$.*

4   Conclusions

We have designed an $O(m \log n)$ algorithm, where $m = |Q \times \Sigma|$ and $n = |Q|$, that computes a hyper-minimized dfa from a given dfa, which may have fewer states than the classical minimized dfa. Its accepted language is almost-equivalent to the original one; i.e., differs in acceptance on a finite number of inputs only. Since hyper-minimization is a very new field of research, most of the standard questions related to descriptional complexity such as, e.g., nondeterministic automata to dfa conversion w.r.t. hyper-minimality, are problems of further research.

Finally, let's argue that minimization linearly reduces to hyper-minimization. This is seen as follows: Let $M = (Q, \Sigma, q_0, \delta, F)$ be a dfa. If $L(M) = \emptyset$, which can be verified in time linear in the number of states, then we are already done since the single state hyper-minimal dfa accepting the emptyset is also minimal. Now let $L(M) \neq \emptyset$ and assume $\#$ to be a new input symbol not contained in Σ. We construct a dfa $M' = (Q, \Sigma \cup \{\#\}, q_0, \delta', F)$ by $\delta'(p,\sigma) = \delta(p,\sigma)$ for $p \in Q$ and $\sigma \in \Sigma$ and $\delta'(p,\#) = q_0$ for $p \in Q$. Observe, that by construction M' consists of kernel states only. Thus, hyper-minimizing M' leads to a dfa M'' that is unique because for two almost-equivalent hyper-minimized automata the kernels are isomorphic to each other [9, Theorem 3.5]—compare this with the characterization of minimal and hyper-minimal dfa mentioned in the Introduction. Thus, M'' is a minimal dfa accepting $L(M')$. Then it is easy to see that taking M'' and deleting the #-transitions yields a minimal dfa accepting $L(M)$. Hence, minimization linearly reduces to hyper-minimization. Thus, our algorithm achieves the optimal worst-case complexity in the light of the recent developments for HOPCROFT's state minimization algorithm, which show that the $O(n \log n)$ bound is tight for that algorithm [7] even under any possible implementation [8].

References

1. Rabin, M.O., Scott, D.: Finite automata and their decision problems. IBM J. Res. Dev. 3, 114–125 (1959)
2. Meyer, A.R., Fischer, M.J.: Economy of description by automata, grammars, and formal systems. In: Annual Symposium on Switching and Automata Theory, pp. 188–191. IEEE Computer Society Press, Los Alamitos (1971)
3. Moore, F.R.: On the bounds for state-set size in the proofs of equivalence between deterministic, nondeterministic, and two-way finite automata. IEEE Transaction on Computing C-20, 1211–1219 (1971)
4. Jiang, T., Ravikumar, B.: Minimal NFA problems are hard. SIAM J. Comput. 22(6), 1117–1141 (1993)
5. Hopcroft, J.E., Ullman, J.D.: Introduction to Automata Theory, Languages, and Computation. Addison Wesley, Reading (1979)
6. Hopcroft, J.E.: An $n \log n$ algorithm for minimizing states in a finite automaton. In: Theory of Machines and Computations, pp. 189–196. Academic Press, London (1971)
7. Berstel, J., Caston, O.: On the complexity of Hopcroft's state minimization algorithm. In: Domaratzki, M., et al. (eds.) CIAA 2004. LNCS, vol. 3317, pp. 35–44. Springer, Heidelberg (2005)
8. Castiglione, G., Restivo, A., Sciotino, M.: Hopcroft's algorithm and cyclic automata. In: Martín-Vide, C., Otto, F., Fernau, H. (eds.) LATA 2008. LNCS, vol. 5196, pp. 172–183. Springer, Heidelberg (2008)
9. Badr, A., Geffert, V., Shipman, I.: Hyper-minimizing minimized deterministic finite state automata. RAIRO Theor. Inf. Appl. 43(1), 69–94 (2009)
10. Badr, A.: Hyper-minimization in $O(n^2)$. In: Ibarra, O.H., Ravikumar, B. (eds.) CIAA 2008. LNCS, vol. 5148, pp. 223–231. Springer, Heidelberg (2008)
11. Câmpeanu, C., Santean, N., Yu, S.: Minimal cover-automata for finite languages. Theoret. Comput. Sci. 267(1-2), 3–16 (2001)
12. Paun, A., Paun, M., Rodríguez-Patón, A.: On the Hopcroft minimization technique for DFA and DCFA. Theoret. Comput. Sci. (to appear, 2009), http://dx.doi.org/10.1016/j.tcs.2009.02.034
13. Tarjan, R.E.: Depth-first search and linear graph algorithms. SIAM J. Comput. 1(2), 146–160 (1972)
14. Cheriyan, J., Mehlhorn, K.: Algorithms for dense graphs and networks. Algorithmica 15(6), 521–549 (1996)
15. Gabow, H.N.: Path-based depth-first search for strong and biconnected components. Inf. Process. Lett. 74(3-4), 107–114 (2000)
16. Kosaraju, S.R.: Strong-connectivity algorithm (unpublished manuscript 1978)
17. Sharir, M.: A strong-connectivity algorithm and its applications in data flow analysis. Computers and Mathematics with Applications 7(1), 67–72 (1981)

On Extremal Cases of Hopcroft's Algorithm

Giusi Castiglione, Antonio Restivo, and Marinella Sciortino

Università di Palermo, Dipartimento di Matematica e Applicazioni,
via Archirafi, 34 - 90123 Palermo, Italy
{giusi,restivo,mari}@math.unipa.it

Abstract. In this paper we consider the problem of minimization of deterministic finite automata (DFA) with reference to Hopcroft's algorithm. Hopcroft's algorithm has several degrees of freedom, so there can exist different sequences of refinements of the set of the states that lead to the final partition. We find an infinite family of binary automata for which such a process is unique. Some recent papers (cf. [3,7,1]) have been devoted to find families of automata for which Hopcroft's algorithm has its worst execution time. They are unary automata associated to circular words. However, automata minimization can be achieved also in linear time when the alphabet has only one letter (cf. [14]), so in this paper we face the tightness of the algorithm when the alphabet contains more than one letter. In particular we define an infinite family of binary automata representing the worst case of Hopcroft's algorithm. They are automata associated to particular trees and we deepen the connection between the refinement process of Hopcroft's algorithm and the combinatorial properties of such trees.

1 Introduction

A deterministic finite automaton (DFA) is a recognizer of a regular language and provides a compact representation of the language itself. Among the equivalent deterministic finite automata (i.e. recognizing the same regular language), there exists a unique one (up to isomorphism) with minimal number of states, called minimal automaton of the language. Describing a regular language by its minimal automaton is important in many applications, such as, for instance, text searching, lexical analysis or coding systems, where space considerations are prominent.

Finding the minimal automaton equivalent to a given DFA is a classical and largely studied problem in Theory of Automata and Formal Languages, also called automata minimization problem. Several methods have been developed to minimize a deterministic finite automaton. Some of them operate by successive refinements of a partition of the states. For instance, we recall the well known algorithm proposed by Moore in 1956 (cf. [13]) with time complexity $O(kn^2)$, where n is the number of states of the DFA and k is the cardinality of the alphabet. More efficient is the algorithm provided by Hopcroft in 1971 (cf. [9]) where the refinements are computed in $O(kn \log n)$. Besides, such an algorithm is the fastest known solution to the automata minimization problem.

S. Maneth (Ed.): CIAA 2009, LNCS 5642, pp. 14–23, 2009.

A taxonomy of finite automata minimization algorithms is given in [15]. Very recently, many papers on experimental comparison of minimization algorithms has been published.

The general complexity of the automata minimization problem is still an open question but there are families of automata for which Hopcroft's algorithm runs effectively in $\Theta(n \log n)$ (cf. [3,7,6]). Such families are unary automata associated to circular words. However, automata minimization can be achieved also in linear time when the alphabet has only one letter (cf. [14]), but the solution does not seem to extend to larger alphabet. In this paper we are focus on finding families of automata defined on more that one letter alphabet representing the worst case of Hopcroft's algorithm. Actually, we provide an infinite family of binary automata defined by binary labelled trees and relate the execution of Hopcroft's algorithm on such automata with some combinatorial properties of the associated binary tree. Moreover, for such automata the refinement process leading from the initial partition of set of the states to the final one is uniquely determined. Recall that, in general, Hopcroft's algorithm has several degrees of freedom since it leaves several choices to the programmer.

The paper is organized as follows. The Section 2 contains the description of Hopcroft's algorithm by focusing on its degrees of freedom. The Section 3 introduces the notion of standard binary tree and standard tree-like automaton. The uniqueness of the execution of Hopcroft's algorithm on standard tree-like automata is studied in Section 4. In Section 5 we deepen the problem of tightness of Hopcroft's algorithm, by providing an infinite family of binary automata representing the worst case of the algorithm. Section 6 describes some sided research topics and future directions.

2   Hopcroft's Algorithm

In 1971 Hopcroft proposed an algorithm for minimizing a deterministic finite state automaton with n states, over an alphabet Σ, in $O(|\Sigma|n \log n)$ time (cf. [9]). This algorithm has been widely studied and described by many authors (see for example [10,12,15]) cause of the difficult to give its theoretical justification, to prove correctness and to compute running time.

In Figure 1 we give a brief description of the algorithm's running.

Given an automaton $\mathcal{A} = (Q, \Sigma, \delta, q_0, F)$, it computes the coarsest congruence that saturates F. Let us observe that the partition $\{F, Q \setminus F\}$, trivially, saturates F. Given a partition $\Pi = \{Q_1, Q_2, ..., Q_m\}$ of Q, we say that the pair (Q_i, a), with $a \in \Sigma$, *splits* the class Q_j if $\delta_a^{-1}(Q_i) \cap Q_j \neq \emptyset$ and $Q_j \not\subseteq \delta_a^{-1}(Q_i)$. In this case, the class Q_j is split into $Q_j' = \delta_a^{-1}(Q_i) \cap Q_j$ and $Q_j'' = Q_j \setminus \delta_a^{-1}(Q_i)$. Furthermore, we have that a partition Π is a congruence if and only if for any $1 \leq i, j \leq m$ and any $a \in \Sigma$, the pair (Q_i, a) does not splits Q_j.

Hopcroft's algorithm operates by a sequence $\Pi_1, \Pi_2, \ldots, \Pi_l$ of successive refinements of a partition of the states and it is based on the so-called "smaller half" strategy. Actually, it starts from the partition $\Pi_1 = \{F, Q \setminus F\}$ and refines it by means of splitting operations until it obtains a congruence, i.e. until

HOPCROFT MINIMIZATION $(\mathcal{A} = (Q, \Sigma, \delta, q_0, F))$
1. $\Pi \leftarrow \{F, Q \setminus F\}$
2. **for all** $a \in \Sigma$ **do**
3. $\mathcal{W} \leftarrow \{(min(F, Q \setminus F), a)\}$
4. **while** $\mathcal{W} \neq \emptyset$ **do**
5.   *choose and delete any* (C, a) *from* $\mathcal{W}$
6.   **for all** $B \in \Pi$ **do**
7.   **if** B **is split from** (C, a) **then**
8. $B' \leftarrow \delta_a^{-1}(C) \cap B$
9. $B'' \leftarrow B \setminus \delta_a^{-1}(C)$
10. $\Pi \leftarrow \Pi \setminus \{B\} \cup \{B', B''\}$
11.   **for all** $b \in \Sigma$ **do**
12.   **if** $(B, b) \in \mathcal{W}$ **then**
13. $\mathcal{W} \leftarrow \mathcal{W} \setminus \{(B, b)\} \cup \{(B', b), (B'', b)\}$
14.   **else**
15. $\mathcal{W} \leftarrow \mathcal{W} \cup \{(min(B', B''), b)\}$

Fig. 1. Hopcroft's algorithm

no split is possible. To do that it maintains the current partition Π_i and a set $\mathcal{W} \subseteq \Pi_i \times \Sigma$, called *waiting set*, that contains the pairs for which it has to check whether some classes of the current partition are split. The main loop of the algorithm takes and deletes one pair (C, a) from $\mathcal{W}$ and, for each class B of Π_i, checks if it is split by (C, a). If it is the case, the class B in Π_i is replaced by the two sets B' and B'' obtained from the split. For each $b \in \Sigma$, if $(B, b) \in \mathcal{W}$, it is replaced by (B', b) and (B'', b), otherwise the pair $(min(B', B''), b)$ is added to $\mathcal{W}$ (with the notation $min(B', B'')$ we mean the set with minimum cardinality between B' and B''). Let us observe that a class is split by (B', b) if and only if it is split by (B'', b), hence, the pair $(min(B', B''), b)$ is chosen for convenience.

We point out that the algorithm has a degree of freedom because the pair (C, a) to be processed at each step is freely chosen. Another free choice intervenes when a set B is split into B' and B'' with the same size and it is not present in $\mathcal{W}$. In this case, the algorithm can, indifferently, add to $\mathcal{W}$ either B' or B''.

Such considerations imply that there can be several sequences of successive refinements that starting from the initial partition $\Pi_1 = \{F, Q \setminus F\}$ lead to the coarsest congruence of the input automaton $\mathcal{A}$.

As regards the running time of the algorithm we can observe that the splitting of classes of the partition, with respect to the pair (C, a), takes a time proportional to the cardinality of the set C. Hence, the running time of the algorithm is proportional to the sum of the cardinality of all sets processed. Hopcroft proved that the running time is bounded by $O(|\Sigma||Q| \log |Q|)$. In [3] the authors proved that this bound is tight, in the sense that they provided a family of unary automata for which there exist a sequence of refinements such that the time complexity of the algorithm is $\Theta(|\Sigma||Q| \log |Q|)$. However, for the same automata there exist other sequences of refinements producing executions that run in linear time. In [7] we presented a family of unary automata for which there is a unique sequence of refinements. Moreover we defined a subclass of such automata for which the running time is $\Theta(|\Sigma||Q|\log|Q|)$. Such a subclass of unary automata was extended in [1]. Actually, unary automata represent a very special case for the automata minimization problem. In fact, the minimization can be achieved also in linear time when the alphabet has only one letter (cf. [14]). So, we are interested in facing both the problem of the uniqueness of the refinements and the tightness of the algorithm when the alphabet contains more than one letter.

In next sections we consider a family of binary automata having a unique sequence of refinements. Moreover we find a class of binary automata for which the running time of Hopcroft's algorithm is $\Theta(|\Sigma||Q|\log|Q|)$.

3   Standard Trees and Tree-Like Automata

In this section we present a class of binary automata defined by using the notion of binary labelled tree.

Let $\Sigma = \{0,1\}$ and $A = \{a,b\}$ be two binary alphabets. A *binary labelled tree* over A is a map $\tau : \Sigma^* \to A$ whose domain $dom(\tau)$ is a prefix-closed subset of Σ^*. The elements of $dom(\tau)$ are called *nodes*, if $dom(\tau)$ has a finite (resp. infinite) number of elements we say that τ is *finite* (resp. *infinite*). The *height* of a finite tree τ, denoted by $h(\tau)$, is defined as $\max\{|u| + 1, u \in dom(\tau)\}$. We say that a tree $\bar{\tau}$ is a *prefix* of a tree τ if $dom(\bar{\tau}) \subseteq dom(\tau)$ and $\bar{\tau}$ is the restriction of τ to $dom(\bar{\tau})$. A *complete infinite tree* is a tree whose domain is Σ^*. Besides, a *complete finite tree* of height n is a tree whose domain is Σ^{n-1}. The *empty tree* is the tree whose domain is the empty set.

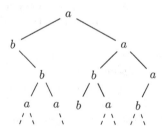

Fig. 2. Binary infinite labeled tree

If $x, y \in dom(\tau)$ are nodes of τ such that $x = yi$ for some $i \in \Sigma$, we say that y is the *father* of x and in particular, if $i = 0$ (resp. $i = 1$) x is the *left son* (resp. *right son*) of y. A node without sons is called *leaf* and the node ϵ is called *the root* of the tree. Given a tree τ, the *outer frontier* of τ is the set $Fr(\tau) = \{xi|x \in dom(\tau), i \in \Sigma, xi \notin dom(\tau)\}$.

Example 1. In Fig.2 an example of an infinite tree τ is depicted. We have, for instance, that $0111, 1011 \in dom(\tau)$ and $0110, 1001, 1000 \in Fr(\tau)$.

Let τ and τ' be two binary labelled trees. We have that τ is a *subtree* of τ' if there exist a node $v \in dom(\tau')$ such that:

i) $v \cdot dom(\tau) = \{vu | u \in dom(\tau)\} \subseteq dom(\tau')$
ii) $\tau(u) = \tau'(vu)$ for all $u \in dom(\tau)$.

In this case we say that τ is a subtree of τ' that *occurs at* node v.

In [11] operations among trees have been introduced. Here, we are interested in the concatenation among trees. Roughly speaking, we can say that in order to concatenate two trees τ_1 and τ_2 we attach the root of τ_2 to one of the element of the outer frontier of τ_1. Obviously, since the outer frontier of τ_1 can have more than one element, by concatenating τ_1 and τ_2 we obtain a set of trees. In what follows we use the notion of *simultaneous concatenation* of τ_2 to all the nodes of $Fr(\tau_1)$ i.e. the tree $\tau_1 \circ \tau_2$ defined as follows:

i) $dom(\tau_1 \circ \tau_2) = dom(\tau_1) \cup Fr(\tau_1)dom(\tau_2)$;
ii) $\forall x \in dom(\tau_1 \circ \tau_2)$, $\tau_1 \circ \tau_2(x) = \begin{cases} \tau_1(x) & \text{if } x \in dom(\tau_1) \\ \tau_2(y) & \text{if } x = zy,\ z \in Fr(\tau_1),\ y \in dom(\tau_2). \end{cases}$

Let τ be a tree, with τ^ω we denote the infinite simultaneous concatenation $\tau \circ \tau \circ \tau \circ \ldots$. Notice that, by infinitely applying the simultaneous concatenation, we obtain a complete infinite tree.

We define *factor* of a tree a finite complete subtree of the tree, and in the following we are interested in particular factors we define by using some notations given in [5].

Let τ be a tree, σ and $\bar{\sigma}$ two factors of τ such that $\bar{\sigma}$ is the complete prefix of σ of height $h(\sigma) - 1$, then σ is called an *extension of $\bar{\sigma}$* in τ. A factor σ of a tree τ is *extendable* in τ if there exists at least one extension of σ in τ.

A factor σ of τ is *2-special* if there exist exactly two different extensions of σ in τ.

We say that γ is a *circular factor* of τ if it is a factor of τ^ω with $h(\gamma) \leq h(\tau)$. A circular factor γ of τ is a *2-special circular factor* if there exist exactly two different extensions of γ in τ^ω (that we can call *circular extensions*). The concept of circular factor can be easily understood by noting that in the case of unary tree it coincides with the well-known notion of circular factor of a word.

With reference to a characterization of the notion of circular standard word given in [4], we say that a finite tree τ is a *standard tree* if for each $0 \leq h \leq h(\tau) - 2$ it has only a 2-special circular factor of height h.

Example 2. An example of standard tree, called *finite uniform tree*, is a complete tree defined by labelling all the nodes at the same level with the same letter taken in the same order it occurs in a given standard word. In Figure 3 we give the uniform tree from the word $abaab$.

Let $\mathcal{A} = (Q, \Sigma, \delta, q_0, F)$ be a *deterministic finite automaton (DFA)* over the finite alphabet Σ, where Q is a finite state set, δ is a *transition function*, $q_0 \in Q$ is the *initial state* and $F \subseteq Q$ the set of *final states*. Let $G = (V, E)$ be the

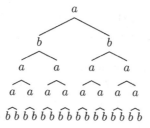

Fig. 3. The finite uniform tree defined from the word *abaab*

transition directed graph associated to $\mathcal{A}$. We say that $\mathcal{A}$ is a *tree-like automaton* if $G = (V, E)$ has a subgraph $G_t = (V, E_t)$, containing all nodes V, which is a tree (called *skeleton*) with root q_0, and such that all edges of $E \backslash E_t$ are edges from a node to an ancestor.

Given a finite binary labelled tree τ we can uniquely associate a tree-like automaton $\mathcal{A}_\tau$ having τ as skeleton and such that for each missing edge we add a transition to the root of the tree. Moreover, the root is the initial state and the states corresponding to nodes labelled by a (resp. b) are non-final (resp. final) states.

Example 3. In Fig.4 a finite labelled tree and the corresponding tree-like automaton are depicted. In the automaton, the initial state labelled by 1 corresponds to the root of the tree.

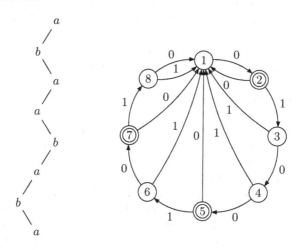

Fig. 4. A tree τ and tree-like automaton $\mathcal{A}_\tau$

4   Hopcroft's Algorithm on Standard Tree-Like Automata

In this section we deepen the connection between the refinements process of Hopcroft's algorithm when applied on a tree-like automaton associated to a standard tree and the combinatorial properties of the tree itself. By using such properties we prove that such a process is uniquely determined.

We define *standard tree-like automaton* a tree-like automaton $\mathcal{A}_\tau$ associated to a standard tree τ. The main theorem of this section gives a characterization of the partitions representing the refinement process of Hopcroft's algorithm on standard tree-like automata.

Let $\mathcal{A}_\tau = (Q, \Sigma, \delta, q_0, F)$ be a standard tree-like automaton. For any circular factor σ of τ, we define the subset Q_σ of states of $\mathcal{A}_\tau$ as the set of occurrences of σ in τ. Trivially, we have that $Q_\epsilon = Q$, $Q_b = F$ and $Q_a = Q \setminus F$. More in general, one can prove that the classes that appear during each execution of Hopcroft's algorithm on a standard tree-like automaton $\mathcal{A}_\tau$ are all of the form Q_σ for some circular factor σ of τ.

The following proposition establishes a close relation between the split operation during the execution of Hopcroft's algorithm on a standard tree-like automaton and the notion of circular special factor of a standard tree.

Proposition 1. *Let $\mathcal{A}_\tau$ be a standard tree-like automaton. Let Q_σ and Q_γ be classes of a partition of Q. If (Q_γ, x) splits Q_σ, for some $x \in \Sigma$, with $h(\gamma) = h(\sigma)$, then σ is a 2-special circular factor of τ. The resulting classes are $Q_{\sigma'}$ and $Q_{\sigma''}$, where σ' and σ'' are the only two possible extensions of σ in τ.*

The following theorem states that, in case of standard tree-like automata, the sequence of partitions created during the refinement process of Hopcroft's algorithm is unique whatever element we choose and delete from the waiting set. The statement of the theorem characterizes each current partition after each split operation of Hopcroft's algorithm on a standard tree-like automaton.

Theorem 1. *Let $\mathcal{A}_\tau$ be a standard tree-like automaton. The sequence of the refinement process $\Pi_1, \Pi_2, ...\Pi_{h(\tau)-2}$ is uniquely determined and*

$$\Pi_k = \{Q_\sigma | \ \sigma \ \text{is a circular factor of} \ \tau \ \text{with} \ h(\sigma) = k\}$$

Note that the theorem states also that, the partition Π_k of the set of the states has exactly $k + 1$ classes. In fact, one can easily prove that a tree τ is standard if and only if, for each $k = 1, \ldots, h(\tau) - 1$, τ has exactly $k + 1$ circular factors of height k. For the sake of brevity, we don't give the proof of the theorem but the following two propositions play a fundamental role in proving the statement. They provide the main reasons for which the sequence of the split operations is uniquely determined during the execution of Hopcroft's algorithm. Indeed, at each step, the splitting classes (if exist) of the waiting set, cause the same unique split in the current partition and with respect to the same letter.

Proposition 2. *Let $\mathcal{A}_\tau$ be a standard tree-like automaton and σ and γ be two circular factors of τ having the same height. If $(Q_\gamma, 0)$ (resp. $(Q_\gamma, 1)$) splits Q_σ then $(Q_\gamma, 1)$ (resp. $(Q_\gamma, 0)$) either does not split Q_σ or splits it in the same way.*

Proposition 3. *Let $\mathcal{A}_\tau$ be a standard tree-like automaton. Each (Q_γ, x) splits at most one class Q_σ, with $h(\gamma) = h(\sigma)$, for some $x \in \Sigma$.*

5   Word Trees

Let $\Sigma = \{0,1\}$ and $A = \{a, b\}$. Given two words $v = v_1 v_2 ... v_{n-1} \in \Sigma^*$ and $w = w_1 w_2 ... w_n \in A^*$, by $\tau_{v,w}$ we denote the labelled tree $\tau_{v,w}$ such that $dom(\tau_{v,w})$ is the set of prefixes of v and the map is defined as follows:

$$\begin{cases} \tau_{v,w}(\epsilon) = w_1 \\ \tau_{v,w}(v_1 v_2 ... v_i) = w_{i+1} \; \forall 1 \leq i \leq n-1 \end{cases}$$

We call *word tree* the finite labelled tree $\tau_{v,w}$. When v is obtained by taking the prefix of length $n-1$ of w and by substituting a's with 0's and b's with 1's, we use the simpler notation τ_w. In Fig. 4 a word tree τ_w with $w = abaababa$ is depicted.

Our investigation is focused on word trees associated to standard words.

We recall the well known notion of standard word. Let $d_1, d_2, ..., d_n, ...$ be a sequence of natural integers, with $d_1 \geq 0$ and $d_i > 0$, for $i = 2, ..., n, ...$. Consider the following sequence of words $\{s_n\}_{n \geq 0}$ over the alphabet A: $s_0 = b$, $s_1 = a$, $s_{n+1} = s_n^{d_n} s_{n-1}$ for $n \geq 1$. Each finite words s_n in the sequence is called *standard word*. It is uniquely determined by the (finite) directive sequence $(d_0, d_1, ..., d_{n-1})$. In the special case where the directive sequence is of the form $(1, 1, ..., 1, ...)$ we obtain the sequence of Fibonacci words.

In this section we consider the trees τ_w, when w is a standard word. One can prove that such trees are standard, so the associated tree-like automata are standard. Actually, they represent an instance of standard trees that is opposite to the finite uniform tree described in Section 3. The difference consists in the fact that the two extension of each 2-special circular factors differ only by a leaf, while in case of uniform tree all the leaves are involved.

The aim of this section is to compute the running time of Hopcroft's algorithm on these automata by using propositions stated in previous section.

With $c(\mathcal{A})$ we denote the running time of Hopcroft's algorithm to minimize $\mathcal{A}$.

Firstly, we recall that the running time is proportional to the cardinality of the classes processed in the waiting set. So, in order to make the computation we have to establish which classes each time go into the waiting set. In this particular case, as we saw in previous section, the split that occurs at each step involves the class Q_σ with σ special factor of the tree. Then, at each step we have a unique split of Q_σ in $Q_{\sigma'}$ and $Q_{\sigma''}$. Furthermore, in order to prove the main result of this section, the following proposition is needed.

Proposition 4. *Let τ_w be a standard word tree. At each step of Hopcroft's algorithm on $\mathcal{A}_{\tau_w}$ any class does not split itself.*

Hence, we can conclude that each time only one class goes into the waiting set (the minimum between $Q_{\sigma'}$ and $Q_{\sigma''}$), with both the letters of the alphabet. By Proposition 2 one can derive that such a class can cause a split with respect only one letter. Such facts lead to the following proposition.

Proposition 5. *Let τ_w be a standard word tree. Then the time complexity of Hopcroft's algorithm on $\mathcal{A}_{\tau_w}$ is*

$$\mathbf{c}(\mathcal{A}_{\tau_w}) = 2 \sum_{\sigma \in sp(\tau_w)} \min(|Q_{\sigma'}|, |Q_{\sigma''}|),$$

where with $sp(\tau_w)$ we denote the set of 2-special circular factor of τ_w.

In [6,1] the authors consider the unary cyclic automaton $\mathcal{A}_w$ associated to a word w and give an exact computation of the running time the algorithm on these automata, when w is a standard word, by using the fact that $\mathbf{c}(\mathcal{A}_w) = \sum_{u \in sp(w)} \min(|Q_{u0}|, |Q_{u1}|)$, where $sp(w)$ is the set of special factors of w. For sake of brevity we refer to [3] for the definition of the notion of unary cyclic automaton.

Remark that, in case of a standard word tree τ_w, there is a one-to-one correspondence between the occurrences of the 2-special circular factors of τ_w and the occurrences of the special factors of w. Consequently, we have the following result.

Proposition 6. *Let τ_w be a standard word tree and w the corresponding standard word.*

$$\mathbf{c}(\mathcal{A}_{\tau_w}) = 2\mathbf{c}(\mathcal{A}_w).$$

The previous proposition states that Hopcroft'algorithm on binary standard tree-like automaton inherits all the worst cases obtained when it is applied on unary cyclic automata associated to standard words. Such worst cases are described in [6,1]. Such a consideration is formalized in the following theorem.

Theorem 2. *Hopcroft's algorithm on tree-like automata $\mathcal{A} = (Q, \Sigma, \delta, q_0, F)$ associated to standard word trees has a uniquely determined refinement process and runs in time $\Theta(|\Sigma||Q|log|Q|)$.*

Hence, we proved that there exist automata on binary alphabet for which Hopcroft's algorithm is tight.

6   Conclusions and Related Works

In this paper we face the problem of minimization of deterministic finite automata with reference to Hopcroft's algorithm. We consider the refinement processes of the algorithm and we find an infinite family of binary automata for which there is a unique process. It would be interesting to give a characterization of the automata for which the sequence of successive refinements is uniquely determined. Moreover we face the tightness of the algorithm when the alphabet contains more than one letter. In particular we define an infinite family of binary automata representing the worst case of Hopcroft's algorithm.

Remark that the here defined standard trees can be arouse an independent interest because they are closely related to a class of infinite trees, called *Sturmian Trees* (cf. [2]). Actually the standard trees allow to construct an infinite family of Sturmian Trees having some interesting combinatorial properties as, for instance, the balance. We investigate such a family in [8].

References

1. Berstel, J., Boasson, L., Carton, O.: Continuant Polynomials and worst-case of Hopcroft's algorithm. Theoretical Computer Science (to appear)
2. Berstel, J., Boasson, L., Carton, O., Fagnot, I.: Sturmian trees. Theory of Computing Systems (to appear)
3. Berstel, J., Carton, O.: On the complexity of Hopcroft's state minimization algorithm. In: Domaratzki, M., Okhotin, A., Salomaa, K., Yu, S. (eds.) CIAA 2004. LNCS, vol. 3317, pp. 35–44. Springer, Heidelberg (2005)
4. Borel, J.P., Reutenauer, C.: On Christoffel classes. RAIRO-Theoretical Informatics and Applications 450, 15–28 (2006)
5. Carpi, A., de Luca, A., Varricchio, S.: Special factors and uniqueness conditions in rational trees. Theory Comput. Syst. 34(4), 375–395 (2001)
6. Castiglione, G., Restivo, A., Sciortino, M.: Circular sturmian words and hopcroft's algorithm. Theoretical Computer Science (to appear)
7. Castiglione, G., Restivo, A., Sciortino, M.: Hopcroft's algorithm and cyclic automata. In: Martín-Vide, C., Otto, F., Fernau, H. (eds.) LATA 2008. LNCS, vol. 5196, pp. 172–183. Springer, Heidelberg (2008)
8. Castiglione, G., Restivo, A., Sciortino, M.: On a family of sturmian trees. Technical report, University of Palermo (2009)
9. Hopcroft, J.E.: An $n \log n$ algorithm for mimimizing the states in a finite automaton. In: Kohavi, Z., Paz, A. (eds.) Theory of machines and computations (Proc. Internat. Sympos. Technion, Haifa, 1971), pp. 189–196. Academic Press, New York (1971)
10. Knuutila, T.: Re-describing an algorithm by Hopcroft. Theoret. Comput. Sci. 250, 333–363 (2001)
11. Mantaci, S., Restivo, A.: Codes and equations on trees. Theor. Comput. Sci. 255(1-2), 483–509 (2001)
12. Matz, O., Miller, A., Potthoff, A., Thomas, W., Valkema, E.: Report on the program AMoRE. Technical Report 9507, Inst. f. Informatik u. Prakt. Math., CAU Kiel (1995)
13. Moore, E.F.: Gedaken experiments on sequential machines. In: Automata Studies, pp. 129–153 (1956)
14. Paige, R., Tarjan, R.E., Bonic, R.: A linear time solution to the single function coarsest partition problem. Theor. Comput. Sci. 40, 67–84 (1985)
15. Watson, B.: A taxonomy of finite automata minimization algorithms. Technical Report 93/44, Eindhoven University of Technology, Faculty of Mathematics and Computing Science (1994)

Compact Normal Form for Regular Languages as Xor Automata

Jean Vuillemin and Nicolas Gama

École normale supérieure and INRIA, France

Abstract. The only presently known normal form for a regular language $\mathcal{L} \in \mathcal{R}\mathrm{eg}$ is its Minimal Deterministic Automaton $\mathrm{MDA}(\mathcal{L})$. We show that a regular language is also characterized by a finite dimension $\dim(\mathcal{L})$, which is always smaller than the number $|\mathrm{MDA}(\mathcal{L})|$ of states, and often exponentially so. The dimension is also the minimal number of states of all *Nondeterministic Xor Automaton* (NXA) which accept the language. NXAs combine the advantages of deterministic automata (normal form, negation, minimization, equivalence of states, accessibility) and of non-deterministic ones (compactness, mirror language). We present an algorithmic construction of the Minimal Non Deterministic Xor Automaton $\mathrm{MXA}(\mathcal{L})$, in cubic time from any NXA for $\mathcal{L} \in \mathcal{R}\mathrm{eg}$. The MXA provides another normal form: $\mathcal{L} = \mathcal{L}' \Leftrightarrow \mathrm{MXA}(\mathcal{L}) = \mathrm{MXA}(\mathcal{L}')$. Our algorithm establishes a missing connection between Brzozowski's mirror-based minimization method for deterministic automata, and algorithms based on state-equivalence.

1 Introduction

Regular languages $\mathcal{R}\mathrm{eg}$ are at the core of formal languages (sets of words), in logic, computer science and linguistics. Finding minimal forms for regular languages has a long history [5,10,11]; yet, minimizing *Non Deterministic Automata* NDA [12] or deciding their equivalence has remained computationally intractable for well over half a century [6,7].

Our contribution is to show that, unlike NDAs, non-deterministic xor automata NXA [3,14] have a unique minimal form which can be effectively computed through linear algebra. The result is novel for alphabet sizes 2 and more: our minimization algorithm proceeds in two mirror passes, and has a cubic bit-level complexity. The result was known for the unary alphabet: the minimization of such NXA is achieved in [15] by reduction to *linear feed-back shift registers* and use of the Berlekamp-Massey algorithm [8].

1.1 Background and Notations

Words and hierarchical order. The alphabet is denoted by Σ, and the set of all words is Σ^*. The shortest word is ϵ of length $0 = |\epsilon|$. Words are ordered by *hierarchical order*: $u \leq v \Leftrightarrow |u| < |v|$ or $(|u| = |v|$ and $u \leq_{\mathrm{lex}} v)$. This well-founded order allows to enumerate every words in increasing order, so that words

S. Maneth (Ed.): CIAA 2009, LNCS 5642, pp. 24–33, 2009.

can be used as indexes in infinite tables. For example, words over the alphabet $\Sigma = \{a, b\}$ are in order $\Sigma^* = \{\epsilon, a, b, aa, ab, ba, bb, aaa, \cdots\}$.

Operations on words and languages. The concatenation of two words u and v is $u.v$, and the mirror of u is $\rho(u)$ with the letters of u in reversed order. Note that $\epsilon.u = u.\epsilon = u$ and $\rho(\epsilon) = \epsilon$. In any word $w = u.v$, u is a prefix of w and v a suffix. The set operators of $\cup, \cap, \backslash$, complement ($\neg$), and symmetric difference ($\oplus$) are used on sets of words, *i.e.* languages. Concatenation and mirror are extended to languages: for U and $V \in \Sigma^*$, $\rho(U) = \{\rho(u), u \in U\}$, and $U.V$ stands for $\{u.v, u \in U, v \in V\}$. This operator can be iterated a fixed number of times: $U^0 = \{\epsilon\}$ and $U^{n+1} = U.U^n$ when $n \geq 1$, or indefinitely of times with Kleene's star $U^* = \bigcup_{n \in \mathbb{N}} U^n$ operation [12].

Non-deterministic finite automata. A NDA is a structure $\mathcal{A}(Q, I, (T_\alpha)_{\alpha \in \Sigma}, F)$, where Q is the finite set of *states*, $I, F \subseteq Q$ are the initial and final states, for each letter $\alpha \in \Sigma$, $T_\alpha : Q \to \mathcal{P}(Q)$ is the transition function of α. An accepting path in $\mathcal{A}$ along a word $w = \alpha_1.\ldots.\alpha_p \in \Sigma^p$ is a tuple $(q_0, \ldots, q_p) \in Q^{p+1}$ such that $q_0 \in I$, $q_{i+1} \in T_{\alpha_i}(q_i)$ and $q_p \in F$.

Schutzenberger [13] introduces the multiplicity $M_{\mathcal{A}}^w$ of a word w in $\mathcal{A}$ as the number of such accepting paths in $\mathcal{A}$ along w. A NDA is equivalently represented by a graph or by matrices. In the matrix representation, Q is the integer interval $[1; n]$. Sets of states, like I and F, are represented by their characteristic vector $I[i] = 1 \Leftrightarrow i \in I$, and transition functions are represented by $n \times n$ row-matrices $(T_\alpha)_{i,j \in [1,n]}$ with $T_\alpha[i, j] = 1 \iff j \in T_\alpha(i)$. Note that with row matrices, an expression like $g(f(x))$ is represented by the product $X \times \text{Matrix}_f \times \text{Matrix}_g$ in this order. Although the coefficients of the matrices above are all 0 or 1, the integer matrix product $*_{\mathbb{N}} =< \times, + >$ yields non-negative integers which count the multiplicity of words between states of $\mathcal{A}$. We note the key matrix expression:

$$M_{\mathcal{A}}^{w_1 \ldots w_p} = I *_{\mathbb{N}} T_{\alpha_1} \ldots T_{\alpha_p} *_{\mathbb{N}} F.$$

Classical automata theory [12] effectively defines recognition in NDA by $w \in \mathcal{L}_{\mathcal{A}} \iff M_{\mathcal{A}}^w \neq 0$. One can equivalently use $w \in \mathcal{L}_{\mathcal{A}} \iff B_{\mathcal{A}}^w = 1$, with

$$B_{\mathcal{A}}^{w_1, \ldots, w_p} = I *_{\mathbb{B}} T_{\alpha_1} \ldots T_{\alpha_p} *_{\mathbb{B}} F,$$

where the matrix operations $*_{\mathbb{B}} =< \cap, \cup >$ now take place in the boolean ring rather than in integer algebra, and $B_{\mathcal{A}}^w = 1 \iff M_{\mathcal{A}}^w \neq 0$. A third expression is

$$P_{\mathcal{A}}^{w_1, \ldots, w_p} = I *_{\mathbb{F}_2} T_{\alpha_1} \ldots T_{\alpha_n} *_{\mathbb{F}_2} F,$$

where matrices are now multiplied $*_{\mathbb{F}_2} =< \cap, \oplus >$ over the 2-element field $\mathbb{F}_2$. This defines the representation of *Nondeterministic Xor Automaton* (NXA) by binary matrices. Acceptance of a word w of length p by a NXA with n states is defined by $w \in \mathcal{L}_{\mathcal{A}} \iff P_{\mathcal{A}}^w \neq 0$ in $O(pn^2)$ boolean operations. Note that $P_{\mathcal{A}}^w$ is the parity of $M_{\mathcal{A}}^w$ and w is accepted by a NXA $\mathcal{A} \iff$ the number of accepting paths in $\mathcal{A}$ along w is odd. For all three above matrix products, we extend the transition matrices to words by $T_w = T_{\alpha_1} \star \cdots \star T_{\alpha_n}$, and the acceptance condition becomes $I \star T_w \star F \neq 0$. Complete deterministic finite automata (DFA) are a subclass of NDA with a single initial state $|I| = 1$, and $\forall q \in Q, \forall \alpha \in \Sigma$ a single element in $T_\alpha(q)$. The transition functions are deterministic, the matrices are stochastic (single 1 per row), and all three matrix products coincide:

$$\mathcal{A} \in DFA \iff \forall w : I *_\text{N} T_w *_\text{N} F = I *_\text{B} T_w *_\text{B} F = I *_{\mathbb{F}_2} T_w *_{\mathbb{F}_2} F.$$

So, a DFA can be equivalently interpreted as a NDA or a NXA.

Furthermore, each NDA and NXA can be transformed into a DFA which accepts the same language. Determinization is achieved by the *subset construction*, in time proportional to that of the output. The difference between NXA and NDA-determinizations is that a subset of states in the output is *final* if and only if its intersection with F is odd, rather than *not-empty*. It follows that NDA, DFA and NXA all recognize the very same class of regular languages.

1.2   Linear Representation of a Language and Dimension

Schutzenberger's theory [13] of automata with multiplicity is extended over semi-rings by Fliess [4] into what are now known as weighted automata [9] and formal power series [1]. Here, we only consider the very special case of these theories over the two element field $\mathbb{F}_2$. We also replace the Hankel matrix used in [1], by the *truth matrix*, so as to establish connections between mirror and negation operations on languages, and classical involutions in linear algebra, and link minimization based on state-equivalence with algorithms in two mirror passes à la Brzozowski.

1.3   Dimension of a Language

The set of all languages $\mathcal{P}(\Sigma^*)$ has a natural structure of vector space over $\mathbb{F}_2$: the sum of two languages is their symmetric difference $\oplus$, the neutral element $\emptyset$ is the empty language, and the external product $\times$ by constants 0 or 1 is trivial. Since regular languages are closed by $\oplus$, the class $\mathcal{R}eg$ of regular languages is a sub-vector space of $\mathcal{P}(\Sigma^*)$. The linear span (over $\mathbb{F}_2$) containing a subset F of a vector space E, is the set of all finite linear combinations of elements of F, denoted by $\text{span}(F)$.

Truth table. A language can be represented by the formal power series of its multiplicities $(\chi_\mathcal{L}^w)_{w \in \Sigma^*} \in \mathbb{F}_2^{\Sigma^*}$ where $\chi_\mathcal{L}^w = 1 \iff w \in \mathcal{L}$, 0 else. In [1], this serie is written as $\sum_{w \in \Sigma^*} \chi_\mathcal{L}^w \cdot w$ where words are monomials on the non-commutative letters. Note that series of two languages $\mathcal{L}$ and $\mathcal{L}'$ can be added pairwise, which yields to the serie of $\mathcal{L} \oplus \mathcal{L}'$. By carefully choosing an order on words, a serie can be uniquely presented as an infinite vector, which we call *truth table*. This particular order is the one of mirrors: the *truth table* of $\mathcal{L}$ contains $\chi_\mathcal{L}^{\rho(w)}$ at position $w \in \Sigma^*$ (recall that here, w represents its integer index in hierarchical increasing order).

Suffix languages. Given a language $\mathcal{L}$ and a word $w \in \Sigma^*$, the *suffix language* $w^{-1}.\mathcal{L}$ is defined by $\{u \in \Sigma^*, w.u \in \mathcal{L}\}$. Note that $\epsilon^{-1}.\mathcal{L} = \mathcal{L}$ and for any words

u and v, $(u.v)^{-1}.\mathcal{L} = v^{-1}.(u^{-1}.\mathcal{L})$. The *suffix linear application* of $\mathcal{L}$ associates any word w to the corresponding suffix of $\mathcal{L}$. It is defined on the canonical basis of $\text{span}(\Sigma^*)$ by:

$$\text{suffix}_{\mathcal{L}} \begin{array}{l} \text{span}(\Sigma^*) \to \mathcal{P}(\Sigma^*) \\ w \in \Sigma^* \to w^{-1}.\mathcal{L} \end{array}$$

The *index* of a language $\mathcal{L}$ is the number of different suffixes of $\mathcal{L}$, i.e. the cardinality of $\{w^{-1}.\mathcal{L}, w \in \Sigma^*\}$. It corresponds to the size of the minimal deterministic automata of $\mathcal{L}$ (MDA($\mathcal{L}$)). The *dimension* of $\mathcal{L}$ is the dimension of $\text{span}\{w^{-1}.\mathcal{L}, w \in \Sigma^*\}$ or equivalently the rank of $\text{suffix}_{\mathcal{L}}$. Since the field $\mathbb{F}_2$ is finite, the dimension satisfies: $\log_2(\text{index}(\mathcal{L})) \le \dim(\mathcal{L}) \le \text{index}(\mathcal{L})$. For example, the following LFSR language $L = \{a^t, t \in \{0,1,2,4\} \bmod 7\}$ has index 8 and dimension $\log_2(8) = 3$. Hence the following [11,13] characterization of regular languages.

Theorem 1 (Myhill,Nerode,Schutzenberger). *A language $\mathcal{L}$ is regular $\Longleftrightarrow$ it has finite index $\Longleftrightarrow$ it has finite dimension over $\mathbb{F}_2$.*

Truth function and Truth matrix. The notion of *truth matrix* is a variant of Hankel's matrix [4]. Both are infinite matrix representations of $\text{suffix}_{\mathcal{L}}$. The *truth matrix* $\mathfrak{T}$ of the language $\mathcal{L}$ is defined by $\mathfrak{T}[i,j] = 1 \iff w_i.\rho(w_j) \in \mathcal{L}$. Its i-th row is the truth table of $w_i^{-1}.\mathcal{L}$. Note that the formula of the truth matrix contains a mirror, whereas Hankel's matrix [4], defined by $H[i,j] = 1 \iff w_i.w_j \in \mathcal{L}$ doesn't. However both matrices have same rank, as they just differ by a permutation of columns. As we can see in the following theorem, the mirror in the truth table is important to make a connection between linear properties of $\mathcal{L}$ and its mirror.

Theorem 2. *Truth matrices of a language $\mathcal{L}$ and its mirror $\rho(\mathcal{L})$ are respective transpose. Let $\mathfrak{T}$ be the truth matrix of $\mathcal{L}$, then the w-th row of $\mathfrak{T}$ is the truth table of $w^{-1}.\mathcal{L}$, and the w-th column of $\mathfrak{T}$ is the truth table of $w^{-1}.\rho(\mathcal{L})$. $\mathcal{L}$ is regular $\Leftrightarrow \mathfrak{T}$ has a finite number of different rows $\Leftrightarrow \mathfrak{T}$ has finite rank $\Leftrightarrow \mathfrak{T}$ has a finite number of different columns. The indexes of $\mathcal{L}$ and $\rho(\mathcal{L})$ are respectively the number of different rows and columns of $\mathfrak{T}$, and $\dim(\mathcal{L}) = \dim(\rho(\mathcal{L})) = \text{rank}(\mathfrak{T})$.*

Proof. We have $\mathfrak{T}_{\mathcal{L}}[i,j] = 1 \Leftrightarrow w_i.\rho(w_j) \in \mathcal{L} \Leftrightarrow \rho(w_i.\rho(w_j)) = w_j.\rho(w_i) \in \rho\mathcal{L} \Leftrightarrow \mathfrak{T}_{\rho\mathcal{L}}[j,i] = 1$. In other words, the truth table of the mirror language is the transpose of the truth table of $\mathcal{L}$. Other properties are in common with Hankel matrices [13,1,4] and are immediate consequences of their definitions, and of the invariance of rank by transposition. □

In the binary field $\mathbb{F}_2$, the truth matrix also reveals that the dimensions of $\mathcal{L}$ and its negation $\neg\mathcal{L}$ satisfy $|\dim(\mathcal{L}) - \dim(\neg L)| \le 1$. Indeed, one negates any truth table by adding the constant infinite vector $[1,1,\ldots,1,\ldots]$. Therefore, $\text{Im}(\text{suffix}_{\neg\mathcal{L}}) \subseteq \text{Im}(\text{suffix}_{\mathcal{L}}) \oplus [1,1,\ldots,1,\ldots]$. This proves the inequality on the dimension.

Note that the index of some languages like $\Sigma^*1\Sigma^n1$ is exponentially larger than the index of its mirror. This clearly motivates the research of normal form for a language which is polynomial in its dimension, which is in turn lower than $\min(\text{index}(\mathcal{L}), \text{index}(\rho L))$, and therefore much smaller than the MDA.

1.4   Consequences on Xor Automata

Following Schutzenberger's terminology [1], regular languages are particular case of recognizable languages, and they admit a linear representation which corresponds to a weighted automata. There exists a similarity equivalence relation, modulo which the minimal linear representation of $\mathcal{L}$ is unique. When the weights are taken from $\mathbb{F}_2$, this linear representation of $\mathcal{L} \in \mathcal{R}eg$ corresponds to the class of NXA which accepts $\mathcal{L}$. The similarity between NXA can be defined with their matrix representation by:

Definition 1. *Two automata $\mathcal{A} = (n, I, (T_\alpha), F)$ and $\mathcal{A}' = (n, I', (T'_\alpha), F')$ are similar if and only if there exists an invertible matrix $P \in GL(\mathbb{F}_2^n)$ such that $I' = IP$, $T'_\alpha = P^{-1}T_\alpha P$ and $F' = P^{-1}F$.*

As similarity preserves products of the form $I \times T_{\alpha_1} \times \cdots \times T_{\alpha_n} \times F$, it follows that two similar automata recognize the same language. We now show why the converse is true when the number of states is minimal. This is a major difference with classical NDA, which lack such a relation. Just like the permutation of states on deterministic automata, similarity between NXA is the key element to perform reduction and minimization of these automata.

Given a Xor automata $\mathcal{A}(n, I, (T_\alpha), F)$ recognizing a language $\mathcal{L}$, two linear applications will be particularly useful. The *configuration function*, which associates to a word the configuration of active states when reading this word:

$$\text{config}_\mathcal{A} : \begin{array}{c} \text{span}(\Sigma^*) \to \mathbb{F}_2^n \\ w \in \Sigma^* \to I \times T_w \end{array}$$

and the *language function*, which associates to any configuration of states the language accepted from this configuration.

$$\mathcal{L}_\mathcal{A} : \begin{array}{c} \mathbb{F}_2^n \to \mathcal{R}eg \\ x \to \text{language of } \mathcal{A}(n, x, (T_\alpha), F) \end{array}$$

Note that by definition of the acceptance, a word $w = u.v$ is accepted by $\mathcal{A}$ if and only if $(I \times T_u) \times T_v \times F = 1$, that is $v \in \mathcal{L}_\mathcal{A}(\text{config}_\mathcal{A}(u))$. Therefore, for all $u \in \Sigma^*$, $u^{-1}.\mathcal{L} = \mathcal{L}_\mathcal{A}(\text{config}_\mathcal{A}(u))$. In particular, we have

$$\text{suffix}_\mathcal{L} = \mathcal{L}_\mathcal{A} \circ \text{config}_\mathcal{A}. \tag{1}$$

The matrix $\text{ram}_\mathcal{A}$ of $\text{config}_\mathcal{A}$ has dimensions $\infty \times n$ and its w-th row is $I \times T_w$. The matrix $\text{cam}_\mathcal{A}$ of $\mathcal{L}_\mathcal{A}$ is the juxtaposition of truth tables (like in Section 1.3) of the languages $\mathcal{L}_\mathcal{A}(e_i)$ of each state $(e_i)_{i \in [1,n]}$. It is a $n \times \infty$ matrix whose w-th column is $T_{\rho w} \times F$. By Equation (1), the truth matrix $\mathfrak{T}_\mathcal{L}$ of $\mathcal{L}$ is $\text{ram}_\mathcal{A} \times \text{cam}_\mathcal{A}$. This leads to the fundamental theorem.

Theorem 3. *The dimension of a language $\mathcal{L}$ is smaller than the number of states n of any NXA $\mathcal{A}$ recognizing $\mathcal{L}$. There is equality $n = \dim(\mathcal{L})$ if and only if $\mathrm{config}_{\mathcal{A}}$ is surjective and $\mathcal{L}_{\mathcal{A}}$ is injective. Furthermore, two minimal NXA (with $n = \dim \mathcal{L}$) recognizing the same language are similar.*

Proof. Both functions $\mathrm{config}_{\mathcal{A}}$ and $\mathcal{L}_{\mathcal{A}}$ have by definition rank $\leq n$. Therefore by (1), $\dim(L) = \mathrm{rank}(\mathrm{suffix}_{\mathcal{L}}) \leq n$. If $n = \dim(\mathcal{L})$, then $\mathrm{rank}(\mathrm{config}_{\mathcal{A}}) = n$ ($\mathrm{config}_{\mathcal{A}}$ is surjective), and $\mathrm{rank}(\mathcal{L}_{\mathcal{A}}) = n$ ($\mathcal{L}_{\mathcal{A}}$ is injective). Reciprocally, if $\mathrm{config}_{\mathcal{A}}$ is surjective and $\mathcal{L}_{\mathcal{A}}$ is injective, $\dim(\mathcal{L}) = \mathrm{rank}(\mathcal{L}_{\mathcal{A}} \circ \mathrm{config}_{\mathcal{A}}) = \dim(\mathcal{L}_{\mathcal{A}}(\mathbb{F}_2^n)) = n$. For the last point, consider another minimal automata $\mathcal{A}'$ recognizing $\mathcal{L}$. Since $\mathrm{ram}_{\mathcal{A}} \times \mathrm{cam}_{\mathcal{A}} = \mathrm{ram}_{\mathcal{A}'} \times \mathrm{cam}_{\mathcal{A}'} (= \mathfrak{T}_{\mathcal{L}})$ and both $\mathrm{cam}_{\mathcal{A}}, \mathrm{cam}_{\mathcal{A}'}$ are injective, there is an invertible $n \times n$ matrix P such that $\mathrm{ram}_{\mathcal{A}'} = \mathrm{ram}_{\mathcal{A}} \times P$. One can show by induction that this specific P defines the similitude between $\mathcal{A}$ and $\mathcal{A}'$. For instance, let W be the n smallest words such that the extracted $\mathrm{ram}_{\mathcal{A}'}(W)$ is invertible, then the transition T_{α}' of $\mathcal{A}'$ is $\mathrm{ram}_{\mathcal{A}'}(W)^{-1} \times \mathrm{ram}_{\mathcal{A}'}(W.\alpha) = P^{-1} \times \mathrm{ram}_{\mathcal{A}}(W)^{-1} \times \mathrm{ram}_{\mathcal{A}}(W.\alpha) \times P = P^{-1} T_{\alpha} P$. $\square$

As suggested by dimension considerations in 1.3, recognizing the mirror language is easy as for classical NDA: from the matrix representation of a NXA $\mathcal{A}(n, I, (T_{\alpha})_{\alpha \in \Sigma}, F)$ accepting a language $\mathcal{L}$, its transpose $\mathcal{A}(n, F^t, (T_{\alpha}^t)_{\alpha \in \Sigma}, I^t)$ recognizes the mirror language $\rho\mathcal{L}$. It is also easy to make an NXA recognize the negation of a language: just add a single isolated state which is always active (that is, both initial and final, and looping back to itself by all letters). In the classical NDA case, recognizing the negation would require determinization.

2   Reduction of Xor Automata

In [1], a formal algorithm was already described to obtain one minimal linear representation of $\mathcal{L}$ up to similarity. Here, we focus on NXA minimization algorithms and their complexity, and we provide unique normal form MXA($\mathcal{L}$) as output. We show how to adjust DFA minimization algorithms to handle NXA within cubic complexity.

In the deterministic case, minimization consist in ensuring *accessibility* (each state must be reached by at least a word $w \in \Sigma^*$) and *distinguishability* (the language recognized from each state must be different). Up to permutation of states, the output is the *minimal deterministic automata* (MDA) of a regular language $\mathcal{L}$ and corresponds to the intrinsic suffix automata $\mathcal{A}(Q, I, (T_{\alpha}), F)$ where $Q = \{w^{-1}.\mathcal{L}, w \in \Sigma^*\}$, $I = \epsilon^{-1}.\mathcal{L}$, $T_{\alpha}(q) = \{\alpha^{-1}.q\}$, $F = \{q \in Q, \epsilon \in q\}$. Various algorithms are known to construct the MDA of a language, and most [16] iteratively construct a partition of states based on their language $\mathcal{L}_{\mathcal{A}}(q)$. According to Watson [16], the only exception is Brzozowski's algorithm [2], which applies successively mirror, determinization, mirror, determinization. Despite its exponential worst-case complexity, Brzozowski's is the only minimization algorithm reported in [17] which can efficiently take NDAs and regular expressions for inputs.

2.1   Linear Accessibility

We still need to show that both conditions of Theorem 3 can be fulfilled at the same time to prove the existence of a minimal xor-automata. We first show how to make the config function surjective. This is analogue of the deterministic accessibility.

Definition 2 (linear accessibility). *An automata is linearly accessible if and only if its configuration function* $\text{config}_A : w \to IT_w$ *is surjective.*

Let's begin with an example of non linearly-accessible NXA. The configuration function always remains in $\text{span}(e_1, e_2)$, and the state e_3 is never active.

$$I = [0\ 1|0], T_0 = \begin{bmatrix} 1 & 1 & | & 0 \\ 0 & 1 & | & 0 \\ 1 & 0 & | & 1 \end{bmatrix} T_1 = \begin{bmatrix} 0 & 1 & | & 0 \\ 1 & 0 & | & 0 \\ 1 & 0 & | & 1 \end{bmatrix}, F = \begin{bmatrix} * \\ * \\ * \end{bmatrix}$$

In this case, we say that the automaton is block-triangular of size 2, which can be formalized by the following definition.

Definition 3 (block triangular automata). *An automata is block-triangular of size* $d < n$ *if* $I_t = 0$ *for* $t > d$ *and* $T_\alpha(i, j) = 0$ *for* $i \leq d$ *and* $j > d$ *(they are blockwise lower-triangular). Then the truncated automata* $A^{(d)} = (I^{(d)}, T_\alpha^{(d)}, F^{(d)})$ *recognizes the same language, where* $I^{(d)}$ *and* $F^{(d)}$ *are the first* d *coefficients of* I *and* F, *and* $T_\alpha^{(d)}$ *is upper-left most* $d \times d$ *submatrix of* T_α.

In fact, up to similarity, every case of non-accessibility can be transformed into the previous example.

Theorem 4. *Every automaton* $\mathcal{A}(n, I, (T_\alpha), F)$ *is similar to a block-triang. automata of size* $d = \text{rank}(\text{config}_A)$. *The truncated automata at level d is linearly accessible and recognizes the same language. Algorithm 1 obtains linear accessibility in place in time* $O(n^2 d)$.

We prove this theorem with Algorithm 1, which basically performs a breadth first search in the subset automata, but unlike the determinization algorithm, it stops the exploration whenever the current subset of states (the configuration) is linearly dependent on previous ones (instead of equal). Tests of linear dependencies are eased by incrementally applying elementary operations like in the Gaussian elimination.

2.2   Linear Distinguishability

In order to minimize a xor-automata, we also need to ensure that its language function $\mathcal{L}_A$ becomes injective. This is the analogue of the *distinguishability* of deterministic automata, which requires that the (suffix) language of each state is different.

Definition 4. *An xor-automata* $\mathcal{A} = (n, I, (T_\alpha)_{\alpha \in \Sigma}, F)$ *is linearly distinguishable if its acceptance function* $\mathcal{L}_A$ *is injective.*

Algorithm 1. Linear Accessibility (LAcc)

Require: An automata $\mathcal{A}(n, I, (T_\alpha), F)$, and the elem. ops and similitudes:
    def $P(i, j, [\lambda_1, \ldots, \lambda_n])$: Do column $C_k \leftarrow C_k + \lambda_k C_j, k \neq j$ then swap (C_i, C_j).
    def $\text{Simi}(i, j, [\lambda_1, \ldots, \lambda_n])$: Apply $P = P(i, j, [\lambda_1, \ldots, \lambda_n])$ on cols, P^{-1} on rows.
Ensure: A similar automata split and truncated at level $b = \text{rank}(\text{config}_\mathcal{A})$
  1: **if** $(I = 0)$ return $\emptyset$.
  2: int a=1, b=1;
  3: Let j be the position of the last non-zero coefficient of I
  4: Apply $\text{Simi}(b, j, I)$ to $\mathcal{A}$; $b++$
  5: **while** $a < b$ **do**
  6:     $q \leftarrow a$; $a++$
  7:     **for** each $\alpha \in \Sigma$ **do**
  8:         Let $v = e_q \cdot T_\alpha$
  9:         Let j the position of the last non-zero coefficient of v
10:         **if** j > b **then**
11:             Apply $\text{Simi}(b, j, v)$ à $\mathcal{A}$; $b++$
12:         **end if**
13:     **end for**
14: **end while**
15: Truncate $\mathcal{A}$ at level $b - 1$ (remove rows and columns $\geq b$), return $\mathcal{A}$.

An analogue of the equivalence relation. The formal algorithm presented in [1] corresponds to this method. It can also be viewed as a linear analogue of Nerode's algorithm [11], based on an equivalence of states. It focuses on $\mathcal{L}_\mathcal{A}(e_1)^{(p)}, \ldots, \mathcal{L}_\mathcal{A}(e_n)^{(p)}$ where $\mathcal{L}_\mathcal{A}(e_i)^{(p)}$ represents the restriction to words of $\leq p$ letters of the language $\mathcal{L}_\mathcal{A}(e_i)$ of the state e_i. Like in the deterministic case, $\mathcal{L}_\mathcal{A}(e_i)^{(p)} \subseteq \mathcal{L}_\mathcal{A}(e_i)^{(p+1)}$, and there is an induction relationship $\mathcal{L}_\mathcal{A}(e_i)^{(p+1)} = \mathcal{L}_\mathcal{A}(e_i)^{(p)} \cup \left(\alpha.\mathcal{L}_\mathcal{A}(e_i \times T_\alpha)^{(p)} \right)_{\alpha \in \Sigma}$. Let $V^{(p)}$ be the (finite) matrix of $\mathcal{L}_\mathcal{A}^{(p)}$: for each index $i \leq n$ and word w of $\leq p$ letters, the coefficient $V^{(p)}[i, w] = 1 \Leftrightarrow w \in \mathcal{L}_\mathcal{A}^{(p)}(e_i)$, 0 else. Note that the union of columns of $V^{(p)}$ and $T_\alpha.V^{(p)}, \alpha \in \Sigma$ contain precisely all columns of $V^{(p+1)}$. Therefore tools like the RCEF (reduced column echelon form) as introduced by Gauss for the Gaussian elimination, can be used to iteratively compute the kernel of $V^{(p)}$ (*i.e.* of $\mathcal{L}_\mathcal{A}^{(p)}$), and thus the kernel of $\mathcal{L}_\mathcal{A}$, which is the first fixed point of kernels of $\mathcal{L}_\mathcal{A}^{(p)}$ when p grows (reached for a $p \leq \dim(\mathcal{L})$).

Effect of the mirror. In fact, linear accessibility and linear distinguishability are equivalent problem. This was almost the case for classical automata, although the proof was horribly unnatural and complicated [2] (mixing notions of accessibility which belong to DFA and mirror which only applies to NDA). In MXA, this is much simpler. Consider the $\infty \times n$ matrix of $\text{config}_\mathcal{A}$ and the $n \times \infty$ matrix of $\mathcal{L}_\mathcal{A}$ of Section 1. Applying the mirror on $\mathcal{A}$ has the effect to exchange and transpose both matrices. Therefore, a simple consideration on the ranks of both matrices lead to the elementary theorem and algorithm:

Theorem 5. *An automata $\mathcal{A}$ is linearly distinguishable $\Leftrightarrow$ its mirror is linearly accessible, and $\mathcal{A}$ is linearly accessible $\Leftrightarrow$ its mirror is linearly distinguishable. Furthermore, the algorithm* mirror∘lin.access∘mirror *ensures linear distinguishability in place and in time $O(n^2 \dim(\mathcal{L}) \cdot |\Sigma|)$.*

2.3   Minimization in Two Passes and MXA Normal Form

Finally, we have shown that from any NXA, one constructs a NXA minimal in number of states which is both lin. accessible and lin. distinguishable. We just need to apply in turn linear distinguishability and accessibility algorithms until the number of states stops decreasing. In fact, only one pass of each algorithm is enough.

Theorem 6 (MXA). *From an NXA $\mathcal{A}$ for $\mathcal{L} \in \mathcal{R}$eg, the output MXA$(\mathcal{A})$ of Algorithm 2 is a minimal NXA for $\mathcal{L}$ with $\dim(\mathcal{L})$ states, which only depends on $\mathcal{L}$. It can be denoted by MXA$(\mathcal{L})$.*

Proof. Applying Algorithm 1 on a linearly distinguishable automata first performs similitudes (which preserve linear distinguishability), followed by a truncation. If $\mathcal{L}_{\mathcal{A}}$ was injective over the whole $\mathbb{F}_2^n$, its restriction to a sub-span remain injective in the end. By Theorem 3, all minimal NXA recognizing $\mathcal{L}$ are similar. But after Algorithm 1, the matrix of config$_{\mathcal{A}}$ is in RCEF normal form, which makes the representative unique. The output is a normal form: MXA$(\mathcal{A}) = $ MXA$(\mathcal{A}') \Leftrightarrow \mathcal{L}(\mathcal{A}) = \mathcal{L}(\mathcal{A}')$. □

Algorithm 2. Minimization algorithm (MXA)

Require: A NXA $\mathcal{A}$ recognizing $\mathcal{L} \in \mathcal{R}$eg
Ensure: Minimize $\mathcal{A}$ in place, compute MXA$(\mathcal{L})$ in place.
  1: Transform $\mathcal{A}$ into its mirror
  2: Apply linear accessibility to $\mathcal{A}$ (Algorithm 1)
  3: Transform $\mathcal{A}$ into its mirror
  4: Apply linear accessibility to $\mathcal{A}$ (Algorithm 1)

We end this study with two important results summarizing the advantages of NXA against classical NDA or DFA.

Testing equality of languages. Two NXA recognize the same language if and only if their Xor is zero. The automaton which recognizes the xor of two languages is simply the (disjoint) union of both graphs. Therefore we just need to minimize this automaton and test whether the final dimension is 0. This test is polynomial in the input. In the opposite, testing equality of languages from two NDA would require an exponential determinization.

Polynomial Brzozowski. From a DFA, the classical Brzozowski minimization algorithm [2] (mirror,determinize,mirror,determinize) computes the MDA in exponential time and space, because of the determinization of the mirror language. The Xor variants provide a better alternative: given as input a DFA, one can compute the same MDA with: mirror, linear accessibility, mirror, then xor-determinization. This construction is now proved polynomial in the input. Indeed, the first three (mirror, lin. acces, mirror) provide linear distinguishability in polynomial time in the input. During the last determinization, the suffix-languages coming from each subset of states are all different (linear combinations of linearly independent $\mathcal{L}_A(e_i)$ are all different!). Therefore after determinization, the automaton is deterministic, accessible and distinguishable: it is the MDA. The last xor-determinization is polynomial in its output, which is smaller than the DFA we started from.

References

1. Berstel, J., Reutenauer, C.: Rational Series and Their Languages. EATCS Monograph. Springer, Heidelberg (1988)
2. Brzozowski, J.A.: Canonical regular expressions and minimal state graphs for definite events. In: Mathematical theory of Automata. MRI Symposia Series, vol. 12, pp. 529–561. Polytechnic Press, Polytechnic Institute of Brooklyn (1962)
3. Domaratzki, M., Kisman, D., Shallit, J.: On the number of distinct languages accepted by finite automata with n states. Journal of Automata, Languages and Combinatorics 7, 469–486 (2002)
4. Fliess, M.: Matrices de Hankel. J. Math pures et appl. 53, 197–224 (1974)
5. Huffman, D.A.: The synthesis of sequential switching circuits. The journal of symbolic logic 20, 69–70 (1955)
6. Jiang, T., Ravikumar, B.: Minimal NFA problems are hard. SIAM Journal on Computing 22(6), 1117–1141 (1993)
7. Kameda, T., Weiner, P.: On the state minimalization of nondeterministic finite. Automata. IEEE Transactions on Computers 19(7), 617–627 (1970)
8. Massey, J.: Shift register synthesis and BCH decoding. Trans. on Information Theory IT-15, 122–127 (1969)
9. Mohri, M.: Weighted automata algorithms. In: Droste, M., Kuich, W., Vogler, H. (eds.) Handbook of weighted automata. Springer, Heidelberg (2009)
10. Moore, E.F.: Gedanken-experiments on sequential machines. The Journal of Symbolic Logic 23, 60 (1958)
11. Nerode, A.: Linear automaton transformations. Proceedings of the AMS 9, 541–544 (1958)
12. Rabin, M.O., Scott, D.: Finite automata and their decision problems. IBM Journal 3, 114–125 (1959)
13. Schützenberger, M.P.: On the definition of a family of automata. Information and Control 4, 245–270 (1961)
14. van Zijl, L.: On binary xor-NFAs and succinct descriptions of regular languages. Theoretical Computer Science 328(1-2), 161–170 (2004)
15. van Zijl, L., Muller, G.: Minimization of unary symmetric difference NFAs. In: Proc. of SAICSIT, pp. 125–134. ACM, New York (2004)
16. Watson, B.W.: A taxonomy of finite automata minimization algorithmes. Computing Science Note 93/44, Eindhoven University of Technology, The Netherlands (1993)
17. Watson, B.W.: Combining two algorithms by Brzozowski. In: Wood, D., Yu, S. (eds.) Proceedings of the Fifth International Conference on Implementing Automata, London, Canada (July 2001)

Cellular Automata with Sparse Communication

Martin Kutrib and Andreas Malcher

Institut für Informatik, Universität Giessen
Arndtstr. 2, 35392 Giessen, Germany
{kutrib,malcher}@informatik.uni-giessen.de

Abstract. We investigate cellular automata whose internal inter-cell communication is bounded. The communication is quantitatively measured by the number of uses of the links between cells. It is shown that even the weakest non-trivial device in question, that is, one-way cellular automata where each two neighboring cells may communicate constantly often only, accept rather complicated languages. We investigate the computational capacity of the devices in question and prove an infinite strict hierarchy depending on the bound on the total number of communications during a computation. Despite their sparse communication even for the weakest devices, by reduction of Hilbert's tenth problem undecidability of several problems is derived. Finally, the question whether a given real-time one-way cellular automaton belongs to the weakest class is shown to be undecidable. This result can be adapted to answer an open question posed in [16].

1 Introduction

We study the parallel computational model of cellular automata which are linear arrays of identical copies of deterministic finite automata, where the single nodes, which are called cells, are homogeneously connected to their both immediate neighbors. They work synchronously at discrete time steps. In the general case, in every time step the state of each cell is communicated to its neighbors. That is, on one hand the state is sent regardless of whether it is really required, and on the other hand, the number of bits sent is determined by the number of states. The latter question has been dealt with in [4,5,11,12,13,17] where the bandwidth of the inter-cell links is bounded by some constant being independent of the number of states. The former question concerns the amount of communication necessary for a computation. In [14,15] two-way cellular automata are considered where the number of proper state changes is bounded. There are strong relations to inter-cell communication. Roughly speaking, a cell can remember the states received from its neighbors. As long as these do not change, no communication is necessary. Here we investigate cellular automata where the communication is quantitatively measured by the number of uses of the links between cells. Bounds on the sum of all communications of a computation as well as bounds on the maximal number of communications that may appear between each two cells are considered.

S. Maneth (Ed.): CIAA 2009, LNCS 5642, pp. 34–43, 2009.

In the next section we present some basic notions and definitions, and introduce the classes of communication bounded cellular automata. Examples of constructions for important types of languages are presented. Then, in Section 3 some computational capacity aspects are investigated, where an infinite strict hierarchy depending on the bound on the total number of communications during an computation is shown. Since the proof methods used in connection with the number of state changes in [14,15] apply also for the devices in question we adapt and summarize some of the known results.

Section 4 is devoted to decidability problems. We consider the weakest nontrivial device in question, that is, one-way cellular automata where each two neighboring cells may communicate constantly often only, and show by reduction of Hilbert's tenth problem undecidability of several problems. It turns out that also the question whether or not a given real-time one-way cellular automaton belongs to the weakest class of cellular automata with sparse communication is undecidable. This result can be adapted to answer an open question posed in [16].

2   Definitions and Preliminaries

We denote the positive integers and zero $\{0, 1, 2, ...\}$ by $\mathbb{N}$. The empty word is denoted by λ, the reversal of a word w by w^R, and for the length of w we write $|w|$. For the number of occurrences of a subword x in w we use the notation $|w|_x$, and for a set of words X, we define $|w|_X = \sum_{x \in X} |w|_x$. We use $\subseteq$ for inclusions and $\subset$ for strict inclusions. For a function $f : \mathbb{N} \to \mathbb{N}$ we denote its i-fold composition by $f^{[i]}$, $i \in \mathbb{N}$, where $f^{[0]}$ denotes the identity.

A cellular automaton is a linear array of identical deterministic finite state machines, sometimes called cells. Except for the leftmost cell and rightmost cell each one is connected to its both nearest neighbors. We identify the cells by positive integers. The state transition depends on the current state of each cell and on the information which is currently sent by its neighbors. The information sent by a cell depends on its current state and is determined by so-called communication functions. The two outermost cells receive a boundary symbol on their free input lines once during the first time step from the outside world. Subsequently, these input lines are never used again. A formal definition is:

Definition 1. A cellular automaton (CA) is a system $\langle S, F, A, B, \#, b_l, b_r, \delta \rangle$, where S is the finite, nonempty set of cell states, $F \subseteq S$ is the set of accepting states, $A \subseteq S$ is the nonempty set of input symbols, B is the set of communication symbols, $\# \notin B$ is the boundary symbol, $b_l, b_r : S \to B \cup \{\bot\}$ are communication functions which determine the information to be sent to the left and right neighbors, where $\bot$ means nothing to send, and $\delta : (B \cup \{\#, \bot\}) \times S \times (B \cup \{\#, \bot\}) \to S$ is the local transition function.

A configuration of a cellular automaton $\langle S, F, A, B, \#, b_l, b_r, \delta \rangle$ at time $t \geq 0$ is a description of its global state, which is actually a mapping $c_t : [1, \ldots, n] \to S$, for $n \geq 1$. The operation starts at time 0 in a so-called initial configuration. For a given input $w = a_1 \cdots a_n \in A^+$ we set $c_{0,w}(i) = a_i$, for $1 \leq i \leq n$. During its course of computation a CA steps through a sequence of configurations, whereby successor configurations are computed according to the global transition function Δ: Let c_t, $t \geq 0$, be a configuration. Then its successor configuration $c_{t+1} = \Delta(c_t)$ is as follows. For $2 \leq i \leq n-1$, $c_{t+1}(i) = \delta(b_r(c_t(i-1)), c_t(i), b_l(c_t(i+1)))$, and for the leftmost and rightmost cell we set $c_1(1) = \delta(\#, c_0(1), b_l(c_0(2)))$, $c_{t+1}(1) = \delta(\bot, c_t(1), b_l(c_t(2)))$, for $t \geq 1$, and $c_1(n) = \delta(b_r(c_0(n-1)), c_0(n), \#)$, $c_{t+1}(n) = \delta(b_r(c_t(n-1)), c_t(n), \bot)$, for $t \geq 1$. Thus, the global transition function Δ is induced by δ.

An input w is accepted by a CA $\mathcal{M}$ if at some time i during its course of computation the leftmost cell enters an accepting state. The *language accepted by* $\mathcal{M}$ is denoted by $L(\mathcal{M})$. Let $t : \mathbb{N} \to \mathbb{N}$, $t(n) \geq n$, be a mapping. If all $w \in L(\mathcal{M})$ are accepted with at most $t(|w|)$ time steps, then $\mathcal{M}$ is said to be of time complexity t.

An important subclass of cellular automata are so-called *one-way cellular automata* (OCA), where the flow of information is restricted to one way from right to left. For a formal definition it suffices to require that b_r maps all states to $\bot$, and that the leftmost cell does not receive the boundary symbol during the first time step.

In the following we study the impact of communication in cellular automata. The communication is measured by the number of uses of the links between cells. It is understood that whenever a communication symbol not equal to $\bot$ is sent, a communication takes place. Here we do not distinguish whether either or both neighboring cells use the link. More precisely, the number of communications between cell i and cell $i+1$ up to time step t is defined by

$$\mathrm{com}(i,t) = |\{\, j \mid 0 \leq j < t \text{ and } (b_r(c_j(i)) \neq \bot \text{ or } b_l(c_j(i+1)) \neq \bot) \,\}|.$$

For computations we now distinguish the maximal number of communications between two cells and the total number of communications. Let $c_0, c_1, \ldots, c_{t(|w|)}$ be the sequence of configurations computed on input w by some cellular automaton with time complexity $t(n)$, that is, the *computation on* w. Then we define $\mathrm{mcom}(w) = \max\{\, \mathrm{com}(i, t(|w|)) \mid 1 \leq i \leq |w| - 1 \,\}$ and $\mathrm{scom}(w) = \sum_{i=1}^{|w|-1} \mathrm{com}(i, t(|w|))$. Let $f : \mathbb{N} \to \mathbb{N}$ be a mapping. If all $w \in L(\mathcal{M})$ are accepted with computations where $\mathrm{mcom}(w) \leq f(|w|)$, then $\mathcal{M}$ is said to be *max communication bounded by* f. Similarly, if all $w \in L(\mathcal{M})$ are accepted with computations where $\mathrm{scom}(w) \leq f(|w|)$, then $\mathcal{M}$ is said to be *sum communication bounded by* f. In general, it is not expected to have tight bounds on the exact number of communications but tight bounds on their numbers in the order of magnitude. For the sake of readability we denote the class of CAs that are max communication bounded by some function $g \in O(f)$ by $\mathrm{MC}(f)$-CA, where it is understood that f gives the order of magnitude. Corresponding notations are used for OCAs and sum communication bounded CAs and OCAs. ($\mathrm{SC}(f)$-CA and $\mathrm{SC}(f)$-OCA).

The family of all languages which are accepted by some device X with time complexity t is denoted by $\mathscr{L}_t(X)$. In the sequel we are particularly interested in fast computations and call the time complexity $t(n) = n$ *real time* and write $\mathscr{L}_{rt}(X)$. To illustrate the definitions we start with an example.

Lemma 1. *The language* $\{a^n b^n \mid n \geq 1\}$ *belongs to* $\mathscr{L}_{rt}(MC(1)\text{-}OCA)$.

Proof. The acceptance of the language is governed by two signals. The rightmost cell is sending a signal B with maximum speed to the left whereas the unique cell which has an a in its input and has a right neighbor with a b in its input is sending a signal A with speed $1/2$ to the left. When both signals meet in a cell, an accepting state is assumed. Obviously, $\{a^n b^n \mid n \geq 1\}$ is accepted and each cell performs only a finite number of communications. ☐

By an obvious generalization of the above construction with suitable signals having a certain speed we obtain that the languages $\{a^n b^n c^n \mid n \geq 1\}$, $\{a^n b^m c^n d^m \mid n, m \geq 1\}$, and $\{a_1^n a_2^n \cdots a_k^n \mid n \geq 1\}$, for $k \geq 1$ and different symbols $a_1, a_2, \dots, a_k$, are accepted by real-time MC(1)-OCAs as well. The languages are non context free.

For the language $\{a^n b^{n_1} c^m b^{n_2} \mid n, m \geq 1 \wedge n_1, n_2 \geq 0 \wedge n_1 + n_2 = n\}$ the above technique of suitable signals having an appropriate speed cannot be applied, since the block of cs may be arbitrary large. Here, the first idea is to use two different signals B and $\circ$. All b-cells send a signal B to the left which is matched against the a-cells. All c-cells send a signal $\circ$ to the left which does not affect the matching of a-cells and B-signals. This approach implies that some cells may forward an arbitrary number of signals B or $\circ$ and leads to a real-time OCA which is not an MC(1)-OCA. But, we can overcome this problem by applying the following technique. Whenever some cell has sent a signal X to the left, it sends $\perp$ in the next time steps as long as no other signal $Y \neq X$ has to be sent to the left. The cells which obtain some signal X for the first time store this in their state. The information $\perp$ arriving in the next time steps can then be interpreted as "nothing has changed," that is, each $\perp$ is interpreted as a signal X and is suitably processed. It can be observed that in this way each cell performs only a finite number of communications as long as only a finite number of blocks of identical signals has to be sent to the left.

Lemma 2. *The language* $\{a^n b^{n_1} c^m b^{n_2} \mid n, m \geq 1 \wedge n_1, n_2 \geq 0 \wedge n_1 + n_2 = n\}$ *belongs to* $\mathscr{L}_{rt}(MC(1)\text{-}OCA)$.

Proof. All b-cells send a signal B which is forwarded by all b-cells and c-cells and is matched against the a-cells. That is, when a signal B arrives in an a-cell it is stopped and the cell is marked as a matched cell. When a signal B arrives at a marked a-cell, the signal is forwarded to the left as long as it arrives at an unmarked a-cell where it is stopped and marks the cell as matched. The c-cells send a signal $\circ$ which is forwarded by b-cells to the left. All a-cells are forwarding $\circ$-signals to the left as long as they are stopped by an a-cell which has not yet sent a signal B to the left. These $\circ$-signals do not affect the matching of a-cells with B-signals, but they carry the information that the first block of b's has been processed. Initially, in the rightmost cell a signal $\triangleleft$ is started which checks the correct formatting and forces a marked a-cell which has not been used to forward a B-signal to enter an accepting state. Additionally, the signal $\triangleleft$ is stopped. In this way, a real-time OCA acceptor has been constructed. By applying the technique described above we obtain a real-time MC(1)-OCA, since we have one block of signals B followed by one block of signals $\circ$, which is followed by another block of signals B. Thus, the assertion follows. $\square$

A straightforward generalization yields the next lemma.

Lemma 3. *Let $k \geq 0$ be a constant. Then language $L_k = \{\, a^n w \mid n \geq 1 \wedge w \in (b^*c^*)^k b^* \wedge |w|_b = n \,\}$ belongs to $\mathscr{L}_{rt}(MC(1)\text{-}OCA)$.*

3   Computational Capacity

In [14,15] two-way cellular automata are considered where the number of proper state changes is bounded. By applying the technique of saving communication steps by storing the last signal received in the state and to interpret an arriving $\perp$ suitably, it is not hard to see, that such a device can be simulated by the corresponding communication bounded device. Whether or not state change bounded devices are strictly weaker than communication bounded ones is an open problem. However, the restrictions introduced in [14,15] have been investigated with respect to communication in cellular automata, and the proof methods used apply also for the devices in question.

Theorem 1 ([14,15]). *1. $\mathscr{L}_{rt}(MC(1)\text{-}CA) \subset \mathscr{L}_{rt}(SC(n)\text{-}CA)$.*
2. $REG \subset \mathscr{L}_{rt}(MC(1)\text{-}CA) \subset \mathscr{L}_{rt}(MC(\sqrt{n})\text{-}CA) \subset \mathscr{L}_{rt}(MC(n)\text{-}CA)$.

Next we turn to show an infinite proper hierarchy of real-time SC(f)-CA families. We start with the top of the hierarchy.

Theorem 2. *Let $f : \mathbb{N} \to \mathbb{N}$ be a function. If $f \in o(n^2/\log(n))$, then language $L = \{\, wcw^R \mid w \in \{a,b\}^+ \,\}$ is not accepted by any real-time SC(f)-CA.*

Proof. In contrast to the assertion, assume that L is accepted by some real-time SC(f)-CA $\mathcal{M}$. We consider accepting computations on wcw^R.

We claim that for any constant $k > 0$, there must exist a length $n_k \geq 2$ such that for all $w \in \{a,b\}^{2n_k}$ there is a cell $j(w)$, where $n_k + 1 \leq j(w) \leq 2n_k$, such that the number of communications occurring between cells $j(w)$ and $j(w) + 1$ is at most $k4n_k/\log(4n_k)$.

If the claim would be wrong, then there would be a constant $k > 0$, such that for all lengths n_k there is a word $w \in \{a,b\}^{2n_k}$ such that for all $n_k + 1 \leq j(w) \leq 2n_k$, the number of communications occurring between cells $j(w)$ and $j(w)+1$ is at least $k4n_k/\log(4n_k)$. Therefore, the total number of communications during an accepting computation on wcw^R is at least $k4n_k(2n_k - n_k - 1)/\log(4n_k)$ which is of order $\Omega(n_k^2/\log(n_k))$. Since for all lengths n_k there is such a word w, a contradiction to the assumption $f \in o(n^2/\log(n))$ follows, and the claim is shown.

Now we turn to derive an upper bound on the number of possibilities for some r communications between two cells in real-time computations. To this end, we have to consider the information to be communicated as well as the time steps at which the communications take place. There are $\binom{n}{r}$ possibilities to choose time steps, and $(|B| + 1)^2 - 1$ possibilities to use a link, where both cells must not send $\perp$ simultaneously in order to have a communication at all. So, there are at most

$$\binom{n}{r}((|B| + 1)^2 - 1)^r \leq \frac{n^r}{(r/2)^{r/2}} 2^{\log(|B|+1)2r} \leq \frac{n^r 2^{r/2}}{r^{r/2}} 2^{\log(|B|+1)2r}$$

$$\leq 2^{\log(n)r + r/2 + \log(|B|+1)2r - \log(r)r/2}$$

$$\leq 2^{k_0 \log(n)r}, \text{ for some constant } k_0 \geq 1,$$

possibilities. Next we choose $k < 1/(16k_0)$ and apply the claim shown above. So, there is an $n_k \geq 2$ such that for all $w \in \{a, b\}^{2n_k}$ there is a cell $j(w)$, where $n_k + 1 \leq j(w) \leq 2n_k$, such that the number of communications occurring between cells $j(w)$ and $j(w) + 1$ is at most $r = k4n_k/\log(4n_k)$. For these communications there are at most $2^{k_0 \log(4n_k+1)r} \leq 2^{k_0 2 \log(4n_k)k\frac{4n_k}{\log(4n_k)}} \leq 2^{k_0 2 \log(4n_k)\frac{1}{16k_0}\frac{4n_k}{\log(4n_k)}} \leq 2^{\frac{n_k}{2}}$ possibilities. Since there are 2^{n_k} words of length n_k, there must exist two words

$$w_1 = u_1 u_2 \cdots u_{n_k} u_{n_k+1} \cdots u_{j(w_1)} u_{j(w_1)+1} \cdots u_{2n_k} \text{ and}$$

$$w_2 = v_1 v_2 \cdots v_{n_k} v_{n_k+1} \cdots v_{j(w_2)} v_{j(w_2)+1} \cdots v_{2n_k}$$

with accepting computations on $w_1 c w_1^R$ and $w_2 c w_2^R$ that differ in their first n_k symbols, and that imply exactly the same communications between cells $j(w_1)$ and $j(w_1) + 1$ on one hand and between cells $j(w_2)$ and $j(w_2) + 1$ on the other hand. Therefore, also the input $u_1 u_2 \cdots u_{n_k} u_{n_k+1} \cdots u_{j(w_1)} v_{j(w_2)+1} \cdots v_{2n_k} c w_2^R$ is accepted, which is a contradiction since it does not belong to L. $\square$

In order to define witness languages that separate the levels of the hierarchy, for all $i \geq 1$, the functions $\varphi_i : \mathbb{N} \to \mathbb{N}$ are defined by $\varphi_1(n) = 2^n$, and $\varphi_i(n) = 2^{\varphi_{i-1}(n)}$, for $i \geq 2$, and we set $L_i = \{ w\$^{\varphi_i(|w|) - 2|w|} w^R \mid w \in \{a, b\}^+ \}$.

Lemma 4. *Let $i \geq 1$ be an integer and $f : \mathbb{N} \to \mathbb{N}$ be a function. If $f \in o((n \log^{[i]}(n))/\log^{[i+1]}(n))$, then language L_i is not accepted by any real-time $SC(f)$-CA.*

Lemma 5. *Let $i \geq 1$ be an integer. Then language L_i is accepted by some real-time $SC(n \log^{[i]}(n))$-CA.*

Theorem 3. *Let $i \geq 0$ be an integer. Then $\mathscr{L}_{rt}(SC(n \log^{[i+1]}(n))$-CA$)$ is properly included in $\mathscr{L}_{rt}(SC(n \log^{[i]}(n))$-CA$)$.*

Proof. The inclusion is trivial. For $i = 0$, consider the linear context-free language $L = \{ wcw^R \mid w \in \{a, b\}^+ \}$. In [10] it is shown that any linear context-free language is accepted by some real-time CA. So, obviously it is accepted by a real-time $SC(n^2)$-CA. Since $n \log(n) \in o(n^2/\log(n))$, language L does not belong to $\mathscr{L}_{rt}(SC(n \log(n))$-CA) by Theorem 2. For $i \geq 1$, a witness for the properness of the inclusion is language L_i. By Lemma 5 it belongs to $\mathscr{L}_{rt}(SC(n \log^{[i]}(n))$-CA).

Since $n \log^{[i+1]}(n) = \frac{n(\log^{[i+1]}(n))^2}{\log^{[i+1]}(n)}$ and

$$\lim_{n \to \infty} \frac{\frac{n(\log^{[i+1]}(n))^2}{\log^{[i+1]}(n)}}{\frac{n \log^{[i]}(n)}{\log^{[i+1]}(n)}} = \lim_{n \to \infty} \frac{n(\log^{[i+1]}(n))^2}{n \log^{[i]}(n)} = \lim_{n \to \infty} \frac{(\log^{[i+1]}(n))^2}{2 \log^{[i+1]}(n)} = 0$$

we have $n \log^{[i+1]}(n) \in o((n \log^{[i]}(n))/\log^{[i+1]}(n))$. Therefore, by Lemma 4 language L_i does not belong to $\mathscr{L}_{rt}(SC(n \log^{[i+1]}(n))$-CA).   □

4   Decidability Questions

Two of the common techniques to show undecidability results are reductions of Post's Correspondence Problem or reductions of the emptiness and finiteness problem on Turing machines using the set of valid computations. Both techniques have been used successfully to obtain results for variants of cellular automata [6,7,8,9]. Here we first show that emptiness is undecidable for real-time MC(1)-OCAs by reduction of Hilbert's tenth problem which is known to be undecidable. The problem is to decide whether a given polynomial $p(x_1, \ldots, x_n)$ with integer coefficients has an integral root. That is, to decide whether there are integers $\alpha_1, \ldots, \alpha_n$ such that $p(\alpha_1, \ldots, \alpha_n) = 0$. In [1] Hilbert's tenth problem has been used to show that emptiness is undecidable for certain multicounter machines. As is remarked in [1], it is sufficient to restrict the variables $x_1, \ldots, x_n$ to take non-negative integers only. If $p(x_1, \ldots, x_n)$ contains a constant summand, then we may assume that it has a negative sign. Otherwise, $p(x_1, \ldots, x_n)$ is multiplied with -1. Such a polynomial then has the following form: $p(x_1, \ldots, x_n) = t_1(x_1, \ldots, x_n) + \ldots + t_r(x_1, \ldots, x_n)$, where each $t_j(x_1, \ldots, x_n)$ $(1 \leq j \leq r)$ is a term of the form $t_j(x_1, \ldots, x_n) = s_j x_1^{i_{j,1}} \ldots x_n^{i_{j,n}}$ with $s_j \in \{+1, -1\}$ and $i_{j,1}, \ldots, i_{j,n} \geq 0$. Additionally, we may assume that the summands are ordered according to their sign, i.e., there exists $1 \leq q \leq r$ such that $s_1 = \ldots = s_q = 1$ and $s_{q+1} = \ldots = s_r = -1$. Moreover, constant terms are occurring only at the end of the sum. I.e., $t_r = \ldots = t_{r-c+1} = -1$, if p contains $c > 0$ constant terms. Finally, let $i_j = \sum_{t=1}^{n} i_{j,t}$.

Now, we consider a polynomial $p(x_1, \ldots, x_n)$ with integer coefficients that has the above form. We first look at the positive terms t_j of $p(x_1, \ldots, x_n)$ with $1 \leq j \leq q$ and define languages $L(t_j)$ as follows.

$$L(t_j) = \{ b_1^{\alpha_1} \ldots b_{i_{j,1}}^{\alpha_1} b_{i_{j,1}+1}^{\alpha_2} \ldots b_{i_{j,1}+i_{j,2}}^{\alpha_2} \ldots b_{i_{j,1}+\ldots+i_{j,n-1}+1}^{\alpha_n} \ldots b_{i_j}^{\alpha_n} .$$
$$f_j(\underbrace{\alpha_1, \ldots, \alpha_1}_{i_{j,1}}, \ldots, \underbrace{\alpha_n, \ldots, \alpha_n}_{i_{j,n}}) \mathord{\text{¢}} \mid \alpha_1, \ldots, \alpha_n \geq 0 \}$$

where $f_j : \mathbb{N}^{i_j} \to \{\$_1, \$_2, \ldots, \$_{i_j}\}^*$ is inductively defined by the following rules with $1 \le i \le i_j - 1$.

$$f_j(\alpha_1, \ldots, \alpha_{i_j}) = \left(f_j^{(i_j-1)}(\alpha_1, \ldots, \alpha_{i_j-1})\$_{i_j} \right)^{\alpha_{i_j}}$$

$$f_j^{(i)}(\alpha_1, \ldots, \alpha_i) = \left(f_j^{(i-1)}(\alpha_1, \ldots, \alpha_{i-1})\$_i \right)^{\alpha_i - 1} f_j^{(i-1)}(\alpha_1, \ldots, \alpha_{i-1})$$

$$f_j^{(0)} = \lambda$$

For the negative, non-constant terms t_j with $q+1 \le j \le r$ the definition of $L(t_j)$ is identical except for the fact that each symbol $\$_k$ is replaced by some symbol $\newcommand{\euro}{\mbox{€}}\euro_k$. For each negative, constant term t_j, we define $L(t_j) = \{\euro_1\}$.

Lemma 6. *For $1 \le j \le r$, $|f_j(\alpha_1, \ldots, \alpha_{i_j})| = \alpha_1 \cdot \alpha_2 \cdot \ldots \cdot \alpha_{i_j}$.*

Thus, if $w \in L(t_j)$ and w contains ℓ symbols $\$$ or $\euro$, respectively, then there exist non-negative integers $\alpha_1, \ldots, \alpha_n$ such that $t_j(\alpha_1, \ldots, \alpha_n) = s_j \cdot \ell$. In other words, the number of symbols $\$$ or $\euro$ occurring in $L(t_j)$ denote all evaluations of t_j on non-negative integers. Furthermore, symbols $\$$ or $\euro$ denote evaluations with positive or negative sign, respectively.

Lemma 7. *For $1 \le j \le r$, let t_j be a non-constant term. Then language $L(t_j)^R$ belongs to $\mathscr{L}_{rt}(MC(1)\text{-}OCA)$.*

We next consider the following regular languages R_k depending on the sign of t_k. We set $R_k = b_1^* \ldots b_{i_{k,1}}^* \ldots b_{i_{k,1}+\ldots+i_{k,n-1}+1}^* \ldots b_{i_k}^* \{\$_1, \ldots, \$_{i_k}\}^* \mathord{\mathrm{¢}}$ if $s_k = 1$, $R_k = b_1^* \ldots b_{i_{k,1}}^* \ldots b_{i_{k,1}+\ldots+i_{k,n-1}+1}^* \ldots b_{i_k}^* \{\euro_1, \ldots, \euro_{i_k}\}^* \mathord{\mathrm{¢}}$ if $s_k = -1$ and t_k is non-constant, and $R_k = \euro_1^* \mathord{\mathrm{¢}}$ otherwise. Then, we define

$$\tilde{L}(t_j) = \{ a_1^{\alpha_1} \ldots a_n^{\alpha_n} w_1 \ldots w_{j-1} b_1^{\alpha_1} \ldots b_{i_{j,1}}^{\alpha_1} \ldots b_{i_{j,n}}^{\alpha_n} \ldots b_{i_{j,1}+\ldots+i_{j,n-1}+1}^{\alpha_n} \ldots b_{i_j}^{\alpha_n} \cdot$$

$$f_j(\underbrace{\alpha_1, \ldots, \alpha_1}_{i_{j,1}}, \ldots, \underbrace{\alpha_n, \ldots, \alpha_n}_{i_{j,n}})\mathord{\mathrm{¢}} w_{j+1} \ldots w_r \mid \alpha_1, \ldots, \alpha_n \ge 0 \text{ and } w_i \in R_i \}$$

and consider $\tilde{L}(p) = \bigcap_{i=1}^r \tilde{L}(t_j)^R$.

Lemma 8. *The language $\tilde{L}(p)$ belongs to $\mathscr{L}_{rt}(MC(1)\text{-}OCA)$.*

Proof. Since $\mathscr{L}_{rt}(MC(1)\text{-}OCA)$ is closed under intersection, we have to show that each $\tilde{L}(t_j)^R$ belongs to $\mathscr{L}_{rt}(MC(1)\text{-}OCA)$. If t_j is a constant term, then $\tilde{L}(t_j)^R$ is a regular language and therefore is in $\mathscr{L}_{rt}(MC(1)\text{-}OCA)$. Now, let t_j be a non-constant term. As in the proof of Lemma 7 we describe a real-time $MC(1)\text{-}OCA$ accepting $\tilde{L}(t_j)$ which has information flow from left to right and accepts in the rightmost cell. Then, $\tilde{L}(t_j)^R$ belongs to $\mathscr{L}_{rt}(MC(1)\text{-}OCA)$. Due to Lemma 7 we know that an $MC(1)\text{-}OCA$ accepting $L(t_j)$ can be constructed. We generalize this construction by concatenating the regular languages $a_1^* \ldots a_n^* R_1 \ldots R_{j-1}$ and $R_{j+1} \ldots R_r$ to $L(t_j)$ from right and left, respectively. It can be observed that this can be done by an $MC(1)\text{-}OCA$. It remains to be shown that for

$1 \leq k \leq n$ the number of symbols a_k is equal to each the number of symbols $b_{i_{j,1}+\ldots+i_{j,k-1}+1}, \ldots, b_{i_{j,1}+\ldots+i_{j,k}}$. This can be achieved by an obvious generalization of the construction given in the proof of Lemma 2. All a_k-cells send signals a_k to the right. Whenever the $(j-1)$st ¢-cell has been passed, the matching of $b_{i_{j,1}+\ldots+i_{j,k-1}+m}$-cells $(1 \leq m \leq i_{j,k})$ with the signal a_k starts. Due to Lemma 2, this task can be done by some MC(1)-OCA. This implies $\tilde{L}(t_j)^R \in \mathscr{L}_{rt}(\text{MC}(1)\text{-OCA})$ and shows the lemma.   □

Finally, let X be the set of all occurring symbols $\$_k$ and Y be the set of all occurring symbols $\text{\euro}_k$. Then, we define $L(p) = \{w \in \tilde{L}(p) \mid |w|_X = |w|_Y\}$.

Lemma 9. *The language $L(p)$ belongs to $\mathscr{L}_{rt}(MC(1)\text{-}OCA)$.*

Theorem 4. *Given an arbitrary real-time MC(1)-OCA $\mathcal{M}$, it is undecidable whether $L(\mathcal{M})$ is empty.*

Proof. Due to Lemma 9 we can construct a real-time MC(1)-OCA $\mathcal{M}$ accepting $L(p)$. By the construction of $L(p)$, it is not difficult to observe that $\mathcal{M}$ accepts the empty set if and only if $p(x_1, \ldots, x_n)$ has no solution in the non-negative integers. Since Hilbert's tenth problem is undecidable, we obtain that the emptiness problem for real-time MC(1)-OCAs is undecidable.   □

Corollary 1. *The problems finiteness, infiniteness, universality, equivalence, inclusion, regularity, and context-freedom are undecidable for arbitrary real-time MC(1)-OCAs.*

Theorem 5. *It is undecidable for an arbitrary real-time OCA $\mathcal{M}$ whether $\mathcal{M}$ is a real-time MC(1)-OCA.*

Proof. Let $\mathcal{M}'$ be a real-time MC(1)-OCA and consider the language $L_{\mathcal{M}'} = \{a^{|w|}w \mid w \in L(\mathcal{M}')\}$ where a is some new alphabet symbol. A real-time OCA $\mathcal{M}$ accepting $L_{\mathcal{M}'}$ can be described as follows. The correct number of a- and non-a-symbols can be checked in the same way as it is done for the language $\{a^n b^n \mid n \geq 1\}$ (see Lemma 1). The cells initially carrying non-a symbols are simulating the given real-time MC(1)-OCA $\mathcal{M}'$. Whenever the leftmost non-a-cell enters an accepting state of $\mathcal{M}'$, which can be detected by its left neighboring cell, some signal A is sent with maximum speed to the left. This signal forces all a-cells to communicate in every time step. In the rightmost cell, some signal is started which checks the correct input and enters an accepting state in the leftmost cell whenever the format is correct, the number of a- and non-a-symbols is correct, and the A-signal has reached the leftmost cell. It can be observed that the number of communication steps in each cell in the first block of a-cells depends on the length of w, if $w \in L_{\mathcal{M}'}$. Thus, $\mathcal{M}$ is an MC(1)-OCA if and only if $L_{\mathcal{M}'}$ is finite. Since finiteness is undecidable for MC(1)-OCAs due to Corollary 1, we obtain that the question whether $\mathcal{M}$ is a real-time MC(1)-OCA is undecidable as well.   □

In conclusion we state that the results can also be adapted to cellular automata where the number of proper state changes is bounded [14,15], which answers an open question posed in [16].

References

1. Ibarra, O.H.: Reversal-bounded multicounter machines and their decision problems. J. ACM 25, 116–133 (1978)
2. Kutrib, M.: Cellular automata – a computational point of view. In: New Developments in Formal Languages and Applications, pp. 183–227. Springer, Heidelberg (2008)
3. Kutrib, M.: Cellular automata and language theory. In: Encyclopedia of Complexity and System Science. Springer, Heidelberg (to appear)
4. Kutrib, M., Malcher, A.: Fast cellular automata with restricted inter-cell communication: Computational capacity. In: Theoretical Computer Science (IFIPTCS 2006). IFIP, vol. 209, pp. 151–164. Springer, Heidelberg (2006)
5. Kutrib, M., Malcher, A.: Fast iterative arrays with restricted inter-cell communication: Constructions and decidability. In: Královič, R., Urzyczyn, P. (eds.) MFCS 2006. LNCS, vol. 4162, pp. 634–645. Springer, Heidelberg (2006)
6. Kutrib, M., Malcher, A.: Fast reversible language recognition using cellular automata. Inform. Comput. 206, 1142–1151 (2008)
7. Malcher, A.: Descriptional complexity of cellular automata and decidability questions. J. Autom., Lang. Comb. 7, 549–560 (2002)
8. Malcher, A.: On the descriptional complexity of iterative arrays. IEICE Trans. Inf. Syst. E87-D, 721–725 (2004)
9. Seidel, S.R.: Language recognition and the synchronization of cellular automata. Technical Report 79-02, Department of Computer Science, University of Iowa (1979)
10. Smith III, A.R.: Cellular automata and formal languages. In: Switching and Automata Theory (SWAT 1970), pp. 216–224. IEEE, Los Alamitos (1970)
11. Umeo, H.: Linear-time recognition of connectivity of binary images on 1-bit inter-cell communication cellular automaton. Parallel Comput. 27, 587–599 (2001)
12. Umeo, H., Kamikawa, N.: A design of real-time non-regular sequence generation algorithms and their implementations on cellular automata with 1-bit inter-cell communications. Fund. Inform. 52, 257–275 (2002)
13. Umeo, H., Kamikawa, N.: Real-time generation of primes by a 1-bit-communication cellular automaton. Fund. Inform. 58, 421–435 (2003)
14. Vollmar, R.: On cellular automata with a finite number of state changes. Computing 3, 181–191 (1981)
15. Vollmar, R.: Some remarks about the 'efficiency' of polyautomata. Internat. J. Theoret. Phys. 21, 1007–1015 (1982)
16. Vollmar, R.: Zur Zustandsänderungskomplexität von Zellularautomaten. In: Beiträge zur Theorie der Polyautomaten – zweite Folge –, Braunschweig, pp. 139–151 (1982) (in German)
17. Worsch, T.: Linear time language recognition on cellular automata with restricted communication. In: Gonnet, G.H., Viola, A. (eds.) LATIN 2000. LNCS, vol. 1776, pp. 417–426. Springer, Heidelberg (2000)

A Cellular Automaton Model for Car Traffic with a Slow-to-Stop Rule

Adam Clarridge and Kai Salomaa

Queen's University, Kingston, Canada
{adam,ksalomaa}@cs.queensu.ca

Abstract. We propose a modification of the widely known Benjamin-Johnson-Hui (BJH) cellular automaton model for single-lane traffic simulation. In particular, our model includes a 'slow-to-stop' rule that exhibits more realistic microscopic driver behaviour than the BJH model. We present some statistics related to fuel economy and pollution generation and show that our model differs greatly in these measures. We give concise results based on extensive simulations using our system.

Keywords: cellular automata, car traffic, highway, single lane, model, simulation.

1 Introduction

An almost universal daily annoyance in most North American cities is getting slowed down or stuck in traffic. Many people spend hours each day in traffic, slowly losing their money and sanity while generating unnecessary pollution. Unfortunately, in many cities the addition of more highways to reduce the growing amount of congestion is far too expensive since the land is already developed. Because of these limitations, if traffic management is to be improved, it is important to understand the dynamics of car traffic flow extremely well to facilitate the planning and prediction of high density traffic. The earliest traffic flow models were based on fluid dynamics, but more recently cellular automata (CA) based models have been gaining popularity. This is partly because simulations are easy to develop and run very quickly (especially on designated parallel hardware), but also since cars in traffic operate under their own power and do not emulate particle flow based on the laws of physics particularly well.

The first study using CA for car traffic simulation was conducted by Nagel and Schreckenberg [1], who develop a simple stochastic CA model to simulate single-lane highway traffic. Essentially, the model says that all cars follow the same basic transition rules, and then move v sites at each time interval. They increase their velocity v by 1 up to some limit as long as there are no cars v spaces ahead of them, slow down to speed $i - 1$ if they see a car i spaces ahead of them, and randomly slow down by one speed unit with some probability p. The authors observe nontrivial, realistic simulation, particularly the transition from laminar traffic flow to start-stop waves as density increases.

S. Maneth (Ed.): CIAA 2009, LNCS 5642, pp. 44–53, 2009.

In this paper, we focus on the microscopic behaviour of cars in the BJH model (a modification of the Nagel-Schreckenberg model) - specifically the fact that they decelerate in a very unrealistic way. Since cars only decelerate to avoid collisions, it is a frequent occurrence that cars drive up to a jam at maximum speed and slow down to a stop in a single time step. In order to more closely simulate the behaviour of human drivers, we propose a modification to the BJH model where cars begin slowing down earlier by an amount which is a function of their speed, the speed of the car ahead, and the distance to the car ahead.

We give a short summary of selected papers relating to CA-based traffic modelling in Section 2. We describe our model in detail in Section 3 and present simulations that compare it with the BJH model. In Section 4 we present a brief comparison of our model with other recent extensions of the NaSch model. Finally, we summarize and conclude the paper in Section 5.

2   Summary of CA-Based Traffic Simulation Models

The Nagel-Schreckenberg (NaSch) model [1] has been studied quite extensively in several papers [2,3,4,5,6].

Another model developed by Benjamin, Johnson, and Hui (BJH model) [7] is quite similar to the NaSch model, but with the addition of a 'slow-to-start' rule. That is, a vehicle which has come to a complete stop moves forward at its first available opportunity with probability $1 - p_{slow}$, and on the time step after that with probability p_{slow}. The authors used this model to study the effect of junctions on highways, finding that setting a speed limit near junctions on single lane roads can greatly decrease the queue length to enter the road.

Since almost all major highways have two lanes or more, several researchers have constructed multi-lane models for highway traffic. The first work in this area was done by Rickert et al. [8], who designed a working model based on the NaSch model. They noticed that checking for extra space when switching lanes ('look-back') is an important feature of their model in order to get the realistic behaviour of laminar to start-stop traffic flow. Wagner et al. [9] design a two-lane simulation which accounts for a faster left lane which is to be used for passing. Using simple rules, they are able to obtain the realistic behaviour that at higher overall densities, the left lane has a higher density than the right one. They remark that this correct macroscopic behaviour is fairly easy to obtain using a CA model, and cite some failed attempts to simulate multi-lane traffic using other types of models. Knospe et al. [10] study heterogeneous two-lane traffic and find that even at low densities, a very small amount of slower cars effectively cause both lanes to slow significantly. Also, they note that a system with mostly slow cars and a small percentage of fast cars is almost identical to a system with all slow cars. Finally, Nagel et al. [11] summarize the existing lane-changing CA models and propose a general scheme according to which realistic lane-changing rules can be developed.

Esser and Schreckenberg designed a complete simulation tool for urban traffic in [12]. The model accounts for realistic traffic light intersections, priority rules, parking capacities, and public transport circulation. The simulation of large traffic networks can be performed in multiple real-time. Several other researchers have devised related schemes [13,14,15,16,17].

3   A Modified Version of the BJH Model

Here we investigate a modification of the well-known Benjamin-Johnson-Hui (BJH) CA model [7] for single-lane highway traffic. This model is able to correctly capture several of the macroscopic characteristics of real traffic using very simple and computationally fast cellular automata, and as a result, has been studied extensively and incorporated into several complex traffic simulators. The primary reason we choose this slightly older model rather than one of the recent more complex models is that it has extremely simple transition rules which are easy to understand, so our extension will be clearer.

The BJH model is based on the NaSch model, which we will now describe in detail. The NaSch model is defined on a one-dimensional cellular space of N cells, usually with the toroidal (periodic) boundary condition. On a particular time step each cell either contains a car or is empty, and each car has an integer velocity v between 0 and v_{max} inclusive. Given some global configuration of cars at various velocities, the NaSch model dictates that cars are advanced along the road on the next time step according to the following rules, which are performed in order and in parallel for all cars. The quantity d is the distance in cells to the next car ahead.

1. Acceleration: if $v < v_{max}$ and $d > v + 1$, then velocity increases ($v \leftarrow v + 1$).
2. Slowing down (collision avoidance): if $d <= v$, then velocity decreases appropriately ($v \leftarrow d - 1$).
3. Randomization: if $v > 0$, with probability p_{fault}, velocity decreases by one ($v \leftarrow v - 1$).
4. Motion: the car advances v cells.

These velocity rules implicitly do not allow collisions or overtaking.

The BJH model is a fairly straightforward extension of the NaSch model - the authors attempt to more accurately simulate the behaviour of drivers which have come to a complete stop in traffic jams on the highway. Cars which have velocity 0 either accelerate at their first available opportunity (as soon as there is an empty space ahead of them) with probability $1 - p_{slow}$, or on the time step immediately after that with probability p_{slow}. Otherwise, they follow the NaSch model. This scheme is intended to reflect the fact that drivers take longer to accelerate from a complete stop, perhaps because they do not immediately notice the car ahead of them moving, or because of the slow pick-up of their car's engine. So the BJH model is essentially the NaSch model with the addition of a 'slow-to-start' rule. An example of cars following the BJH model on a small road is given in Figure 1, and a more complete picture on a larger road for a longer period of time is given in Figure 2. In these examples, the initial configuration is a random placement of ρN cars ($0 < \rho < 1$) with velocity 1, where N is the size of the road in cells.

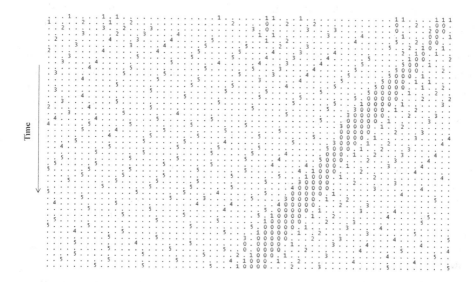

Fig. 1. A small example of cars following the BJH model. The dots refer to empty cells, and the numbers represent the velocities of cars. Here the density $\rho = 0.2$, $p_{fault} = 0.1$, and $p_{slow} = 0.5$. Cars drive from left to right.

Fig. 2. A 'zoomed-out' view of a larger simulation of the BJH model. Black dots refer to cars, while white space is empty road. Here the density $\rho = 0.15$, $v_{max} = 5$, $p_{fault} = 0.1$, and $p_{slow} = 0.5$. The road is 1000 cells wide and the last 1000 evolutions out of 2000 are shown (to reach a steady state). Cars drive from left to right, and time 0 is at the top.

We noticed that cars following these models behave in an unrealistic fashion when approaching a jam; if a car B ahead has velocity 0, then a car A may drive up to B at velocity v_{max} only to brake down to 0 velocity in one time step in the cell right behind B. This microscopically inaccurate behaviour may not be a big issue since these models are only meant to be macroscopically realistic in some ways, but we believe it could be interesting to explore the addition of a 'slow-to-stop' rule. That is, we want to modify the BJH model so that cars look farther ahead than v cells and slow down earlier in certain situations. People typically pay attention to the velocity of the car directly ahead of them, so we use this information to aid in the decision of how much and when to slow down. A car's change in velocity is then a function of its current velocity, the velocity of the car ahead of it, and the distance between them.

In our model, the cars' velocities are adjusted at each time step according to the following rules. Recall that d is the distance to the next car, v is the velocity of the current car, v_{next} is the velocity of the next car, p_{slow} is the probability that the slow-to-start rule is applied, and p_{fault} is the probability that the car slows down randomly. We fix $v_{max} = 5$.

1. Slow-to-Start: As in the BJH rule, if $v = 0$ and $d > 1$ then with probability $1 - p_{slow}$ the car accelerates normally (this step is ignored), and with probability p_{slow} the car stays at velocity 0 on this time step (does not move) and accelerates to $v = 1$ on the next time step.
2. Deceleration (when the next car is near): if $d <= v$ and either $v < v_{next}$ or $v <= 2$, then the next car is either very close or going at a faster speed, and we prevent a collision by setting $v \leftarrow d - 1$, but do not slow down more than is necessary. Otherwise, if $d <= v$, $v >= v_{next}$, and $v > 2$ we set $v \leftarrow \min(d - 1, v - 2)$ in order to possibly decelerate slightly more, since the car ahead is slower or the same speed and the velocity of the current car is substantial.
3. Deceleration (when the next car is farther): if $v < d <= 2v$, then if $v >= v_{next} + 4$, decelerate by 2 ($v \leftarrow v - 2$). Otherwise, if $v_{next} + 2 <= v <= v_{next} + 3$ then decelerate by 1 ($v \leftarrow v - 1$).
4. Acceleration: if the speed has not been modified yet by one of rules 1-3 and $v < v_{max}$ and $d > v + 1$, then $v \leftarrow v + 1$.
5. Randomization: if $v > 0$, with probability p_{fault}, velocity decreases by one ($v \leftarrow v - 1$).
6. Motion: the car advances v cells.

These rules prevent collisions and overtaking. We now attempt to justify the second and third of these rules, which differ from the BJH model.

Consider the following scenario: a car with velocity 5 has a car 5 spaces ahead of it with velocity 0. The BJH model would change the car's velocity to 4, and assuming the car ahead still has not moved, the car would be forced to decelerate to 0 on the next time step. Our model's second rule decelerates the car to 3 in this case so that it is two spaces away, then on the next time step to 1 so that it is one space away, then finally to 0. We believe this is much more realistic behaviour, since cars which see a stopped car ahead of them would certainly attempt to slow

Fig. 3. A 'zoomed-out' view of a larger simulation of our 'slow-to-stop' model. Black dots refer to cars, while white space is empty road. The simulation parameters used to produce this output are the same as those used for Figure 2. Cars drive from left to right, and time 0 is at the top.

down gradually. In less extreme situations, our model behaves the same way as the BJH model in terms of collision avoidance. Note that we are assuming for both models that the car ahead does not move and the randomization rule has not been applied.

Now consider another situation: a car with velocity 5 has a car 6 spaces ahead of it with velocity 0. The BJH model would not change the velocity of the car, resulting in a very sharp deceleration on the next time step as it decelerates from 5 to 0. Our model's third rule decelerates the car to 3 so that it is 3 spaces away on the next time step, then the second rule decelerates the car to 1 so that it is two spaces away, then the car continues at 1 to the last space, then stops. Again, we believe that this type of gradual deceleration is typical of real drivers, and again we have assumed in this scenario that the car ahead does not move and that the randomization rule has not been applied.

Although both examples involved cars ahead which were stopped, the deceleration rules apply whenever a car is going significantly faster than the car ahead of it. While the car ahead with velocity 0 is the most illustrative case, the above examples could also be considered for different 'car ahead' speeds of 1 or 2.

An example of cars following our 'slow-to-stop' model is given in Figure 3. In this example, the simulation parameters are exactly the same as in Figure 2.

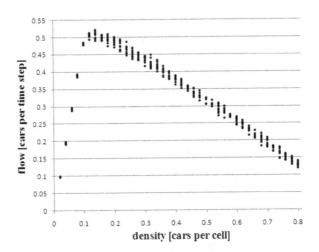

Fig. 4. The 'fundamental diagram' for our model. Each point represents the result from the latter 1000 iterations out of 2000 iterations (to reach steady state) on a road of length 1000 starting from a random configuration. Car density was set from 0 to 0.8, in intervals of 0.02, and ten simulations were performed for each density. p_{fault} was set to 0.1, and $p_{slow} = 0.5$.

One would think that on a real highway with a fairly low car density, where a small jam is visible from a distance, drivers would slow down enough beforehand to allow the stopped cars to continue. The 'slow-to-stop' rule causes drivers to go slower when approaching jams, and as we conjectured this added foresight seems to help to slow down cars enough before the jam so as to let it dissipate on its own over time. There are fewer long jams with many cars at a complete stop, and instead there appear to be many slowdowns to avoid these situations, which we think is fairly accurate behaviour at medium traffic densities.

In Figure 4 we give the so-called 'fundamental diagram' for our model.

We were interested to discover the impact on fuel economy that the 'slow-to-stop' rule would have on the BJH model, so the average number of acceleration cycles and loops driven per car were recorded. The number of accelerations per car was recorded by simply incrementing a counter at each time step by an amount equal to the number of cars whose velocity increased by 1 on that time step. The number of loops driven per car was counted by incrementing a counter each time a car reached the end of the road and started back at the beginning of it. These two quantities provide at least a rough idea of fuel economy. For the simulation parameters used in Figures 2 and 3 averaged over 10 iterations, it was found that the average number of acceleration cycles per car for the BJH model and the slow-to-stop model was 134.3 and 216.7 respectively, and average number of loops driven per car was 3.7 and 3.4 respectively. It is very interesting that although the 'slow-to-stop' cars had several more acceleration cycles (about 61% more), cars travelled a very similar distance in the same amount of time. Since 'slow-to-stop' cars tend

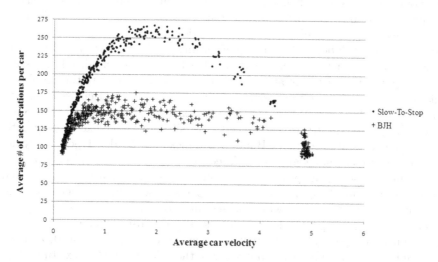

Fig. 5. A fuel economy diagram comparing our model with the BJH model. Each point represents the result from the latter 1000 iterations out of 2000 iterations (to reach steady state) on a road of length 1000 starting from a random configuration. The same simulation parameters as in Figure 4 were used, but average car speed and average number of acceleration cycles per car were recorded instead.

to slow down more often, the two models probably had similar distance results because in the BJH model cars spend more time in complete jams, whereas in our model cars tend to slow down rather than stop completely.

This type of fuel economy indicator (comparing average number of acceleration cycles per car among simulations with a similar average car velocity) can be seen more clearly in Figure 5. We can see that for very low or very high average car velocities (resp. very high or very low ρ values), the two models have fairly similar fuel consumption characteristics, but in the middle range our slow-to-stop model causes cars to accelerate much more often. We think this is probably more realistic, since in the BJH model cars are mostly either at a complete stop, or are going at maximum speed (as in Figure 2).

4   Comparison with Recent Models

After most of the work for this paper had been completed, a slightly more extensive search of the literature yielded a few strongly related papers. We feel that it is important to address some of the differences in our work, since there are several papers which present modifications to the NaSch model.

One of the first papers to propose a modification of the NaSch model was by Emmerich and Rank [18]. They devise a scheme which describes the change in velocity by a matrix M, whose indices correspond to the velocity of the current car and the gap (distance to the next car) and whose entries correspond to the speed of the car on the next time step. This model indeed provides a very general braking scheme, but does not depend on the velocity of the car ahead. A model by Knospe et al. [19] suggested many modifications to the NaSch model, the most relevant to our work being the braking according to an 'effective gap'. This term is defined to be a function of the 'anticipated' velocity of the car ahead, the 'security gap' (a fixed quantity set at simulation time), and distance to the car ahead. This is intuitive, however one possible criticism is that the 'anticipated' velocity of the car ahead is a function of that car's distance to the car ahead of it. Since drivers cannot always see two cars ahead, this behaviour may lead to unrealistic car decisions in some situations. Bham and Benekohal [20] developed a very detailed model which they claim is validated at the microscopic and macroscopic levels using two sets of empirical data. Chakroborty and Maurya [21] compared this and other models against several macroscopic benchmarking criteria, and gave their own model as well which passed all of their criteria.

Our model is perhaps simpler to implement than most of these models, since we use only the speed of the current car, the speed of the car ahead, and the distance between them in order to determine the velocity on the next time step. Our modification to the BJH model, though perhaps minor, produces interesting output and we provide at least some indication of the fuel economy or pollution generation statistics, a characteristic that is lacking in most of the literature.

5   Conclusion and Future Work

We have presented a modification of the well-known BJH model for single lane car traffic, designed to simulate the braking behaviour of cars more correctly. We have provided the fundamental diagram for our model as well as some supplemental simulation results, and have recorded a statistic proportional to fuel economy and the amount of pollution generated. The simulator[1] we have constructed is fairly simple to understand and modify, and could be a useful tool for future researchers to incorporate into their work in this area. It performs an iteration of cars moving on a road in $O(L)$ time, where L is the length of the road - of course, a parallel implementation could do this in constant time.

Comparison with empirical traffic data is needed in order to tell if our model provides realistic figures for fuel economy and general driving and jamming characteristics. We believe it may be interesting to compare traffic data from North American traffic networks, since there currently appears to be a shortage of this type of comparison in the literature.

References

1. Nagel, K., Schreckenberg, M.: A cellular automaton model for freeway traffic. Journal de Physique I 2(12), 2221–2229 (1992)
2. Nagel, K.: Particle hopping models and traffic flow theory. Phys. Rev. E 3(5), 4655–4672 (1996)

---

[1] Email the first author for a working copy.

3. Sasvári, M., Kertész, J.: Cellular automata models of single-lane traffic. Phys. Rev. E 56(4), 4104–4110 (1997)

4. Schadschneider, A.: The nagel-schreckenberg model revisited. Eur. Phys. J. B 10, 573–582 (1999)

5. Schadschneider, A., Schreckenberg, M.: Cellular automaton models and traffic flow. J. Phys. A Math. Gen. 26, 679–683 (1993)

6. Wagner, P.: Traffic simulations using cellular automata: Comparison with reality. In: Traffic and Granular Flow. World Scientific, Singapore (1996)

7. Benjamin, S.C., Johnson, N.F., Hui, P.M.: Cellular automata models of traffic flow along a highway containing a junction. Journal of Physics A: Mathematical and General 29(12), 3119–3127 (1996)

8. Rickert, M., Nagel, K., Schreckenberg, M., Latour, A.: Two lane traffic simulations using cellular automata. Physica A: Statistical and Theoretical Physics 231(4), 534–550 (1996)

9. Wagner, P., Nagel, K., Wolf, D.E.: Realistic multi-lane traffic rules for cellular automata. Physica A: Statistical and Theoretical Physics 234(3-4), 687–698 (1997)

10. Knospe, W., Santen, L., Schadschneider, A., Schreckenberg, M.: Disorder effects in cellular automata for two-lane traffic. Physica A: Statistical and Theoretical Physics 265(3-4), 614–633 (1999)

11. Nagel, K., Wolf, D.E., Wagner, P., Simon, P.: Two-lane traffic rules for cellular automata: A systematic approach. Phys. Rev. E 58(2), 1425–1437 (1998)

12. Esser, J., Schreckenberg, M.: Microscopic simulation of urban traffic based on cellular automata. International Journal of Modern Physics C 8(5), 1025–1036 (1997)

13. Simon, P.M., Nagel, K.: Simplified cellular automaton model for city traffic. Phys. Rev. E 58(2), 1286–1295 (1998)

14. Chowdhury, D., Schadschneider, A.: Self-organization of traffic jams in cities: Effects of stochastic dynamics and signal periods. Phys. Rev. E 59(2), R1311–R1314 (1999)

15. Brockfeld, E., Barlovic, R., Schadschneider, A., Schreckenberg, M.: Optimizing traffic lights in a cellular automaton model for city traffic. Phys. Rev. E 64(5), 056132 (2001)

16. Barlovic, R., Brockfeld, E., Schadschneider, A., Schreckenberg, M.: Optimal traffic states in a cellular automaton model for city traffic. In: Traffic and Granular Flow 2001. Springer, Heidelberg (2003)

17. Deo, P., Ruskin, H.J.: Simulation of heterogeneous motorised traffic at a signalised intersection. In: El Yacoubi, S., Chopard, B., Bandini, S. (eds.) ACRI 2006. LNCS, vol. 4173, pp. 522–531. Springer, Heidelberg (2006)

18. Emmerich, H., Rank, E.: An improved cellular automaton model for traffic flow simulation. Physica A: Statistical and Theoretical Physics 234(3-4), 676–686 (1997)

19. Knospe, W., Santen, L., Schadschneider, A., Schreckenberg, M.: Towards a realistic microscopic description of highway traffic. Journal of Physics A: Mathematical and General 33(1), L477–L485 (2000)

20. Bham, G.H., Benekohal, R.F.: A high fidelity traffic simulation model based on cellular automata and car-following concepts. Transportation Research Part C: Emerging Technologies 12(1), 1–32 (2004)

21. Chakroborty, P., Maurya, A.K.: Microscopic analysis of cellular automata based traffic flow models and an improved model. Transport Reviews 28(18), 717–734 (2008)

On Parallel Implementations of Deterministic Finite Automata[*]

Jan Holub and Stanislav Štekr

Department of Computer Science and Engineering,
Faculty of Electrical Engineering,
Czech Technical University in Prague,
Karlovo náměstí 13, 121 35, Prague 2, Czech Republic
holub@fel.cvut.cz

Abstract. We present implementations of parallel DFA run methods and find whether and under what conditions is worthy to use the parallel methods of simulation of run of finite automata.

First, we introduce the parallel DFA run methods for general DFA, which are universal, but due to the dependency of simulation time on the number of states $|Q|$ of automaton being run, they are suitable only for run of automata with the smaller number of states.

Then we show that if we apply some restrictions to properties of automata being run, we can reach the linear speedup compared to the sequential simulation method. We designed methods benefiting from k-locality that allows optimum parallel run of exact and approximate pattern matching automata.

Finally, we show the results of experiments conducted on two types of parallel computers (Cluster of workstations and Symmetric shared-memory multiprocessors).

1 Introduction

Finite automata (also known as *finite state machines*) are the formal system for solving many tasks in Computer Science. The finite automata run very fast and there exists many efficient implementations (e.g., [Tho68, NKW05, NKW06]).

The increase of computation power of available computers is based not only on the increase of CPU frequency but also on other modern technologies. The finite automata implementations have to consider these technologies. A recent paper [Hol07] provides a survey of various finite automata implementations considering CPU (like [NKW05, NKW06]). One of the latest technologies used is a usage of multiple CPU core. The speed of sequential run of the finite automata cannot follow the increase of computation power of computers that is mostly based on dual-core and quad-core processors. Therefore a demand on parallel run of the finite automata strengthens.

---

[*] This research has been partially supported by the Ministry of Education, Youth and Sports under research program MSM 6840770014 and the Czech Science Foundation as project No. 201/09/0807.

S. Maneth (Ed.): CIAA 2009, LNCS 5642, pp. 54–64, 2009.

The parallel run of deterministic finite transducer was first described in [LF80]. We implement deterministic finite automata run on two parallel computer architectures: Cluster of Workstations (COW) and Symmetric Shared-Memory Multiprocessors (SMP). Since finite automata are very often used in the approximate and exact pattern matching, we also describe methods of parallel simulation on these automata exploiting their special properties—they are synchronizing automata.

2 Finite Automata

Nondeterministic finite automaton (NFA) is a quintuple $(Q, \Sigma, \delta, q_0, F)$, where Q is a finite set of states, Σ is a set of input symbols, δ is a mapping $Q \times (\Sigma \cup \{\varepsilon\}) \mapsto \mathcal{P}(Q)$, $q_0 \in Q$ is an initial state, and $F \subseteq Q$ is a set of final states. *Deterministic finite automaton* (DFA) is a special case of NFA, where δ is a mapping $Q \times \Sigma \mapsto Q$. We define $\hat{\delta}$ as an extended transition function: $\hat{\delta}(q, \varepsilon) = q$, $\hat{\delta}(q, ua) = p \iff \hat{\delta}(q, u) = q', \delta(q', a) = p, a \in \Sigma, u \in \Sigma^*$.

A *configuration of DFA* is a pair $(q, w) \in Q \times \Sigma^*$. The *initial configuration of DFA* is a pair (q_0, w) and a *final (accepting) configuration of DFA* is a pair (q_f, ε), where $q_f \in F$. A *move of DFA* $M = (Q, \Sigma, \delta, q_0, F)$ is a relation $\vdash_M \subseteq (Q \times (\Sigma^* \setminus \{\varepsilon\})) \times (Q \times \Sigma^*)$ defined as $(q_1, aw) \vdash_M (q_2, w)$, where $\delta(q_1, a) = q_2$, $a \in \Sigma$, $w \in \Sigma^*$, $q_1, q_2 \in Q$. The symbol $\vdash_M^*$ denotes a transitive and reflexive closure of relation $\vdash_M$.

3 DFA Run

3.1 Sequential DFA Run

The sequential run of DFA uses the fact that there is always just one state[1] active during the computation. *The run of accepting automaton* consists of one **for** loop over the length of the input text (with iterator j) which contains only one statement: $q \leftarrow \delta[q, t_j]$. Variable q holds the number of active state. When the **for** loop finishes we check if we reached a final state ($q \in F$) and thus DFA accepts the text. On the other hand in *the run of pattern matching automaton* [Mel95, Mel96, Hol96, HIMM01] we check if we reached a final state in each position of the text to report all occurrences of the pattern. In both cases DFA runs in time $\mathcal{O}(n)$ and space $\mathcal{O}(|Q||\Sigma|)$, where n is the length of the input text.

3.2 DFA Run on a COW

In this section we describe a method of parallel run of DFA on a COW. Let us remind that on COW-based parallel computers *message passing* is used for exchanging data among processors.

---

[1] In this text, we suppose run of completely defined automaton. Any partially defined automaton can be converted to the equivalent complete one by adding a sink state.

DFA run method. When running DFA sequentially on input text T of size n, we start in one initial state and after n steps we reach a state from set Q.

The basic idea of run of DFA on a COW is to divide the input text among all processors, run the automaton on each of them, and then join all subresults.

Let us have a DFA M and a COW with $|P|$ processors. The input text is sliced into $|P|$ parts $T_1, T_2, \ldots T_{|P|}$ using block data decomposition. On every part T_i of input text, M is run and after reading all symbols a state is reached.

A problem comes with joining of subresults. We need to connect the last active state of processor P_i to the first active state of processor P_{i+1} (so that the initial state of processor P_{i+1} is the last active state of P_i). The problem is that the last active state of processor P_i is known after reading whole part T_i of input text. If each P_{i+1} would need to wait for the last active state P_i and then process part T_{i+1}, we reach sequential complexity (or even worse because sending results between processors is very expensive operation).

To solve this problem we have to consider all states (one after other) as initial states and to find the corresponding last active state for each of them. After doing so, we get mappings of one *initial state* to one *last active state*. This mapping can be simply reduced by parallel binary reduction [LF80].

Algorithm 3.1 shows the basic DFA run on a COW. We suppose (for both COW and SMP), that:

- each processor has built the transition table δ,
- each processor has the set of final states F,
- processors are ranked by *continuous linear sequence of IDs starting with zero* and each of them knows its own as a value of variable[2] P_i,
- processor P_0 knows which state is the initial state (q_0),
- each processor has access to its part of the input text (see below),
- at least two processors execute this algorithm,
- the number $|P|$ of processors executing the algorithm does not change during algorithm execution and all processors know the value.

We implement a mapping of *possible initial states* to *possible last active states* as vector $\mathcal{L}_{P_i} = [l_0, l_1, \ldots, l_{|Q|-1}]$, where l_j, $0 \leq j < |Q|$, is the last active state assuming that processor P_i starts in state j and processes part T_i of the input text (i.e., $\hat{\delta}(q_j, T_i) = l_j$). The set F of final states is implemented as bit vector $\mathcal{F} = [f_0, f_1, \ldots, f_{|Q|-1}]$, where bit $f_j = 1$, if $q_j \in F$, or $f_j = 0$, otherwise.

We also need to implement a vector $\mathcal{R}_{P_i} = [r_0, r_1, \ldots, r_{|Q|-1}]$ in which we store information about the automaton run. It depends on our requirements what kind of information we want to store. We can store a complete sequence of configurations $(q_0, w) \vdash_M^* (q_f, \varepsilon)$, but for our purposes (without loss of generality) we store only a count of final states reached. Each element r_i of this vector contains a number of reached final states assuming initial state being q_i.

Finally, the transition function δ is implemented as a transition table $\mathcal{T}$ of size $(|Q| \times |\Sigma|)$, where $a \in \Sigma$ and $q_j \in Q$ such that $q_j = \delta(q_i, a)$: $\mathcal{T}[i, a] = q_j, q_j \in Q$.

---

[2] This variable is often named 'my_rank' in MPI programs.

Algorithm 3.1 (Basic run of DFA on a COW)
Input: $\mathcal{T}$, $\mathcal{F}$, $\mathcal{L}$ and $\mathcal{R}$, input text $T = t_1 t_2 \ldots t_n$ and q_0
Output: Output of run of DFA
Method: Set S of active states is used, each processor has its unique number P_i, number of processors is $|P|$.

for all $P_0, P_1 \ldots P_{|P|-1}$ **do in parallel**
$\quad j \leftarrow \lfloor P_i \frac{n}{|P|} \rfloor$
$\quad end\_position \leftarrow \lfloor (P_i + 1) \frac{n}{|P|} \rfloor - 1$
$\quad$**for** $k \leftarrow 0, 1 \ldots |Q| - 1$ **do**
$\quad\quad \mathcal{L}_{P_i}[k] \leftarrow k$ /* initialize vector $\mathcal{L}_{P_i}$ */
$\quad\quad \mathcal{R}_{P_i}[k] \leftarrow 0$ /* initialize vector $\mathcal{R}_{P_i}$ */
$\quad$**endfor**
$\quad$**while** $j \leq end\_position$ **do**
$\quad\quad$**for** $\ell \leftarrow 0 \ldots |Q| - 1$ **do**
$\quad\quad\quad \mathcal{L}_{P_i}[\ell] \leftarrow \mathcal{T}[\mathcal{L}_{P_i}[\ell], t_j]$ /* evaluate transition */
$\quad\quad\quad$**if** $\mathcal{L}_{P_i}[\ell] \in \mathcal{F}$ **then**
$\quad\quad\quad\quad \mathcal{R}_{P_i}[\ell] \leftarrow \mathcal{R}_{P_i}[\ell] + 1$
$\quad\quad\quad$**endif**
$\quad\quad$**endfor**
$\quad\quad j \leftarrow j + 1$
$\quad$**endwhile**
endfor
MPI_Barrier() /* wait for the slowest processor */
$result \leftarrow$ **perform_parallel_reduction()**

Distributing and finishing partial results. After running DFA in parallel, each processor P_i has built mapping $\mathcal{L}_{P_i}$ (*possible initial state* to *possible last active state*) in local memory. In order to finish parallel DFA run, we need to join these mappings (reduce results from processors).

The trivial reduction is based on fact, that only the processor P_0 knows the initial state of automaton M. Hence, only the processor P_0 can send the last active state l_0 and the number of reached final states r_0 to the next processor P_1. This processor uses incoming value l_0 to determine which of possible last active states is correct and sends it to the next processor as an active start state. Incoming value r_0 is added to a corresponding value and also sent to the next processor.

$$
\mathcal{L}_{P_i P_j} = \begin{bmatrix} \mathcal{L}_{P_j}[\mathcal{L}_{P_i}[0]] \\ \mathcal{L}_{P_j}[\mathcal{L}_{P_i}[1]] \\ \vdots \\ \mathcal{L}_{P_j}[\mathcal{L}_{P_i}[|Q| - 1]] \end{bmatrix} . \tag{1}
$$

In the binary reduction, many reductions are made in one parallel step and complete vectors $\mathcal{L}$ and $\mathcal{R}$ are reduced. We define binary operator $\oplus_{DFA}$, which makes one mapping $\mathcal{L}_{P_i P_j}$ from mappings $\mathcal{L}_{P_i}$ and $\mathcal{L}_{P_j}$, where P_i and P_j are processors performing actual step of binary reduction. This newly created mapping $\mathcal{L}_{P_i P_j}$ is built as shown in Formula 1.

This vector $\mathcal{L}_{P_i P_j}$ is either the final result of the binary reduction or will be used in the next reduction operation. At the end of the binary reduction we have got mapping $\mathcal{L}_{P_i P_j}$, where $i = 0$ and $j = |P| - 1$, hence value of $\mathcal{L}_{P_i P_j}[q_0]$ is the last active state of run of automaton M.

Vector $\mathcal{R}$ is reduced similarly:

$$
\mathcal{R}_{P_i P_j} =
\begin{bmatrix}
\mathcal{R}_{P_i}[0] + \mathcal{R}_{P_j}[\mathcal{L}_{P_i}[0]] \\
\mathcal{R}_{P_i}[1] + \mathcal{R}_{P_j}[\mathcal{L}_{P_i}[1]] \\
\vdots \\
\mathcal{R}_{P_i}[|Q| - 1] + \mathcal{R}_{P_j}[\mathcal{L}_{P_i}[|Q| - 1]]
\end{bmatrix}.
\tag{2}
$$

Theorem 3.1
The time of the run of general DFA shown in Algorithm 3.1 using Parallel trivial reduction is $\mathcal{O}(\frac{|Q|n}{|P|} + \log|P| + |P|)$, where $|Q|$ is the number of states of the DFA, n is the length of input text and $|P|$ is the number of processors in COW.

Theorem 3.2
The time of the run of general DFA shown in Algorithm 3.1 using Parallel binary reduction is $\mathcal{O}(\frac{|Q|n}{|P|} + \log|P| + |Q|\log|P|)$, where $|Q|$ is number of states of the DFA, n is the length of input text and $|P|$ is the number of processors in COW.

Analysis of DFA run method. The sequential method of DFA run has time complexity $\mathrm{SU}(n) = \mathcal{O}(n)$. Theorems 3.1 and 3.2 show that parallel method of DFA run depends in addition on $|P|$ and on the number of states of M being run.

If we suppose that the length of the input text is far greater than the number of processors ($|P| \ll n$), we can ignore the barrier part $\mathcal{O}(\log|P|)$ in the complexity formula. This overhead is common in parallel algorithms and barrier is made only once per run of the algorithm. Contrary to the sequential run of DFA, the parallel run depends also on the number of states $|Q|$. This dependency is present because of precomputing possible terminal states (there is a lot of subresults computed by each processor, but only on of them is used).

If we use the trivial reduction, we need time $\mathrm{T}(n, |P|) = \mathcal{O}(\frac{|Q|n}{|P|} + \log|P| + |P|)$. If we suppose $|P| \ll n$ and $|P| \ll |Q|$, we can omit the barrier and reduction parts of complexity formula, so we get $\mathrm{T}(n, |P|) = \mathcal{O}(\frac{|Q|n}{|P|})$. Speedup is then

$$
S(n, |P|) = \mathcal{O}\left(\frac{\mathrm{SU}(n)}{\mathrm{T}(n, |P|)}\right) = \mathcal{O}\left(\frac{n}{\frac{|Q|n}{|P|}}\right) = \mathcal{O}\left(\frac{|P|}{|Q|}\right)
\tag{3}
$$

We can see that parallel speedup depends on the number of processors $|P|$ and the number of states $|Q|$. If we increase $|P|$, we speed up the run of the algorithm. If we run a DFA with more states than the number of processors, we do not reach the optimum time of computation. On the other hand the run of DFAs with less states is faster than the sequential algorithm.

If we use the parallel binary reduction, we run DFA in time $\mathcal{O}(\frac{|Q|n}{|P|} + \log|P| + |Q|\log|P|)$. At this formula, we can not simply omit the reduction part of formula $\mathcal{O}(|Q|\log|P|)$ because it depends not only on the number of processors $|P|$, but also on the number of states $|Q|$. As mentioned above, this method of DFA run is not suitable DFAs with more states than the number of processors, so if we accept this, we can get rough approximation of speedup which is the same as in Formula 3.

Summary of DFA run method on COW. The algorithm does not need any communication operation during reading of input text, but the penalty for this is necessity to precompute possible initial states, which has increased complexity $|Q|$ times. This method is not suitable for run of DFAs with large number of states, but may fit for parallel run of small DFAs with a large input text.

3.3   Run of DFA on a SMP

In this section we describe a method of parallel run of DFA on SMP. Contrary to processors of *COW*, *SMP* processors have shared address space, so that each processor can access memory of another one.

Basic DFA run. We divide the input text among processors, run the automaton on each of them, supposing each state of automaton as initial state, and join partial results into the result of the run. Since we have a share memory at disposal, we do not need to send messages in order to join subresults. At the beginning of the DFA run we can allocate shared memory for all processors, let each processor to work on its part of memory and compute final result of DFA run using this memory at the end of the DFA run.

Remark 3.3
Here, we suppose usage of *OpenMP* library, its pragmas and functions, so all variables, memory allocations, and memory writes in the algorithm, executed before entering a parallel section (pragma **#pragma omp parallel** is used in the source code) are made over the shared memory. It means that in the parallel section these values can be accessed by processors and even if they are at the beginning of parallel section marked as *private*, they will contain original values.

Algorithm 3.2 shows the basic run of DFA on a SMP. As in DFA run on a *COW*, we need to implement vectors $\mathcal{L}$ and $\mathcal{R}$. These vectors have similar purpose. Since in *SMP* the memory is shared, vectors $\mathcal{L}$ and $\mathcal{R}$ for all processors compose matrices (vectors of vectors). Vectors in the matrices are indexed by the processor number. Vector $\mathcal{F}$ and matrix $\mathcal{T}$ remain the same. Since they are shared, they are set up only at beginning of run of algorithm and then the are used by all processors only for reading.

$$\mathcal{L}[p] = \begin{bmatrix} l_0 \\ l_1 \\ \vdots \\ l_{|Q|-1} \end{bmatrix}, \quad \mathcal{R}[p] = \begin{bmatrix} r_0 \\ r_1 \\ \vdots \\ r_{|Q|-1} \end{bmatrix} \qquad (4)$$

Mapping of *possible initial states* to *possible last active states* is implemented as matrix $\mathcal{L}$ of size $|Q| \times |P|$ ($\mathcal{L}[i] = [l_0, l_1, \ldots, l_{|Q|-1}]$), where $i \in 0, \ldots, |P|-1$ is a number of processor, $l_j, 0 \leq j < |Q|$, is the last active state assuming that processor i starts in state j and processes part T_i of the input text (i.e., $\hat{\delta}(q_j, T_i) = l_j$). The count of reached final states[3] is stored in matrix $\mathcal{R}$ of size $|Q| \times |P|$ and each processor P_i has its own column (vector $\mathcal{R}[i] = [r_0, r_1, \ldots, r_{|Q|-1}]$). Each item r_j of this vector contains the number of reached final states assuming initial state q_j.

Algorithm 3.2 (Basic run of DFA on a SMP)
Input: A transition table $\mathcal{T}$, set of final states $\mathcal{F}$, mapping from possible initial state to possible last visited state $\mathcal{L}$ and a set $\mathcal{R}$ of possibly reached final states of DFA, input text $T = t_1 t_2 \ldots t_n$ and initial state q_0
Output: Output of run of DFA
Method: Set S of active states is used, each processor has its unique number P_i, number of processors is $|P|$.

> **for all** $P_0, P_1 \ldots P_{|P|-1}$ **do in parallel**
> $\quad j \leftarrow \lfloor P_i \frac{n}{|P|} \rfloor$
> $\quad end\_position \leftarrow \lfloor (P_i + 1) \frac{n}{|P|} \rfloor - 1$
> $\quad$ **for** $k \leftarrow 0 \ldots |Q| - 1$ **do**
> $\quad \quad \mathcal{L}[P_i][k] \leftarrow k$ /* initialize vector $\mathcal{L}$ */
> $\quad \quad \mathcal{R}[P_i][k] \leftarrow 0$ /* initialize vector $\mathcal{R}$ */
> $\quad$ **endfor**
> $\quad$ **while** $j \leq end\_position$ **do**
> $\quad \quad$ **for** $k \leftarrow 0 \ldots |Q| - 1$ **do**
> $\quad \quad \quad \mathcal{L}[P_i][k] \leftarrow \mathcal{T}[\mathcal{L}[P_i][k], t_j]$ /* evaluate transition */
> $\quad \quad \quad$ **if** $\mathcal{L}[P_i][k] \in \mathcal{F}$ **then**
> $\quad \quad \quad \quad \mathcal{R}[P_i][k] \leftarrow \mathcal{R}[P_i][k] + 1$
> $\quad \quad \quad$ **endif**
> $\quad \quad$ **endfor**
> $\quad \quad j \leftarrow j + 1$
> $\quad$ **endwhile**
> **endfor**
> **#pragma omp barrier** /* wait for the slowest processor */
> $result \leftarrow$ **perform_parallel_reduction()**

---

[3] As we have mentioned in Section 3.2, we can store more complex information than is the count of reached final states.

The reduction of partial results is made either sequentially by one processor, which accesses shared memory and computes the final result, or by all processors using the binary reduction, where more processors access different memory cells and join them into the final result.

Theorem 3.4

The time of the run of general DFA shown in Algorithm 3.2 using the sequential reduction is $\mathcal{O}(\frac{|Q|n}{|P|} + \log|P| + |P|)$, where $|Q|$ is the number of states of the DFA, n is the length of the input text and $|P|$ is number of processors of SMP.

Theorem 3.5

The time of the run of general DFA shown in Algorithm 3.2 using the parallel binary reduction is $\mathcal{O}(\frac{|Q|n}{|P|} + \log|P| + |Q|\lceil\log|P|\rceil)$, where $|Q|$ is number of states of the DFA, n is the length of input text and $|P|$ is number of processors of SMP.

Analysis of DFA run method. The complexity is the same as for *COW* but we do not need to explicitly send messages. We benefit from the shared memory.

4   Experiments

The algorithms were implemented in **C** programming language using *MPI* environment and *OpenMP* environment. We measured time of execution on *SMP* and *COW* computers.

Star is a cluster of workstations with 16 nodes (Intel Pentium III 733 MHz, 256 MB RAM, HD 30 GB) interconnected by Myrinet and Ethernet network. The program for this cluster was written using *MPI*.

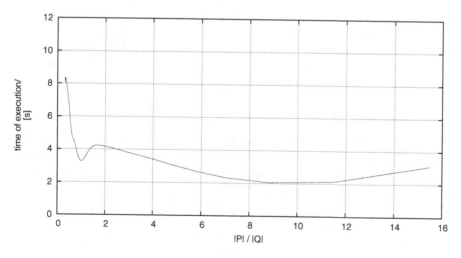

Fig. 1. Dependency of execution time of parallel run of DFA on $|P|/|Q|$ (Altix, $|P| = 31$, $n = 10^8$)

Altix is a symmetric shared-memory multiprocessor with 32 processors (16x 1,3 GHz 3MB L3 cache, 16x 1,5 GHz 6MB L3 cache) interconnected by *NUMA-link* network. Each processor has its own local memory, which is fast and can access to shared memory (but accessing of shared memory is much slower).

Figure 1 shows execution time of parallel run related to number of processors to one state of automaton. We can see that for $|P|/|Q| < 1$ is performance low, but if we increase the number of processors, we speedup the computation. For $|P|/|Q| > 10$ performance descends due to collisions on bus and higher time needed for reduction of results.

5   Parallel Run of Pattern Searching DFAs

In this section, we show parallel runs of pattern matching finite automata. They can be run in parallel without necessity to precompute possible initial states, so the complexity of the run does not depend on the number of states of automaton being run. All these runs are based on synchronization of automaton. We suppose running this run on a *COW*, because it can be simply executed also on *SMP* with only few modifications.

5.1   Synchronization of Finite Automata

In the run of general DFA we do not know in which state the DFA run should start[4]. If we restrict the DFA to a subset of k-local automata, we do not have to precompute the possible initial states, because we can synchronize the DFA of each processor and start the DFA run at the correct state.

We say that $w = a_0 a_1 \ldots a_{k-1}$ is a *synchronizing word* for M if $\forall p, q \in Q, \hat{\delta}(p, w) = \hat{\delta}(q, w)$. We say that M is *k-local automaton* if there exists an integer k such that any word of length k is synchronizing. We say, that M is *synchronizing automaton*, if there exists a word $w = \Sigma^*$ of length at least k, which is synchronizing. The number k can be called the synchronization delay of automaton M. Černý's conjecture [Čer64, ČPR71] gives a relation between the size of synchronizing automaton and the length of its synchronizing word.

5.2   Parallel Run of k-Local DFA

Method of the parallel run of k-local DFA. Let M be a k-local DFA. We divide the input text among $|P|$ processors using block data decomposition, but here we give extra last k symbols of the preceding block of input text to each processor. This overlapping by k symbols synchronizes the DFA into correct initial state before it reads its part of the input text.

The method is shown in Algorithm 5.1. At the beginning the left boundary is extended by k symbols to the left for all processors (except P_0). Since we should not count reached final states during synchronizing the automaton we add condition $j \geq \lfloor P_i \frac{n}{|P|} \rfloor$ to the last *if* statement.

---

[4] Except of the first processor, which has this information—the initial state q_0 of M.

Algorithm 5.1 (Basic run of k-local DFA)
Input: A transition table $\mathcal{T}$, set of final states $\mathcal{F}$, input text $T = t_1 t_2 \ldots t_n$, initial state q_0 and the length of the synchronizing word in variable k
Output: Number of reached final states
Method: Set S of active states is used, each processor has its unique number P_i, number of processors is $|P|$.

> **for all** $P_0, P_1 \ldots P_{|P|-1}$ **do in parallel**
> $\quad j \leftarrow \lfloor P_i \frac{n}{|P|} \rfloor$
> $\quad found \leftarrow 0 \;/*$ number of reached final states $*/$
> $\quad$ **if** $P_i > 0$ **then** $/*$ The first proc. does not need to synchronize $*/$
> $\quad\quad j \leftarrow j - k \;/*$ Shift the left boundary. $*/$
> $\quad$ **endif**
> $\quad end\_position \leftarrow \lfloor (P_i + 1) \frac{n}{|P|} \rfloor - 1$
> $\quad q \leftarrow q_0$
> $\quad$ **while** $j \leq end\_position$ **do**
> $\quad\quad q \leftarrow \mathcal{T}[q, t_j] \;/*$ evaluate transition $*/$
> $\quad\quad$ **if** $\mathcal{L}[i] \in \mathcal{F}$ **and** $j \geq \lfloor P_i \frac{n}{|P|} \rfloor$ **then**
> $\quad\quad\quad found \leftarrow found + 1$
> $\quad\quad$ **endif**
> $\quad\quad j \leftarrow j + 1$
> $\quad$ **endwhile**
> $\quad$ **MPI_Reduce**($data \; found \; using \; operator + store \; results \; on \; P_0$)
> **endfor**
> **for all** P_0 **do in parallel**
> $\quad$ **return**($found$)
> **endfor**

Theorem 5.1
The time of the run of k-local DFA shown in Algorithm 5.1 is $\mathcal{O}(k + \frac{n}{|P|} + \log |P|)$, where $|Q|$ is the number of states of automaton M, n is the length of the input text and $|P|$ is the number of processors.

Analysis of DFA run method. The complexity of run of k-local DFA depends on the length of synchronizing word k. Contrary to the run of general DFA, the complexity is not multiplied by $|Q|$. It means, that if we omit the time needed to reduce results and expect $k \ll n$ (which is usual assumption in pattern matching automata), we get the speedup:

$$S(n, |P|) = \mathcal{O}\left(\frac{n}{k + \frac{n}{|P|} + \log |P|} \right) \doteq \mathcal{O}\left(\frac{n}{\frac{n}{|P|}} \right) = \mathcal{O}(|P|)$$

We can see, that we get the linear speedup for DFAs with $n \gg |Q|$, which is the upper bound of speedup achievable by parallelization of sequential algorithm.

6   Conclusion and Future Work

We have designed and implemented DFA run on two different parallel computer architectures. First we implement the parallel run of general DFA. On both architectures it runs in time $\mathcal{O}(\frac{|Q|n}{|P|} + \log|P| + |P|)$ when using parallel trivial reduction and in time $\mathcal{O}(\frac{|Q|n}{|P|} + \log|P| + |Q|\log|P|)$ when using parallel binary reduction. $|Q|$ is the number of states of automaton M, n is the length of input text and $|P|$ is number of processors. We did some experiments that show it is not so efficient in practice due to bus collisions.

We have shown that for a class of DFA called k-local automata widely used in pattern matching the situation is much better. We designed and implemented very efficient parallel algorithm. It runs in time $\mathcal{O}(k + \frac{n}{|P|} + \log|P|)$.

Our next research will focus on parallel simulation of nondeterministic finite automata.

References

[Čer64]   Černý, J.: Poznámka k homogénnym experimentom s konečnými automatmi. Mat. fyz. čas. SAV 14, 208–215 (1964)

[ČPR71]   Černý, J., Pirická, A., Rosenauerová, B.: On directable automata. Kybernetika 7(4), 289–297 (1971)

[HIMM01]   Holub, J., Iliopoulos, C.S., Melichar, B., Mouchard, L.: Distributed pattern matching using finite automata. J. Autom. Lang. Comb. 6(2), 191–204 (2001)

[Hol96]   Holub, J.: Reduced nondeterministic finite automata for approximate string matching. In: Holub, J. (ed.) Proceedings of the Prague Stringologic Club Workshop 1996, Czech Technical University in Prague, Czech Republic, pp. 19–27. Collaborative Report DC–96–10 (1996)

[Hol07]   Holub, J.: Finite automata implementations considering CPU cache. Acta Polytechnica 47(6), 51–55 (2007)

[LF80]   Ladner, R.E., Fisher, M.J.: Parallel prefix computation. J. Assoc. Comput. Mach. 27(4), 831–838 (1980)

[Mel95]   Melichar, B.: Approximate string matching by finite automata. In: Hlaváč, V., Šára, R. (eds.) CAIP 1995. LNCS, vol. 970, pp. 342–349. Springer, Heidelberg (1995)

[Mel96]   Melichar, B.: String matching with k differences by finite automata. In: Proceedings of the 13th International Conference on Pattern Recognition, Vienna, Austria, vol. II, pp. 256–260. IEEE Computer Society Press, Los Alamitos (1996)

[NKW05]   Ngassam, E.K., Kourie, D.G., Watson, B.W.: Reordering finite automatata states for fast string recognition. In: Holub, J., Šimánek, M. (eds.) Proceedings of the Prague Stringology Conference 2005, Czech Technical University in Prague, Czech Republic, pp. 69–80 (2005)

[NKW06]   Ngassam, E.K., Kourie, D.G., Watson, B.W.: On implementation and performance of table-driven DFA-based string processors. In: Holub, J., Žďárek, J. (eds.) Proceedings of the Prague Stringology Conference 2006, Czech Technical University in Prague, Czech Republic, pp. 108–122 (2006)

[Tho68]   Thompson, K.: Regular expression search algorithm. Commun. ACM 11, 419–422 (1968)

FAdo and GUItar: Tools for Automata Manipulation and Visualization*

André Almeida, Marco Almeida**, José Alves, Nelma Moreira,
and Rogério Reis

DCC-FC & LIACC, Universidade do Porto
R. do Campo Alegre 1021/1055, 4169-007 Porto, Portugal
{bernarduh,sobuy,mfa,nam,rvr}@ncc.up.pt

Abstract. **FAdo** is an ongoing project which aims to provide a set
of tools for symbolic manipulation of formal languages. To allow high-
level programming with complex data structures, easy prototyping of
algorithms, and portability (to use in computer grid systems for example), are its main features. Our main motivation is the theoretical and
experimental research, but we have also in mind the construction of a
pedagogical tool for teaching automata theory and formal languages. For
the graphical visualization and interactive manipulation a new interface
application, **GUItar**, is being developed. In this paper, we describe the
main components of the **FAdo** system as well as the basics of the graphical interface and editor, the export/import filters and its generic interface
with external systems, such as **FAdo**.

1 Introduction

The **FAdo** [pro08] project aims to provide an open source extensible high-perfor-
mance software library for the symbolic manipulation of automata and other
models of computation. A first implementation currently includes most standard operations for the manipulation of regular languages [MR05], a Turing
machine simulator and parsing tools for context-free languages. An automata
random generator package was released, based on previous theoretical work
on enumeration and generation of initially connected deterministic finite automata (ICDFA) [AMR07]. Although there are several software packages for
the symbolic manipulation of formal languages they either are not open source,
have restricted purposes, or are no longer being maintained. Examples include:
Grail+ [RW94, Yu09], *Automate* [CH91], *Amore* [JPTW90], *Fire Station* [FW09]
and *OpenFst* [Ril09]. An exception to this is the *Vaucanson* package [LRGS04]
whose basic structures, due to its orientation to more algebraic applications
of automata, are too heavy for the combinatorial and algorithmic simulations
we think useful for complexity studies of formal languages. *JFLAP* [RF06] is

---

* This work was partially funded by Fundação para a Ciência e Tecnologia (FCT) and
  Program POSI, and by project ASA (PTDC/MAT/65481/2006).
** Marco Almeida is funded by FCT grant SFRH/BD/27726/2006.

S. Maneth (Ed.): CIAA 2009, LNCS 5642, pp. 65–74, 2009.

a specialized pedagogical tool with an extensive coverage of formal language topics taught in undergraduate computer science courses. The possibility of interactively experimenting with the construction proofs is a major feature of this system. The **FAdo** system was first developed for pedagogical purposes. However the necessity of easily prototyping new algorithms, testing algorithm performance with large datasets, and the combinatorial nature of formal languages representations led us to continue **FAdo** development. The use of *Python*, a high-level object-oriented language with high-level data types and dynamic typing, ensures a system which is modular, extensible, clearly and easily implemented, and portable. Specialized and optimized data structures and performance critical algorithms may be written in a low-level language like *C*, and easily interfaced with *Python*, via the *Cython* language extension [BB09]. Here, we will describe the main components of the **FAdo** system for regular languages manipulation.

GUItar is a visualization software tool for various types of automata (standard, weighted, pushdown, transducers, Turing machines, etc.). Its purposes include automatic and assisted diagram drawing, algorithm animation, interactive editing and export/import filters. Automatic graph drawing has been a very active research area and several commercial software packages are now available for general and specific applications (database design, information systems, bioinformatics, social networks, etc.) [BERT99, Gra08, JM04]. In contrast, automata diagrams (labelled multi-digraphs) require additional aesthetics and graphical constraints: left-to-right reading, initial states on the left and final states on the right, edge shapes and label placements, etc. We intend to design and implement tools for automatic drawing of automata diagrams according to common accepted aesthetics principles. As a first step, in this paper, we describe the basic **GUItar** framework that includes assisted diagram drawing, interactive editing, and export/import filters.

2   FAdo: Tools for Regular Languages Manipulation

Regular languages can be represented by regular expressions (r.e.) or finite automata, among other formalisms. Finite automata may be deterministic (DFA) or non-deterministic (NFA). In **FAdo** these representations are implemented as *Python* classes, as presented in Figure 1. The class *FA* implements the basic structure of a finite automaton shared by DFAs and NFAs. This class also provides methods for manipulating these structures. The class *DFA* and *NFA* implements DFAs and NFAs, respectively. The class *EFA* implements generalized NFAs that are used in the conversion between finite automata and r.e. There are two representations for r.e.: the class *RE* implements, in a object-oriented manner, the usual inductive definition (it is elegant, but not efficient) and the class *ACIRE* implements irreducible regular expressions modulo *ACIA*, i.e., *associativity* of the concatenation and disjunction, *commutativity* of the disjunction, and *idempotence* of both disjunction and Kleene star operations. Disjunctions are represented as sets, which are efficiently implemented in *Python*. Concatenated r.e. are kept in an ordered list. The idempotence of the Kleene star

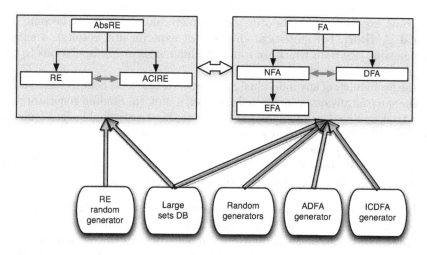

Fig. 1. FAdo classes for regular languages

is assured by not allowing double stared r.e. Whether or not a r.e. accepts the empty word is tabulated as a *ACIRE* attribute, to avoid unnecessary recursive calls. Elementary regular languages operations as union, intersection, concatenation, complementation and reverse are implemented for each class. Several conversions between these representations are implemented: $NFA \to DFA$: subset construction; $NFA \to RE$: recursive method; $EFA \to RE$: state elimination, with possible choice of state orderings; $RE \to NFA$: Thompson method, Glushkov method, follow, Brzozowski, and partial derivatives.

For DFAs several minimization algorithms are available (some with C implementations): Moore, Hopcroft, incremental algorithms of Watson and Daciuk. Brzozowski minimization is available for NFAs. Language equivalence of two DFAs can be determined by reducing their correspondent minimal DFA to a canonical form [AMR07], or by the Hopcroft and Karp algorithm. Language equivalence of two r.e. is implemented in the *ACIRE* class using variants of a rewrite system [AMR08a]. The class *ACIRE* has also several simplification methods for r.e.

2.1 Generators and Random Samples

We have designed and implemented several exact and random generators for some classes of automata and regular expressions. An exact and a uniform random generator are available for ICDFAs [AMR07]. Based on new canonical forms we also developed exact generators for acyclic (trim) deterministic finite automata (ADFA)[AMR08b], and for minimal ADFA (MADFA) [AMR08c]. For the uniform generation of random r.e. we implemented the method described by Mairson [Mai94] for the generation of context-free languages. Random (non-uniform) generators for NFAs that allow to generate initially connected NFAs (with one initial state) and to control the transition density are also implemented.

For a given number of states and symbols, the number of DFAs grows in a way that experimental tests over the complete universe quickly become impractical [AMR07]. For statistical analysis (or experimental results), a subset of manageable size from which we can make inferences or extrapolations to the whole universe may be used.

As the probability of any individual member of the universe being selected is exactly the same as any other individual member, a uniform random generator produces a true, unbiased, random sample. In order to have a reasonable sized (enough for statistically significant results), consistent, random sample readily available, we designed and implemented an SQL database to store the uniformly generated DFAs (and r.e.). We used the PostgreSQL open source relational database system [DBM08] to store the random samples of both DFAs and r.e.

Database. The ICDFAs database keeps and makes available random samples of automata with $n \in \{10, 20, \dots, 90, 100\}$ states, each over an alphabet of $k \in \{2, 3, 4, \dots, 18, 20, 25, 30, \dots, 45, 50\}$ symbols. Besides the automaton structure, the database stores some properties such as minimality, being trimmed, acyclic, etc. This allows to obtain, with a simple SQL query, some automata datasets with specific properties. For efficiency reasons, besides its unique string representation [AMR07], the database is used to store the pre-parsed internal **FAdo** representation of each ICDFA. This avoids the need to parse an automaton's description every single time we need to manipulate it. By similar reasons, each automaton's final states set is stored in two different ways: as a comma separated list of integers and as a bitmap.

REs Database. The r.e. database is similar to the ones pertaining to finite automata. Pre-parsed representations of each object is kept in the database, both in the *ACIRE* and *RE* representation, to avoid overhead parsing time in any algorithm process.

3   GUItar: Interactive Visualization

The **GUItar** graphical interface allows the interactive visualization of generic graph diagrams and the execution of external graph manipulation tools. It is implemented with the *wxPython* [SRZD06] graphical toolkit. Figure 2 shows the interactive diagram editor. The basic frame has a *menu bar*, a *tool bar*, and a notebook that manipulates multiple pages. The *menu bar* and the *tool bar* are dynamically built from *XML* [Con08a] configuration files and event handler files, allowing an easy extensibility and modularity. Each notebook page contains a canvas for diagram drawing and manipulation. The canvas is based on the *wxPython's Floatcanvas component* [Bar08] which allows to draw and to interact with graphic objects. It provides zooming, panning and binding mouse clicks on object to callbacks. It allows the addition of new objects and to alter its interactive behavior. To draw graph transitions a new *FloatCanvas* object called *ArrowSpline* was created. This object defines splines with or without arrow heads. It allows the access to the spline interpolation points, which was not

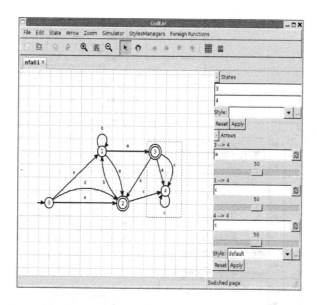

Fig. 2. GUItar graphical interface

possible in the native implementation. The main classes of **GUItar** are presented
in Figure 3, and are summarized in the next subsections.

3.1   Drawing a Graph

A graph is defined by a set of nodes and a set of edges. The class *DrawGraph*
allows the display and the editing of a graph diagram, and its main components
are a canvas, a set of node objects, a set of edge objects and a grid. Nodes and
edges can be added, edited, moved or deleted. Node labels can be automatically
generated according to a given specification. The grid uses a general coordinate
system to manage node positions and prevent objects to overlap. Each object
can occupy several grid cells. To assist diagram editing a specialized graphical
user interface (GUI) mode, a draw assistant and an undo/redo manager were
implemented. Objects properties can be inspected and changed in the *properties
panel*.

Nodes. The *Node* class has an identifier (ID), a position, canvas objects and a
style. This class has methods to change node position and to determine borders
for docking edges.

Edges. The *Edge* class has an ID, an origin and an target nodes, a canvas *ArrowSpline* object, and a label object (with side and position).This class has methods to edit *ArrowSpline* control points, change nodes dock points and change
label location.

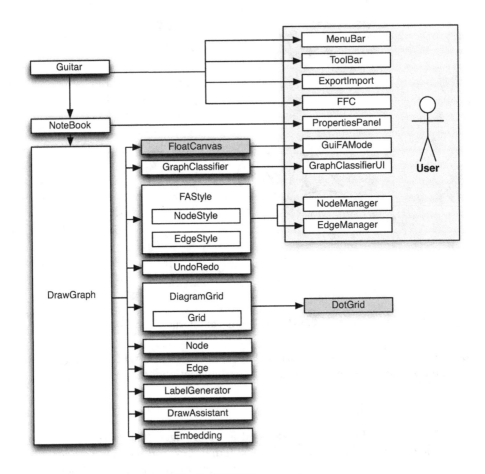

Fig. 3. A **GUItar** overview

Labels. A label can be simple (text string) or composed of several components.

Embeddings. The embedding is the layout of the nodes and edges in the plane. Currently a integer coordinate embedding is provided.

Editing Mode. The *GUIFAMode* class implements an user interface that allows several interactions with the graphical objects, essentially mouse based events, such as addition, deletion, selection, or movement of objects, as well as activation of pop-up menus. It also provides movement in the canvas viewport. The *DrawAssistant* class helps to place the edges and the loops. The edges can be edited by dragging their control points freely or using stepwise movements. To support undo and redo actions, the Undo/Redo manager assigns an ID to each kind of action, a method that handles the undo event, and the ID of the reverse action. The handler method receives as an argument the information needed to undo/redo the action. For each performed action, its ID and the information that the Undo handler method needs are pushed into the Undo stack. The Undo and the Redo methods pop an action from the stack and call the handler method with the appropriated information.

Complex style managers. In general, automata diagrams provide several graphical information on state or transition representations. For instance, an initial state representation can have a side arrow, or a final state representation can have a doubled line border. Instead of having a few special styles built-in, **GUItar** provides a *Node Style Manager* that allows the construction of node styles with complex graphical objects. A node style can have several graphic objects, as components. Two of these are mandatory: the *primary* object and the *primary* label. Primary objects must be ellipses or rectangles, and they ensure that there is always a docking object for the edges. The primary label must be text. For each object, its usual style properties such as line color, line width, line style, fill color, fill style, sizes, fonts, etc. can be defined. A node style can be previewed while it is being defined (or edited), and saved in the **GUItar** internal database. A set of tags (key/value pairs) may also be associated with each node style. The *Edge Style Manager* permits the definition of edge styles. An edge style is characterized by the graphical properties of the edge's *ArrowSpline* canvas object. It is possible to specify the number of heads and their shapes, line style properties, and loop properties.

Graph Classifier. The *GraphClassifer* class allows the definition of graph classes by specifying graphic properties of each object. The *GraphClassifica-tionUI* class provides an user interface to visualize and to create new classes. *Graph*, *digraph*, or *multidigraph* are the default classes.

Automatic graph drawing. A simple layout algorithm for visualizing graphs without any embedding information is implemented. An automatic placement based on physical forces simulation is also available.

3.2   Foreign Function Calls

GUItar provides a generic *foreign function calls* (FFC) interface between the diagram graphical editor and external manipulation tools, as the **FAdo** toolkit. The FFCs have two components: a description on a *XML* configuration file and a *Python* module. The description includes the module path and the methods that will be imported by **GUItar**. Each method must have a *name*, a *return type*, and, for each argument its *type* and a possible *default value*. Each module may have a menu in the main **GUItar**'s frame, or be accessed from a general FFC menu. At startup, **GUItar** loads the FFC configurations and builds the FFC menus.

3.3   Export/Import

Diagram descriptions and embeddings are saved in a *XML* format that was defined as a dialect of the *GraphML* language [Gro08]. *GraphML* is a simple language to describe the structural properties of a graph and has a flexible extension mechanism to add application-specific data. Extensions are provided by a key/data mechanism that can be added to each graph element. For efficiency reasons, for the **GUItar** internal information our dialect encodes this mechanism directly. A fragment of the **GUItar** *Relax NG* schema, is presented below, where diag_data represent the embedding information, and draw_data correspond to general drawing information.

```
include "styles.rnc"                graph_diag,
guitar = element guitar {            graph_class,
   attribute version {text},           style*
   graph*                           }
}                                   node_diag = element diag_data {
graph = element graph {                 attribute x {text},
   attribute id {text},                 attribute y {text}}
   element node {                    node_draw = element draw_data {
      attribute id {text},              attribute style {text},
      label,                            attribute x {text},
      node_diag,                        attribute y {text} }
      node_draw,                     node_auto = element auto_data {
      node_automata                     attribute initial {1 | 0},
   }*,                                  attribute final {1 | 0} }
   element edge {                    edge_draw = element draw_data {
      attribute id {text},              attribute style {text},
      attribute source {text},          element point{
      attribute target {text},             attribute x {text},
      label,                               attribute y {text}} * }
      edge_diag,                     label = element label {
      edge_draw                         attribute type {"sim"|"com"},
   }*,                                  (dict*|text),
                                       label_draw }
```

GUItar exports its objects in three other formats: basic *GraphML*, *dot* and *Vaucanson-g* [LS08]. **GUItar** can also import from *GraphML* and **FAdo** automata format. These export/import methods are implemented as *XSLT* transformations [Con08b] from the **GUItar** format. We are developing *XSLT* transformations for the *fsmxml* format [Gro09].

4   Conclusions

The development of a solid and reliable symbolic manipulation package for formal languages is not a simple task. Being written in a high-level programming language and kept in an free software license promotes its usability by the scientific community. Visualization tools, and specially automatic drawing of automata diagrams, are challenging and important for both research and pedagogical purposes.

References

[AMR07]   Almeida, M., Moreira, N., Reis, R.: Enumeration and generation with a string automata representation. Theoret. Comput. Sci. 387(2), 93–102 (2007)

[AMR08a]   Almeida, M., Moreira, N., Reis, R.: Antimirov and Mosses's rewrite system revisited. In: Ibarra, O.H., Ravikumar, B. (eds.) CIAA 2008. LNCS, vol. 5148, pp. 46–56. Springer, Heidelberg (2008)

[AMR08b]   Almeida, M., Moreira, N., Reis, R.: Exact generation of acyclic deterministic finite automata. In: DCFS 2008, Charlottetown, Canada (2008)

[AMR08c]   Almeida, M., Moreira, N., Reis, R.: Exact generation of minimal acyclic deterministic finite automata. I. J. of F. of Com. Sci. 19(4), 751–765 (2008)

[Bar08]   Barker, C.: Floatcanvas, http://morticia.cs.dal.ca/FloatCanvas/ (access date: 1.12.2008)

[BB09]   Behnel, S., Bradshaw, R.: Cython: C-extensions for Python, http://www.cython.org/ (access date: 03.01.2009)

[BERT99]   Battista, G., Eades, P., Tamassia, R., Tolli, I.G.: Graph Drawing, Algorithms for the Visualisation of Graphs. Prentice Hall, Englewood Cliffs (1999)

[CH91]   Champarnaud, J.M., Hanset, G.: AUTOMATE, a computing package for automata and finite semigroups. J. of Symb. Comput. 12, 197–220 (1991)

[Con08a]   World Wide Web Consortium. XML specification WWW page, http://www.w3.org/TR/xml (access date: 1.12.2008)

[Con08b]   World Wide Web Consortium. XSLT specification WWW page, http://www.w3.org/TR/xslt (access date: 1.12.2008)

[DBM08]   PostgreSQL DBMS. PostgreSQL website, http://www.postgresql.org (access date: 1.12.2008)

[FW09]   Frishert, M., Watson, B.W.: Fire Station, http://www.fastar.org/ (access date: 1.4.2009)

[Gra08]   Graphviz — Graph Visualization Software. The dot language, http://www.graphviz.org/ (access date: 1.12.2008)

[Gro08]   GraphML Working Group. Graphml file format, http://graphml.graphdrawing.org/ (access date: 01.12.2008)

[Gro09]   Vaucanson Group. FSMXML format, http://www.lrde.epita.fr/cgi-bin/twiki/view/Vaucanson/XML (access date: 1.3.2009)

[JM04]   Jünger, M., Mutzel, P. (eds.): Graph Drawing Software. Mathematics and visualization. Springer, Heidelberg (2004)

[JPTW90]   Jansen, V., Potthoff, A., Thomas, W., Wermuth, U.: A short guide to the AMoRE system. Aachener informatik-berichte (90) 02, Lehrstuhl fur Informatik II, Universitat Aachen (January 1990)

[LRGS04]   Lombardy, S., Régis-Gianas, Y., Sakarovitch, J.: Introducing Vaucanson. Theoret. Comput. Sci. 328, 77–96 (2004)

[LS08]   Lombardy, S., Sakarovitch, J., Vaucanson, G.: http://igm.univ-mlv.fr/~lombardy/ (access date: 1.12.2008)

[Mai94]   Mairson, H.G.: Generating words in a context-free language uniformly at random. Information Processing Letters 49, 95–99 (1994)

[MR05]   Moreira, N., Reis, R.: Interactive manipulation of regular objects with FAdo. In: ITiCSE 2005, pp. 335–339. ACM, New York (2005)

74   A. Almeida et al.

[pro08]   FAdo project. FAdo: tools for formal languages manipulation, http://www.ncc.up.pt/FAdo (access date: 1.12.2008)

[RF06]   Rodger, S., Finlea, T.: JFLAP - An Interactive Formal Languages and Automata Package. Jones and Bartlett (2006)

[Ril09]   Riley, M.: OpenFst, http://www.openfst.org (access date: 1.4.2009)

[RW94]   Raymond, D., Wood, D.: Grail: A C++ Library for automata and expressions. J. Symb. Comp. 17(4), 341–350 (1994)

[SRZD06]   Smart, J., Roebling, R., Zeitlin, V., Dunn, R.: wxWidgets 2.6.3: A portable C++ and Python GUI toolkit (2006)

[Yu09]   Yu, S.: Grail+, http://www.csd.uwo.ca/Research/grail/ (access date: 1.3.2009)

A Testing Framework for Finite-State Morphology

François Barthélemy

CNAM (Cédric), Paris, France
INRIA (Alpage), Rocquencourt, France
francois.barthelemy@cnam.fr

Abstract. This paper describes a unit testing framework for the languages which rely on rational relations to describe Natural Language Morphology. A test is divided into two parts: firstly compute a finite-state machine; secondly inspect this machine to compute its cardinality. The first part involves the finite-state machines to be tested and finite-state machines encoding the inputs of the test. A dependency relation is used to relate tests and the components of the description.

1 Introduction

Morphology is the subarea of Linguistics which deals with the structure and content of word forms. It describes the structure of these forms and their flexion (conjugation, agreement, declension). Finite-State Morphology is an approach of Natural Language Processing where the morphology is described using contextual rules which are compiled into finite-state transducers. Several languages have been proposed since the mid-eighties. They have been used for a lot of languages with different kinds of morphologies, belonging to several families (Indo-European, Semitic, Altaic, Finno-Ougrian, etc). Mechanisms such as affixation, interdigitation and to some extend, reduplication, are handled.

The most popular instance of finite-state morphology is the Xerox Finite State Tool (Xfst) described in [1]. This system proposes a powerful language, based on a clean semantics, with an efficient implementation. Other systems have more or less the same properties, and there are several finite-state toolkits which may be used to develop new systems quite easily, such as for instance, Google's openFST [2].

A weakness of these systems is their relatively poor development environments. For instance, the Xfst system comes with a top-level and a basic scripting facility. This is relatively poor compared to the Integrated Development Environments (IDE) of programming languages. Such environments provide an editor, a compiler, a notion of project, support for documentation, debugging and test. Eclipse is an instance of popular, modern and versatile IDE.

An increasing effort has been done to improve software quality. An important approach consists in the testing frameworks Xunit, which is instantiated for different languages such as Java (Junit), C (CUnit), C++ (CppUnit) and so on. These frameworks are based on unit black-box tests which perform runtime execution

S. Maneth (Ed.): CIAA 2009, LNCS 5642, pp. 75–83, 2009.
© Springer-Verlag Berlin Heidelberg 2009

of pieces of code (typically, a method or a function) and compares the actual result which an expected result. The testing is automated, which is important for non-regression testing, namely testing that modifications in the code do not alterate its quality. Programming styles are promoted where tests are written at the same time or even before the code to be tested. Tests are to be run on components before a system is completed (cf. *extreme programming* [3]).

Some other approaches of software quality rely on static checks performed at compile-time. Syntax and type checking are the first level of verification, fully automated and usually integrated in the compilers. Some other techniques (abstract interpretation, model-checking, binary decision diagram) allow the proof of some properties. They are only partly automated and therefore expansive, but they also are more powerful. They give positive proofs of properties which hold for all the possible executions. Results of tests cannot achieve the same level of certainty. The result of a test may only be a negative proof: if the test fails, one knows that there is a bug in the program. The success does not prove that there is no bug. It says nothing on other executions.

In this paper, we propose a test framework for the languages used to describe Natural Language morphology using finite-state machines. Some ideas of the XUnit frameworks are applied. For instance, the notion of unit testing and the automation of the test activity. In the next section, the JUnit framework is briefly presented. Afterwards, some specificities of finite-state machines and their consequences on tests are discussed. A language for tests is then proposed and a prototype implementation described.

2   The Example of JUnit

JUnit is the most popular instance of the XUnit test framework proposed for software testing. Its precursor was the Smalltalk instance SUnit proposed by Kent Beck. JUnit was created in 1997 by Kent Beck and Erich Gamma [4]. This framework promotes automated tests of parts of a system. Concretely, a part of a Java program is a method. Each method is tested separately using a black-box approach where some parameters are given to the method and the actual result is compared to an expected result.

The test is written in Java, as a method. In previous versions of JUnit, test methods had to belong to test classes inheriting from a given class `TestCase`, but it is no more the case. Now, tests are identified using an assertion, a construction which appeared in the version 1.5 of the Java Language. The inheritance is no more used, so a test method may appear in any java class. The test method has no parameters and gives no result. It calls the method to be tested and then calls one or several *assert methods*. There are 8 such methods to test some properties of the computed result.

The 8 assert methods are the following: `assertEquals` to test the equality of two values (objects compared using the `equals` method or primitive values), `assertSame` and `assertNotSame` to test the identity and difference of two references, `assertNull` and `assertNotNull` to test if a reference is `null` (the empty pointer) or not, and finally, `assertTrue` and `assertFalse` to test the value of a boolean expression, and `fail` to enforce a failure of a test.

The test framework is completely embedded in the Java language. It is implemented through a library which automates the running of tests. Ultimately, a test is a Java boolean expression. There are constructions around this expression to print reports according to its value. If it is `true`, the test succeeds, if it is `false`, the test fails. Reporting is the main contribution of the assert methods with respect to the equivalent genuine boolean expression (for instance, `assertNull(e)` w.r.t. `e==null`). The test mechanism uses Java exceptions and especially the predefined `java.lang.AssertionError` which is thrown when a test fails. Running the tests consist in calling a program of the JUnit library and giving it the classes containing the tests as parameters.

A test is a call of the tested method which may involve some parameters. JUnit calls *fixtures* the objects which are build to be passed as parameters to the tested methods. They may be instances of classes from the tested system, identical to the objects used in this system, or instances of classes written to perform the test. Fixtures are declared as ordinary variables and they are initialized either in the test method or in a method called before the test, declared using the `@Before` assertion.

3   Finite-State Morphology

Finite-State Morphology is a technique which represents the morphology of a natural language using a rational relation defined using a combination of numerous small parts. The relation relates a concrete level with the words as they appear in actual texts to a more or less abstract level which explains the structure of the words. The two levels are called respectively the *surface form* and the *lexical form*. The small parts are defined using regular expressions possibly extended with the Cartesian Product, and *contextual rules*. Instances of contextual rules are the two-level rules by Koskenniemi, the rewrite rules by Kaplan and Kay and the generalized restriction rules by Yli-Jyrä and Koskenniemi. These rules express constraints which characterize the pairs in a rational relation that they define. They are compiled into finite-state transducers [5], [6].

The combination of small parts uses rational operations, Cartesian product and also some other operations defined on finite-state machines. There are two approaches: one which rely mainly on intersection (two-level morphology, [7]); another one which uses mainly composition (rewrite rules, [5]). For the first approach, small part describe simultaneous constraints; for the second one, the constraints are applied sequentially.

The complete morphology of a language is usually described by the combination of a few dozen constraint combined into a unique finite-state transducer, which may be quite big (up to a few million transitions and states).

The notion of *execution* of a finite-state machine may be expressed as a graph traversal trying to recognize or generate a string or a tuple. But a more general and declarative view is to define it as a new machine definition. For instance, suppose that the morphology of a natural language is described by a binary rational relation R and that one wants to analyze a surface form x. The analysis consist in composing the regular language {x} with R and then project the result on its second component. The composition and projection are standard finite-state operations. The result is the rational language containing the different analysis of the form.

So, unlike other kinds of software, there is no difference between static tests and runtime tests: they are both tests of finite-state machines. The execution involve some algorithms applied on finite-state machines (in our example, the composition and projection algorithms), but the progress of these algorithms is usually not informative for the developer. The algorithms run on the compiled forms which are not easily understood. Algorithms work locally in the graph, state by state, transition by transition. So a classical debugger following the execution of the algorithms is not useful. There are a small number of algorithms involved. Only their data structures with the relation. The interesting properties of a machine are not local properties, which may be observed at the state level, but global properties such as the existence of cycles and of final states.

Another great difference with a programming language is that a test is not naturally an object of the language. A test is a boolean function which succeeds or fails. It is natural to implement them using a method returning a boolean in java. There is no native implementation of booleans in rational relations. Tests are more easily described as a global observation of a machine than as relations. Furthermore, it is not obvious whether all the interesting properties are expressible as rational relations.

4   Tests of Finite-State Machines

In this section, we address the problem of adding new features to a morphological description system in order to write and run easily and automatically unit tests. We suppose that there exists a language to define rational relations, such as for instance Pc-kimmo, Xfst or Mmorph. Any subpart of the description which is compilable into a finite-state machine may be tested separately. For instance, a contextual rule and a regular expression are such a unit.

We propose a framework where 5 assertions are available to test machines: two of them are binary operators comparing two machines, the other ones are unary, asserting some property of one machine. The binary assertions test respectively the equivalence and the inclusion of two machines. The unary assertions test the cardinality of its operand, either numerically or qualitatively. The cardinality may be compared to an integer using equality, difference and order comparators. The qualitative operators separate cyclic (infinite cardinality) from acyclic machines (finite cardinality).

There are algorithms to implement all these tests. The equivalence and inclusion may be tested by first computing the difference between two machines and then testing that the result is empty. The difference is not always defined on rational relations. This point is discussed in section 5. The numerical cardinality tests may be performed either by enumerating the members or by using an n-best algorithm. An equality test consists in verifying that the machine is equivalent to the machine computed by applying the n-best operation on it, with the asserted cardinality as value for n. Inequality tests use inclusion instead of equivalence. There are algorithms to search for cycles in a machine. All the algorithms are tractable, although some of them have a high complexity.

The test framework involves also fixtures which are ordinary finite state machines written only to test a unit of the system. The language to write the fixtures is the same as the one used to write the system itself. When fixtures are involved, the assertion tests a property of a fixture and not directly of the tested unit.

Let us take an example. Suppose that a finite state transducer encodes the conjugation of all the verbs of a language, the abstract representation containing the verbal root and information about tense and relevant morphological features, the concrete representation being actual conjugated forms. A meaningful test consists in testing the machine for a given verb. This involves two fixtures: the first one is the abstract representation defining the verb's root. The second fixture consist in computing the image of the first fixture by the transducer, i.e. all the conjugated forms. Then an assertion may test the cardinality of this second fixture. A more precise test defines the expected image as a third fixture, and asserts the equivalence of the second and third fixtures.

In order to make the non-regression tests automatic, we propose to relate each test to one or several machines using a dependency relation. A test (resp. a machine) *immediately depends* on a machine m if m appears in its definition (for instance, the definition is an expression where m appears as an operand). The dependency relation is the transitive closure of the immediate dependency. A test t is a test for a non-fixture machine m if i) t depends on m and ii) there exists a path between t and m in the dependency graph such that all the machines in the path are fixtures. In the following of the paper, we will call a machine m a successor (resp. a predecessor) of another machine m' if (m', m) (resp. (m, m')) belongs to the dependency relation.

The dependency relation is important in the compilation process: a machine may be compiled only after all the machines it depends on. Whenever the definition of a machine changes (for instance to fix a bug), all the machines which depend on it must be re-computed. Similarly, all the tests which depend on this machine must be re-run.

5   Intersection, Difference and Tests

Tests of equivalence and inclusion are not always possible for finite-state transducers. The intersection and difference of rational relations are not necessarily rational The two operations are closely related.

An example of intersection which is not rational is the following. $(a : x)^*(b : \epsilon)^* \cap (a : \epsilon)^*(b : x)^* = (a, x)^n(b : \epsilon)^n$ which is a variant of the language $a^n b^n$, a typical example of non rational language. The intersection algorithm applied on such relations does not terminate, new states being computed continually.

Regular languages are closed under intersection, difference and complementation. This allows for the typical test of the image of a given string (or language) by a relation, since such an image is a regular language.

Some subclasses of relations are closed under intersection. It is the case of length-preserving relations, also called same-length relations. Each pair in such a relation is composed of two strings which have the same length. There is an equivalence between such a pair $(a_1 \ldots a_n, b_1 \ldots b_n)$ and the string of symbol pairs $(a_1 : b_1) \ldots (a_n : b_n)$. A length preserving relation may be expressed as a regular language where the alphabet is a finite set of symbol pairs. This subclass is the one used to express the semantics of a Two-Level Grammar [7]. Two-Level rules are expressed using symbol pairs and rational operators over these pairs. Length-preserving relation are closed under intersection and difference, so there is no limitation for testing equivalence and inclusion for Two-Level Grammars.

The problem is more tedious for contextual rewrite rules as used by Xfst, since such rules describe rational relations which are not length-preserving. Another subclass of relations is interesting and gives a way to perform some tests, namely the *bounded delay* relations. These relations are such that the same-length constraint applies on cycles only. They have been defined in [8], also studied by [9] and [10]. An interesting point is that the intersection is rational even if only one of the two intersected relations is bounded delay. The upper bound of this operand is used to break loops in the computations. The bounded delay property is fulfilled by all the finite relations. Therefore, the test of inclusion of a finite fixture and any rational relation, such as for instance the one defined by a rewrite rule, is feasible.

6   Interactive Bug Tracking

When a test fails, it is the sign that there is a bug either in the tested machine or in the test itself. It is sometimes possible to exhibit a counter-example of the asserted property. For instance, if the test predicts that a machine is included in another one, the computation consists in testing the emptiness of their difference. If not empty, it is possible to exhibit one or several strings belonging to this difference. A n-best algorithm is able to extract the n smallest strings to be displayed in the failure report.

If a machine is defined by an expression involving some predecessors, it is possible to search the bug in the predecessors. This may be done automatically in some cases. For instance, if a tuple expected to belong to a relation is missing and the relation is the result of an intersection, the tuple is also expected to belong to all the predecessors. The membership test may be perform to all the predecessors. Conversely, if an unexpected tuple appears in a relation which is the result of an union, it is possible to search for the predecessor which introduced this tuple.

In most cases, however, the debugging process needs some information from the user in order to be efficient. If a relation is the result of a composition, and a pair is missing in the relation, it is often necessary to know the expected intermediate form to determine which operand of the composition is faulty. The introduction of this intermediate form by the user results in two new tests on the two predecessors. The development interface should allow such an enrichment and give the choice between performing these two tests only once or adding them permanently to the description to be run every time a modification of the description is done, as non-regression tests.

When a cardinality test fails, if the cardinality is not too high, the better help is to enumerate the tuples in order to determine what is missing or what is in surplus. Here again, this may result in new tests which may be added to the test suite, or not.

7   Preliminary Experiments

The testing framework presented in this paper has been implemented in *Karamel*, a prototype of Interface Development Environment for morphological descriptions described in [11]. It implements a language to write, compile and test such descriptions. It uses a subclass of n-ary rational relations which is closed under intersection and difference [12], so there is no restriction on the equivalence and inclusion assertions.

The language offers three ways for defining relations: regular expressions extended with a typed Cartesian product which allows the definition of relations and not only languages; generalized restriction contextual rules [6]; and finally a calculus over finite-state machines with various operations (rational operations, projection, intersection, etc).

Fixtures are defined using the same language as the core of a description. They are clearly identified in the syntax by the keyword test. A project in the system consists in a declaration of the alphabet and the types of feature structures and Cartesian products, followed by definition of machines, fixtures and tests. The environment maintains the graph of dependencies and uses it to ensure the consistency of the machines. For instance, when the definition of a machine is changed, the machines which depend on it are marked as out-dated. They cannot be used for computations before recompilation.

Karamel is implemented by python scripts, executed within a python HTTP server which is used to offer simply a graphical interface through standard html/css forms. It offers a poor support for editing but operations are available through menus and buttons. The system uses the FSM toolkit by AT&T for implementing finite-state machines. Karamel n-ary relations are compiled into FSM finite-state automata. Some operations on relations are directly implemented by the same operation applied on the automata (e.g.: concatenation, closure, intersections). Some other operations are implemented by a python script (e.g.: the projection).

Our experience of grammar developer is that cardinality tests are very efficient: they are easy to write and give a significant information about the coverage of a machine. For instance, the number of forms in a verbal paradigm is usually known or easy to find out. The most difficult case is to track a failure where the tests derived on all the predecessors succeed. In this case, the problem is not clearly in one predecessor but in the interaction of several machines. We encountered such a problem with a system obtained by intersecting a dozen of predecessors. A string missing in the intersection was present in all the predecessors, the incompatibility being in other members of tuples. In such a situation, one would like to identify the minimal subset of machines for which the intersection fails to the membership test. This minimal subset is possibly not unique and this search implies the computation of many intersections. Some of them may be very costly and even intractable.

8   Conclusion

Existing system usually provide commands to inspect finite-state machines. For instance, Xfst provides nine commands which are boolean testing of machines, including equivalence, inclusion, emptiness. The FSM toolkit used to implement the Karamel system provides a command to test the equivalence of two machines and another one called fsminfo to display various information about the machine such as the existence of cycles. Both system also provide graphical display of small machines.

The difference between these facilities and the assert construction proposed in our language is that the expected result is given in the assert so that the assert is a boolean test which may be done automatically every time something changes in the definition of a machine. The dependency relation is used to know if a test applies on a machine and if a modification of a machine impacts another one. This relation allows to recompile only the successors of the modified machine. The user may not only ask for executing a given test, but also for executing all the tests of a given machine, the relevant test suite being automatically inferred.

The framework presented in this paper is interesting for all the finite-state descriptions which are obtained by the combination of several parts (the units considered) and are quite big, so that the graphical representation is not readable. This includes, but of course is not limited to, Finite-State Morphology.

References

1. Beesley, K.R., Karttunen, L.: Finite State Morphology. CSLI Publications (2003)
2. Allauzen, C., Riley, M., Schalkwyk, J., Skut, W., Mohri, M.: Openfst: A general and efficient weighted finite-state transducer library. In: Holub, J., Žďárek, J. (eds.) CIAA 2007. LNCS, vol. 4783, pp. 11–23. Springer, Heidelberg (2007)
3. Beck, K., Andres, C.: Extreme Programming Explained: Embrace Change, 2nd edn. Addison-Wesley Professional, Reading (2004)
4. Beck, K., Gamma, E.: Test-infected: programmers love writing tests. Java Report 3 (1998)
5. Kaplan, R.M., Kay, M.: Regular models of phonological rule systems. Computational Linguistics 20(3), 331–378 (1994)
6. Yli-Jyrä, A.M., Koskenniemi, K.: Compiling contextual restrictions on strings into finite-state automata. In: Proceedings of the Eindhoven FASTAR Days 2004, Eindhoven, The Netherlands, September 3-4 (2004)

7. Koskenniemi, K.: Two-level model for morphological analysis. In: IJCAI 1983, Karlsruhe, Germany, pp. 683–685 (1983)
8. Eilenberg, S.: Automata, Languages, and Machines. Academic Press, Inc., Orlando (1976)
9. Frougny, C., Sakarovitch, J.: Synchronized rational relations of finite and infinite words. Theoretical Computer Science 108, 45–82 (1993)
10. Kempe, A., Champarnaud, J.M., Eisner, J.: A note on join and auto-intersection of n-ary rational relations. In: Watson, B., Cleophas, L. (eds.) Proc. Eindhoven FASTAR Days, Eindhoven, Netherlands (2004)
11. Barthélemy, F.: The karamel system and semitic languages: Structured multi-tiered morphology. In: Proceedings of the EACL 2009 Workshop on Computational Approaches to Semitic Languages (2009)
12. Barthélemy, F.: Multi-grain relations. In: Holub, J., Žďárek, J. (eds.) CIAA 2007. LNCS, vol. 4783, pp. 243–252. Springer, Heidelberg (2007)

A Table Compression Method for Extended Aho-Corasick Automaton

Yanbing Liu[1,2], Yifu Yang[1,2], Ping Liu[1], and Jianlong Tan[1]

[1] Institute of Computing Technology, Chinese Academy of Sciences, Beijing, 100190
[2] Graduate School of Chinese Academy of Sciences, Beijing, 100190
{liuyanbing,yangyifu}@software.ict.ac.cn, {liuping,tjl}@ict.ac.cn

Abstract. The Aho-Corasick algorithm is a classic method for matching a set of strings. However, the huge memory usage of Aho-Corasick automaton prevents it from being applied to large-scale pattern sets. Here we present a simple but efficient table compression method to reduce the automaton's space. The basic idea of our method is based on equivalent rows elimination, which groups state rows into equivalent classes and eliminates the duplicates. Experiments demonstrate that the proposed method significantly reduces the memory usage and still runs at linear searching time comparable to that of extended Aho-Corasick algorithm. Our method provides good trade-off between memory usage and searching time.

1 Introduction

Multiple string matching is a classic problem of computer science, and plays a fundamental role in many fields. Aho-Corasick (abbr. as AC) algorithm[1] is the most famous automaton-based method for matching a set of strings. AC algorithm searches a text T in linear time $O(|T|)$, and therefore is widely used in many network security systems such as Snort and ClamAV which need a strict guarantee on worst case performance. As the signature databases grow larger and larger, however, network security systems are troubled with the huge memory space used by string matching automaton. Take Anti-Virus system ClamAV for example, the AC automaton built from 79560 ClamAV signatures uses more than 7.5 Gigabytes memory. Furthermore, the growing disparity of speed between CPU and memory, called "memory wall", remains a longstanding problem. Automaton-base string matching is a typical memory-bound application, and suffers from large memory usage and poor cache locality. So it's highly necessary to devise table compression methods to reduce AC automaton's space.

In this paper we propose an efficient table compression method for extended AC automaton[2]. Our method is based on the observation that extended AC automaton's transitions are not uniformly distributed but rather aggregated, that is, most of the transitions lead to states in top levels of the automaton. This provides us the chance to employ equivalent rows elimination, which groups state rows into equivalent classes and eliminates the duplicates. However, equivalent rows elimination technique is not directly applicable because of the interference between the forward transitions and the backward transitions in AC automaton.

S. Maneth (Ed.): CIAA 2009, LNCS 5642, pp. 84–93, 2009.

In our method we firstly split the automaton into two sub-tables, one holding the forward transitions and the other holding the backward transitions. And then we employ equivalent rows elimination on the sub-tables with further optimization techniques. Besides great reduction in memory space, our method also runs in linear searching time comparable to that of extended AC algorithm. Experiments are also carried out to justify the method's efficiency.

The rest of this paper is organized as follows. We first summarize the classic table compression methods in section 2. Next, in section 3 we present our table compression method for extended AC automaton. And finally, we compare our method with extended AC algorithm and report the experimental results in section 4. Section 5 is the concluding remark.

2 Related Work

Research on table compression has a long history and many ingenious compression methods have been designed to store sparse arrays, matrices, DFA state tables, tries, etc. Row displacement, which is mentioned in many articles including [3,4], overlaps rows with displacement to store sparse matrices. Tarjan et al. [4] analyzed this method theoretically and proposed double-displacement for improvement. Aho et al.[5] proposed Triple Array to compress sparse DFA state table. Aoe et al.[6] simplified Triple Array to Double Array for trie structure. Kiraz[7] also proposed compression method for finite-state transducers. Perfect hashing is another efficient method for storing tables. Fredman et al.[8] constructs perfect hash function like $f(x) = (kx \bmod p) \bmod q$ to represent sparse table. The method stores a sparse table with $6n$ memory space and $O(1)$ worst case access time. Galli et al.[9] combines perfect hashing and row displacement for table compression. The method firstly randomizes a table into a sparse matrix using hash function like $f(x) = (kx \bmod p) \bmod n^2$ and then employs row displacement method to compress the sparse matrix. It achieves $2n$ memory space and $O(1)$ worst case access time. Andersson et al.[10] proposed LC-trie to compress binary tries. Most of the methods work well on sparse tables, but they do not cater to the problem of compressing dense tables with high redundancy.

In addition to the general-purposed table compression techniques, some studies have also been conducted to optimize AC automaton's size. For example, Aoe et al. [11] invented Double Array trie structure to represent AC trie structure. Norton [12] proposed banded row method to optimize AC's space and speed, which gains 17% performance improvement. In a hardware implementation of string matching[13], bitmap compression and path compression techniques were adopted to compress AC trie. Nieminen et al. [14] studied different implementations of AC automaton using Unicode. Its experiments show that Triple Array and Double Array structure perform best. It also should be mentioned that the general automaton minimization technique[15] might be useful for reducing AC automaton's states. Most of these methods are designed for the basic AC trie structure, while compression methods for extended AC automaton still need to be studied.

As most of the above methods are designed either to compress sparse tables or to represent trie structures, they are not directly applicable to full state tables like extended AC automaton. Specially tailored compression method is devised to compress the extended AC automaton in this paper.

3   A Table Compression Method for Extended Aho-Corasick Automaton

In this section, we present our table compression method for extended AC automaton. Extended AC automaton[2] refers to the full AC automaton that has eliminated failure transitions. State switching in extended AC automaton takes exactly one memory access per text character, without tracing the failure transitions. Extended AC automaton is widely adopted for practical implementation.

We first outline our compression method from an overall perspective in subsection 3.1. The method consists of splitting extended AC automaton into two sub-tables and employing equivalent rows elimination technique to compress the sub-tables. Then we describe the detail of equivalent rows elimination in subsection 3.2. Finally, the detailed compression techniques for each sub-table are presented in subsection 3.3 and 3.4.

3.1   Overall Description of the Table Compression Method

Our table compression method employs equivalent rows elimination technique to reduce redundancy in extended AC automaton. To use the technique effectively, we split the automaton into two sub-tables, one table T_1 holding the forward transitions and the other table T_2 holding the backward transitions. This splitting eliminates the interference between forward transitions and backward transitions. Then further optimization techniques are devised to compress the sub-tables respectively.

The compression techniques for the sub-tables are slightly different:

 - For the first sub-table T_1, we firstly subtract a base value $base[s]$ from each row s and then apply equivalent rows elimination on the remaining table. R_1 is the reduced table after row elimination, and $EQ_1[s]$ points to the equivalent row in R_1 for row s. It also should be pointed out that the first sub-table is essentially a trie structure and the technique presented here is applicable to general trie and tree. The detail is described in section 3.3.
 - For the second sub-table T_2, we firstly extract the most frequent element from each column c as the default state $default[c]$, and then apply equivalent rows elimination on the remaining table. Accordingly, R_2 is the reduced table and $EQ_2[s]$ points to the equivalent row in R_2 for row s. We use a bitmap to indicate whether the next state is a default state or in the remaining table R_2. The detail is described in section 3.4.

The compressing and lookup procedure of our method is described in algorithm 1.

Algorithm 1. Table compression and lookup for extended AC automaton

---

```
1: procedure COMPRESS(T, N)
2:     rearrange extended AC automaton's state label in breadth first traversing order
3:     for i ← 0, N − 1 do
4:         for each c ∈ Σ do
5:             if the transition from i to T[i, c] is forward then
6:                 T₁[i, c] ← T[i, c]
7:                 T₂[i, c] ← −1
8:             else
9:                 T₁[i, c] ← −1
10:                T₂[i, c] ← T[i, c]
11:            end if
12:        end for
13:    end for
14:    (base, EQ₁, R₁) ←COMPRESS1(T₁, N)
15:    (default, bitmap, EQ₂, R₂) ←COMPRESS2(T₂, N)
16: end procedure

1: procedure NEXTSTATE(s, c)
2:     next ← base[s] + R₁[EQ₁[s], c]
3:     if next < 0 then
4:         if bitmap[s, c] = 1 then
5:             next ← default[c]
6:         else
7:             next ← R₂[EQ₂[s], c]
8:         end if
9:     end if
10:    return next
11: end procedure
```

3.2 Equivalent Rows Elimination

The idea of equivalent rows elimination is very simple: if multiple rows are equivalent, we can just store one copy and replace other rows by pointers.

In the first sub-table, rows that are exactly the same are considered equivalent. It's formally stated in definition 1:

Definition 1. *Row r and row s in table T_1 is equivalent iff $T_1[r, c] = T_1[s, c]$ for any $c \in \Sigma$.*

In the second sub-table, the definition of row equivalence is slightly different. Whenever we take a lookup operation in the second sub-table, we can definitely find the next state. So two rows have the same nonempty cells are considered equivalent. Here is the formal definition of row equivalence in the second sub-table:

Definition 2. *Row r and row s in table T_2 is equivalent iff $T_2[r, c] = -1$ or $T_2[s, c] = -1$ or $T_2[r, c] = T_2[s, c]$ for any $c \in \Sigma$.*

Algorithm for equivalent rows elimination is also straightforward. We use table R_i ($i = 1, 2$) to hold all distinct rows and process the rows in table T_i one by one. If the current row $T_i[j]$ is found equivalent to a row in R_i, then $EQ_i[j]$ points to that equivalent row, otherwise row $T_i[j]$ is added into R_i. The time complexity of this naive method is $O(N|\Sigma|\log N)$. Algorithmic description is omitted due to limited pages.

3.3   Compress the First Sub-table

The key idea to compress the first sub-table is rearranging AC automaton's state label in breadth first traversing order, which is stated in algorithm 1 line 2, then extracting the label of each state's first child as the base value, and finally applying equivalent rows elimination on the offset table.

Since the first sub-table is essentially a trie structure, for any state s, its children are labeled in consecutive numbers. Let f denotes the first child's label, then the last child's label will be less than $f+256$. Therefore, we extract $base[s] = f$ as the base value and only store the offsets in table. Note that the offsets are less than 256, so a single byte is enough for each offset.

Now we analyze the efficiency of equivalent rows elimination on the offset table. For trie nodes with out degree 1, there are at most $|\Sigma|$ distinct equivalent rows. And according to Theorem 1, the number of trie nodes with out degree greater than 1 is less than $|P|$ (P is the pattern set). In all, number of distinct equivalent rows is less than $|P| + |\Sigma|$. Compared to the row number $m|P|$ (m is the average pattern length) in the offset table, our method achieves a high compression ratio bounded by $\frac{1}{m}$.

Theorem 1. *Let $Trie(P)$ be the trie built from pattern set P, and n_i be the number of trie nodes with out degree i, then $\sum_{i\geq 2} n_i < |P|$.*

Proof. The number of nodes in $Trie(P)$ is $n = n_0+n_1+\cdots+n_k$. The number of edges in $Trie(P)$ is $e = n_1+2n_2+\cdots+kn_k$. According to the inherent property $n = e+1$, we have $n_0 + n_1 + \cdots + n_k = n_1 + 2n_2 + \cdots + kn_k + 1$, which implies $\sum_{i\geq 2} n_i < n_0$. Because the terminal nodes number n_0 is bounded by $|P|$, it follows $\sum_{i\geq 2} n_i < n_0 \leq |P|$. ∎

The procedure for compressing the first sub-table is described in algorithm 2.

3.4   Compress the Second Sub-table

Space reduction is very limited when directly applying equivalent rows elimination on the second sub-table. Fortunately, we observed that there is always a frequent element in each column of the second sub-table, so we extract the most frequent element from each column as the default state. Again equivalent rows elimination is applied on the remaining table.

The idea of extracting a default state from each column can be explained informally. According to the construction of AC automaton, most states have

---

Algorithm 2. Compress the first table T_1

1: **procedure** COMPRESS1(T_1, N)
2:     **for** $i \leftarrow 0$, $N - 1$ **do**
3:         $base[i] \leftarrow -1$
4:         **for** each $c \in \Sigma$ **do**
5:             **if** $T_1[i, c] \geq 0$ **then**
6:                 **if** $base[i] = -1$ **then**
7:                     $base[i] \leftarrow T_1[i, c]$
8:                 **end if**
9:                 $T_1[i, c] \leftarrow T_1[i, c] - base[i]$
10:             **end if**
11:         **end for**
12:     **end for**
13:     apply equivalent rows elimination on T_1: R_1 is the reduced table and $EQ_1[s]$ points to equivalent row in R_1 for each row s.
14:     **return** ($base$, EQ_1, R_1)
15: **end procedure**

Algorithm 3. Compress the second table T_2

1: **procedure** COMPRESS2(T_2, N)
2:     **for** each $c \in \Sigma$ **do**
3:         $default[c] \leftarrow$ most frequent element in the c-th column $\{T_2[i, c] \mid 0 \leq i < N\}$
4:         **for** $i \leftarrow 0$, $N - 1$ **do**
5:             **if** $T_2[i, c] = default[c]$ **then**
6:                 $T_2[i, c] \leftarrow -1$
7:                 $bitmap[s, c] \leftarrow 1$
8:             **else**
9:                 $bitmap[s, c] \leftarrow 0$
10:             **end if**
11:         **end for**
12:     **end for**
13:     apply equivalent rows elimination on T_2: R_2 is the reduced table and $EQ_2[s]$ points to equivalent row in R_2 for each row s.
14:     **return** ($default$, $bitmap$, EQ_2, R_2)
15: **end procedure**

---

failure links pointing to the initial state, so their transitions on a character c lead to a same state. This state is extracted as the default state.

The step of extracting default states is important. A great portion of non-empty elements in each column is removed by employing this technique, making it possible to apply equivalent rows elimination for further space reduction. However, the percent of extracted elements decreases as the number of automaton states grows larger.

The procedure for compressing the second sub-table is described in algorithm 3.

4   Experimental Results

In this subsection, we compare our table compression method (extendedAC-optimize) with the basic AC algorithm (AC), the extended AC algorithm (extendedAC) and the extended AC algorithm with default states (extendedAC-default) in terms of memory usage and searching time.

We did our experiments both on random and real pattern sets, including:

- Random strings and text: A set of 30000 random strings with each character uniformly generated from 256-alphabet. All the strings are of the same length 8. The strings are searched against a 10MB random text generated in the same way.
- Chinese words: A set of 75717 commonly used Chinese words. The words are searched against a 25.3MB text from "People's Daily" (www.people.com.cn).
- English words: A set of 3599 English words randomly chosen from the Bible. The words are searched against the Bible.
- Snort signatures: A set of 5029 signatures extracted from the open source NIDS system Snort (www.snort.org). The signatures are searched against the MIT intrusion detection dataset mit_1999_training_week1_friday_inside.dat (www.ll.mit.edu/IST/ideval).
- ClamAV signatures: A set of 8000 signatures extracted from the open source Anti-Virus system ClamAV (www.clamav.org). The signatures are searched against the MIT intrusion detection dataset as above.
- DNA sequences: A set of 5000 DNA sequences. The DNA sequences are searched against a 21.6MB DNA database. (www.bioinfo.org.cn)

We use compression ratio to evaluate the efficiency of equivalent rows elimination on the sub-tables. *Compression ratio* is defined as the ratio of number of distinct rows after compression to number of rows in original table. Results in Table 1 and Table 2 show that equivalent rows elimination works fine on both sub-tables. Take random pattern set for example, the compression ratio is about 1.9% for the first sub-table and 5.1% for the second sub-table. We can see from table 2 that extracting default states from each column contributes most to the

Table 1. Compression ratio of 1st sub-table on different pattern sets. The 3rd column is number of rows eliminated and the 4th column is the number of distinct rows after applying equivalent rows elimination on the sub-table. The last column presents the percent of distinct state rows compared to the number of automaton states.

Test	# of States	Eliminated Rows	Distinct Rows	Compression Ratio
Random	204270	200358	3912	1.9%
Chinese	173801	161462	12339	7.1%
English	10448	9816	633	6.05%
Snort	59081	57631	1450	2.45%
ClamAV	307881	305582	2299	0.75%
DNA	122566	122550	16	0.01%

Table 2. Compression ratio of 2nd sub-table on different pattern sets. The 3rd column presents the percent of removed elements by extracting a default state from each column of the state table. The last column is the percent of distinct state rows compared to the number of automaton states.

Test	# of States	Percent of Default (%)	Eliminated Rows	Distinct Rows	Compression Ratio (%)
Random	204270	62.86%	193916	10354	5.1%
Chinese	173801	72.53%	155940	17861	10.2%
English	10448	95.97%	9569	879	8.4%
Snort	59081	91.74%	57117	1964	3.3%
ClamAV	307881	89.57%	302922	4959	1.6%
DNA	122566	0.29%	107605	14961	12.2%

Table 3. Memory usage (MB) comparison between the algorithms on different pattern sets

Test	AC	extendedAC	extendedAC-default	extendedAC-optimize
Random	1.753	199.482	94.157	13.524
Chinese	1.492	169.728	59.614	22.821
English	0.090	10.203	0.594	1.153
Snort	0.507	57.696	6.407	2.993
ClamAV	2.643	300.655	41.564	8.999
DNA	1.052	1.870	3.266	1.631

Table 4. Searching time (seconds) comparison between the algorithms on different pattern sets

Test	AC	extendedAC	extendedAC-default	extendedAC-optimize
Random	1.437	0.625	3.016	0.266
Chinese	3.829	1.797	4.734	1.359
English	1.859	1.564	1.563	1.544
Snort	8.156	0.999	1.969	1.610
ClamAV	9.593	0.984	1.953	1.124
DNA	2.578	0.985	1.968	1.641

space reduction. On the English, Snort and ClamAV datasets, the percentage of elements extracted as default states is up to 90%. However, the percentage is extremely low on the DNA dataset, because on small alphabet the distribution of state transitions is rather random.

The comparison of total memory usage and searching time is presented in Table 3. The memory used by our method is greatly less than that used by the extended AC, but it is still larger than the memory usage of the basic AC algorithm. On small alphabet, the overheads of our method offset the profit brought by equivalent rows elimination. With regard to searching time, our method performs better than extended AC on random dataset, Chinese dataset and English dataset, but slower on other datasets. Though the memory usage of the basic AC algorithm is low, its searching phase is rather time-consuming. Therefore, our method provides better trade-off between memory usage and searching time than the extended AC algorithm and the basic AC algorithm.

5   Conclusion

We proposed an efficient table compression method for extended AC automaton. Our method is based on equivalent rows elimination which groups state rows into equivalent classes and then eliminates the duplicates. To employ the technique efficiently, we split the extended AC automaton into two sub-tables. Further more, special optimization techniques are devised to compress the sub-tables using equivalent rows elimination. Besides great reduction in memory space, our method also runs in linear searching time comparable to that of extended AC algorithm. Experiments on both random and real pattern sets justified the method's efficiency.

Acknowledgment

This work is supported by the National Basic Research Program of China (973) under grant. No. 2007CB311100. We would like to thank the anonymous referees for their insightful comments.

References

1. Aho, A.V., Corasick, M.J.: Efficient String Matching: An Aid to Bibliographic Search. Communication of the ACM 18(6), 333–340 (1975)
2. Navarro, G., Raffinot, M.: Flexible Pattern Matching in Strings – Practical on-line search algorithms for texts and biological sequences, p. 54. Cambridge University Press, Cambridge (2002)
3. Dencker, P., Dorre, K., Heuft, J.: Optimization of Parser Tables for Portable Compilers. ACM Transactions on Programming Languages and Systems 6(4), 546–572 (1984)
4. Tarjan, R.E., Yao, A.C.: Storing a Sparse Table. Communications of the ACM 22(11), 606–611 (1979)
5. Aho, A.V., Sethi, R., Ullman, J.D.: Compilers: Principles, Techniques, and Tools, p. 145. Addison-Wesley Publishing Co., Reading (1986)
6. Aoe, J., Morimoto, K., Sato, T.: An Efficient Implementation of Trie Structures. Software - Practice and Experience 22(9), 695–721 (1992)
7. Kiraz, G.A.: Compressed Storage of Sparse Finite-State Transducers. In: 4th International Workshop on Automata Implementation, pp. 109–121 (1999)
8. Fredman, M.L., Komlos, J., Szemeredi, E.: Storing a Sparse Table with $O(1)$ Worst Case Access Time. Journal of the ACM 31(3), 538–544 (1984)
9. Galli, N., Seybold, B., Simon, K.: Tetris-hashing or Optimal Table Compression. Discrete Applied Mathematics 110(1), 41–58 (2001)

10. Andersson, A., Nilsson, S.: Improved Behavior of Tries by Adaptive Branching. Information Processing Letters 46(6), 295–300 (1993)
11. Aoe, J.: An Efficient Implementation of Static String Pattern Matching Machines. IEEE Transactions on Software Engineering 15(8), 1010–1016 (1989)
12. Norton, M.: Optimizing Pattern Matching for Intrusion Detection (2004), http://www.idsresearch.org
13. Tuck, N., Sherwood, T., Calder, B., Varghese, G.: Deterministic Memory-Efficient String Matching Algorithms for Intrusion Detection. In: IEEE INFOCOM (2004)
14. Nieminen, J., Kilpel, P.: Efficient Implementation of Aho-Corasick Pattern Matching Automata Using Unicode. Software - Practice and Experience 37(6), 669–690 (2007)
15. Hopcroft, J.E.: An $n \log n$ Algorithm for Minimizing States in a Finite Automaton. Technical Report: CS-TR-71-190, Stanford University, Stanford, CA, USA (1971)

Compact Representation for Answer Sets of n-ary Regular Queries

Kazuhiro Inaba and Haruo Hosoya

The University of Tokyo
{kinaba,hahosoya}@is.s.u-tokyo.ac.jp

Abstract. An n-ary query over trees takes an input tree t and returns a set of n-tuples of the nodes of t. In this paper, a compact data structure is introduced for representing the answer sets of n-ary queries defined by tree automata. Despite that the number of the elements of the answer set can be as large as $|t|^n$, our representation allows to store the set using only $O(3^n|t|)$ space. Several basic operations on the sets are shown to be efficiently executable on the representation.

1 Introduction

Finite state automaton is a well-known model for representing properties for trees and strings. The class of queries definable by finite state automata is called *regular* and is widely used both in theory and in practice. A number of query formalisms are shown to be equivalent or subsumed by regular queries. Examples of such formalisms include, regular expression pattern [1], monadic second-order logic [2], μ-calculus [3], Core XPath [4], monadic Datalog [5], boolean attribute grammar [6], etc.

In this paper, we are interested in the space complexity of the n-ary queries defined by tree automata. An n-ary query over trees takes an input tree t and returns a set of n-tuples of the nodes of t. The number of elements in the answer set of an n-ary query may be as large as $|t|^n$ where $|t|$ is the number of the nodes of t. And, usually, storing a set of $|t|^n$ elements requires at least $c|t|^n$ space where c is the space required to store a single element (in this case, one n-tuple of nodes). The $O(|t|^n)$ space consumption is unavoidable if the elements are chosen in a perfectly random manner; it is a well-known consequence from the information theory. Note, however, we are interested in more practical, less random queries. Queries defined by tree automata have much more structure than random ones. By exploiting the structural characteristics of regular queries, we can represent the answer sets in some *compressed* form.

Let us explain the idea by an example. Consider the regular query "select all pair of nodes (x, y) such that x is in the left subtree of the root node and y is in the right subtree of the root node" with the input tree t as in the figure. Then the answer set consists of nine elements: $\{(v_1, v_4), (v_2, v_4), (v_3, v_4), (v_1, v_5),$ $(v_2, v_5), (v_3, v_5), (v_1, v_6), (v_2, v_6), (v_3, v_6)\}$. Obviously, if an input tree has n nodes both in the left and the right subtrees, the size of the answer set will be n^2, which is quadratic in the number $2n + 1$ of the nodes. Our approach for avoiding the quadratic blow-up is to represent the answer set by a symbolic *expression*, instead of computing the concrete list of elements. For this example, we represent the answer

S. Maneth (Ed.): CIAA 2009, LNCS 5642, pp. 94–104, 2009.

set by the expression $\{v_1, v_2, v_3\} \times \{v_4, v_5, v_6\}$ where $\times$ denotes the product of two sets. Counting the number of variables v_i and the operator, the length of the expression is 7 instead of 9. Analogously, for the general case with n nodes in both the left and the right subtrees, the answer set can be represented by the expression of length $2n + 1$, which consumes only linear space with respect to the size of the input tree.

The contribution of our work is in establishing the expression-based compact representation as illustrated above. In fact, only two operators—$\uplus$ (*disjoint union*) and $*$ (a slight variant of *product*)—are necessary for achieving the linear-size representation of the answer sets of regular queries. We show that for any fixed n-ary regular query and an input tree t, the answer set can always be represented by an expression on $\uplus$ and $*$ with every leaf expression being a singleton set of an input node. By sharing common sub-expressions, the expression can be represented by a dag of size $O(3^n|t|)$. That is, regardless of the arity n of the query, the data complexity with respect to the size $|t|$ of the input is always linear! The factor 3^n is sufficiently low for queries with small n such as binary or ternary queries, which are the most cases occur in practice (after all, it is quite rare to run, say, a 100-ary query).

Furthermore, the dag representation is extended to a data structure named *SRED (Set Representation by Expression Dags)*, which enjoys good time complexity as well as the size-efficiency. The SRED representation of the answer set can always be computed from the input tree t in time $O(3^n|t|)$, regardless how large the actual answer set is. Also, evaluation (or we could say, *decompression*) of a SRED to yield the concrete list of answer tuples can be done in time $O(3^n a)$, where a is the number of the answers. By combining these two steps, we obtain an algorithm for regular queries in the optimal data complexity $O(|t| + a)$. More than that, on SRED, we can carry out the following two important operations *without decompressing* it: (1) SELECTION: for an answer set s, the SRED representation of the set $s_{[i:u]} = \{(v_1, \ldots, v_{i-1}, v_{i+1}, \ldots, v_n) \mid (v_1, \ldots, v_{i-1}, u, v_{i+1}, \ldots, v_n) \in s\}$ can be computed in time $O(3^n h)$ where h is the height of the input tree for binary trees and is the height times $\log|t|$ for unranked trees, and (2) PROJECTION: the set $s_{@i} = \{v_i \mid (v_1, \ldots, v_n) \in s\}$ can be computed in time $O(6^n h|s_{@i}|)$. The key idea of SRED is to remember for every sub-expression the least common ancestor of the nodes contained in the set represented by the sub-expression. The information allows to locate the leaf expressions containing each input node in time proportional only to the height of the expression-dag.

Related Work. SRED has much similarity to the Complete Answer Aggregate (CAA) introduced by Meuss, Schulz, and Bry [7] as a compact representation of answer sets of queries. The size of a CAA is $O(nh|t|)$ which is competitive to our $O(3^n|t|)$. CAA is also suitable for applying several operations such as membership testing. The main advantage of our work is that it supports arbitrary regular queries, which is strictly more expressive than the query language used in [7]. Though an attempt to represent the answer sets of regular queries with CAA is given by Filiot and Tison [8] through a decomposition of queries, the space complexity is $O(n|t|^{d_\phi})$ for some constant d_ϕ depending on the query, which grows to n in the worst case. Besides, precise complexity of operations like selection or projection for CAA was not estimated.

An algorithm (FFG algorithm) for answering regular n-ary queries in the optimal time complexity $O(|t| + a)$ is shown by Flum, Frick, and Grohe [9]. Since no compact data structure was used in their work, the FFG algorithm requires $O(a)$ space to be carried out. In fact, our algorithm can be regarded as a space-efficient variant of the FFG algorithm. The expression dag generated in our algorithm precisely corresponds to the set operations executed in the FFG algorithm. On the other hand, the class of queries that the FFG algorithm can be applied is more general than our algorithm. The FFG algorithm can also be used for querying n-tuples of *sets of* nodes of *graphs* that have a tree decomposition, while our algorithm only supports queries for n-tuples of nodes of trees. It is future work whether our compact representation of the answer sets can be extended to more general class of queries.

2 Preliminaries

In this paper, we mainly consider *binary trees*, in which every node has either zero or two children. Generalization to the trees with other arity is briefly mentioned in the end of Section 4. Let Σ be a finite alphabet that is a disjoint union of two alphabets $\Sigma^{(0)}$ and $\Sigma^{(2)}$. A *binary tree* (or simply, a *tree*) over Σ is a tuple $t = (V_t, label_t, lt_t, rt_t, root_t)$ where V_t is the disjoint union $V_t^{(0)} \uplus V_t^{(2)}$ of finite sets of *nodes*, $label_t : V_t^{(0)} \to \Sigma^{(0)} \uplus V_t^{(2)} \to \Sigma^{(2)}$ is the *label* function, $lt_t, rt_t : V_t^{(2)} \to V_t$ is the *left-* and *right-child* function respectively, and $root_t \in V_t$ is the *root* node. We require a tree to satisfy the following conditions: (1) rooted: there is no node $v \in V_t$ such that $lt_t(v) = root_t$ or $rt_t(v) = root_t$, (2) acyclic: there is no node $v \in V_t$ that is reachable from itself by finite applications of lt_t and rt_t, and (3) tree-formed: for any non-root node $v \in V_t \setminus \{root_t\}$, there exists unique node u called the *parent* of v such that $lt_t(u) = v \vee rt_t(u) = v$. A structure only satisfying (1) and (2) is called a *dag*. For $v_1, v_2 \in V_t$, the binary order relation $v_1 \leq_t v_2$ is defined to hold if and only if v_2 is reachable from v_1 by zero or finitely many applications of lt_t and rt_t. We usually omit the subscript t if clear from the context. By $|t|$ we denote the number $|V_t|$ of the nodes. We use the notation $a\langle v_1, v_2 \rangle$ to denote a node v such that $label_t(v) = a$, $lt_t(v) = v_1$, and $rt_t(v) = v_2$.

For a tree t, we assume that each node $v \in V_t$ can be stored on memory in constant space independent from $|t|$. In practice, this implies the assumption that the tree t fits in the address space of the computer and each node can be represented by a single pointer. We also assume that the operations $label$, lt, rt, and $\leq$ can be executed in constant time. In particular, we can test the relation $\leq$ in constant time by, e.g., the preorder/postorder numbering [10]. Again by the assumption that $|t|$ fits in the address space, preorder and postorder numbers can be stored in constant space.

A *tree language* over Σ is a set of trees over Σ. By T_Σ, we denote the set of all trees over Σ. An important class of tree languages are those defined in terms of tree automata. A *bottom-up deterministic tree automaton* over Σ is a tuple $\mathcal{A} = (Q_\mathcal{A}, \delta_\mathcal{A}, F_\mathcal{A})$ where $Q_\mathcal{A}$ is the set of states, $\delta_\mathcal{A} : (\Sigma^{(0)} \cup \Sigma^{(2)} \times Q_\mathcal{A} \times Q_\mathcal{A}) \to Q_\mathcal{A}$ is the transition function, and $F_\mathcal{A} \subseteq Q_\mathcal{A}$ is the set of accepting states. The subscript $\mathcal{A}$ is omitted if clear from the context. A *run* of a tree automaton $\mathcal{A}$ on the input tree t is the unique function $\rho : V_t \to Q_\mathcal{A}$ such that $\rho(v) = \delta_\mathcal{A}(label_t(v))$ if $label_t(v) \in \Sigma^{(0)}$ and $\rho(v) = \delta_\mathcal{A}(label_t(v), \rho(lt_t(v)), \rho(rt_t(v)))$ if $label_t(v) \in \Sigma^{(2)}$. The automaton *accepts* t if and only if $\rho(root_t) \in F_\mathcal{A}$. By $\mathcal{L}(\mathcal{A})$, we denote the set of trees accepted by $\mathcal{A}$. A tree language is said to be *regular* if it is equal to $\mathcal{L}(\mathcal{A})$ for some tree automaton $\mathcal{A}$.

3 N-ary Regular Tree Queries

As a basis of our algorithm for computing the compact representation of answer sets, we first explain a basic bottom-up algorithm for regular queries with $O(|t|^{n+1})$ time complexity, which has already been known in the literature. Our new algorithm is obtained by changing the data structure used in the algorithm, as explained later in Section 4.

An n-ary *query* for trees over Σ is a function ψ that maps each tree $t \in T_\Sigma$ to a set of n-tuples of its nodes. Let $\mathbb{B} = \{0, 1\}$, $\Sigma_n^{(0)} = \Sigma^{(0)} \times \mathbb{B}^n$, $\Sigma_n^{(2)} = \Sigma^{(2)} \times \mathbb{B}^n$, and $\Sigma_n = \Sigma_n^{(0)} \cup \Sigma_n^{(2)}$. For a tree language $L \subseteq \Sigma_n$, an n-ary *query defined by* L is the function $\psi_L(t) = \{(v_1, \ldots, v_n) \mid mark(t, v_1, \ldots, v_n) \in L\}$ where $mark(t, v_1, \ldots, v_n)$ is a tree $m = (V_t, label_m, lt_t, rt_t, root_t)$ with $label_m(v) = (label_t(v), b_1 \cdots b_n)$ where $b_i = 1$ if $v = v_i$ and 0 otherwise. Intuitively, a query defined by a language L selects a tuple $(v_1, \ldots, v_n)$ if and only if L contains a tree obtained by marking each selected node v_i with 1. A query defined by a regular language L is called a *regular query*. In the rest of the paper, we assume the regular language L to be given as a tree automaton $\mathcal{A}$ such that $L = \mathcal{L}(\mathcal{A})$. Nevertheless, our algorithm can be applied, without changing the data complexity, to many other query formalisms as long as they define regular languages by first compiling them into tree automata and then running the algorithm.

The most naive algorithm for a regular n-ary query is, to try all possible markings. Given an automaton $\mathcal{A}$ over Σ_n and a tree t, for all $(v_1, \ldots, v_n) \in V_t^n$ we generate the marked tree $mark(t, v_1, \ldots, v_n)$ and test whether it is accepted by $\mathcal{A}$. If it is, $(v_1, \ldots, v_n)$ is an answer and hence we output it. This algorithm takes $O(|t|^{n+1})$ time, because computing each run of $\mathcal{A}$ takes $O(|t|)$ time and we try $|t|^n$ runs in total.

Another approach is to try all marking parallelly by a single bottom-up run. The following recursive procedure QUERY-RUN$_\mathcal{A}$ takes a node v of t and computes a table containing the result of the parallel marking run.

```
QUERY-RUN_A (v)
 1:   r ← new 2-dimensional array of size |Q_A| × 2^n with each element initialized to ∅
 2:   if label(v) ∈ Σ^(0) then
 3:       for each ((label(v), b_0) ↦ q_0) ∈ δ_A do
 4:           r[q_0, b_0] ← singleton(v, b_0)
 5:   else if label(v) ∈ Σ^(2) then
 6:       r_1 ← QUERY-RUN_A (lt(v));  r_2 ← QUERY-RUN_A (rt(v))
 7:       for each ((label(v), b_0), q_1, q_2 ↦ q_0) ∈ δ_A do
 8:           for each disjoint b_0, b_1, b_2 in 00 . . . 00 to 11 . . . 11 do
 9:               r[q_0, b_0|b_1|b_2] ← r[q_0, b_0|b_1|b_2] ⊎ singleton(v, b_0) * r_1[q_1, b_1] * r_2[q_2, b_2]
10:   return r
```

By $singleton(v, \beta_1 \cdots \beta_n)$ we denote the singleton set $\{(u_1, \ldots, u_n)\}$ where $u_i = v$ if $\beta_i = 1$ and $u_i = \bot$ if $\beta_i = 0$. Here, $\bot$ is a special symbol not contained in V_t. In line 7, **for each disjoint** iterates over pairs of form $(b_1 = \beta_{11} \cdots \beta_{1n}, b_2 = \beta_{21} \cdots \beta_{2n}) \in (\mathcal{B}^n)^2$ such that for all $1 \leq i \leq n$, at most one of $\{\beta_{0i}, \beta_{1i}, \beta_{2i}\}$ is 1, with $\beta_{01} \cdots \beta_{0n} = b_0$. The operator $|$ is for bitwise-or and $\uplus$ is disjoint union of sets (the operands are indeed disjoint, as explained later). The operator $*$ is a kind of "product" operation that combines two sets of tuples, defined as follows: $S * T = \{(u_1, \cdots, u_n) \mid (s_1, \cdots, s_n) \in S, (t_1, \ldots, t_n) \in T, \forall i : (u_i = s_i \wedge \bot = t_i) \vee (\bot = s_i \wedge u_i = t_i)\}$. For example, $\{(v_1, \bot, \bot), (v_2, \bot, \bot)\} * \{(\bot, \bot, v_3), (\bot, \bot, v_4)\}$ is equal to $\{(v_1, \bot, v_3), (v_1, \bot, v_4),$

$(v_2, \bot, v_3), (v_2, \bot, v_4)\}$. Let us remark that we never take $*$-product of sets that have tuples with non-$\bot$ nodes on the same position, as will be shown in Lemma 1.

Let us explain how the algorithm works. Let $r = $ QUERY-RUN$_{\mathcal{A}}(v)$ for a node $v \in V_t$. For each $q \in Q_{\mathcal{A}}$ and $b = \beta_1 \cdots \beta_n \in \mathbb{B}^n$, $r[q, b]$ is a set of n-tuples over the set $V_t \cup \{\bot\}$. A tuple in $(V_t \cup \{\bot\})^n$ is called a *partial answer* to the query. For example, $(v_1, \bot)$ is a partial answer that selects the node v_1 as the first coordinate and leaves the second coordinate to be selected later. Intuitively, $r[q, b]$ is the set of partial answers α such that, if a tree is marked according to α, then at the node v, the run of the automaton $\mathcal{A}$ reaches the state q. For example, if $(v_1, \bot) \in r[q, b]$, it means that "if the node v_1 is marked as the first component of the answer and no node in the subtree under v is marked as the second component, $\mathcal{A}$ reaches the state q at node v". As an example, let us assume v to be a leaf node labeled $\sigma \in \Sigma^{(0)}$ and $\mathcal{A}$ to define a binary query. Suppose $\delta_{\mathcal{A}}$ has the following four rules: $\delta_{\mathcal{A}}((\sigma, 00)) = q_1$, $\delta_{\mathcal{A}}((\sigma, 01)) = q_2$, $\delta_{\mathcal{A}}((\sigma, 10)) = q_1$, and $\delta_{\mathcal{A}}((\sigma, 11)) = q_2$. Then, the table $r = $ QUERY-RUN$_{\mathcal{A}}(v)$ is:

$$r[q_1, 00] = \{(\bot, \bot)\} \quad r[q_1, 01] = \emptyset \quad\quad r[q_1, 10] = \{(v, \bot)\} \quad r[q_1, 11] = \emptyset$$
$$r[q_2, 00] = \emptyset \quad\quad\quad r[q_2, 01] = \{(\bot, v)\} \quad r[q_2, 10] = \emptyset \quad\quad\quad r[q_2, 11] = \{(v, v)\}.$$

The set $r[q_1, 00]$ contains $(\bot, \bot)$ because if we do not select any node below v, the automaton reaches the state q_1. On the other hand, the set $r[q_2, 00]$ is empty, because we cannot reach the state q_2 at node v if we do not select any node. Similarly, $r[q_1, 01]$ is empty, because we cannot reach the state q_1 if we select the second coordinate of the answer. On the other hand, we have $r[q_2, 01] = \{(\bot, v)\}$, because if we choose v as the second coordinate, the automaton reaches the state q_2.

The index b of r called *flag* denotes the already selected coordinates. Formally, the following lemma can be shown by induction on the structure of the tree rooted at v.

Lemma 1. *Let* $r = $ QUERY-RUN$_{\mathcal{A}}(v)$ *for some* v *and* $(u_1, \ldots, u_n) \in r[q, \beta_1 \cdots \beta_n]$. *For all* $1 \leq i \leq n$, *we have* $(u_i \in V_t$ *and* $v \leq_t u_i)$ *if* $\beta_i = 1$, *and* $u_i = \bot$ *if* $\beta_i = 0$.

The lemma ensures the two disjointness in the procedure QUERY-RUN$_{\mathcal{A}}$. First, the $*$-product is always taken between the sets with disjoint selected-coordinates. That is, we need to compute $S * T$ only for the sets S, T such that $(\ldots, v_i, \ldots) \in S$ and $(\ldots, u_i, \ldots) \in T$ implies either v_i or u_i is $\bot$. For such a case, we have $|S * T| = |S| \cdot |T|$. Second, $\uplus$ is always taken between disjoint sets, because the operands of $\uplus$ are constructed by $*$-product over different flags.

The answer set of the query can be calculated from the result of QUERY-RUN$_{\mathcal{A}}$ applied to the root node, namely, $r = $ QUERY-RUN$_{\mathcal{A}}(root_t)$. For each $q \in F_{\mathcal{A}}$, recall that the set $r[q, 1 \cdots 1]$ is the set of tuples such that "if the tree is marked according to the tuple, $\mathcal{A}$ reaches the state q at the root node", which is by definition the answer set.

Theorem 2. $\psi_{\mathcal{L}(A)}(t) = \bigcup_{q \in F_{\mathcal{A}}} \text{QUERY-RUN}_{\mathcal{A}}(root_t)[q, 11 \cdots 11].$

Proof (sketch; for more detail, consult Claim 1 of [9]). Let $v_1, \ldots, v_n \in V_t$ to be fixed and ρ be the unique run on the tree $mark(t, v_1, \ldots, v_n)$ by $\mathcal{A}$. Let $v \in V_t$. For each i, if $v \leq_t v_i$ then let $u_i = v_i$ and $\beta_i = 1$. Otherwise let $u_i = \bot$ and $\beta_i = 0$. We can prove by induction on the structure of v the following claim: if $\rho(v) \neq q$ the set

QUERY-RUN$_A(v)[q, b]$ is empty for any $b \in \mathbb{B}^n$, and if $\rho(v) = q$ then $(u_1, \ldots, u_n) \in$ QUERY-RUN$_A(v)[q, b]$ if and only if $b = \beta_1 \cdots \beta_n$. By applying the claim to the root node $v = root_t$, we have $(v_1, \ldots, v_n) \in$ QUERY-RUN$_A(root_t)[q, 11 \cdots 11]$ if and only if $q = \rho(root_t)$, which, together with the definition of $\psi_{\mathcal{L}(A)}$, proves the desired result. $\square$

What is the complexity of this algorithm? For each node $v \in V_t$, the procedure QUERY-RUN$_A$ is applied exactly once. In other words, the procedure is called $|t|$ times. In the body of the procedure, the case for $\Sigma^{(2)}$ labels is computationally harder; the outer loop requires $|\delta_A|$ iterations, the inner loop for b_0, b_1, b_2 requires 3^n iterations, and inside the loop, one $\cup$ operation and two $*$ operations are required. Note that the result of those set operations can be as large as $O(|t|^n)$ in the worst case. As long as we represent such sets as a concrete collection of tuples, the operation $*$ need to enumerate all its output elements. Hence it takes at least $O(|t|^n)$ time. Altogether, the total time complexity is still high: $O(3^n |\delta_A| |t|^{n+1})$. In fact, the complexity can be reduced by a 2-pass preprocessing proposed in [9]. Their preprocessing detects, for each node, whether or not each entry $r[q, b]$ really needs to be computed. By omitting the computations that turned out not to be need, the complexity is reduced to $O(3^n |\delta_A| (|t| + a))$ where a is the size of the answer set.

In the next section, we take a completely different approach for reducing the complexity. Rather than changing the structure of the algorithm (like adding preprocessing passes), we introduce a novel data structure for representing sets of tuples. Just by using the data structure to represent sets in the QUERY-RUN$_A$ procedure, we obtain linear running time with respect to $|t|$, as well as a compact representation of the answer set.

4   SRED: Set Representation by Expression Dags

The idea of our compact representation is quite simple. To represent a set s, we use a syntax tree r of an expression that evaluates to s. For example, let r_1 and r_2 be the root nodes of the syntax-tree representations of sets s_1 and s_2 (we write $s_1 = [\![r_1]\!]$). Then we denote the set $s_1 \cup s_2$ by the tree $r = \text{cup}\langle r_1, r_2 \rangle$. To denote the set $[\![r_1]\!] \cup ([\![r_2]\!] * [\![r_3]\!])$, we use $\text{cup}\langle r_1, \text{star}\langle r_2, r_3 \rangle \rangle$. Note that, by allowing sharing of subtrees (i.e., using syntax-*dags* instead of syntax-trees, which allows a node like $\text{cup}\langle r_1, r_1 \rangle$), each operation can be executed in constant time, because it is just a creation of one new node. Since the algorithm QUERY-RUN$_A$ carries out set operations at most $O(3^n |\delta_A| |t|)$ times, under this representation of sets, the running time of QUERY-RUN$_A$ is in $O(3^n |\delta_A| |t|)$, and so is the size of the output dag representing the answer set.

Let us formally explain the syntax-dag-based representation, which we call *SRED* (*Set Representation by Expression Dags*). An answer set of an n-ary query over a tree t is represented by a dag of the following BNF, for $\beta_1 \cdots \beta_n \in \mathbb{B}^n$:

$$ST_{\beta_1 \cdots \beta_n} ::= \text{emp}\langle\rangle \mid \text{unit}\langle\rangle \mid \text{ne}\langle NST_{\beta_1 \cdots \beta_n} \rangle$$
$$NST_{\beta_1 \cdots \beta_n} ::= \text{cup}\langle v, NST_{\beta_1 \cdots \beta_n}, NST_{\beta_1 \cdots \beta_n} \rangle \text{ with } v \in V_t$$
$$\mid \text{star}\langle v, NST_{\alpha_1 \cdots \alpha_n}, NST_{\gamma_1 \cdots \gamma_n} \rangle \text{ with } v \in V_t \text{ and } \alpha_i \oplus \gamma_i = \beta_i$$
$$\mid \text{sing}\langle v, \beta_1 \cdots \beta_n \rangle \text{ with } v \in V_t$$

EVAL (r)
  1: **if** $r \equiv \mathrm{emp}\langle\rangle$ **then return** $\emptyset$
  2: **else if** $r \equiv \mathrm{unit}\langle\rangle$ **then return** $\{(\bot,\cdots,\bot)\}$
  3: **else if** $r \equiv \mathrm{ne}\langle r'\rangle$ **then return** EVAL-NE(r')

UNION-AT (v, r_1, r_2)
  1: **if** $r_1 \equiv \mathrm{emp}\langle\rangle$ **then**
  2:     **return** r_2
  3: **else if** $r_2 \equiv \mathrm{emp}\langle\rangle$ **then**
  4:     **return** r_1
  5: **else if** $r_1 \equiv \mathrm{ne}\langle r_1'\rangle$ **and** $r_2 \equiv \mathrm{ne}\langle r_2'\rangle$ **then**
  6:     **return** $\mathrm{ne}\langle\mathrm{cup}\langle v, r_1', r_2'\rangle\rangle$

SINGLETON-AT $(v, \beta_1 \cdots \beta_n)$
  1: **if** $\beta_1 \cdots \beta_n = 0 \cdots 0$ **then**
  2:     **return** $\mathrm{unit}\langle\rangle$
  3: **else return** $\mathrm{ne}\langle\mathrm{sing}\langle v, \beta_1 \cdots \beta_n\rangle\rangle$

EVAL-NE (r)
  1: **if** $r \equiv \mathrm{cup}\langle v, r_1, r_2\rangle$ **then**
  2:     **return** EVAL-NE(r_1) $\uplus$ EVAL-NE(r_2)
  3: **else if** $r \equiv \mathrm{star}\langle v, r_1, r_2\rangle$ **then**
  4:     **return** EVAL-NE(r_1) $*$ EVAL-NE(r_2)
  5: **else if** $r \equiv \mathrm{sing}\langle v, b\rangle$ **then**
  6:     **return** $singleton(v, b)$

PRODUCT-AT (v, r_1, r_2)
  1: **if** $r_1 \equiv \mathrm{emp}\langle\rangle$ **or** $r_2 \equiv \mathrm{emp}\langle\rangle$ **then**
  2:     **return** $\mathrm{emp}\langle\rangle$
  3: **else if** $r_1 \equiv \mathrm{unit}\langle\rangle$ **then**
  4:     **return** r_2
  5: **else if** $r_2 \equiv \mathrm{unit}\langle\rangle$ **then**
  6:     **return** r_1
  7: **else if** $r_1 \equiv \mathrm{ne}\langle r_1'\rangle$ **and** $r_2 \equiv \mathrm{ne}\langle r_2'\rangle$ **then**
  8:     **return** $\mathrm{ne}\langle\mathrm{star}\langle v, r_1', r_2'\rangle\rangle$

Fig. 1. Basic Operations on SRED

where $a \oplus c = b$ if and only if $a \neq c$ and $b = 1$ or $a = b = c = 0$. Note that, for enabling fast navigation as will be explained later, we record the node $v \in V_t$ at each operator. Also for the efficiency, we specially treat the empty set (represented by $\mathrm{emp}\langle\rangle$) and the *unit set* ($\{(\bot,\ldots,\bot)\}$, represented by $\mathrm{unit}\langle\rangle$), so that they do not occur at operand positions. For example, $\mathrm{cup}\langle v, \mathrm{emp}\langle\rangle, \mathrm{emp}\langle\rangle\rangle$ is ill-formed because $\mathrm{emp}\langle\rangle$ occurs as operands of cup. By avoiding $\mathrm{emp}\langle\rangle$ and $\mathrm{unit}\langle\rangle$ to occur at non-root position, we can evaluate the syntax-dag by a simple recursion shown in Fig. 1, in the data complexity proportional to the size of the answer set.

Lemma 3 (EVALUATION). *Assume the disjoint union $s_1 \uplus s_2$ can be computed in constant time and the product $s_1 * s_2$ can be computed in time $O(n|s_1 * s_2|)$ for $s_1, s_2 \neq \emptyset$. Then EVAL(r) (EVAL-NE(r), respectively) runs in time $O(3^k n|\mathrm{EVAL}(r)|)$ ($O(3^k n |\mathrm{EVAL\text{-}NE}(r)|)$) where k is the maximum number of star nodes in every path from r to any leaf.*

Proof. The proof is by induction on the structure of r. For the case of emp, unit, sing, and cup nodes, it is trivial and hence omitted here. For the case $r \equiv \mathrm{star}\langle v, r_1, r_2\rangle$, by induction hypothesis, $s_1 = \mathrm{EVAL\text{-}NE}(r_1)$ and $s_2 = \mathrm{EVAL\text{-}NE}(r_1)$ can be computed in $3^{k-1}n(|s_1| + |s_2|)$ steps. Since neither s_1 nor s_2 is empty, their sizes are less than or equal to $|s_1 * s_2|$. Thus, $3^{k-1}n(|s_1| + |s_2|)$ is no more than $2 \cdot 3^{k-1}n|s_1 * s_2|$. By the assumption, their *-product can be computed in time $n|s_1 * s_2|$. Altogether, the total time consumption for EVAL(r) in this case is $3^k n|s_1 * s_2| = 3^k n|\mathrm{EVAL\text{-}NE}(r)|$ as desired. □

The complexity assumption is satisfied by, for instance, representing the sets by a doubly-linked list of elements. Disjoint union can be implemented by the list concatenation, and the *-product is implemented by a double-loop over two operand sets. Note that, the number k of star node in a path is at most n, because the star operation strictly increases the number of non-$\bot$ coordinates in the element tuples.

The basic three operations used in the algorithm QUERY-RUN$_{\mathcal{A}}$ are defined on SRED as in Figure 1. Note that, to avoid $\mathrm{emp}\langle\rangle$ and $\mathrm{unit}\langle\rangle$ to occur in operand positions, we deal with the nodes specially. For example, since $\emptyset \cup s = s$ for any set s, when either

```
PROJ (i, r)                          PROJ-NE (i, r)
  1:  if r ≡ emp⟨⟩ then                1:  if r ≡ cup⟨v, r₁, r₂⟩ then
  2:      return ∅                      2:      return PROJ-NE(i, r₁) ∪ PROJ-NE(i, r₂)
  3:  else if r ≡ ne⟨r'⟩ then           3:  else if r ≡ star⟨v, r₁, r₂⟩ (with r₁ ∈ NST_{β₁···βₙ}) then
  4:      return PROJ-NE(i, r')         4:      if β_i = 1 then return PROJ-NE(i, r₁) else return PROJ-NE(i, r₂)
                                        5:  else if r ≡ sing⟨v, β₁ ··· βₙ⟩ then
                                        6:      return {v}

SELECT (i, u, r)                     SEL-NE (i, u, r)
  1:  if r ≡ emp⟨⟩ then                1:  if r ≡ cup⟨v, r₁, r₂⟩ and v ≤ u then
  2:      return emp⟨⟩                  2:      return UNION-AT(v, SEL-NE(i, u, r₁), SEL-NE(i, u, r₂))
  3:  else if r ≡ ne⟨r'⟩ then           3:  else if r ≡ star⟨v, r₁, r₂⟩ (with r₁ ∈ NST_{β₁···βₙ}) and v ≤ u then
  4:      return SEL-NE(i, u, r')       4:      if β_i = 1 then return PRODUCT-AT(v, SEL-NE(i, u, r₁), r₂)
                                        5:      else return PRODUCT-AT(v, r₁, SEL-NE(i, u, r₂))
                                        6:  else if r ≡ sing⟨v, β₁ ··· βₙ⟩ and v = u then
                                        7:      return SINGLETON-AT(v, β₁ ··· β_{i-1} 0 β_{i+1} ··· βₙ)
                                        8:  else return emp⟨⟩
```

Fig. 2. Projection and Selection on SRED

one of the operands of the UNION-AT operation is an emp⟨⟩ node, it returns the other operand rather than constructing a new cup node. The correctness is easily verified by induction on the structure of SRED, and we have the following results:

Lemma 4 (Correctness). $\text{EVAL}(\text{UNION-AT}(v, r_1, r_2)) = \text{EVAL}(r_1) \uplus \text{EVAL}(r_2)$, $\text{EVAL}(\text{PRODUCT-AT}(v, r_1, r_2)) = \text{EVAL}(r_1) * \text{EVAL}(r_2)$, and $\text{EVAL}(\text{SINGLETON-AT}(v, b)) = singleton(v, b)$.

Theorem 5. *Let* S-QUERY-RUN$_A$ *be a procedure obtained by replacing* $\emptyset$ *in the procedure* QUERY-RUN$_A$ *with* emp⟨⟩, $x \uplus y$ *with* UNION-AT(v, x, y), $x * y$ *with* PRODUCT-AT(v, x, y), *and* $singleton(v, b)$ *with* SINGLETON-AT(v, b). *Then,* S-QUERY-RUN$_A(t)$ *runs in time* $O(3^n |\delta_A| |t|)$ *and outputs a SRED* r *with at most* $3^n |\delta_A| |t|$ *nodes, such that* $\text{EVAL}(r) = \text{QUERY-RUN}_A(t)$.

Rather than enumerating the all elements of the answer set, we sometimes want to extract a sub-part of the answer set. Here, we give an implementation of two important operations on SRED, namely, PROJECTION and SELECTION. For a set s of n-tuples and $1 \le i \le n$, PROJECTION $s_{@i} = \{v_i \mid (v_1, \ldots, v_n) \in s\}$ is the set of i-th coordinates of s. Given an element u, SELECTION $s_{[i:u]} = \{(v_1, \ldots, v_{i-1}, v_{i+1}, \ldots, v_n) \mid (v_1, \ldots, v_{i-1}, u, v_{i+1}, \ldots, v_n)\}$ is the set of tuples in s such that the i-th coordinate is u. As an example of a use-case of the two operations, consider the following scenario: first we apply PROJECTION $_{@1}$ to an answer set, sort the result in some preferable order, and with each element u of the projected set, apply SELECTION $_{[1:u]}$ to get the remaining coordinates. In this way, we can enumerate the answers of queries in a user-specified order, rather than in the default order of EVALUATION procedure.

On SRED representation of the answer sets, those two operations can be carried out in time proportional to the *height* of the input tree. That is, we do not need to traverse the whole structure of SRED, nor to re-traverse the original input tree. Fig. 2 is the implementation, which is straightforwardly obtained from the distributivity of projection and selection over disjoint union, etc.

Theorem 6 (PROJECTION). *By using memoization, the procedure* $\mathrm{PROJ}(i, r)$ *computes the set* $\mathrm{EVAL}(r)_{@i}$ *in time* $O(6^n h |\delta_\mathcal{A}| |\mathrm{EVAL}(r)_{@i}|)$ *where* h *is the height of the original input tree* t.

Proof. Correctness is proved by induction on the structure of r, which is omitted here due to the lack of the space. For the complexity, we assume the procedure PROJ-NE to be memoized, i.e., if it is applied to the same arguments second time, it immediately returns the previous result in constant time. We can implement such memoization by using hash table. Then the body of the procedure PROJ-NE is executed at most once per each node of r. In fact, it can be shown that PROJ-NE is applied only to the nodes that are an ancestor of a $\mathrm{sing}\langle v, \cdots \rangle$ node with $v \in \mathrm{EVAL}(r)_{@i}$. By the definition of the QUERY-RUN$_\mathcal{A}$ procedure, the number of such sing nodes is at most $2^n |\mathrm{EVAL}(r)_{@i}|$, and for each of them, the number of the ancestors is at most $3^n h |\delta_\mathcal{A}|$. By using list-concatenation for representing set-union[1], the body of PROJ-NE can be executed in constant time. Hence, we obtain the desired complexity. □

Theorem 7 (SELECTION). *By using memoization, the procedure* $\mathrm{SEL}(i, u, r)$ *computes the set* $\mathrm{EVAL}(r)_{[i:u]}$ *in time* $O(3^n h |\delta_\mathcal{A}|)$.

Proof. Correctness is proved by induction on the structure of r. For the complexity, memoization ensures that the procedure SEL-NE is called at most once per each node of r. By Lemma 1, the test $v \leq u$ succeeds only at the node constructed at an ancestor (in the tree t) of u. Hence, SEL-NE is executed only on the nodes constructed at an ancestor of u, or their direct child. Since the number of the ancestor nodes is at most h and on each of such nodes at most $3^n |\delta_\mathcal{A}|$ SRED-node is created, SEL-NE is executed only $O(3^n h |\delta_\mathcal{A}|)$ times, which proves the desired complexity. □

As a corollary, given a tuple $(u_1, \ldots, u_n)$, we can test whether a SRED contains the tuple in time $O(3^n nh |\delta_\mathcal{A}|)$ by applying SELECTION n times.

Generalizations to Unranked Trees. So far, we have considered only binary trees. In many applications, however, we are interested in *unranked* trees with varying number of child nodes. To deal with unranked trees, we encode such trees to binary trees. A widely used encoding is *fc-ns encoding*. In a binary tree obtained as the fc-ns encoding of an unranked tree, the first child of each node is mapped to the *first child* of the corresponding node in the original unranked tree, and the second child of each node is mapped to the *next sibling* in the unranked tree. It is a folklore result that the encoding preserves the regularity of queries, i.e., any regular query for unranked trees can be converted to a regular query on the encoded trees. Hence, by first encoding the unranked input trees and the queries to the binary-tree form and then running S-QUERY-RUN$_\mathcal{A}$, we can compute the linear-size representation of the answer sets of regular queries. One problem of fc-ns encoding is the time complexity of operations on SRED that depends on the factor h, the height of the tree. Suppose an original unranked tree has small height h_0 and nodes with large number $w_0 (\simeq |t|)$ of children (which is often the case for most XML documents). The problem is that the height of the fc-ns encoded tree

---

[1] Precisely speaking, since it is not a *disjoint* union this time, list-concatenation based implementation may cause duplication. It, however, can be remove by a linear time 'uniq' algorithm.

is $O(h_0 w_0)$. To deal with such trees, we recommend to use another encoding, namely, the *bb encoding*, to reduce the complexity to $O(h_0 \log w_0)$. In bb encoding, the list of children of each node is encoded to a *balanced binary tree* whose left-to-right sequence of leaf nodes corresponds to the child sequence in the original tree. Such an encoding also preserves regularity, because the 'first-child' and the 'next-sibling' relations remain regular. Moreover, since the height of a balanced binary tree is in the logarithmic order of the number of the leaves, the height of the bb-encoded tree reduces to $O(h_0 \log |t|)$.

Application. SRED is developed for the XML transformation language MTran [11]. Let us illustrate the benefits of SRED by the following pseudo code for XML translation:

```
{gather x | x:<person> do
  <row><col>{gather y | (x//<name>/y) do y}</col>
    {gather z | z:<person> & document-order(z,x) do <col>···</col>}</row>}
```

The program takes a document containing a list of <person> elements and generates some triangular matrix table. The first query "x:<person>" lists up all the <person> elements, and for each of them, the second query "$(x//$<name>$/y)$" selects a descendant y of x labeled <name> (for simplicity, we assume that such y uniquely exists). If we really run for each x the second query, which takes in general $O(|t|)$ time where $|t|$ is the size of the tree, total running time of the query becomes quadratic, because there may be linearly many <person> nodes. Rather, as pointed out in [12], it is better to regard the second query as a *binary query* for selecting pairs (x, y). By using SRED, the answer set of such a binary query can be computed in linear time. Furthermore, by the SELEC-TION operation followed by the EVALUATION operation, for each x we can obtain the corresponding y in time $O(h_0 \log |t|)$. Total running time reduces to $O(h_0|t| \log |t|)$. So far, we could have used the FFG algorithm (or equivalently, query with SRED directly followed by EVALUATION) for the same purpose, because its running time is linear under the assumption that y uniquely exists for each x. Consider, then, the third query that selects all <person> elements z preceding x in the document order (preorder). Similarly, we run the query as a binary query for selecting pairs (x, z). In this case, the size of the answer set is quadratic. If we use the FFG algorithm, we need $O(|t|^2)$ working space for carrying out the binary-query based approach. While, with SRED, it requires only $O(|t|)$ working space. This makes feasible to run the transformation over larger inputs, which could not be done without SRED due to memory shortage.

Thanks. This work was supported by the Japan Society for the Promotion of Science.

References

1. Hosoya, H., Pierce, B.C.: Regular expression pattern matching for XML. Journal of Functional Programming 13, 961–1004 (2003)
2. Thatcher, J.W., Wright, J.B.: Generalized finite automata theory with an application to a decision problem of second-order logic. Mathematical Systems Theory 2, 57–811 (1968)
3. Niwinski, D.: Fixed points vs. infinite generation. In: LICS, pp. 402–409 (1988)
4. Gottlob, G., Koch, C., Pichler, R.: Efficient algorithms for processing XPath queries. ACM Transactions on Database Systems 30, 444–491 (2005)
5. Gottlob, G., Koch, C.: Monadic datalog and the expressive power of languages for Web information extraction. Journal of the ACM 51, 74–113 (2004)

6. Neven, F., Bussche, J.V.D.: Expressiveness of structured document query languages based on attribute grammars. Journal of the ACM 49, 56–100 (2002)
7. Meuss, H., Schulz, K.U., Bry, F.: Towards aggregated answers for semistructured data. In: Van den Bussche, J., Vianu, V. (eds.) ICDT 2001. LNCS, vol. 1973, pp. 346–360. Springer, Heidelberg (2000)
8. Filiot, E., Tison, S.: Regular n-ary queries in trees and variable independence. In: International Conference on Theoretical Computer Science (TCS), pp. 429–443 (2008)
9. Flum, J., Frick, M., Grohe, M.: Query evaluation via tree-decompositions. Journal of the ACM 49, 716–752 (2002)
10. Dietz, P.F.: Maintaining order in a linked list. In: STOC, pp. 122–127 (1982)
11. Inaba, K., Hosoya, H.: XML transformation language based on monadic second order logic. In: Programming Language Technologies for XML (PLAN-X), pp. 49–60 (2007)
12. Berlea, A., Seidl, H.: Binary queries for document trees. Nordic Journal of Computing 11, 41–71 (2004)

Recognition of a Spanning Tree of Directed Acyclic Graphs by Tree Automata

Akio Fujiyoshi

Department of Computer and Information Sciences, Ibaraki University
4-12-1 Nakanarusawa, Hitachi, Ibaraki, 316-8511, Japan
fujiyosi@mx.ibaraki.ac.jp

Abstract. In this paper, we study tree automata for directed acyclic graphs (DAGs). We define the movement of a tree automaton on a DAG so that a DAG is accepted by a tree automaton if and only if a DAG has a spanning tree accepted by a tree automaton. The NP-completeness of the membership problem of DAGs for a tree automaton is shown, and a linear-time recognition algorithm of series-parallel graphs for a tree automaton is presented.

1 Introduction

This paper proposes the use of tree automata [3] for the recognition of directed acyclic graphs (DAGs). Since DAGs are one of the most popular data structures in computer science and have many important applications, it is natural to study automata models for DAGs.

There are several ways to relate tree automata to DAGs. Many papers, e.g., [2,1,6] and Chap. 4 of [3], regarded DAGs as a compressed representation of trees and defined that a DAG is accepted by a tree automaton if the unfolded tree of a DAG is accepted by a tree automaton. For the sake of the motivation of this study, this paper defines the movement of a tree automaton on a DAG so that a DAG is accepted by a tree automaton if and only if a DAG has a spanning tree accepted by a tree automaton.

The motivation of this study is to establish a powerful and efficient recognition method for a mathematical OCR system [5]. As shown in Fig. 1, an OCR system constructs a DAG representing the adjacency relation of bounding boxes of symbols in a mathematical formula from a scanned image. From the DAG, we want to obtain a spanning tree representing connections of symbols, which should be syntactically reasonable.

It is shown that the membership problem of DAGs for a tree automaton is NP-complete. Thus, we need to think over restrictions on DAGs in order to obtain a recognition algorithm for practical use.

We introduce a linear-time recognition algorithm of series-parallel graphs (SPGs) for a tree automaton. SPGs are DAGs formed recursively by two simple composition operations. SPGs are of interest in algorithmic graph theory because a number of standard problems on graphs are solvable in linear time for SPGs including some NP-complete problems [7].

S. Maneth (Ed.): CIAA 2009, LNCS 5642, pp. 105–114, 2009.
© Springer-Verlag Berlin Heidelberg 2009

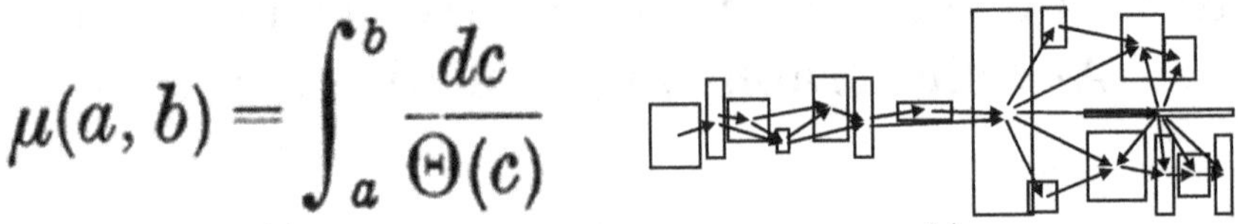

$$\mu(a, b) = \int_a^b \frac{dc}{\Theta(c)}$$

(a)

(b)

Fig. 1. (a) A scanned image, and (b) the adjacency relation of bounding boxes

2   Preliminaries

In this section, we give some definitions.

A *directed graph* is an ordered pair $G = (V, E)$, where V is a set, called *vertices*, and E is a set of ordered pairs of vertices, called *edges*. When $u, v \in V$, $e \in E$, and $e = (u, v)$, e is called an *outgoing edge* of u and also called an *incoming edge* of v, u is called a *parent* of v, and v is called a *child* of u. A directed graph is a *directed acyclic graph (DAG)* if it has no directed cycles. For a DAG, a *source* is a vertex with no incoming edges, while a *sink* is a vertex with no outgoing edges. A DAG is *single-source* if it has exactly one source. Likewise, a DAG is *single-sink* if it has exactly one sink. A single-source DAG is a *tree* if every vertex except the source has exactly one incoming edge. The source of a tree is also called the *root*, while sinks of a tree are also called *leaves*.

Let $G = (V, E)$ be a directed graph. Let Σ be a finite set of *vertex labels*, and let Γ be a finite set of *edge labels*. A *vertex-labeling* is a function $\sigma : V \to \Sigma$. Likewise, an *edge-labeling* is a function $\gamma : E \to \Gamma$. When σ is defined over V, G is called *vertex-labeled*. When both σ and γ are defined over V and E, G is called *vertex-edge-labeled*. In this paper, we assume that every graph to be vertex-labeled. Consequently, we use the term "edge-labeled" to mean "vertex-edge-labeled."

In this paper, a tree means an unranked, unordered tree. However, an ordered tree can be realized as a special case of an edge-labeled tree where the outgoing edges of each vertex are uniquely labeled as 1, 2, 3, ...

Spanning trees are defined for both vertex-labeled case and vertex-edge-labeled case as follows: (i) Let $D = (V_1, E_1)$ be a DAG with a vertex-labeling σ_1, and let $T = (V_2, E_2)$ be a tree with a vertex-labeling σ_2. T is a *spanning tree* of D if $V_1 = V_2$, $\sigma_1 = \sigma_2$, and $E_2 \subseteq E_1$. (ii) Let $D = (V_1, E_1)$ be a edge-labeled DAG with a vertex-labeling σ_1 and edge-labeling γ_1, and let $T = (V_2, E_2)$ be a edge-labeled tree with a vertex-labeling σ_2 and edge-labeling γ_2. T is a *edge-labeled spanning tree* of D if $V_1 = V_2$, $\sigma_1 = \sigma_2$, $E_2 \subseteq E_1$, and $\gamma_1(e) = \gamma_2(e)$ for all $e \in E_2$. Since a DAG must be single-source to have a spanning tree, we consider only single-source DAGs in this paper.

Let $\mathcal{X} = \{x_1, x_2, \ldots\}$ be a fixed countable set of *variables*.

Example 1. The following is an example of a DAG: $D = (V, E)$, where $V = \{v_1, v_2, v_3, v_4, v_5\}$, $E = \{(v_1, v_2), (v_1, v_3), (v_2, v_3), (v_2, v_4), (v_2, v_5), (v_3, v_5)\}$,

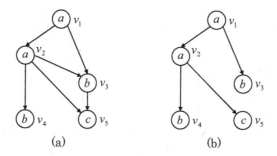

(a)   (b)

Fig. 2. (a) A DAG, and (b) one of the spanning trees of the DAG

$\Sigma = \{a, b, c\}$, and $\sigma = \{(v_1, a), (v_2, a), (v_3, b), (v_4, b), (v_5, c)\}$. An example of a spanning tree of D is $T = (V, E')$, where $E' = \{(v_1, v_2), (v_1, v_3), (v_2, v_4), (v_2, v_5)\}$. D and T are illustrated as (a) and (b) in Fig. 2.

3   Tree Automata Recognizing a Spanning Tree of DAGs

In this section, we introduce tree automata recognizing spanning trees of DAGs. The definition of tree automata is the same as well-known top-down tree automata for ordered trees [3]. Though only a top-down type of tree automata is introduced in this paper, it is easy to define a bottom-up sibling of tree automata with equivalent recognition capability.

Definition 1. A *nondeterministic top-down tree automaton* (top-down TA) over Σ is a four-tuple $\mathcal{A} = (Q, \Sigma, q_0, R)$ where Q is a finite set of *states*, $q_0 \in Q$ is the *initial state*, and R is a finite set of *rules* of the following form:

$$q(f(x_1, \ldots, x_n)) \rightarrow f(q_1(x_1), \ldots, q_n(x_n)),$$

where $n \geq 0$, $f \in \Sigma$, $q, q_1, \ldots, q_n \in Q$, and $x_1, \ldots, x_n \in \mathcal{X}$.

Let $D = (V, E)$ be a single-source DAG with a vertex-labeling σ, and let $\mathcal{A} = (Q, \Sigma, q_0, R)$ be a top-down TA. A *state mapping* is a function $S : V \rightarrow Q \cup \{\Box, \times\}$. The *initial state mapping* S_0 is the state mapping such that, for $v \in V$, $S_0(v) = q_0$ if v is the source of D, otherwise $S_0(v) = \Box$. The *final state mapping* S_f is the state mapping such that $S_f(v) = \times$ for all $v \in V$. We define a relation $\Rightarrow$ over state mappings as follows: For state mappings S and S', $S \Rightarrow S'$ if there exists $v \in V$ such that $S(v) = q$, $\sigma(v) = f$, $n \geq 0$, $q(f(x_1, \ldots, x_n)) \rightarrow f(q_1(x_1), \ldots, q_n(x_n))$ is a rule in R, and v has at least n children, $S(v_1) = \Box, \ldots, S(v_n) = \Box$ where $v_1, \ldots, v_n \in V$ are children of v such that $v_i \neq v_j$ for $i \neq j$, and S' is obtained from S by modifying as $S'(v) = \times$ and $S'(v_1) = q_1, \ldots, S'(v_n) = q_n$. Here, q is called the *state assigned to* v. Let $\overset{*}{\Rightarrow}$ be the reflective, transitive closure of $\Rightarrow$. D is *accepted by* $\mathcal{A}$ if $S_0 \overset{*}{\Rightarrow} S_f$.

When D is accepted by $\mathcal{A}$, a spanning tree of D, called *a recognition tree*, is obtained as follows: Let $S_0, \ldots, S_k$ be state mappings such that S_0 is the initial

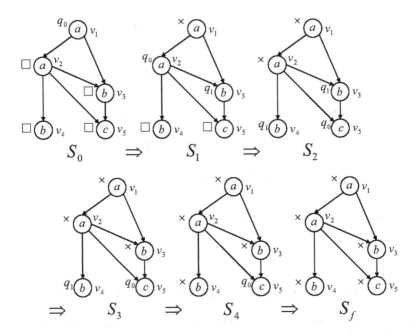

Fig. 3. A successful sequence of state mappings on D

state mapping, S_k is the final state mapping, and $S_i \Rightarrow S_{i+1}$ for any $0 \le i \le k-1$. For $0 \le i \le k-1$, let v^i and $v_1^i, \ldots, v_{n_i}^i$ be the vertices that attracted attention when S_{i+1} was obtained from S_i. Let $E' = \{(v^i, v_j^i) \mid 0 \le i \le k-1 \text{ and } 1 \le j \le n_i\}$. Then, the tree $T = (V, E')$ is a spanning tree of D.

From the definitions, the following proposition clearly holds:

Proposition 1. *A DAG D is accepted by $\mathcal{A}$ if and only if there exists a tree T such that T is a spanning tree of D, and T is accepted by $\mathcal{A}$.*

Example 2. The following is an example of a tree automaton which accepts the DAG D in Example 1: $\mathcal{A} = (Q, \Sigma, q_0, R)$, where $Q = \{q_0, q_1\}$, and $R = \{q_0(a(x_1, x_2)) \rightarrow a(q_0(x_1), q_1(x_2)), q_1(b(x_1)) \rightarrow b(q_0(x_1)), q_1(b) \rightarrow b, q_0(c) \rightarrow c\}$. A successful sequence of state mappings on D is illustrated in Fig. 3; the outputs of the state mappings for vertices are denoted at the left shoulder of vertices.

Concerning S_0, we can apply the rule $q_0(a(x_1, x_2)) \rightarrow a(q_0(x_1), q_1(x_2))$ to v_1, and S_1 is obtained by applying the rule by choosing v_2 for x_1 and v_3 for x_2. Regarding S_1, the rule that can be applied to v_2 is the same as for v_1. We need to choose v_4 and v_5 for the rule because $S_1(v_3) \ne \square$. Thus S_2 is obtained by applying the rule by choosing v_5 for x_1 and v_4 for x_2. By applying the rule $q_1(b) \rightarrow b$ to v_3 and v_4, and applying $q_0(c) \rightarrow c$ to v_5, the final state mapping S_f is successfully obtained.

The corresponding recognition tree is the same tree as T in Example 1.

4   NP-Completeness of the Membership Problem of DAGs for a Tree Automaton

In this section, we show the NP-completeness of the membership problem of DAGs for a tree automaton.

Theorem 1. *The membership problem of DAGs for a tree automaton is NP-complete, and the problem is still NP-complete even if the set of vertex labels is singleton.*

Proof. We will show the NP-completeness of the membership problem of DAGs for tree automata by reducing the Boolean satisfiability problem (SAT) to that problem.

Let $\Sigma = \{f\}$ be the set of vertex labels. Consider the top-down TA $\mathcal{A} = (Q, \Sigma, q_0, R)$ where:

$Q = \{q_0, q_1, q_2\}$, and
$$R = \{q_0(f(x_1, x_2)) \to f(q_1(x_1), q_3(x_2)),$$
$$q_1(f(x_1, x_2)) \to f(q_0(x_1), q_2(x_2)), \; q_1(f(x_1)) \to f(q_2(x_1)),$$
$$q_2(f(x_1, x_2)) \to f(q_2(x_1), q_2(x_2)), \; q_2(f(x_1)) \to f(q_2(x_1)), \; q_2(f) \to f,$$
$$q_3(f(x_1)) \to f(q_3(x_1)), \; q_3(f) \to f\}.$$

Let $\mathcal{F}$ be a given Boolean formula in conjunctive normal form (CNF), where $\mathcal{C} = \{c_1, \ldots, c_m\}$ is the set of clauses composing $\mathcal{F}$, and $\mathcal{V} = \{v_1, \ldots, v_n\}$ is the set of Boolean variables appearing in $\mathcal{F}$.

From $\mathcal{F}$, we construct a single-source DAG $D = (V, E)$ as follows:

$$V = \{v_1, \ldots, v_n\} \cup \{\bar{v}_1, \ldots, \bar{v}_n\} \cup \{c_1, \ldots, c_m\}$$
$$\cup \{s_{v_1}, \ldots, s_{v_n}\} \cup \{t_{v_1}, \ldots, t_{v_n}, t_{\bar{v}_1}, \ldots, t_{\bar{v}_n}\} \cup \{u_{v_1}, \ldots, u_{v_n}, u_{\bar{v}_1}, \ldots, u_{\bar{v}_n}\}$$
$$\cup \{w_{[v_i, c_j]}, w_{[\bar{v}_i, c_j]} \mid 1 \leq i \leq n \text{ and } 1 \leq j \leq m\}, \text{ and}$$
$$E = \{(s_{v_i}, v_i), (s_{v_i}, \bar{v}_i) \mid 1 \leq i \leq n\} \cup \{(v_i, s_{v_{i+1}}), (\bar{v}_i, s_{v_{i+1}}) \mid 1 \leq i \leq n-1\}$$
$$\cup \{(v_i, u_{v_i}), (\bar{v}_i, u_{\bar{v}_i}) \mid 1 \leq i \leq n\}$$
$$\cup \{(u_{v_i}, w_{[v_i, c_1]}), (u_{\bar{v}_i}, w_{[\bar{v}_i, c_1]}) \mid 1 \leq i \leq n\}$$
$$\cup \{(w_{[v_i, c_j]}, w_{[v_i, c_{j+1}]}), (w_{[\bar{v}_i, c_j]}, w_{[\bar{v}_i, c_{j+1}]}) \mid 1 \leq i \leq n \text{ and } 1 \leq j \leq m-1\}$$
$$\cup \{(w_{[v_i, c_m]}, t_{v_i}), (w_{[\bar{v}_i, c_m]}, t_{\bar{v}_i}) \mid 1 \leq i \leq n\}$$
$$\cup \{(w_{[v_i, c_j]}, c_j) \mid 1 \leq i \leq n, 1 \leq j \leq m, \text{ and } v_i \text{ appears in } c_j\}$$
$$\cup \{(w_{[\bar{v}_i, c_j]}, c_j) \mid 1 \leq i \leq n, 1 \leq j \leq m, \text{ and } \bar{v}_i \text{ appears in } c_j\}.$$

The vertex labeling is defined as $\sigma(v) = f$ for all $v \in V$.

Note that every vertex has at most two children. The source is s_{v_1}, while the sinks are $c_1, \ldots, c_m, t_{v_1}, \ldots, t_{v_n}, t_{\bar{v}_1}, \ldots, t_{\bar{v}_n}$.

For example, we consider the Boolean formula $(v_1 \vee \bar{v}_2 \vee v_3) \wedge (v_1 \vee v_3 \vee \bar{v}_4) \wedge (\bar{v}_2 \vee \bar{v}_3 \vee v_4)$. The DAG corresponding to the formula is illustrated in Fig. 4.

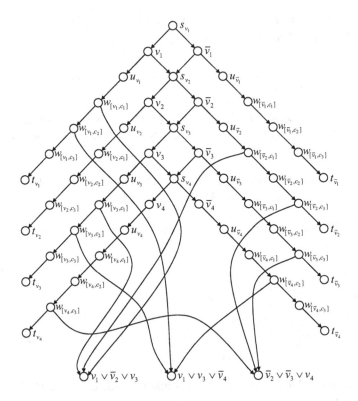

Fig. 4. The DAG corresponding to $(v_1 \vee \bar{v}_2 \vee v_3) \wedge (v_1 \vee v_3 \vee \bar{v}_4) \wedge (\bar{v}_2 \vee \bar{v}_3 \vee v_4)$

Because the labels of vertices are all the same, labels are omitted. A recognition tree with a successful assignment of states to vertices is illustrated in Fig.5.

When D is accepted by $\mathcal{A}$, a recognition tree and a successful assignment of states to vertices have the following features:

- The state assigned to each $s_{v_1}, \ldots, s_{v_n}$ is only q_0, and q_0 must not be assigned to any other vertices.
- q_1 is assigned only to one of each pair $v_i, \bar{v}_i$ for $1 \leq i \leq n$.
- The state assigned to each $c_1, \ldots, c_m$ is only q_2.
- The vertices assigned q_3 have at most one child in a recognition tree, while the vertices assigned q_2 may have two children.
- The state assignment for $v_1, \ldots, v_n$ yields a truth assignment for the Boolean variables of $\mathcal{F}$. If we assign TRUE to the variables with q_1 and assign FALSE to the variables with q_3, then a truth assignment is obtained.

It is clear that D is accepted by $\mathcal{A}$ if and only if there exists a truth assignment for the Boolean variables of $\mathcal{F}$. This means that the problem is NP-hard. On the other hand, given a DAG D, we can nondeterministically obtain a recognition tree T and check if T is accepted by $\mathcal{A}$ in polynomial time. This means that the problem is in the class NP. Therefore, the problem is NP-complete.   □

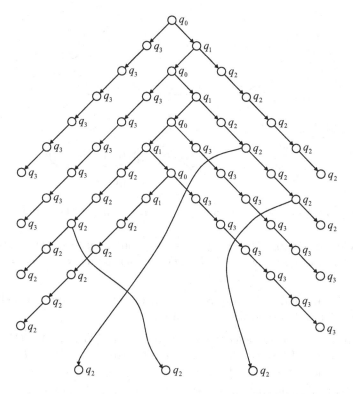

Fig. 5. A recognition tree with a successful assignment of states to vertices

5 Linear-Time Recognition Algorithm of Series-Parallel Graphs for a Tree Automaton

In this section, we introduce a linear-time recognition algorithm of series-parallel graphs (SPGs) for a tree automaton. SPGs are single-source, single-sink DAGs formed recursively by two simple composition operations. It is known that a number of standard problems on graphs are solvable in linear time for SPGs though some of these problems are NP-complete for general graphs [7].

Let us write $D(s,t)$ to mean that a single-source, single-sink DAG D has the source s and the sink t.

5.1 Series-Parallel Graphs

Definition 2. A single-source, single-sink DAG is a *series-parallel graph (SPG)* if (1) it is a single edge graph, or (2) it can be produced by a sequence of the following two operations:

Series Composition: Given two series-parallel graphs $D_1(s_1,t_1)$ and $D_2(s_2,t_2)$, form a new graph $D(s,t)$ by identifying $s = s_1$, $t_1 = s_2$, and $t = t_2$.

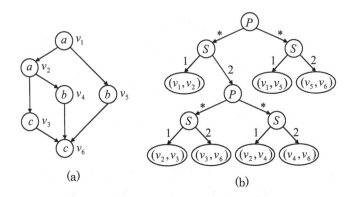

Fig. 6. (a) An SPG, and (b) one of the corresponding SPTs to the SPG

Parallel Composition: Given two series-parallel graphs $D_1(s_1, t_1)$ and $D_2(s_2, t_2)$, form a new graph $D(s, t)$ by identifying $s = s_1 = s_2$, and $t = t_1 = t_2$.

Due to the recursive definition of SPGs, we can obtain an edge-labeled tree in accordance with a decomposition of an SPG.

Definition 3. A *series-parallel tree (SPT)* T for an SPG $D(s, t) = (V, E)$ is an edge-labeled tree defined as follows: The set of vertex labels is $\{S, P\} \cup E$, and the set of edge labels is $\{*, 1, 2\}$.

- If $D(s, t)$ is a single edge graph, then $T = (\{(s, t)\}, \emptyset)$, and $\sigma((s, t)) = (s, t)$.
- If $D(s, t)$ is obtained by a series composition of $D_1(s_1, t_1)$ and $D_2(s_2, t_2)$, and $T_1 = (V_1, E_1)$ and $T_2 = (V_2, E_2)$ are SPTs of them, then $T = (\{r\} \cup V_1 \cup V_2, \{(r, r_1), (r, r_2)\} \cup E_1 \cup E_2)$ where r is a new vertex, and r_1 and r_2 are the roots of T_1 and T_2, $\sigma(r) = S$, $\gamma((r, r_1)) = 1$, and $\gamma((r, r_2)) = 2$.
- If $D(s, t)$ is obtained by a parallel composition of $D_1(s_1, t_1)$ and $D_2(s_2, t_2)$, and $T_1 = (V_1, E_1)$ and $T_2 = (V_2, E_2)$ are SPTs of them, then $T = (\{r\} \cup V_1 \cup V_2, \{(r, r_1), (r, r_2)\} \cup E_1 \cup E_2)$ where r is a new vertex, and r_1 and r_2 are the roots of T_1 and T_2, $\sigma(r) = P$, $\gamma((r, r_1)) = *$, and $\gamma((r, r_2)) = *$.

An example of an SPG and a corresponding SPT is illustrated in Figure 6.

Note that the children of a vertex labeled S are ordered, while the children of a vertex labeled P are unordered. All edges of D appear exactly once as a label of leaves. An SPG may have many corresponding SPTs since the above decomposition is not unique in general.

It is known that an SPT is obtained from any SPG in linear time depending on the number of edges of an SPG [7].

5.2 Recognition Algorithm of SPGs

Let $\mathcal{A} = (Q, \Sigma, q_0, R)$ be a top-down TA, and let $\mathcal{X}_\mathcal{A}$ be the set of variables appearing in R. For a rule $r = q(f(x_1, \ldots, x_n)) \to f(q_1(x_1), \ldots, q_n(x_n))$ in R, let state(r) mean the state q, and let var(r) mean the set $\{x_1, \ldots, x_n\}$.

The algorithm takes as input an SPG $D(s,t) = (V, E)$ and a corresponding SPT $T = (V_T, E_T)$, where T is prepared to give an appropriate order to process D. The main task of the algorithm is to calculate two sets A and B.

Main:
    input: an SPG $D(s,t) = (V, E)$ and a corresponding SPT $T = (V_T, E_T)$;
    output: *accept* or *reject*;
begin
1   Let u be the root vertex of T;
2    $(A, B) := \mathbf{Calculate}(u)$;
3   if A includes an element $(r, \mathcal{X}', q)$ such that state$(r) = q_0$, var$(r) = \mathcal{X}'$,
      and $q(\sigma(t)) \to \sigma(t)$ is in R **then return** *accept* **else return** *reject*;
end.

Calculate:
    input: a vertex $u \in V_T$;
    output: $A \subseteq R \times 2^{\mathcal{X}_A} \times Q$ and $B \subseteq R \times 2^{\mathcal{X}_A}$;
begin
1   if $\sigma(u) = (v_1, v_2) \in E$ **then begin**
2        $A := \emptyset$, and $B := \emptyset$;
3   **for each** $r = q(f(x_1, \ldots, x_n)) \to f(q_1(x_1), \ldots, q_n(x_n))$ in R **do**
4   **if** $n \geq 1$, and $\sigma(v_1) = f$ **then** $A := A \cup \{(r, \{x_i\}, q_i) \mid 1 \leq i \leq n\}$
5   **else if** $n = 0$, and $\sigma(v_1) = f$ **then** $B := B \cup \{(r, \emptyset)\}$;
    end
6   **else if** $\sigma(u) = S$ **then begin**
7   Let u_1 be the first child of u, and let u_2 be the second child of u;
8        $(A_1, B_1) := \mathbf{Calculate}(u_1)$, and $(A_2, B_2) := \mathbf{Calculate}(u_2)$;
9        $A := \{(r_1, \mathcal{X}_1, q_2) \mid (r_1, \mathcal{X}_1, q_1) \in A_1, (r_2, \mathcal{X}_2, q_2) \in A_2, \text{state}(r_2) = q_1,$
           and $\mathcal{X}_2 = \text{var}(r_2)\}$;
10     $B := \{(r_1, \mathcal{X}_1) \mid (r_1, \mathcal{X}_1, q_1) \in A_1, (r_2, \mathcal{X}_2) \in B_2, \text{state}(r_2) = q_1, \text{ and}$
           $\mathcal{X}_2 = \text{var}(r_2)\}$;
    end
11   **else if** $\sigma(u) = P$ **then begin**
12   Let u_1 and u_2 be the children of u;
13     $(A_1, B_1) := \mathbf{Calculate}(u_1)$, and $(A_2, B_2) := \mathbf{Calculate}(u_2)$;
14     $A := \{(r, \mathcal{X}_1 \cup \mathcal{X}_2, q_1) \mid (r, \mathcal{X}_1, q_1) \in A_1, (r, \mathcal{X}_2) \in B_2, \text{ and } \mathcal{X}_1 \cap \mathcal{X}_2 = \emptyset\}$
           $\cup \{(r, \mathcal{X}_1 \cup \mathcal{X}_2, q_2) \mid (r, \mathcal{X}_1) \in B_1, (r, \mathcal{X}_2, q_2) \in A_2, \text{ and } \mathcal{X}_1 \cap \mathcal{X}_2 = \emptyset\}$;
15     $B := \{(r, \mathcal{X}_1 \cup \mathcal{X}_2) \mid (r, \mathcal{X}_1) \in B_1, (r, \mathcal{X}_2) \in B_2, \text{ and } \mathcal{X}_1 \cap \mathcal{X}_2 = \emptyset\}$;
    end;
16 **return** (A, B);
end.

Theorem 2. *The recognition algorithm works correctly and terminates in linear time depending on the number of edges of D.*

Proof. Omitted.

6   Tree Automata for the Edge-Labeled Case

Though ordered trees are mainly discussed in the theory of tree automata, DAGs without edge labels are not a generalization of ordered trees. Therefore, we consider tree automata dealing with edge-labeled DAGs.

For reasons of space, only the definition of edge-labeled tree automata is introduced. A linear-time recognition algorithm of edge-labeled SPGs can be obtained with small modifications to the recognition algorithm in Section 5.

Definition 4. An *edge-labeled tree automaton* (edge-labeled TA) over Σ and Γ is a five-tuple $\mathcal{A} = (Q, \Sigma, \Gamma, q_0, R)$ where Q is a finite set of *states*, $q_0 \in Q$ is the *initial state*, and R is a finite set of *rules* of the following form:

$$q(f(c_1(x_1), \ldots, c_n(x_n))) \rightarrow f(c_1(q_1(x_1)), \ldots, c_n(q_n(x_1))),$$

where $n \geq 0$, $f \in \Sigma$, $c_1, \ldots, c_n \in \Gamma$, $q, q_1, \ldots, q_n \in Q$, and $x_1, \ldots, x_n \in \mathcal{X}$.

7   Conclusion and Future Works

We have studied the recognition of a spanning tree of DAGs by tree automata. The NP-completeness of the membership problem of DAGs for a tree automaton was shown, and a linear-time recognition algorithm of series-parallel graphs for a tree automaton was presented.

For future works, we want to extend the recognition algorithm in Section 5 so that it recognizes more general graphs such as partial k-trees. It is also interesting to think of the recognition of DAGs by linear pushdown tree automata [4].

References

1. Anantharaman, S., Narendran, P., Rusinowitch, M.: Closure properties and decision problems of dag automata. Information Processing Letters 94(5), 231–240 (2005)
2. Charatonik, W.: Automata on dag representations of finite trees. Technical Report MPI-I-1999-2-001, Max-Planck-Institut für Informatik (1999)
3. Comon, H., Dauchet, M., Gilleron, R., Jacquemard, F., Lugiez, D., Löding, C., Tison, S., Tommasi, M.: Tree automata techniques and applications (2007), http://www.grappa.univ-lille3.fr/tata (release October 12, 2007)
4. Fujiyoshi, A., Kawaharada, I.: Deterministic recognition of trees accepted by a linear pushdown tree automaton. In: Farré, J., Litovsky, I., Schmitz, S. (eds.) CIAA 2005. LNCS, vol. 3845, pp. 129–140. Springer, Heidelberg (2006)
5. Fujiyoshi, A., Suzuki, M., Uchida, S.: Verification of mathematical formulae based on a combination of context-free grammar and tree grammar. In: Autexier, S., Campbell, J., Rubio, J., Sorge, V., Suzuki, M., Wiedijk, F. (eds.) AISC 2008, Calculemus 2008, and MKM 2008. LNCS (LNAI), vol. 5144, pp. 415–429. Springer, Heidelberg (2008)
6. Lohrey, M., Maneth, S.: Tree automata and XPath on compressed trees. In: Farré, J., Litovsky, I., Schmitz, S. (eds.) CIAA 2005. LNCS, vol. 3845, pp. 225–237. Springer, Heidelberg (2006)
7. Takamizawa, K., Nishizeki, T., Saito, N.: Linear-time computability of combinatorial problems on series-parallel graphs. J. ACM 29(3), 623–641 (1982)

Random Generation of Deterministic Tree (Walking) Automata[*]

Pierre-Cyrille Héam[1,3], Cyril Nicaud[2], and Sylvain Schmitz[3]

[1] LIFC, Université de Franche-Comté & INRIA, Besançon, France
[2] LIGM, Université Paris Est & CNRS, Marne-la-Vallée, France
[3] LSV, ENS Cachan & CNRS & INRIA, Cachan, France

Abstract. Uniform random generators deliver a simple empirical means to estimate the average complexity of an algorithm. We present a general rejection algorithm that generates sequential letter-to-letter transducers up to isomorphism. We tailor this general scheme to randomly generate deterministic tree walking automata and deterministic top-down tree automata. We apply our implementation of the generator to the estimation of the average complexity of a deterministic tree walking automata to nondeterministic top-down tree automata construction we also implemented.

1 Introduction

The widespread use of automata as primitive bricks in computer science motivates an ever renewed search for efficient algorithms taking automata as input (see for some recent examples [1,2,3]). Developing new algorithms and heuristics raises crucial evaluation issues, as improved worst-case complexity upper-bounds do not always transcribe into clear practical gains [4].

A suite for software performance evaluation can usually gather three types of entries:[1]

1. benchmarks, i.e. large sets of typical samples, which can be prohibitively difficult to collect, and thus only exist for a few general problems,
2. hard instances, that provide good estimations of the worst case behaviour, but are not always relevant for average case evaluations,
3. random inputs, that deliver average complexity estimations, for which the catch resides in obtaining a meaningful random distribution (for instance a uniform random distribution). As the mathematical computation of the average complexity of an algorithm is an intricate task that cannot be undertaken in general, random inputs can prove themselves invaluable for its empirical estimation.

---

[*] This work was supported in part by ANR GAMMA - project BLAN07-2_195422 and ANR RAVAJ - project SETIN-2006.
[1] All of the three types are used in SAT-solver competitions like http://www.satcompetition.org/

S. Maneth (Ed.): CIAA 2009, LNCS 5642, pp. 115–124, 2009.

This paper is dedicated to the random generation of deterministic top-down tree automata and of deterministic tree-walking automata. Tree automata have witnessed a recent surge of interest in connection with XML applications [5,6], fostering a wealth of theoretical results (e.g. [7,8,9]). This paper makes the following contributions:

- Section 2 proposes a generic rejection algorithm for uniformly generating sequential letter-to-letter transducers. Thanks to the structural properties of these transducers, the algorithm can be used for the generation of various kinds of finite automata.
- We apply this algorithm in Sect. 3 to the generation of deterministic tree walking automata. The approach was implemented, and we provide in Sect. 3.3 an empirical estimation of the average size of the nondeterministic top-down tree automaton equivalent to a given deterministic tree walking automaton.
- Section 4 presents a bijection between a class of letter-to-letter transducers and deterministic top-down tree automata, providing a uniform random generator for this class of tree automata.

Our approach consists in reducing the problem to the uniform random generation of deterministic word automata, as developed by Bassino et al. [10,11].

Related Work. In the case of deterministic accessible word automata, two main approaches to the random generation with uniform distribution on complete automata stand out: one based on a recursive decomposition [12] and one using Boltzmann samplers [10]. The latter algorithm has been extended to possibly incomplete automata by Bassino et al. [11]. An implementation of these algorithms is available in the C++ package REGAL [13].[2]

The random generation of non deterministic finite word automata is still mostly open. Two recent papers propose such random generation algorithms: Tabakov and Vardi [14] apply theirs to the evaluation of inclusion testing procedures, whereas Chen et al. [15] evaluate the performance of a learning algorithm. Both algorithms are *ad hoc* and fail to provide statistically exploitable distributions.

Notations. If i and j are positive integers, we denote by $[i, j]$ the set of integers k such that $i \leq k$ and $k \leq j$. If K is a set, $\mathcal{P}(K)$ (resp. $\mathcal{P}^*(K)$) denotes the set of subsets (resp. the set of non empty subsets) of K. The domain of a function φ is denoted $\mathrm{Dom}(\varphi)$.

A *sequential letter-to-letter transducer* (SLT) from input alphabet Σ_1 to output alphabet Σ_2 is a tuple $\mathcal{T} = (\Sigma_1, \Sigma_2, Q, q_{\mathrm{init}}, \delta, \gamma, \rho, a_{\mathrm{init}})$ where Q is the finite set of *states*, $q_{\mathrm{init}} \in Q$ is the *initial state*, δ is a partial *transition function* from $Q \times \Sigma_1$ into Q, γ is a partial *output function* from $Q \times \Sigma_1$ into Σ_2 such that $\mathrm{Dom}(\delta) = \mathrm{Dom}(\gamma)$, ρ is a partial *final function* from Q into Σ_2, and $a_{\mathrm{init}} \in \Sigma_2$ is the *initial output*. An SLT is *complete* if $\mathrm{Dom}(\delta) = Q \times \Sigma_1$. *Accessible* states of an SLT are inductively defined by: q_{init} is accessible and if q is accessible, for every $a \in \Sigma_1$, $\delta(q, a)$ is accessible. An SLT is *accessible* if all its states are accessible. An example of complete and accessible SLT is depicted in Fig. 1.

---

[2] http://regal.univ-mlv.fr/

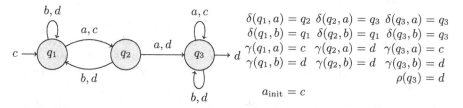

$$\delta(q_1, a) = q_2 \quad \delta(q_2, a) = q_3 \quad \delta(q_3, a) = q_3$$
$$\delta(q_1, b) = q_1 \quad \delta(q_2, b) = q_1 \quad \delta(q_3, b) = q_3$$
$$\gamma(q_1, a) = c \quad \gamma(q_2, a) = d \quad \gamma(q_3, a) = c$$
$$\gamma(q_1, b) = d \quad \gamma(q_2, b) = d \quad \gamma(q_3, b) = d$$
$$\rho(q_3) = d$$
$$a_{\text{init}} = c$$

Fig. 1. A sequential letter-to-letter transducer

Let $\mathcal{T}_1 = (\Sigma_1, \Sigma_2, Q_1, q_{\text{init1}}, \delta_1, \gamma_1, \rho_1, a_{\text{init1}})$ and $\mathcal{T}_2 = (\Sigma_1, \Sigma_2, Q_2, q_{\text{init2}}, \delta_2, \gamma_2, \rho_2, a_{\text{init2}})$ be two SLTs. A function φ from Q_1 to Q_2 is an *isomorphism* from $\mathcal{T}_1$ to $\mathcal{T}_2$ if it satisfies the following conditions: (1) φ is bijective, (2) $\varphi(q_{\text{init1}}) = q_{\text{init2}}$, (3) $\delta_1(q, a) = p$ iff $\delta_2(\varphi(q), a) = \varphi(p)$, (4) $\gamma_1(q, a) = b$ iff $\gamma_2(\varphi(q), a) = b$, (5) $\rho_1(q) = \rho_2(\varphi(q))$ and (6) $a_{\text{init1}} = a_{\text{init2}}$. If such an isomorphism exists, we say that $\mathcal{T}_1$ and $\mathcal{T}_2$ are isomorphic. Informally, $\mathcal{T}_1$ and $\mathcal{T}_2$ are isomorphic if they encode the same SLT, up to state names. The relation *is isomorphic to* is trivially an equivalence relation.

In this paper, we are interested in the uniform random generation of SLTs up to isomorphism, i.e. we want to equiprobably generate equivalence classes for the isomorphic relation (and for a given number of states). Since the approach is purely syntactic and will be applied to different classes of finite automata, we do not need to define a semantic for SLTs.

2   Generating Sequential Transducers

We propose in this section a general method to generate randomly and uniformly deterministic and accessible automata-like structures with n states. For this purpose, we develop an algorithm that generates sequential letter-to-letter accessible transducers with n states, that can be further parametrized by giving some *restrictions* on the possible outputs for each input letter. The idea thereafter, for each given problem, is to find an effective *bijection* φ between the structures one wants to generate and such a family of transducers. The algorithm is in fact more general, since by Proposition 1, one can build an effective random generator even if φ is only an injection, provided that all the complete transducers are in the image of φ. This method will be applied in Sect. 3 and Sect. 4 to build random generators for deterministic tree walking automata and deterministic top-down tree automata.

Note that we are only interested here in the combinatorial structures of transducers, not on what their models are. Indeed, our approach will be used in order to generate several kinds of finite automata. Also note that we are interested in the uniform random generation of isomorphic classes of SLTs. The algorithms proposed in this section fulfill this criterion. However, in order to simplify the exposition, we will write about random generation of SLTs rather than of equivalence classes of SLT, but keep in mind that we randomly generate witnesses of equivalence classes.

2.1   Rejection Algorithms

Before we describe the generation algorithm, let us recall the definition of a *rejection algorithm*: Suppose we want to generate elements of a set X, according to a probability distribution p_X. Furthermore, suppose that X is a subset of Y, and that we have a probability distribution p_Y on Y, whose restriction to X is p_X. If we have an algorithm to generate elements of Y according to p_Y, we may use this algorithm to generate elements of X as follows: repeatedly draw an element of Y, reject it if it is not in X, and stop if it is in X.

The average complexity of this rejection algorithm depends on the complexity of the generation algorithm on Y, on the complexity of the test whether an element of Y is in X, and on the average number of rejects. One can show that if $p_Y(X)$ is the probability for an element of Y to be in X, the average number of iterations is $1/p_Y(X)$.

2.2   Families of Transducers

Let us consider the family $\mathcal{D}_n(\Sigma_1, \Sigma_2, r, r_i, r_F)$ of accessible SLTs with n states, where Σ_1 is the input alphabet, Σ_2 is the output alphabet, $r : \Sigma_1 \to \mathcal{P}^*(\Sigma_2)$ is the restriction on transitions, $r_i \in \mathcal{P}^*(\Sigma_2)$ is the restriction on initialization and $r_F \in \mathcal{P}^*(\Sigma_2)$ is the restriction on finalizations. An n-states accessible SLT $(\Sigma_1, \Sigma_2, Q, i, \delta, \gamma, \rho, a_i)$ belongs to $\mathcal{D}_n(\Sigma_1, \Sigma_2, r, r_i, r_F)$ if the following conditions are met: (i) $a_i \in r_i$, (ii) $\rho(Q) \subseteq r_F$, and (iii) for all $a \in \Sigma_1$, $\gamma(Q, a) \subseteq r(a)$.

We denote by $\mathcal{C}_n(\Sigma_1, \Sigma_2, r, r_i, r_F)$ the subset of $\mathcal{D}_n(\Sigma_1, \Sigma_2, r, r_i, r_F)$ that contains all the complete transducers. In order to generate a random element of $\mathcal{D}_n(\Sigma_1, \Sigma_2, r, r_i, r_F)$ or $\mathcal{C}_n(\Sigma_1, \Sigma_2, r, r_i, r_F)$, we split the problem into three parts: the underlying graph with input symbols, the transitions outputs, and the set of final states. For complete transducers, one can perform these parts independently and still ensure equiprobability. A rejection algorithm is used to adapt this method to possibly incomplete ones.

2.3   Generation Algorithm

The idea to generate deterministic and accessible word automata developed by Bassino et al. [10,11] is to exhibit an effective injection ι from automata with n states on a k-letter alphabet to partitions of $[1, kn+1]$ in n parts in the complete case and of $[1, kn+2]$ in $n+1$ parts in the possibly incomplete case. The inverse ι^{-1} can also be computed, and though all partitions are not the image of an automaton, there are enough of them to guarantee that a rejection algorithm is efficient. The algorithm therefore consists in randomly generating a partition, using a Boltzmann sampler, until the partition is the image of an automaton, and then compute its preimage. Its average complexity is $\mathcal{O}(n^{3/2})$.

The algorithm to generate a random element of $\mathcal{C}_n(\Sigma_1, \Sigma_2, r, r_i, r_F)$ consists in the following three steps:

1. Randomly generate a complete deterministic and accessible automaton with n states on Σ_1.

2. For each $q \in Q$ and each $a \in \Sigma_1$, randomly and uniformly choose $\gamma(q, a)$ in $r(a)$.
3. For each $q \in Q$, randomly and uniformly choose an element x of $r_F \uplus \{\#\}$, where $\#$ is a new symbol indicating that the state is not final; then define $\rho(q) = x$ if $x \neq \#$ and leave $\rho(q)$ otherwise undefined.

One can give the number of final states as a parameter f and change Step 3 into: Choose a random subset F with f elements of Q, and for each $q \in F$, choose $\rho(q)$ in r_F. The average complexity of the algorithm remains in $\mathcal{O}(n^{3/2})$.

To generate a random element of $\mathcal{D}_n(\Sigma_1, \Sigma_2, r, r_i, r_F)$, we proceed as before, except that we generate a possibly incomplete automaton at Step 1. The problem here is that the distribution is not uniform anymore, since we consider multiple choices of $\gamma(q, a)$ when the transition does not exist, leading to the same transducer. In order to obtain uniformity, we arbitrarily order Σ_2 and only keep, using a rejection algorithm, transducers such that $\gamma(q, a)$ is set to the minimum in $r(a)$ for every undefined transition. Corollary 1 of [11] ensures that a proportion greater than c, where $c > 0$ is a real number, of possibly incomplete automata are complete. The average number of rejects of this method is therefore in $\mathcal{O}(1)$, as complete structures are not rejected and are numerous enough. The average complexity is in $\mathcal{O}(n^{3/2})$ as well. Observe that if we had generated the image of $\gamma(q, a)$ for defined transitions only, we would have lost the uniformity.

Using the same argument about the proportion of complete automata given in Corollary 1 of [11], we can prove the following fairly general proposition:

Proposition 1. *Let E_n be a subset of $\mathcal{D}_n(\Sigma_1, \Sigma_2, r, r_i, r_F)$ such that E_n contains $\mathcal{C}_n(\Sigma_1, \Sigma_2, r, r_i, r_F)$. The rejection algorithm consisting in generating uniformly an element of $\mathcal{D}_n(\Sigma_1, \Sigma_2, r, r_i, r_F)$ until it is in E_n performs $\mathcal{O}(1)$ iterations on average.*

Therefore, we have a straightforward method to build a random generator for such a class E_n, which is efficient if one can quickly test if a given transducer is in E_n. In particular, if the membership test can be done in linear time, then the average complexity of this method is in $\mathcal{O}(n^{3/2})$. Note that the constant factor might grow quickly, e.g. when $|\Sigma_1|$ grows.

3   Application to Tree Walking Automata

3.1   Deterministic Tree Walking Automata

A *deterministic tree walking automaton* (DTWA) on binary trees is a tuple $\mathcal{A} = (Q, \Sigma, \Delta, q_{init}, F)$ where Q is a finite set of states, $q_{init} \in Q$ is the initial state, $F \subseteq Q$ the set of final states and Δ is a partial transition function from $Q \times \text{TYPE} \times \Sigma$ to $\{\varepsilon, \uparrow, \swarrow, \searrow\} \times Q$, where $\text{TYPE} = \{\text{root}, \text{left}, \text{right}\} \times \{\text{internal}, \text{leaf}\}$. A deterministic tree walking automaton is *complete* if Δ is a complete function. Accessible states of a DTWA are defined inductively: q_{init} is accessible, and if q is accessible and $\Delta(q, t, a) = (d, p)$ for some $(t, a) \in \text{TYPE} \times \Sigma$, then p is accessible. An example of a DTWA is shown in Fig. 2.

Fig. 2. A deterministic tree walking automaton

An *isomorphism* from a DTWA $\mathcal{A}_1 = (Q_1, \Sigma, \Delta_1, q_{\text{init1}}, F_1)$ to a DTWA $\mathcal{A}_2 = (Q_2, \Sigma, \Delta_2, q_{\text{init2}}, F_2)$ is a bijective function from Q_1 to Q_2 satisfying the three conditions (1) $\varphi(q_{\text{init1}}) = q_{\text{init2}}$, (2) $\varphi(q) \in F_2$ iff $q \in F_1$, and (3) $\Delta_1(q, t, a) = (d, p)$ iff $\Delta_2(\varphi(q), t, a) = (d, \varphi(p))$.

3.2 From SLTs to DTWAs

We define in this section a rather straightforward bijection τ between DTWAs and a class of SLTs, called *DTWA-coherent* SLTs, that contains all the complete SLTs. We obtain thereafter a random generation algorithm for DTWAs thanks to the restriction mechanisms introduced in Sect. 2.

We first observe that a tree walking automaton can be viewed as a "classical" finite automaton on the alphabet $\Sigma_1 \times \Sigma_2$ defined by $\Sigma_1 = \text{TYPE} \times \Sigma$ and $\Sigma_2 = \{\varepsilon, \uparrow, \nearrow, \searrow\}$. Let $\mathcal{A} = (Q, \Sigma, \Delta, q_{\text{init}}, F)$ be a DTWA; we define $\tau(\mathcal{A})$ by

$$\tau(\mathcal{A}) = (\Sigma_1, \Sigma_2 \uplus \{\$, 1\}, Q, q_{\text{init}}, \delta, \gamma, \rho, \$) ,$$

with $\delta(q, (t, a)) = p$ and $\gamma(q, (t, a)) = d$ iff $\Delta(q, t, a) = (d, p)$, and $\text{Dom}(\rho) = F$ with $\rho(q) = 1$ iff $q \in F$. For the example depicted in Fig. 2,

$$\delta(q_1, ((\text{root}, \text{intern}), a)) = q_2 \qquad \gamma(q_1, ((\text{root}, \text{intern}), a)) = \searrow$$
$$\delta(q_2, ((\text{right}, \text{leaf}), b) = q_1 \qquad \gamma(q_2, ((\text{right}, \text{leaf}), b) = \uparrow \qquad \rho(q_1) = 1 .$$

An SLT on $\Sigma_1, \Sigma_2 \uplus \{\$, 1\}$ is *DTWA-coherent* if its initial output symbol is $\$$.

Let us now provide an algorithm for random generation up to isomorphism of DTWAs. We reuse for this purpose the SLT generation algorithm, and need the following two propositions.

Proposition 2. *The function τ is a bijection from DTWAs to DTWA-coherent SLTs. Moreover, for every DTWA $\mathcal{A}$, $\tau(\mathcal{A})$ is complete (resp. accessible) if and only if $\mathcal{A}$ is complete (resp. accessible).*

Proposition 3. *Two DTWAs $\mathcal{A}_1$ and $\mathcal{A}_2$ are isomorphic if and only if $\tau(\mathcal{A}_1)$ and $\tau(\mathcal{A}_2)$ are isomorphic.*

Proof. It suffices to note that the same isomorphism holds between $\mathcal{A}_1$ and $\mathcal{A}_2$ and $\tau(\mathcal{A}_1)$ and $\tau(\mathcal{A}_2)$.

Moreover, the restrictions introduced in Sect. 2 are helpful in order to generate *nicer* tree walking automata. Indeed, in a tree walking automaton, a transition labeled by $((t, a), d)$, with $(t, a) \in \Sigma_1$ and $d \in \Sigma_2$ is *useless* (i.e. can never be fired) in either of the following two cases:

1. t is in $\{root\} \times \{internal, leaf\}$ and $d = \uparrow$, or
2. t is in $\{root, left, right\} \times \{leaf\}$ and $d \in \{\swarrow, \searrow\}$.

Let us denote by r^{DTWA} the subset of $\Sigma_1 \times \Sigma_2$ of the pairs (a, b) that do not match any of the above two cases. The class E_n^{DTWA} of useful DTWA-coherent SLTs with n states then contains $\mathcal{C}_n(\Sigma_1, \Sigma_2 \uplus \{\$, 1\}, r^{DTWA}, \{\$\}, \{1\})$ and is included in $\mathcal{D}_n(\Sigma_1, \Sigma_2 \uplus \{\$, 1\}, r^{DTWA}, \{\$\}, \{1\})$. Thus, random generation of DTWAs can be performed by first using Proposition 1 to obtain a SLT $\mathcal{T}$ and then by computing $\tau^{-1}(\mathcal{T})$.

3.3 Experimentation: From DTWAs to Top-Down Tree Automata

Tree walking automata enjoy a tight connection with several logical formalisms [7,9], including some XPath fragments. Formula satisfiability then reduces to the emptiness of the language of a tree walking automaton. Nevertheless, the latter problem is rather hard to decide: it is an EXPTIME-complete problem, for which the known algorithms consist essentially in constructing an exponentially larger equivalent top-down tree automaton, and (on the fly) checking this automaton for emptiness in linear time.

We have implemented a prototype tool for converting DTWAs into coaccessible nondeterministic top-down tree automata (under the form of RELAX NG grammars [6]). Given a DTWA with n states, the resulting top-down tree automaton can hold as many as $\mathcal{O}(2^{n^2})$ states, that encode which pairs (p, q) of states allow a run of the DTWA to start from state p on a given tree node and return to it in state q without ever visiting its parent node.

We ran the algorithm on 100 randomly generated incomplete DTWA for each n and report the mean number of states in the computed equivalent top-down tree automaton in Fig. 3. Due to very high standard deviation values, we exclude the 10 smallest and 10 largest output automata from the mean computation, and display their mean number of states on separate plots. All three plots display an exponential behaviour. Overall, the translation results in a $\mathcal{O}(2^n)$ size increase on average, which is significantly better than the worst-case $\mathcal{O}(2^{n^2})$ bound.

4 Application to Top-Down Tree Automata

4.1 Deterministic Top-Down Tree Automata

In this section, $\mathcal{F}$ denotes a finite ranked alphabet, i.e. there is an arity function ar from $\mathcal{F}$ into $\mathbb{N}$. We denote by $\mathcal{F}_i$ the subset of elements C of $\mathcal{F}$ such that $ar(C) = i$. We assume that $\$ \notin \mathcal{F}$. Let $\overline{\mathcal{F}} = \{(f, i) \mid f \in \mathcal{F} \setminus \mathcal{F}_0, \ 1 \leq i \leq ar(f)\}$.

A *deterministic top-down tree automata* (DTDA) is a tuple $(Q, \mathcal{F}, \theta, q_{init})$ where Q is a finite set of *states* satisfying $0 \notin Q$, $q_{init} \in Q$ is the *initial state*,

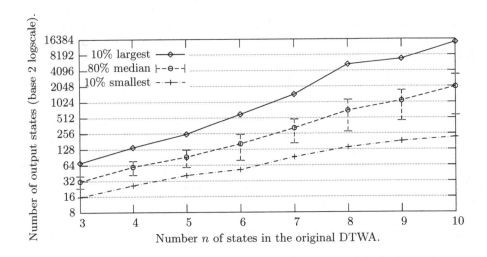

Fig. 3. Average number of states in the 10 smallest, the 10 largest, and the 80 median top-down tree automata obtained from transforming 100 2-letter DTWAs with n states

and θ is a partial *transition function* mapping elements of $Q \times \mathcal{F}_i$ to Q^i (for all $i \geq 1$) and elements of $Q \times \mathcal{F}_0$ to 0. One can inductively define accessible states of a DTDA by: the initial state q_{init} is accessible and for every $f \notin \mathcal{F}_0$, if q is accessible and $\theta(q, f) = (q_1, \ldots, q_{ar(f)})$ then the q_i's are accessible. A DTDA is *complete* if $Q \times (\mathcal{F} \setminus \mathcal{F}_0) \subseteq \text{Dom}(\theta)$. For more information on top-down tree automata, the reader is referred to [16].

Let $\mathcal{A}_1 = (Q_1, \mathcal{F}, \theta_1, q_{\text{init}1})$ and $\mathcal{A}_2 = (Q_2, \mathcal{F}, \theta_2, q_{\text{init}2})$ be two DTDAs. An *isomorphism* φ is a bijective function φ from Q_1 to Q_2 such that (1) for every state q, every $f \in \mathcal{F} \setminus \mathcal{F}_0$, $\theta_1(q, f) = (q_1, \ldots, q_{ar(f)})$ iff $\theta_2(\varphi(q), f) = (\varphi(q_1), \ldots, \varphi(q_{ar(f)}))$, (2) $\varphi(q_{\text{init}1}) = q_{\text{init}2}$, and (3) for every state q, every $C \in \mathcal{F}_0$, $\theta_1(q, C) = 0$ iff $\theta_2(\varphi(q), C) = 0$.

4.2   From SLTs to DTDAs

We define in this section a bijection ψ from DTDAs to a subclass of SLTs, called *DTDA-coherent* SLTs, that contains all the complete SLTs. For every DTDA $\mathcal{A} = (Q, \mathcal{F}, \theta, q_{\text{init}})$, let $\psi(\mathcal{A})$ be the SLT

$$\psi(\mathcal{A}) = (\overline{\mathcal{F}}, \mathcal{P}(\mathcal{F}_0) \uplus \{\$\}, Q, q_{\text{init}}, \delta, \gamma, \rho, \$)$$

defined by: $\gamma(q, (f, i)) = \emptyset$ and $\delta(q, (f, i)) = p_i$ iff $\theta(q) = (p_1, \ldots, p_n)$, and $\rho(q) = \{A \in \mathcal{F}_0 \mid \theta(q, A) = 0\}$ iff this set is not empty, and $\rho(q)$ is undefined otherwise. For example, let $\mathcal{F}_0 = \{A, B\}$, $\mathcal{F}_1 = \{h\}$ and $\mathcal{F}_2 = \{f\}$ in $\mathcal{A}_{\text{exe}} = (\{q_1, q_2\}, \mathcal{F}, \theta_{\text{exe}}, \{q_1\})$ with $\theta_{\text{exe}}(q_1, f) = (q_1, q_2)$, $\theta_{\text{exe}}(q_2, h) = q_2$, and $\theta_{\text{exe}}(q_1, A) = \theta_{\text{exe}}(q_1, B) = \theta_{\text{exe}}(q_2, A) = 0$. This entails $\overline{\mathcal{F}} = \{(h, 1), (f, 1), (f, 2)\}$ in the SLT $\psi(\mathcal{A}_{\text{exe}})$ depicted in Fig. 4.

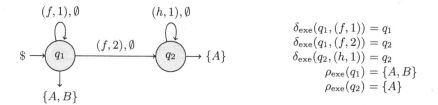

Fig. 4. The SLT $\psi(\mathcal{A}_{\mathrm{exe}}) = (\overline{\mathcal{F}}, \mathcal{P}^*(\{A, B\}) \uplus \{\$\}, \{q_1, q_2\}, q_1, \delta_{\mathrm{exe}}, \gamma_{\mathrm{exe}}, \rho_{\mathrm{exe}}, \$)$

A SLT $(\overline{\mathcal{F}}, \mathcal{P}^*(\mathcal{F}_0) \uplus \{\$\}, Q, q_{\mathrm{init}}, \delta, \gamma, \rho, \$)$ is *DTDA-coherent* if (1) for every state q, every $(f, i) \in \overline{\mathcal{F}}$, $\delta(q, (f, i))$ is defined iff $\delta(q, (f, j))$ is defined for all $j \in [1, ar(f)]$, (2) $\gamma(q, (f, i))$ is either undefined or equal to $\emptyset$, and (3) its initial output is $\$$.

Proposition 4. *The function ψ is a bijection from DTDA to DTDA-coherent SLTs. Moreover, for every DTDA $\mathcal{A}$, $\psi(\mathcal{A})$ is complete (resp. accessible) if and only if $\mathcal{A}$ is complete (resp. accessible).*

Proof. If $\mathcal{A}$ is a DTDA, then it is clear that $\psi(\mathcal{A})$ is DTDA-coherent. Now let $\mathcal{A}_1 = (Q_1, \mathcal{F}, \theta_1, q_{\mathrm{init1}})$ and $\mathcal{A}_2 = (Q_2, \mathcal{F}, \theta_2, q_{\mathrm{init2}})$ be DTDAs such that $\psi(\mathcal{A}_1) = \psi(\mathcal{A}_2)$. By definition of ψ, $Q_1 = Q_2$ and $q_{\mathrm{init1}} = q_{\mathrm{init2}}$. Set $\psi(\mathcal{A}_1) = \psi(\mathcal{A}_2) = (\overline{\mathcal{F}}, \mathcal{P}(\mathcal{F}_0) \uplus \{\$\}, Q_1, q_{\mathrm{init1}}, \delta, \gamma, \rho, \$)$. Reasoning on δ shows that θ_1 and θ_2 are equal for letters in $\mathcal{F} \setminus \mathcal{F}_0$. Reasoning on ρ shows that θ_1 and θ_2 are equal for letters in $\mathcal{F}_0$. It follows that ψ is injective. The remaining points of the proposition are straightforward verifications.

Proposition 5. *Two DTDAs $\mathcal{A}_1$ and $\mathcal{A}_2$ are isomorphic if and only if $\psi(\mathcal{A}_1)$ and $\psi(\mathcal{A}_2)$ are isomorphic.*

Proof. It suffices to note that the same isomorphism holds between $\mathcal{A}_1$ and $\mathcal{A}_2$ and $\psi(\mathcal{A}_1)$ and $\psi(\mathcal{A}_2)$.

Let $r^{\mathrm{DTDA}} = \overline{\mathcal{F}} \times \{\emptyset\}$. The class E_n^{DTDA} of DTDA-coherent SLTs with n states contains $\mathcal{C}_n(\overline{\mathcal{F}}, \mathcal{P}(\mathcal{F}_0) \uplus \{\$\}, r^{\mathrm{DTDA}}, \{\$\}, \mathcal{P}^*(\mathcal{F}_0))$ and is included in $\mathcal{D}_n(\overline{\mathcal{F}}, \mathcal{P}(\mathcal{F}_0) \uplus \{\$\}, r^{\mathrm{DTDA}}, \{\$\}, \mathcal{P}^*(\mathcal{F}_0))$. Thus, random generation of DTDAs can be performed using Proposition 1 to obtain a SLT $\mathcal{T}$ and by computing $\psi^{-1}(\mathcal{T})$.

5   Conclusion

In this paper we define a rejection algorithm to randomly and uniformly generate sequential letter-to-letter transducers with some restrictions. We also exhibit two bijections from this class of transducers to the class of deterministic tree walking automata and deterministic top-down tree automata respectively, and report on an empirical evaluation of a $\mathcal{O}(2^n)$ average complexity instead of a $\mathcal{O}(2^{n^2})$ worst-case bound for turning a deterministic tree walking automaton into an equivalent nondeterministic top-down tree automaton.

The approach we propose in this paper can easily be extended to some other classes of finite automata, like deterministic pebble tree walking automata. A much less obvious variation would be needed in order to randomly generate deterministic bottom-up tree automata or hedge automata.

References

1. Wulf, M.D., Doyen, L., Henzinger, T.A., Raskin, J.F.: Antichains: A new algorithm for checking universality of finite automata. In: Ball, T., Jones, R.B. (eds.) CAV 2006. LNCS, vol. 4144, pp. 17–30. Springer, Heidelberg (2006)
2. van Glabbeek, R.J., Ploeger, B.: Five determinisation algorithms. In: Ibarra, O.H., Ravikumar, B. (eds.) CIAA 2008. LNCS, vol. 5148, pp. 161–170. Springer, Heidelberg (2008)
3. Schewe, S.: Büchi complementation made tight. In: [17], pp. 661–672
4. Bassino, F., David, J., Nicaud, C.: On the average complexity of Moore's state minimization algorithm. In: [17], pp. 123–134
5. Neven, F.: Automata theory for XML researchers. SIGMOD Record 31(3), 39–46 (2002)
6. Murata, M., Lee, D., Mani, M., Kawaguchi, K.: Taxonomy of XML schema languages using formal language theory. ACM Transactions on Internet Technology 5(4), 660–704 (2005)
7. Engelfriet, J., Hoogeboom, H.J.: Tree-walking pebble automata. In: Karhumäki, J., Maurer, H.A., Paun, G., Rozenberg, G. (eds.) Jewels are Forever, pp. 72–83. Springer, Heidelberg (1999)
8. Bojańczyk, M., Colcombet, T.: Tree-walking automata do not recognize all regular languages. SIAM Journal on Computing 38(2), 658–701 (2008)
9. ten Cate, B., Segoufin, L.: XPath, transitive closure logic, and nested tree walking automata. In: Lenzerini, M., Lembo, D. (eds.) PODS 2008, pp. 251–260 (2008)
10. Bassino, F., Nicaud, C.: Enumeration and random generation of accessible automata. Theoretical Computer Science 381(1-3), 86–104 (2007)
11. Bassino, F., David, J., Nicaud, C.: Enumeration and random generation of possibly incomplete deterministic automata. Pure Mathematics and Applications (2009)
12. Champarnaud, J.M., Paranthoën, T.: Random generation of DFAs. Theoretical Computer Science 330(2), 221–235 (2005)
13. Bassino, F., David, J., Nicaud, C.: REGAL: A library to randomly and exhaustively generate automata. In: Holub, J., Žďárek, J. (eds.) CIAA 2007. LNCS, vol. 4783, pp. 303–305. Springer, Heidelberg (2007)
14. Tabakov, D., Vardi, M.Y.: Experimental evaluation of classical automata constructions. In: Sutcliffe, G., Voronkov, A. (eds.) LPAR 2005. LNCS, vol. 3835, pp. 396–411. Springer, Heidelberg (2005)
15. Chen, Y.F., Farzan, A., Clarke, E.M., Tsay, Y.K., Wang, B.Y.: Learning minimal separating DFA's for compositional verification. In: Kowalewski, S., Philippou, A. (eds.) TACAS 2009. LNCS, vol. 5505. Springer, Heidelberg (2009)
16. Comon, H., Dauchet, M., Gilleron, R., Löding, C., Jacquemard, F., Lugiez, D., Tison, S., Tommasi, M.: Tree Automata Techniques and Applications (2007)
17. Albers, S., Marion, J.Y. (eds.): STACS 2009. Dagstuhl Seminar Proceedings, vol. 09001 (2009)

Hedge Pattern Partial Derivative*

Taro Suzuki[1] and Satoshi Okui[2]

[1] University of Aizu, Japan
taro@u-aizu.ac.jp
[2] Chubu University, Japan
okui@cs.chubu.ac.jp

Abstract. We propose hedge pattern partial derivatives, an extension of Antimirov's partial derivatives, in order to give an operational semantics of pattern matching of regular hedge expression patterns, which is crucial in XML processing. We show that correct and small matching automata can be constructed from hedge pattern partial derivatives.

1 Introduction

As the importance of XML has been increasing, the study of statically typed XML processing languages has gained in popularity. The pioneer of such languages is XDuce[11] and there are several subsequent ones such as CDuce[2], Xtatic[9] and XQuery[3]. One of the prominent features of these languages is matching of hedges by regular hedge expression patterns. A regular hedge expression pattern is an adaptation of regular expressions to hedges, and also it contains several positions marked by several variables. When a hedge h is matched by a regular hedge expression pattern p, subhedges of h corresponding to the marked positions in p are output as the result of matching.

We propose *hedge pattern partial derivatives* of a regular hedge expression pattern, which gives an operational semantics of regular hedge expression pattern matching. Hedge pattern partial derivative is an extension of partial derivative of a regular (word) expression, proposed by Antimirov [1], to regular hedge expression patterns. From hedge pattern partial derivatives of a regular hedge expression pattern p, a matching automaton performing matching against p is constructed such that the upper bound of the number of states is as many as the number of labels and names involved in the pattern, though it is often much smaller.

The paper is organized as follows. In Sect. 2 we present the formal definitions of syntax and semantics (denotation) of regular hedge expression patterns and a denotational semantics of pattern matching. Section 3 describes hedge pattern partial derivatives and its property. Operational semantics of pattern matching by hedge pattern partial derivatives and its correctness with respect

---

* This work has been partially supported by JSPS Grants-in-Aid for Scientific Research (B) No.20300001 and JSPS Grants-in-Aid for Scientific Research (C) No.19540042.

S. Maneth (Ed.): CIAA 2009, LNCS 5642, pp. 125–134, 2009.

to the denotational semantics of matching is also given. In Sect. 4 a construction of matching automata from hedge pattern partial derivatives and operational semantics of pattern matching by matching automata is presented. Finally, in Sect. 5 we conclude this paper with some remarks.

2   Regular Hedge Expression Pattern

We denote the set of the subsets of a set X by 2^X and the set of the finite subsets of a set X by $\mathbf{Fin}(X)$. We denote sets of *labels*, of *names* and of *variables* by **Lab**, **Name** and **Var**, respectively. We assume that **Lab** and **Name** are finite and **Var** countably infinite and that they are pairwisely disjoint. The empty sequence is denoted by ε.

A *hedge* h over **Lab** is a sequence of (possibly empty) *unranked trees*. An unranked tree with label $a \in \mathbf{Lab}$ is of the form $a[h]$, where h is a hedge. We often use the following equivalent definition: $h ::= \varepsilon \mid a[h]\,h$, where $a \in \mathbf{Lab}$. The set of hedges over **Lab** is denoted by $\mathbf{H}$. An unranked tree such as $a[\varepsilon]$ is simply written $a[\,]$.

We follow [12] for the definition of regular hedge expression patterns. A *regular hedge expression pattern* (*pattern*, for short) p over **Lab**, **Name** and **Var** is defined as follows:

$$p ::= 0 \mid 1 \mid a[n] \mid p \cdot p \mid p + p \mid p^* \mid p@x .$$

Here $n \in \mathbf{Name}$, $a \in \mathbf{Lab}$ and $x \in \mathbf{Var}$. The pattern of the form $a[n]$ and $p@x$ are called *tree patterns* with label a and *variable binders*, respectively. The set of patterns over **Lab**, **Name** and **Var** is denoted by $\mathcal{T}_{\mathrm{Pat}}$. A pattern in $\mathcal{T}_{\mathrm{Pat}}$ is associated with the *name definition*, a function from **Name** to $\mathcal{T}_{\mathrm{Pat}}$. In this paper we always use the symbol E to denote a name definition.

We say a pattern p' is reachable from a pattern p if either p' is a subpattern of p, or p' is reachable from a pattern $E(n)$, where n is a name occurring in p. Let $\mathcal{V}_{\mathrm{r}}(p)$ be the union of sets of variables occurring in each reachable pattern from p. We call $\mathcal{V}_{\mathrm{r}}(p)$ a set of *reachable variables* from a pattern p. For instance, $\mathcal{V}_{\mathrm{r}}(((a[n_1]@y) \cdot c[n_3])@x) = \{x, y, z, w\}$ if $E(n_1) = (b[n_2] + 1)@z$, $E(n_2) = 1@w$ and $E(n_3) = 1$.

A pattern p is *linear* if every reachable pattern p' from p, i.e., a pattern reachable via the associated name definition E from p, satisfies the following conditions.

- $\mathcal{V}_{\mathrm{r}}(p_1) \cap \mathcal{V}_{\mathrm{r}}(p_2) = \emptyset$ if $p' = p_1 \cdot p_2$,
- $\mathcal{V}_{\mathrm{r}}(p_1) = \mathcal{V}_{\mathrm{r}}(p_2)$ if $p' = p_1 + p_2$,
- $\mathcal{V}_{\mathrm{r}}(p_1) = \emptyset$ if $p' = p_1^*$,
- $x \notin \mathcal{V}_{\mathrm{r}}(p_1)$ if $p' = p_1@x$.

The pattern $((a[n_1]@y) \cdot c[n_3])@x$ in the previous example is linear. If we, however, replace the definition of n_1 with $E(n_1) = (b[n_1] + 1)@z$ then $E(n_1)$ is not linear and hence the pattern is not linear either. In this paper we assume that *every pattern is linear*;

As Emir did in [7] for regular word expression patterns, we regard a pattern p as a regular set of hedges over $\mathbf{Fin}(\mathcal{V}_r(p)) \times \mathbf{Lab}$ such that each element in the regular set is regarded as an encoding of a pair of a hedge over $\mathbf{Lab}$ matched by p and a binding environment, a function assigning a hedge to a variable as its value, yielded by the matching. We define such hedges with labels annotated with sets of variables as follows.

Definition 1 (Annotated Hedges). *An annotated hedge μ over* $\mathbf{Lab}$ *and* $\mathbf{Var}$ *is defined as follows:* $\mu \ ::= \ \varepsilon \ | \ a^X[\mu]\,\mu$, *where* $a \in \mathbf{Lab}$ *and* $X \in \mathbf{Fin}(\mathbf{Var})$. *The set of annotated hedges over* $\mathbf{Lab}$ *and* $\mathbf{Var}$ *is denoted by* $\mathbf{AH}$.

The projection function proj $: \mathbf{AH} \to \mathbf{H}$ *of a hedge from an annotated hedge is defined as follows.*

$$\mathsf{proj}(\varepsilon) = \varepsilon \qquad \mathsf{proj}(a^X[\mu_1]\,\mu_2) = a[\mathsf{proj}(\mu_1)]\,\mathsf{proj}(\mu_2)$$

The extraction function env $: \mathbf{AH} \times \mathbf{Var} \to \mathbf{H}$ *of the value of a variable from an annotated hedge is defined as follows.*

$$\begin{aligned}
\mathsf{env}(\varepsilon, x) &= \varepsilon \\
\mathsf{env}(a^X[\mu_1]\,\mu_2, x) &= a[\mathsf{proj}(\mu_1)]\,\mathsf{env}(\mu_2, x) && \textit{if } x \in X \\
\mathsf{env}(a^X[\mu_1]\,\mu_2, x) &= \mathsf{env}(\mu_1, x)\,\mathsf{env}(\mu_2, x) && \textit{otherwise}
\end{aligned}$$

For simplicity we usually omit the annotation $\emptyset$ of the labels. Thus $a^\emptyset[b^{\{x,y\}}[\,]\,]$ is simply written $a[b^{\{x,y\}}[\,]\,]$.

Thus we regard a pattern p as a regular set of annotated hedges, called the denotation of p.

Definition 2 (Denotation of Patterns). *The denotation of a pattern p, denoted by* $[\![p]\!]$, *is a set of annotated hedges, which are regarded as hedges matched by p together with their bindings. The denotation function* $[\![\,\cdot\,]\!]$ *is the least solution of the following system of equations.*

$$\begin{aligned}
[\![0]\!] &= \emptyset & [\![1]\!] &= \{\varepsilon\} \\
[\![a[n]]\!] &= \{a^\emptyset[\mu] \mid \mu \in [\![E(n)]\!]\} & [\![p_1 \cdot p_2]\!] &= [\![p_1]\!] \cdot [\![p_2]\!] \\
[\![p_1 + p_2]\!] &= [\![p_1]\!] \cup [\![p_2]\!] & [\![p^*]\!] &= [\![p]\!]^* \\
[\![p@x]\!] &= \{\mu \mathord{\uparrow} x \mid \mu \in [\![p]\!]\}
\end{aligned}$$

The set operator $\cdot$ *and* $*$ *are defined as usual. The function* $\mathord{\uparrow}: \mathbf{AH} \times \mathbf{Var} \to \mathbf{AH}$ *is inductively defined as follows:* $\varepsilon \mathord{\uparrow} x = \varepsilon$ *and* $a^X[\mu_1]\mu_2 \mathord{\uparrow} x = a^{X \cup \{x\}}[\mu_1](\mu_2 \mathord{\uparrow} x)$.

The last case of the above definition, i.e., $[\![p@x]\!]$, is most crucial; it annotates x to the labels occurring in the top level of the annotated hedges in $[\![p]\!]$, which enables env to extract the values bound to x. Note that this annotation relies on linearity; if a non-linear pattern like $q = a[n]@x \cdot b[n]@x$ with $E(n) = 1$ is allowed, $[\![q]\!]$ contains $\mu = a^{\{x\}}[\,]\,b^{\{x\}}[\,]$ and hence $ev(\mu, x) = a[\,]\,b[\,]$, the concatenation of different values of x. The restriction to linear patterns prevents such problems. The linearity condition is weaker than Emir's restriction that only the concatenations of variable binders are allowed [7], which is included in the linearity condition.

Example 1. Consider the pattern $p = (a[n_1] \cdot b[n_2]^* @y)@x \cdot c[n_2]$ with $E(n_1) = a[n_2]@z$ and $E(n_2) = 1$. From Definition 2, $\mu = a^{\{x\}}[a^{\{z\}}[\,]]\, b^{\{x,y\}}[\,]\, c[\,] \in [\![p]\!]$. Then $\mathsf{env}(\mu, x) = a[a[\,]]\, b[\,]$, $\mathsf{env}(\mu, y) = b[\,]$ and $\mathsf{env}(\mu, z) = a[\,]$ stand for the values of x, y and z, respectively, obtained from the matching of the hedge $\mathsf{proj}(\mu) = a[a[\,]]\, b[\,]\, c[\,]$ by p.

This implies a denotational semantics of matching of regular hedge expression patterns against hedges.

Definition 3 (Denotational Semantics of Matching). *A hedge h is matched by a pattern p, yielding a binding environment V if and only if*

$$\exists \mu.[\mathsf{proj}(\mu) = h \,\wedge\, \mu \in [\![p]\!] \,\wedge\, \forall x \in \mathcal{V}_\mathrm{r}(p).\, \mathsf{env}(\mu, x) = V(x)] \ .$$

Hence matching of h by p is reduced to finding an annotated hedge belonging to $[\![p]\!]$ and projected to h.

3   Hedge Pattern Partial Derivatives

In [1] Antimirov proposed *partial derivative*, a generalization of Brzozowski's word derivative[5] in a nondeterministic way; while Brzozowski's derivative leads to the construction of deterministic finite automata, Antimirov's partial derivative leads to the construction of *nondeterministic* finite automata. The most notable property of partial derivatives is the following: given a (word) regular expression e over an alphabet Σ, the cardinality of the set of partial derivatives of e with respect to Σ^* is at most the number of symbols in e plus 1. Furthermore, the cardinality is often much less than its upper bound. Because the set of partial derivatives of e corresponds to the set of states of the non-deterministic automaton constructed from partial derivatives, the obtained automaton is much smaller than the corresponding position automaton[10,14,4].

In this section we extend Antimirov's partial derivative. Our extension is twofold: one is from words to hedges, and the other is to include the result of matching of a pattern p against a hedge h, namely an annotated hedge, into the result of partial derivatives of p with respect to h. We omit proofs of some statements here; see [15] for more details.

Antimirov's partial derivative is based on a so-called *nondeterministic linear factorization*: for instance, the regular expression $a^*(ab + 1)$ over an alphabet $\{a, b\}$ is semantically equivalent to $1 + a \cdot a^*(ab + 1) + a \cdot b$. Note that there are two summands starting with the same symbol a and no summand starting with b. Considering $a^*(ab + 1)$ and b as states of an automaton, the summands correspond to nondeterministic transition from $a^*(ab + 1)$ by reading the symbol a and hence this linear factorization is considered as nondeterministic.

Given regular expression r, there are several nondeterministic linear factorization semantically equal to r. In order to determine the linear factorization to r uniquely, Antimirov defined a *linear form* of r, which gives all the summands other than 1 in the uniquely chosen nondeterministic linear factorization of r [1]. We first generalize linear forms by Antimirov to *hedge pattern linear forms*.

Definition 4. *A* hedge pattern monomial *is a quadruple* $\langle a, X, p, q \rangle$, *where* $a \in$ **Lab**, $X \in$ **Fin(Var)**, $p, q \in \mathcal{T}_{\text{Pat}}$. *A* hedge pattern linear form *is a finite set of hedge pattern monomials. The set of hedge pattern linear forms is denoted by* **PLin**. *The hedge pattern linear form of a pattern* p, *denoted by* $\text{plf}(p)$, *is defined as follows:*

$$\text{plf}(0) = \emptyset \qquad\qquad \text{plf}(1) = \emptyset$$
$$\text{plf}(a[n]) = \{\langle a, \emptyset, E(n), 1 \rangle\} \qquad \text{plf}(q_1 \cdot p_2) = \text{plf}(q_1) \odot p_2$$
$$\text{plf}(r_1 \cdot p_2) = \text{plf}(r_1) \odot p_2 \cup \text{plf}(p_2) \qquad \text{plf}(p_1 + p_2) = \text{plf}(p_1) \cup \text{plf}(p_2)$$
$$\text{plf}(p^*) = \text{plf}(p) \odot p^* \qquad\qquad \text{plf}(p@x) = \text{plf}(p) \uparrow x$$

where $\varepsilon \notin [\![q_1]\!]$ *and* $\varepsilon \in [\![r_1]\!]$. *The functions* $\odot : \textbf{PLin} \times \mathcal{T}_{\text{Pat}} \rightarrow \textbf{PLin}$ *and* $\uparrow : \textbf{PLin} \times \textbf{Var} \rightarrow \textbf{PLin}$ *are defined as follows:*

$$\emptyset \odot p = \emptyset \qquad\qquad L \odot 1 = L$$
$$L \odot 0 = \emptyset \qquad\qquad \{\langle a, X, r, 1 \rangle\} \odot q = \{\langle a, X, r, q \rangle\}$$
$$\{\langle a, X, r, 0 \rangle\} \odot q = \emptyset \qquad \{\langle a, X, r, p \rangle\} \odot q = \{\langle a, X, r, p \cdot q \rangle\}$$
$$(L_1 \cup L_2) \odot p = L_1 \odot p \cup L_2 \odot p$$

and $L \uparrow x = \{\langle a, X \cup \{x\}, p_1, p_2@x \rangle \mid \langle a, X, p_1, p_2 \rangle\}$ *for all* $p, q \in \mathcal{T}_{\text{Pat}} \backslash \{0, 1\}$, $r, p_1, p_2 \in \mathcal{T}_{\text{Pat}}$, $L, L_1, L_2 \in \textbf{PLin}$, $a \in \textbf{Lab}$, $X \in \textbf{Fin(Var)}$, $x \in \textbf{Var}$.

The above definition refers to the denotation of patterns. But for any pattern p the condition $\varepsilon \in [\![p]\!]$ is decidable by checking the syntactic structure of p. Hence the hedge pattern linear form of a pattern is computable in a syntactic way.

We adapt the notion of partial derivatives to regular hedge expression patterns using hedge pattern linear forms.

Definition 5 (Hedge Pattern Partial Derivative). *Let* p *be a regular hedge expression pattern and* h *a hedge. A hedge pattern partial derivative of* p *with respect to* h *is a pair of a pattern and an annotated hedge that belongs to the set* $\partial_h(p)$, *where* $\partial_h : \mathcal{T}_{\text{Pat}} \rightarrow \textbf{Fin}(\mathcal{T}_{\text{Pat}} \times \textbf{AH})$ *is defined as follows:*

$$\partial_\varepsilon(p) = \{\langle p, \varepsilon \rangle\} ,$$

$$\partial_{a[h_1]h_2}(p) = \left\{ \langle q_2, a^X[\mu_1]\mu_2 \rangle \;\middle|\; \begin{array}{l} \langle a, X, p_1, p_2 \rangle \in \text{plf}(p), \\ \exists q_1 [\langle q_1, \mu_1 \rangle \in \partial_{h_1}(p_1) \wedge \varepsilon \in [\![q_1]\!]], \\ \langle q_2, \mu_2 \rangle \in \partial_{h_2}(p_2) \end{array} \right\} .$$

It is extended for all $H \subseteq \textbf{H}$, $h \in \textbf{H}$, $p \in \mathcal{T}_{\text{Pat}}$ *and* $P \subseteq \mathcal{T}_{\text{Pat}}$ *as follows:*

$$\partial_H(p) = \bigcup_{h \in H} \partial_h(p) , \qquad \partial_h(P) = \bigcup_{p \in P} \partial_h(p) .$$

From Definition 5, an easy induction reveals that for any $p, q \in \mathcal{T}_{\text{Pat}}$, $h \in \textbf{H}$ and $\mu \in \textbf{AH}$ if $\langle q, \mu \rangle \in \partial_h(p)$ then $\text{proj}(\mu) = h$. Intuitively, a hedge pattern derivative $\langle q, \mu \rangle$ in $\partial_h(p)$ represents a *partial* matching of h by p. The word "partial" is derived from the fact $\{\mu\} \cdot [\![q]\!] \subseteq [\![p]\!]$, which shall be guaranteed by Proposition 1 later. Hence if $\varepsilon \in [\![q]\!]$ then μ, satisfying $\text{proj}(\mu) = h$, belongs to $[\![p]\!]$, which means that h is matched by p from Definition 3.

Example 2. Consider the pattern $p = a[n]^* \cdot a[n]@x \cdot b[n]^*$ with $E(n) = b[n]^*$. Let $q = b[n]^*$. From Definition 4 we obtain $\mathsf{plf}(p) = \{\langle a, \emptyset, q, p \rangle, \langle a, \{x\}, q, q \rangle\}$ and $\mathsf{plf}(q) = \{\langle b, \emptyset, q, q \rangle\}$.

Because of the presence of Kleene star at the top level of q, we know that $\varepsilon \in [\![q]\!]$ holds. Hence, from Definition 5 we obtain

$$\begin{aligned}
\partial_\varepsilon(q) &= \{\langle q, \varepsilon \rangle\} & \partial_{b[\,]}(q) &= \{\langle q, b[\,] \rangle\} \\
\partial_{a[\,]}(p) &= \{\langle p, a[\,] \rangle, \langle q, a^{\{x\}}[\,] \rangle\} & \partial_{a[b[\,]]}(p) &= \{\langle p, a[b[\,]] \rangle, \langle q, a^{\{x\}}[b[\,]] \rangle\} \\
\partial_{a[\,]\,b[\,]}(p) &= \{\langle q, a^{\{x\}}[\,]\,b[\,] \rangle\} & \partial_{a[b[\,]]\,b[\,]}(p) &= \{\langle q, a^{\{x\}}[b[\,]]\,b[\,] \rangle\} \\
\partial_{a[\,]\,a[b[\,]]}(p) &= \{\langle p, a[\,]\,a[b[\,]] \rangle, \langle q, a[\,]a^{\{x\}}[b[\,]] \rangle\}
\end{aligned}$$

Note that for some pattern p the set $\partial_{\mathbf{H}}(p)$ may be infinite due to the second elements of the hedge pattern partial derivatives; for instance, with $E(n) = \varepsilon$, we have $\langle a[n]^*, \mu \rangle \in \partial_{\mathbf{H}}(a[n]^*)$ where μ is a sequence of $a[\,]$ of arbitrary length. The following theorem, however, states that the set of the first elements of the hedge pattern partial derivatives of a pattern are finite.

Theorem 1. *Let $\|p\|$ be the number of labels in p and $\mathsf{pat} : 2^{T_{\mathrm{Pat}} \times \mathbf{AH}} \to 2^{T_{\mathrm{Pat}}}$ be a function defined as $\mathsf{pat}(X) = \{q \mid \langle q, \mu \rangle \in X\}$. For any $p \in T_{\mathrm{Pat}}$ the cardinality of $\mathsf{pat}(\partial_{\mathbf{H}}(p))$ is at most $\|p\| + 1$.*

The proof of this theorem is similar to that of Theorem 3.4 in [1]. We remark that the presence of names in p hardly changes the structure of the proof of Theorem 3.4 in [1].

Now we attempt to relate hedge pattern partial derivatives with the denotational matching semantics. First we introduce left quotients of sets of annotated hedges with respect to annotated hedges. Let A be a set of annotated hedges and μ an annotated hedge. Then $\mu^{-1}A$ is called the *left quotient* of A with respect to μ defined as $\mu^{-1}A = \{\mu' \mid \mu\mu' \in A\}$.

The left quotients and hedge pattern partial derivatives have the following relationship.

Proposition 1. *For any $p \in T_{\mathrm{Pat}}$ and $\mu \in \mathbf{AH}$,*

$$\bigcup_{\langle q, \mu \rangle \in \partial_{\mathsf{proj}(\mu)}(p)} [\![q]\!] = \mu^{-1}[\![p]\!]$$

An operational matching semantics by hedge pattern partial derivatives and its correctness with respect to the denotational matching semantics are immediately derived from the above proposition.

Theorem 2. *For any $p \in T_{\mathrm{Pat}}$ and $\mu \in \mathbf{AH}$, $\exists q.[\varepsilon \in [\![q]\!] \wedge \langle q, \mu \rangle \in \partial_{\mathsf{proj}(\mu)}(p)]$ if and only if $\mu \in [\![p]\!]$.*

Proof. The desired property is derived from the following equivalences.

$$\exists q.[\varepsilon \in [\![q]\!] \wedge \langle q, \mu \rangle \in \partial_h(p)] \iff \varepsilon \in \bigcup_{\langle q, \mu \rangle \in \partial_h(p)} [\![q]\!] \iff \varepsilon \in \mu^{-1}[\![p]\!] \iff \mu \in [\![p]\!]$$

The second equivalence stems from Proposition 1.   □

Corollary 1 (Matching Semantics by Hedge Pattern Partial Derivatives). *A hedge h is matched by a pattern p, yielding a binding environment V if and only if*

$$\exists \mu \, [\exists q.[\varepsilon \in [\![q]\!] \wedge \langle q, \mu \rangle \in \partial_h(p)] \wedge \forall x \in \mathcal{V}_r(p).\mathsf{env}(\mu, x) = V(x)] \, .$$

Example 3. Consider the pattern p and the name definition shown in Example 2. Matching of p against the hedge $a[\,]\,a[b[\,]]$ is performed by computing hedge pattern partial derivatives in $\partial_{a[\,]\,a[b[\,]]}(p)$; from Example 2 they are $\langle p, a[\,]\,a[b[\,]]\rangle$ and $\langle q, a[\,]\,a^{\{x\}}[b[\,]]\rangle$. Since p contains $a[n]@x$, the condition $\varepsilon \in [\![p]\!]$ does not hold. Hence $a[\,]\,a[b[\,]]$ is not included in $[\![p]\!]$. On the other hand, we have already known that $\varepsilon \in [\![q]\!]$ holds and hence $a[\,]\,a^{\{x\}}[b[\,]] \in [\![p]\!]$. Therefore, $a[\,]a[b[\,]]$ matches by p and the value of x is $a[b[\,]]$.

4 Construction of Matching Automata

As demonstrated in the previous section, we can perform pattern matching using hedge pattern partial derivatives. If all the hedge pattern partial derivatives of a pattern p with respect to **H** are computed in advance, we can directly construct a pattern matching automaton and perform pattern matching using it. In this section we present a construction of pattern matching automata from partial derivatives of patterns.

Definition 6. *A matching automaton is a 6-tuple* $\langle Q, \mathbf{Lab}, \mathbf{Var}, I, F, \tau \rangle$, *where Q is the set of states, I the set of the initial states, F the set of the final states and τ the set of transition relations, a subset of* $Q \times \mathbf{Fin}(\mathbf{Var}) \times \mathbf{Lab} \times Q \times Q$.
If $(q, X, a, q', q'') \in \tau$ *then it is denoted by* $q \xrightarrow{X:a[q']} q''$. *The acceptance relation on* $\mathbf{H} \times Q \times \mathbf{AH}$ *for a matching automaton* $\mathcal{M}$, *denoted by* $\mathcal{M} \vdash h \in q \Rightarrow \mu$, *is defined by the the following derivation rules:*

(T-Fin)
$$\frac{q \in F}{\mathcal{M} \vdash \varepsilon \in q \Rightarrow \varepsilon}$$

(T-Lab)
$$\frac{q \xrightarrow{X:a[q_1]} q_2 \quad \mathcal{M} \vdash h_1 \in q_1 \Rightarrow \mu_1 \quad \mathcal{M} \vdash h_2 \in q_2 \Rightarrow \mu_2}{\mathcal{M} \vdash a[h_1]\,h_2 \in q \Rightarrow a^X[\mu_1]\,\mu_2} \, .$$

The matching automaton defined above is the same as the one presented in [12] except for the absence of ε-transitions. Note that if a pattern has no variable binder then the obtained matching automaton is essentially regarded as an NFHA(NFA), a nondeterministic finite hedge automaton with NFA for accepting horizontal languages[6].

Definition 7. *The matching automaton* $\mathcal{M}_p$ *constructed from p is a 6-tuple* $\langle Q_p, \mathbf{Lab}, \mathbf{Var}, \{p\}, F_p, \tau_p \rangle$ *such that*

$$Q_p = \mathsf{pat}(\partial_{\mathbf{H}}(p) \cup \bigcup_{n \in \mathbf{Name}} \partial_{\mathbf{H}}(E(n)))$$
$$F_p = \{q \in Q \mid \varepsilon \in [\![q]\!]\}$$
$$\tau_p = \{q \xrightarrow{X:a[q_1]} q_2 \mid \langle a, X, q_1, q_2 \rangle \in \mathsf{plf}(q)\} \, .$$

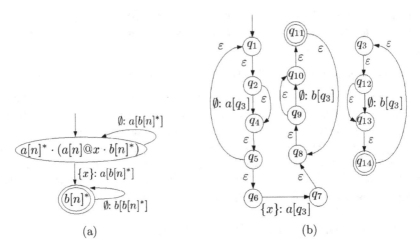

Fig. 1. Matching automata constructed by (a) hedge pattern partial derivative and (b) Thompson's method

Example 4. The automaton constructed from the pattern p in Example 2 by hedge pattern partial derivatives is shown in Fig. 1(a). On the other hand, Fig. 1(b) presents a matching automaton constructed by the method described in [12], which is essentially an adaptation of Thompson's method to regular hedge expression patterns. The number of states in the former automaton is much less than the latter.

Actually the automaton in Fig. 1(a) has much less states than its theoretical upper bound stated in the following theorem.

Theorem 3. *The size of Q_p is at most* $\|p\| + \sum_{n \in \mathbf{Name}} \|E(n)\| + |\mathbf{Name}| + 1$.

Proof. An immediate consequence of Theorem 1.   □

From the above theorem the upper bound of the number of the states of the matching automaton constructed from the pattern shown in Example 4 is $\|(a[n]^* \cdot (a[n]@x \cdot b[n]^*)\| + \|b[n]^*\| + |\{n\}| + 1 = 4$. The automaton shown in Fig. 1(a), however, has 2 states, as many as the half of the upper bound.

The following theorem states the relationship between the acceptance relation for a matching automaton constructed from p and the hedge pattern partial derivatives of p.

Theorem 4. $\mathcal{M}_p \vdash \mathsf{proj}(\mu) \in p \Rightarrow \mu$ *if and only if* $\exists q.[\varepsilon \in [\![q]\!] \wedge \langle q, \mu \rangle \in \partial_{\mathsf{proj}(\mu)}(p)]$.

Proof. We only show the only if part of the theorem. The if part is proved similarly. The proof is done by induction on the structure of μ. If $\mu = \varepsilon$ the relation $\mathcal{M}_p \vdash \varepsilon \in p \Rightarrow \varepsilon$ is equivalent to $\varepsilon \in [\![p]\!]$ from (T-Fin). Since $\partial_\varepsilon(p) = \langle p, \varepsilon \rangle$, the property holds for the base case.

Suppose $\mu = a^X[\mu_1]\,\mu_2$. If $\mathcal{M}_p \vdash a[\mathsf{proj}(\mu_1)]\,\mathsf{proj}(\mu_2) \in p \Rightarrow a^X[\mu_1]\,\mu_2$ holds, there exists a transition $p \xrightarrow{X:[p_1]} p_2$ and $\mathcal{M}_p \vdash \mathsf{proj}(\mu_i) \in p_i \Rightarrow \mu_i$ $(i=1,2)$ hold. From the induction hypothesis $\exists q_i[\varepsilon \in [\![\, q_i \,]\!] \wedge \langle q_i, \mu_i \rangle \in \partial_{\mathsf{proj}(\mu_i)}(p_i)]$ $(i=1,2)$ hold. Furthermore, the transition implies $\langle a, X, p_1, p_2 \rangle \in \mathrm{plf}(p)$. Therefore from the definition of partial derivatives $\exists q[\varepsilon \in [\![\, q \,]\!] \wedge \langle q, a^X[\mu_1]\mu_2 \rangle \in \partial_{\mathsf{proj}(a^X[\mu_1]\mu_2)}(p)]$ holds. $\qquad\square$

The following corollary gives an operational matching semantics by the matching automata, which is correct with respect to the denotational matching semantics. It is immediately obtained by combining Theorems 2 and 4.

Corollary 2 (Matching Semantics by Matching Automata). *A hedge h is matched by a pattern p, yielding a binding environment V if and only if*

$$\exists \mu.\,[\mathcal{M}_p \vdash h \in p \Rightarrow \mu \wedge \forall x \in \mathcal{V}_r(p).\mathsf{env}(\mu, x) = V(x)].$$

5   Conclusion

In this paper we have defined hedge pattern partial derivatives of regular hedge expression patterns. We have shown two operational matching semantics by (1) the hedge pattern partial derivatives and by (2) the matching automata constructed from hedge pattern partial derivatives. We have shown correctness of these matching semantics with respect to denotational semantics of pattern matching. As far as we know it is the first work on the application of partial derivatives to pattern matching in XML processing. Hence, our work is an answer to the question posed by Kuske and Meinecke[13], who has wondered whether the concept of partial derivatives can lead to fruitful results and algorithms in this area.

Our construction using hedge pattern partial derivatives gives much smaller matching automata than the construction described in [12] based on Thompson's construction since the latter is proportional to the structure of patterns. A method based on position automata construction may be applicable to obtain matching automata for regular hedge expression pattern matching (Emir has claimed that it would be possible[7]). However, it would always generate the states as many as the upper bound of our construction; thus the number of states generated is usually much greater than our construction.

One further research has to be done on disambiguation of pattern matching [8,16]. Incorporation of disambiguation in our framework would provide a compilation technique for the efficient execution of disambiguous pattern matching.

References

1. Antimirov, V.: Partial derivatives of regular expression and finite automaton constructions. Theoretical Computer Science 155, 291–319 (1996)
2. Benzaken, V., Castagna, G., Frisch, A.: CDuce: An XML-centric general-purpose language. In: Proc. of the 8th ACM SIGPLAN International Conference on Functional Programming (ICFP 2003), pp. 51–63 (2003)

3. Boag, S., Chamberlin, D., Fernandez, M., Florescu, D., Robie, J., Siméon, J.: XQuery 1.0: An XML Query Language. W3C Recommendation (2007)
4. Berry, G., Sethi, R.: From Regular Expressions to Deterministic Automata. Theoretical Computer Science 48, 117–126 (1986)
5. Brzozowski, J.A.: Derivatives of regular expressions. Journal of ACM 11(4), 481–494 (1964)
6. Comon, H., Dauchet, M., Gilleron, R., Jacquemard, F., Lugiez, D., Löding, C., Tison, S., Tommasi, M.: Tree Automata Techniques and Applications. Draft book, November 18 (2008), http://www.grappa.uni-lille3.fr/tata
7. Emir, B.: Compiling Regular Patterns to Sequential Machines, Technical Report IC/2004/72, EPF Lausanne (2004); Also appeared in: Proc. of ACM Symposium on Applied Computing (SAC 2005), pp. 1385–1389 (2005)
8. Frisch, A., Cardelli, L.: Greedy Regular Expression Matching. In: Díaz, J., Karhumäki, J., Lepistö, A., Sannella, D. (eds.) ICALP 2004, vol. 3142, pp. 618–629. Springer, Heidelberg (2004)
9. Gapeyev, V., Levin, M., Pierce, B.C., Schmitt, A.: XML goes native: Run-time representations for Xtatic. In: Bodik, R. (ed.) CC 2005, vol. 3443, pp. 43–58. Springer, Heidelberg (2005)
10. Glushkov, V.N.: The abstract theory of automata. Russian Mathematical Surveys 16, 1–53 (1961)
11. Hosoya, H., Pierce, B.: XDuce: A Typed XML Processing Language (Preliminary Report). In: Suciu, D., Vossen, G. (eds.) WebDB 2000, vol. 1997, pp. 226–244. Springer, Heidelberg (2001)
12. Hosoya, H.: Regular Expression Pattern Matching — a simpler design —, Technical report 1397, RIMS, Kyoto Univ. (2003)
13. Kuske, D., Meinecke, I.: Construction of Tree Automata from Regular Expressions. In: Ito, M., Toyama, M. (eds.) DLT 2008. LNCS, vol. 5257, pp. 491–503. Springer, Heidelberg (2008)
14. McNaughton, R., Yamada, H.: Regular expressions and state graphs for automata. IRE Transaction on Electronic Comput. EC-9(1), 38–47 (1960)
15. Suzuki, T., Okui, S.: Hedge Pattern Partial Derivative. Technical Report, Univ. of Aizu (forthcoming, 2009)
16. Vansummeren, S.: Type Inference for Unique Pattern Matching. ACM Transactions on Programming Languages and Systems 28(3), 389–428 (2006)

TAGED Approximations for Temporal Properties Model-Checking[*]

Roméo Courbis[1], Pierre-Cyrille Héam[1,2], and Olga Kouchnarenko[1]

[1] INRIA/CASSIS,
LIFC/University of Franche-Comté,
16 route de Gray, F-25030 Besançon Cedex
[2] LSV CNRS/INRIA/ENS Cachan
61 av. du Président Wilson
F-94235 Cachan Cedex
{rcourbis,okouchnarenko}@lifc.univ-fcomte.fr,
pcheam@lsv.ens-cachan.fr

Abstract. This paper investigates the use of tree automata with global equalities and disequalities (TAGED for short) in reachability analysis over term rewriting systems (TRSs). The reachability problem being in general undecidable on non terminating TRSs, we provide TAGED-based construction, and then design approximation-based semi-decision procedures to model-check useful temporal patterns on infinite state rewriting graphs. To show that the above TAGED-based construction can be effectively carried out, complexity analysis for rewriting TAGED-definable languages is given.

1 Introduction

Model-checking techniques [24,23] are commonplace in computer aided verification. Model checking refers to the following problem: given a desired property, expressed as a temporal logic formula φ, and a structure M with initial state s, decide if $M, s \models \varphi$. The use of model-checking techniques and tools is however limited to systems whose state space can be finitely and concisely represented.

Recently, reachability analysis turned out to be a very efficient verification technique for proving properties on infinite systems modeled by term rewriting systems (TRSs for short). In the rewriting theory, the reachability problem is the following: given a TRS $\mathcal{R}$ and two terms s and t, can we decide whether $s \to_{\mathcal{R}}^* t$ or not? This problem, which can easily be solved on strongly terminating TRSs, is undecidable on non terminating TRSs. However, on the one hand, there exist several syntactic classes of TRSs for which this problem becomes decidable [15,19,31]. On the other hand, in addition to classical proof tools of rewriting, given a set $\mathcal{E} \subseteq \mathcal{T}(\mathcal{F})$ of initial terms, provided that $s \in \mathcal{E}$, one can prove $s \not\to_{\mathcal{R}}^* t$ by using over-approximations of $\mathcal{R}^*(\mathcal{E})$ [20,15] and proving that t does not belong to these approximations. Recently, the verification of temporal

---

[*] This work has been funded by the French ANR-06-SETI-014 RAVAJ project.

S. Maneth (Ed.): CIAA 2009, LNCS 5642, pp. 135–144, 2009.
© Springer-Verlag Berlin Heidelberg 2009

properties of systems modeled by TRSs has been investigated [14,27,26]. To apply these very interesting and promising theoretical results to applications in practice, the authors look for finite abstractions to model-check temporal properties, and use proof theory methods. Unlike these works, we develop an approximation and tree automata based approach, which can provide a fully automatic verification framework.

Motivations. Recently, some of the most successful experiments using reachability analysis were done on cryptographic protocols, [17,7], and on Java byte code programs [6]. Presently, Java MIDLet applications security properties are verified through $\mathcal{R}^*(\mathcal{E})$ over-approximations[1]. To this end, following works on CEGAR [8], we developed in [5] over-approximations refinement depending on a security property to be verified. To go further, we are interested in verifying temporal properties.

Contributions. The main question is: *Is it possible to exploit rewriting approximations for verifying temporal properties on infinite state rewriting graphs?* This paper addresses this question and offers a solution for three useful patterns of temporal properties. This solution automatically attempts to show that $M, s \models \varphi$ by exploiting TAGED approximations over M, without building M.

More precisely, the present paper makes the following contributions: Given an LTL formula (of a certain pattern) to be evaluated over M, the *first contribution* is the feasibility of a systematic translation of this formula into a language rewriting equality to be checked. Language equalities being undecidable in general, the *second contribution* is approximation-based semi-decision procedures to model-check temporal properties of three useful patterns coming from static analysis domain and having practical applications. This contribution is obtained using the recent TAGED model (Tree Automata with Global Equality and Disequality Constraints) in [16]. For a lack of space, the proofs of this paper are available at `http://hal.inria.fr/inria-00380048/fr/`.

Structure of the paper. Section 2 introduces preliminary notions on TRSs, tree-automata, and rewriting-based linear temporal logic. Section 3 explains the interest of the proposed approach via three temporal property patterns and relates them to language rewriting equations. The main contribution in Section 4 concerns rewriting-based (semi-)decision procedures and complexity analysis for rewriting related TAGED-definable languages. Then, semi-algorithms, including approximation steps are given. Finally, Section 5 concludes and sums up related works.

2   Preliminaries

2.1   Terms, TRSs and Tree Automata

Comprehensive surveys can be found in [12,2] for TRSs, in [10,18] for tree automata and tree language theory, and in [16] for TAGEDs.

---

[1] In the framework of the French ANR Ravaj project.

Terms and TRSs. Let $\mathcal{F}$ be a finite set of symbols, associated with an arity function $ar : \mathcal{F} \to \mathbb{N}$, and let $\mathcal{X}$ be a countable set of variables. $\mathcal{T}(\mathcal{F}, \mathcal{X})$ denotes the set of terms, and $\mathcal{T}(\mathcal{F})$ denotes the set of ground terms (terms without variables). The set of variables of a term t is denoted by $Var(t)$. A substitution is a function σ from $\mathcal{X}$ into $\mathcal{T}(\mathcal{F}, \mathcal{X})$, which can be extended uniquely to an endomorphism of $\mathcal{T}(\mathcal{F}, \mathcal{X})$. A position p for a term t is a word over $\mathbb{N}$. The empty sequence ϵ denotes the top-most position. The set $\mathcal{P}os(t)$ of positions of a term t is inductively defined by $\mathcal{P}os(t) = \{\epsilon\}$ if $t \in \mathcal{X}$ and by $\mathcal{P}os(f(t_1, \ldots, t_n)) = \{\epsilon\} \cup \{i.p \mid 1 \leq i \leq n \text{ and } p \in \mathcal{P}os(t_i)\}$ otherwise. If $p \in \mathcal{P}os(t)$, then $t|_p$ denotes the subterm of t at position p and $t[s]_p$ denotes the term obtained by replacement of the subterm $t|_p$ at position p by the term s. We also denote by $t(p)$ the symbol occurring in t at position p. Given a term $t \in \mathcal{T}(\mathcal{F}, \mathcal{X})$, we denote $\mathcal{P}os_A(t) \subseteq \mathcal{P}os(t)$ the set of positions of t such that $\mathcal{P}os_A(t) = \{p \in \mathcal{P}os(t) \mid t(p) \in A\}$. Thus $\mathcal{P}os_{\mathcal{F}}(t)$ is the set of functional positions of t. A TRS $\mathcal{R}$ is a set of *rewrite rules* $l \to r$, where $l, r \in \mathcal{T}(\mathcal{F}, \mathcal{X})$ and $l \notin \mathcal{X}$. A rewrite rule $l \to r$ is *left-linear* (resp. right-linear) if each variable of l (resp. r) occurs only once within l (resp. r). A TRS $\mathcal{R}$ is left-linear (resp. right-linear) if every rewrite rule $l \to r$ of $\mathcal{R}$ is left-linear (resp. right-linear). A TRS $\mathcal{R}$ is linear if it is right and left-linear. The TRS $\mathcal{R}$ induces a rewriting relation $\to_{\mathcal{R}}$ on terms whose reflexive transitive closure is written $\to_{\mathcal{R}}^*$. The set of $\mathcal{R}$-descendants of a set of ground terms $\mathcal{E}$ is $\mathcal{R}^*(\mathcal{E}) = \{t \in \mathcal{T}(\mathcal{F}) \mid \exists s \in \mathcal{E} \text{ s.t. } s \to_{\mathcal{R}}^* t\}$. Symmetrically, the set of $\mathcal{R}$-ancestors of a set of ground terms $\mathcal{E}$ is $\mathcal{R}^{-1*}(\mathcal{E}) = \{s \in \mathcal{T}(\mathcal{F}) \mid \exists t \in \mathcal{E} \text{ s.t. } s \to_{\mathcal{R}}^* t\}$.

Note that $\mathcal{R}^*(\mathcal{E})$ is possibly infinite: $\mathcal{R}$ may not terminate and/or $\mathcal{E}$ may be infinite. In general, the set $\mathcal{R}^*(\mathcal{E})$ is not computable [18]. However, it is possible to over-approximate it [15] using completion procedure over tree automata, i.e. a finite representation of infinite (but regular) sets of terms.

Tree automata. Let $\mathcal{Q}$ be a finite set of symbols, of arity 0, called *states* such that $\mathcal{Q} \cap \mathcal{F} = \emptyset$. $\mathcal{T}(\mathcal{F} \cup \mathcal{Q})$ is called the set of *configurations*. A *transition* is a rewrite rule $c \to q$, where $c \in \mathcal{T}(\mathcal{F} \cup \mathcal{Q})$ is of the form $c = f(q_1, \ldots, q_n)$, $f \in \mathcal{F}$, $ar(f) = n$, and $q_1, \ldots, q_n \in \mathcal{Q}$.

A *bottom-up non-deterministic finite tree automaton* (tree automaton for short) over $\mathcal{F}$ is a 3-tuple $\mathcal{A} = (\mathcal{Q}, \mathcal{Q}_f, \Delta)$, $\mathcal{Q}_f \subseteq \mathcal{Q}$ and Δ is a finite set of transitions. The rewriting relation on $\mathcal{T}(\mathcal{F} \cup \mathcal{Q})$ induced by Δ of $\mathcal{A}$ is denoted $\to_\Delta$ or $\to_{\mathcal{A}}$. The tree language $\{t \in \mathcal{T}(\mathcal{F}) \mid t \to_{\mathcal{A}}^* q\}$ is denoted $L(\mathcal{A}, q)$ and called the *tree language recognised by* $\mathcal{A}$ *in* q. The language *recognised* by $\mathcal{A}$, denoted $L(\mathcal{A})$, is the language $\bigcup_{q \in \mathcal{Q}_f} L(\mathcal{A}, q)$. A tree language is *regular* if and only if it is recognised by a tree automaton. A *run* of a tree automaton $\mathcal{A} = (\mathcal{Q}, \mathcal{Q}_f, \Delta)$ on a term $t \in \mathcal{T}(\mathcal{F})$ is a function $\rho : \mathcal{P}os(t) \to \mathcal{Q}$ such that $\rho(p) = q$ for all $p \in \mathcal{P}os(t)$, where $q \in \mathcal{Q}$ and $t|_p = f(t_1, \ldots, t_n)$, $ar(f) = n$, $f(\rho(p.1), \ldots, \rho(p.n)) \to q \in \Delta$. A run is *successful* if $\rho(\epsilon) \in \mathcal{Q}_f$.

Positive TAGEDs. A positive TAGED[16] is a 4-tuple $\mathcal{A} = (\mathcal{Q}, E, F, \Delta)$, where $(\mathcal{Q}, F, \Delta)$ is a tree automaton over $\mathcal{F}$, and $E \subseteq \mathcal{Q} \times \mathcal{Q}$ is a binary reflexive symmetric relation on a subset of $\mathcal{Q}$. The tree automaton $(\mathcal{Q}, F, \Delta)$ is denoted $ta(\mathcal{A})$. A successful run of a positive TAGED $\mathcal{A} = (\mathcal{Q}, E, F, \Delta)$ on a term $t \in \mathcal{T}(\mathcal{F})$ is a successful run ρ of $ta(\mathcal{A})$ on t satisfying: for all positions $p_1, p_2 \in \mathcal{P}os(t)$, if $(\rho(p_1), \rho(p_2)) \in E$ then $t|_{p_1} = t|_{p_2}$. For positive TAGEDs, the emptiness problem is in EXPTIME [16, Theorem 1], and universality and inclusion problems are both undecidable [16, Proposition 5]. Following the respective definitions of runs, it is straightforward that for every positive TAGED $\mathcal{A}$, $L(\mathcal{A}) \subseteq L(ta(\mathcal{A}))$.

2.2 Linear Temporal Logic and Term Rewriting

In this section, linear temporal properties are put in a rewriting context. The approach is based on the well-known and widely used Linear Temporal Logic (LTL for short) [29]. Our goal is to express and to verify temporal constraints on the order of rewriting rules in $\rightarrow^*_{\mathcal{R}}$. The approach is very close to that in [25] when reducing the equational theory to the identity.

Let $\mathcal{R}$ be a TRS and L_0 be a set of terms. We denote by $G(L_0, \mathcal{R})$ the $\mathcal{R}$-labelled graph $(\mathcal{T}(\mathcal{F}), L_0, \Delta)$ where $\Delta = \{t_i \overset{l \rightarrow r}{\rightarrow} t_j \mid l \rightarrow r \in \mathcal{R} \text{ and } t_j \in \{l \rightarrow r\}(t_i)\}$. A path π in $G(L_0, \mathcal{R})$ is a (finite or infinite) sequence $(p_1, a_1, q_1) \ldots (p_i, a_i, q_i) \cdots$ of elements of Δ such that $p_1 \in L_0$, for every $i \geq 1$ if p_{i+1} exists, then $q_i = p_{i+1}$. The (finite or infinite) word $a_1 \ldots a_i \ldots$ over the alphabet $\mathcal{R}$ is called the label of π. A path π is full if it is either infinite or if there exists an integer i such that $\pi = (p_1, a_1, q_1), \ldots, (p_i, a_i, q_i)$ and $\{p \mid \exists a \in \mathcal{R}, (q_i, a, p) \in \Delta\}$ is empty.

LTL formulas over $\mathcal{R}$ are inductively defined by: $\mathcal{R}_0 \subseteq \mathcal{R}$ is an LTL formula, and if φ and ψ are LTL formulas over $\mathcal{R}$, then $\top$, $\neg\varphi$, $(\varphi \vee \psi)$, $\circ\varphi$ and $\varphi\mathcal{U}\psi$ are also LTL formulas. Following formulas are classically defined: $\square\varphi = \neg(\top\mathcal{U}\neg\varphi)$, $(\varphi \wedge \psi) = \neg(\neg\varphi \vee \neg\psi)$ and $\varphi \Rightarrow \psi = (\neg\varphi \vee \psi)$.

Let w be a finite or infinite word over $\mathcal{R}$ (considered as an alphabet). The i-th letter of w, if it exists, is denoted $w(i)$. We inductively define the satisfaction of an LTL formula φ by w at position i, denoted $(w, i) \models \varphi$ by:

$(w, i) \models \top$	iff $w(i)$ exists,
$(w, i) \models \mathcal{R}_0$, with $\mathcal{R}_0 \subseteq \mathcal{R}$	iff $w(i)$ exists and $w(i) \in \mathcal{R}_0$,
$(w, i) \models \neg\varphi$	iff $(w, i) \not\models \varphi$,
$(w, i) \models (\varphi_1 \vee \varphi_2)$	iff $(w, i) \models \varphi_1$ or $(w, i) \models \varphi_2$,
$(w, i) \models \circ\varphi$	iff $(w, i + 1) \models \varphi$,
$(w, i) \models (\varphi_1\mathcal{U}\varphi_2)$	iff there exists $j \geq i$ such that $(w, i) \models \varphi_2$ and for every $i \leq k < j$, $(w, k) \models \varphi_1$.

We say that w is a model of φ if $(w, 1) \models \varphi$. A graph $G(L_0, \mathcal{R})$ satisfies an LTL formula φ, denoted $G \models \varphi$, if and only if the label of each full path in $G(L_0, \mathcal{R})$ satisfies φ. Illustrated examples are given in Section 3.

3 Three LTL Patterns and Related Language Equalities

In this section, we study three LTL formula patterns which are useful to express security requirements when performing Java MIDLet applications static analysis.

- Formula $\square(\mathcal{R}_1 \Rightarrow \circ\mathcal{R}_2)$ intuitively means that if an accessible term is rewritten using a rule in $\mathcal{R}_1$, then the obtained term can be rewritten using a rule in $\mathcal{R}_2$ and only by a rule in $\mathcal{R}_2$, as illustrated on an abstract graph in Fig. 1. In our application domain, this temporal pattern is used to express that if a method m_1 is invoked, then a method m_2 must be invoked just after. For instance, if the method asks the user to authentify using his PINCODE, then the next invoked method is either the authentication or the cancellation of the authentication.

- Formula $\neg \mathcal{R}_2 \wedge \square(\circ\mathcal{R}_2 \Rightarrow \mathcal{R}_1)$ is the dual of the above temporal pattern: if an accessible term is rewritten using a rule in $\mathcal{R}_2$, then just before it was rewritten using a rule in $\mathcal{R}_1$, as illustrated on an abstract graph in Fig. 2. For instance, this temporal formula pattern expresses that if a SMS is sent, then the user has just before provided his agreement.

- Formula $\square(\mathcal{R}_1 \Rightarrow \square\neg\mathcal{R}_2)$ encodes that if a rule in $\mathcal{R}_1$ is used in a rewriting derivation, then no rule of $\mathcal{R}_2$ can be used in the future, as shown in Fig. 3. Thanks to this temporal formula pattern, one can express that if a particular application accesses to the user's private data, like his address book, no message can be sent by this application in the future. So, the user's private data cannot be exploited unbeknown to him. Notice that, according to [13], this formula pattern appears to be commonly used for system specification.

3.1   Formula $\square(\mathcal{R}_1 \Rightarrow \circ\mathcal{R}_2)$

We explore in this section how the model-checking of the formula $\square(\mathcal{R}_1 \Rightarrow \circ\mathcal{R}_2)$ can be translated into language equations. A $\mathcal{R}$-labelled graph satisfying this formula is depicted in Fig. 1.

Proposition 1. *Let $\mathcal{R}$ be a TRS, $\mathcal{R}_1, \mathcal{R}_2 \subseteq \mathcal{R}$ and L_0 be a tree language. One has $G(L_0, \mathcal{R}) \models \square(\mathcal{R}_1 \Rightarrow \circ\mathcal{R}_2)$ iff $(\mathcal{R} \setminus \mathcal{R}_2)(\mathcal{R}_1(\mathcal{R}^*(L_0))) = \emptyset$ and $\mathcal{R}_1(\mathcal{R}^*(L_0)) \cap \mathcal{R}_2^{-1}(\mathcal{T}(\mathcal{F})) = \mathcal{R}_1(\mathcal{R}^*(L_0))$.*

Example 1. Let $\mathcal{F} = \{\bot, a, b, c, f, g\}$ where $ar(\bot) = 0$, $ar(a) = ar(b) = ar(c) = 1$, and $ar(f) = ar(g) = 2$. Let consider the TRS $\mathcal{R} = \{r_1, \ldots, r_5\}$ with $r_1 = f(b(x), b(x)) \to g(x, x)$, $r_2 = a(x) \to a(a(x))$, $r_3 = a(\bot) \to b(\bot)$, $r_4 = a(b(x)) \to$

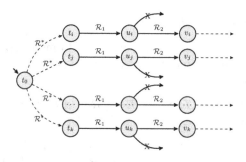

Fig. 1. A graph satisfying $\square(\mathcal{R}_1 \Rightarrow \circ\mathcal{R}_2)$

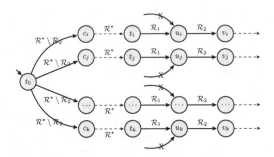

Fig. 2. A graph satisfying $\neg \mathcal{R}_2 \wedge \Box(\circ \mathcal{R}_2 \Rightarrow \mathcal{R}_1)$

$b(b(x))$ and $r_5 = g(x,y) \rightarrow c(g(x,y))$. Finally, let $L_0 = \{f(a(u(\bot)), v(a(\bot))) \mid u \in \{a,b\}^*$ and $v \in a^*\}$. One has $\{r_1\}(\mathcal{R}^*(L_0)) \subseteq g(b^*(\bot), b^*(\bot))$. Thus $(\mathcal{R} \setminus \{r_5\})(\{r_1\}(\mathcal{R}^*(L_0))) = \emptyset$. Moreover, $\{r_5\}^{-1}(\mathcal{T}(\mathcal{F}))$ is the set of terms where g occurs once at least. Consequently, $\{r_1\}(\mathcal{R}^*(L_0)) \cap \{r_5\}^{-1}(\mathcal{T}(\mathcal{F})) = \{r_1\}(\mathcal{R}^*(L_0))$. It follows that $G(L_0, \mathcal{R}) \models \Box(\{r_1\} \Rightarrow \circ \{r_5\})$.

3.2 Formula $\neg \mathcal{R}_2 \wedge \Box(\circ \mathcal{R}_2 \Rightarrow \mathcal{R}_1)$

In this section the formula $\neg \mathcal{R}_2 \wedge \Box(\circ \mathcal{R}_2 \Rightarrow \mathcal{R}_1)$ is compiled to into a language equation to be checked. A $\mathcal{R}$-labelled graph satisfying this formula is depicted in Fig. 2.

Proposition 2. *Let $\mathcal{R}$ be a TRS, $\mathcal{R}_1, \mathcal{R}_2 \subseteq \mathcal{R}$ and L_0 be a tree language. One has $G(L_0, \mathcal{R}) \models \neg \mathcal{R}_2 \wedge \Box(\circ \mathcal{R}_2 \Rightarrow \mathcal{R}_1)$ iff $\mathcal{R}_2((\mathcal{R} \setminus \mathcal{R}_1)(\mathcal{R}^*(L_0))) = \emptyset$ and $\mathcal{R}_2(L_0) = \emptyset$.*

Example 2. In the setting of Example 1, one has $\{r_5\}(L_0) = \emptyset$. Moreover, one can check that g does not occur in terms of $\mathcal{R} \setminus \{r_1, r_5\}(\mathcal{R}^*(L_0))$, proving that $\{r_5\}(\mathcal{R} \setminus \{r_1, r_5\}(\mathcal{R}^*(L_0))) = \emptyset$. Consequently, $G(L_0, \mathcal{R}) \models \neg \{r_5\} \wedge \Box(\circ \{r_5\} \Rightarrow \{r_1, r_5\})$.

3.3 Formula $\Box(\mathcal{R}_1 \Rightarrow \Box \neg \mathcal{R}_2)$

This section shows how the model-checking of the formula $\Box(\mathcal{R}_1 \Rightarrow \Box \neg \mathcal{R}_2)$ can be done thanks to language equations. A $\mathcal{R}$-labelled graph satisfying this formula is depicted in Fig. 3.

Proposition 3. *Let $\mathcal{R}$ be a TRS, $\mathcal{R}_1, \mathcal{R}_2 \subseteq \mathcal{R}$ and L_0 be a tree language. One has $G(L_0, \mathcal{R}) \models \Box(\mathcal{R}_1 \Rightarrow \Box \neg \mathcal{R}_2)$ if and only if $\mathcal{R}_2(\mathcal{R}^*(\mathcal{R}_1(\mathcal{R}^*(L_0)))) = \emptyset$.*

Example 3. In Example 1 setting, one has $\{r_1\}(\mathcal{R}^*(L_0)) \subseteq g(b^*(\bot), b^*(\bot))$. It follows that a never occurs in terms of $\mathcal{R}^*(\{r_1\}(\mathcal{R}^*(L_0)))$. Consequently, $\{r_2\}(\mathcal{R}^*(\{r_1\}(\mathcal{R}^*(L_0)))) = \emptyset$, proving that $G(L_0, \mathcal{R}) \models \Box(\{r_1\} \Rightarrow \Box \neg \{r_2\})$.

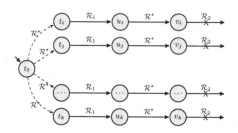

Fig. 3. A graph satisfying $\Box(\mathcal{R}_1 \Rightarrow \Box\neg\mathcal{R}_2)$

4 Semi-decision Procedures

In Section 4.1, we first show that for the above properties, model-checking is un-decidable; That is not surprising. To obtain semi-decision procedures for model-checking these properties, we then provide TAGED-based construction presented in this section. As explained in Sect. 1, given a set $\mathcal{E} \subseteq \mathcal{T}(\mathcal{F})$ of initial terms, over-approximations of the set of reachable terms $\mathcal{R}^*(\mathcal{E})$ can be computed [20,15]. In Sect. 4.2, we explain how to exploit these over-approximations and use constructions of Sect. 4.1 to verify three rewriting temporal properties introduced in Sect. 3.

4.1 Language Equalities and Positive TAGEDs

First we claim that the model-checking of the three pointed out formulas is undecidable.

Proposition 4. *Given a TRS $\mathcal{R}$, $\mathcal{R}_1, \mathcal{R}_2 \subseteq \mathcal{R}$ and a term t_0, one cannot decide whether $G(\{t_0\}, \mathcal{R})) \models \Box(\mathcal{R}_1 \Rightarrow \circ\mathcal{R}_2)$ (resp. whether $G(\{t_0\}, \mathcal{R}) \models \Box(\circ\mathcal{R}_2 \Rightarrow \mathcal{R}_1))$ (resp. whether $G(\{t_0\}, \mathcal{R})) \models \Box(\mathcal{R}_1 \Rightarrow \Box\neg\mathcal{R}_2))$.*

Now we provide several positive TAGED-based constructions in order to cope with the language equalities involved in Sect. 3.

Proposition 5. *Let $\mathcal{R}$ be a TRS. One can compute in polynomial time a positive TAGED accepting $\mathcal{R}^{-1}(\mathcal{T}(\mathcal{F}))$.*

Notice that if $\mathcal{R}$ is left-linear, the obtained TAGED is a tree automaton as for any variable x, the state q_x occurs at most once in runs; This is a well-known result.

Proposition 6. *Let $\mathcal{A}$ be a positive TAGED automaton and $\mathcal{R}$ be a TRS. Deciding whether $\mathcal{R}(L(\mathcal{A}))$ is empty is in EXPTIME.*

Proposition 7. *Let $\mathcal{A}$ be a tree automaton and $\mathcal{R}$ be a TRS. The language $\mathcal{R}(L(\mathcal{A}))$ is accepted by a positive TAGED.*

4.2   Algorithms

In order to semi-decide whether the temporal properties are satisfied or not, we introduce the following procedures.

- Approx($\mathcal{A}$,$\mathcal{R}$), where $\mathcal{A}$ is a tree automaton and $\mathcal{R}$ is a TRS, returns a tree automaton $\mathcal{B}$ such that $\mathcal{R}^*(L(\mathcal{A})) \subseteq L(\mathcal{B})$. This can be done using the procedure defined in [7].
- ta($\mathcal{A}$), where $\mathcal{A}$ is a positive TAGED, returns the tree automaton $ta(\mathcal{A})$.
- OneStep($\mathcal{A}$,$\mathcal{R}$), where $\mathcal{A}$ is a tree automaton and $\mathcal{R}$ is a TRS, returns the positive TAGED $\mathcal{B}$ accepting $\mathcal{R}(L(\mathcal{A}))$ built as in Proposition 7.
- Backward($\mathcal{R}$), where $\mathcal{R}$ is a TRS, returns the positive TAGED $\mathcal{B}$ accepting $\mathcal{R}^{-1}(\mathcal{T}(\mathcal{F}))$ built as in Proposition 5.
- IsEmpty($\mathcal{A}$,$\mathcal{R}$), where $\mathcal{A}$ is a positive TAGED and $\mathcal{R}$ is a TRS, returns true if $\mathcal{R}(L(\mathcal{A}))$ is empty and false, otherwise.

The above procedures and the results in Section 3 allow to deduce the following result.

Proposition 8. *Let $\mathcal{R}$ be a TRS, $\mathcal{R}_1, \mathcal{R}_2 \subseteq \mathcal{R}$ and $\mathcal{A}$ be a tree automaton. The following properties hold:*

(1) If $\mathcal{R}_2$ is left-linear and if IsEmpty(OneStep(Approx($\mathcal{A}$,$\mathcal{R}$),$\mathcal{R}_1$),$\mathcal{R} \setminus \mathcal{R}_2$)= true *and if* OneStep(Approx($\mathcal{A}$,$\mathcal{R}$),$\mathcal{R}_1$)$\subseteq$ Backward($\mathcal{R}_2$), *then* $G(L(\mathcal{A}), \mathcal{R}) \models$ $\square(\mathcal{R}_1 \Rightarrow \circ \mathcal{R}_2)$.

(2) If IsEmpty($\mathcal{A}$,$\mathcal{R}_2$) *and if* IsEmpty(OneStep(Approx($\mathcal{A}$,$\mathcal{R}$),$\mathcal{R} \setminus \mathcal{R}_1$),$\mathcal{R}_2$)= true, *then* $G(L(\mathcal{A}), \mathcal{R}) \models \square(\circ \mathcal{R}_2 \Rightarrow \mathcal{R}_1)$.

(3) If IsEmpty(Approx(ta(OneStep(Approx($\mathcal{A}$,$\mathcal{R}$),$\mathcal{R}_1$)),$\mathcal{R}$),$\mathcal{R}_2$)= true, *then* $G(L(\mathcal{A}), \mathcal{R}) \models \square(\mathcal{R}_1 \Rightarrow \square \neg \mathcal{R}_2)$.

Notice that in *(1)* $\mathcal{R}_2$ is required to be left-linear in order to make the inclusion test decidable.

5   Conclusion and Related Work

We proposed to exploit abstraction-based rewriting approximations to model-check some LTL temporal properties on infinite state systems, and to combat a combinatorial state-space blow up faced by model-checking tools. Our approach is based on the reachability analysis through rewriting approximations as well as tree automata with global equality constraints. We address static analysis problems. Approximation techniques were already implemented in [3]. In the future we plan to integrate TAGED-based algorithms into this tool in order to treat practical applications.

Related work

Temporal properties and rewriting. Hundreds of works exist using LTL [29] in order to model and to verify systems properties. We refer the interested reader to the Spin Model-Checker home page[2].

---

[2] http://spinroot.com/spin/whatispin.html

Rewriting logics [25] is a very general theoretical framework allowing one to model various systems. In this context, rewriting graphs are considered: nodes of these graphs are labeled by equivalence classes of an equational theory. There is an edge between two nodes if an element of the first node can be rewritten into an element of the second node, using a rule of TRS $\mathcal{R}$. When the considered equational theory is the identity, these rewriting graphs are exactly the graphs underlying our labeled transition systems. In this framework, the works in [14,27,26] focus on LTL approaches. In [1] the authors propose a general model for security protocols based on the set-rewriting formalism in a decidable context (considered underlying graphs are finite).

Tree automata with constraints. Tree automata were intensively studied in the literature, in particular for program verification, where tree automata provide abstraction-based approximations of program configurations. In this direction, several classes of extended automata were defined in order to provide finer approximations [4,11,9,16,30,22,28,21].

References

1. Armando, A., Carbone, R., Compagna, L.: Ltl model checking for security protocols. In: CSF, pp. 385–396 (2007)
2. Baader, F., Nipkow, T.: Term Rewriting and All That. Cambridge University Press, Cambridge (1998)
3. Balland, E., Boichut, Y., Genet, T., Moreau, P.-E.: Towards an efficient implementation of tree automata completion. In: Meseguer, J., Roşu, G. (eds.) AMAST 2008. LNCS, vol. 5140, pp. 67–82. Springer, Heidelberg (2008)
4. Bogaert, B., Tison, S.: Equality and disequality constraints on direct subterms in tree automata. In: Finkel, A., Jantzen, M. (eds.) STACS 1992, vol. 577, pp. 161–171. Springer, Heidelberg (1992)
5. Boichut, Y., Courbis, R., Héam, P.-C., Kouchnarenko, O.: Finer is better: Abstraction refinement for rewriting approximations. In: Voronkov, A. (ed.) RTA 2008. LNCS, vol. 5117, pp. 48–62. Springer, Heidelberg (2008)
6. Boichut, Y., Genet, T., Jensen, T., Le Roux, L.: Rewriting approximations for fast prototyping of static analyzers. In: Baader, F. (ed.) RTA 2007. LNCS, vol. 4533, pp. 48–62. Springer, Heidelberg (2007)
7. Boichut, Y., Héam, P.-C., Kouchnarenko, O.: Approximation-based tree regular model-checking. Nordic Journal of Computing (to appear, 2009)
8. Clarke, E.M.: Counterexample-guided abstraction refinement. In: TIME-ICTL, p. 7. IEEE Computer Society, Los Alamitos (2003)
9. Comon, H., Cortier, V.: Tree automata with one memory set constraints and cryptographic protocols. Theoretical Computer Science (TCS 2005) 331 (2005)
10. Comon, H., Dauchet, M., Gilleron, R., Jacquemard, F., Lugiez, D., Tison, S., Tommasi, M.: Tree Automata Techniques and Applications (2002), http://www.grappa.univ-lille3.fr/tata/
11. Dauchet, M., Caron, A.-C., Coquidé, J.-L.: Automata for reduction properties solving. J. Symb. Comput. 20(2), 215–233 (1995)
12. Dershowitz, N., Jouannaud, J.-P.: ch. 6: Rewrite Systems. In: Handbook of Theoretical Computer Science, vol. B, pp. 244–320. Elsevier Science Publishers B. V., Amsterdam (1990)

13. Dwyer, M.B., Avrunin, G.S., Corbett, J.C.: Property specification patterns for finite-state verification. In: Proceedings of the Second Workshop on Formal Methods in Software Practice, pp. 7–15. ACM Press, New York (1998)
14. Escobar, S., Meseguer, J.: Symbolic model checking of infinite-state systems using narrowing. In: Baader, F. (ed.) RTA 2007. LNCS, vol. 4533, pp. 153–168. Springer, Heidelberg (2007)
15. Feuillade, G., Genet, T., VietTriemTong, V.: Reachability analysis over term rewriting systems. Journal on Automated Reasoning 33(3-4) (2004)
16. Filiot, E., Talbot, J.-M., Tison, S.: Tree automata with global constraints. In: Ito, M., Toyama, M. (eds.) DLT 2008. LNCS, vol. 5257, pp. 314–326. Springer, Heidelberg (2008)
17. Genet, T., Klay, F.: Rewriting for Cryptographic Protocol Verification. In: McAllester, D. (ed.) CADE 2000, vol. 1831, pp. 271–290. Springer, Heidelberg (2000)
18. Gilleron, R., Tison, S.: Regular tree languages and rewrite systems. Fundamenta Informatica 24(1/2), 157–174 (1995)
19. Gyenizse, P., Vágvölgyi, S.: Linear Generalized Semi-Monadic Rewrite Systems Effectively Preserve Recognizability. Theoretical Computer Science 194(1-2), 87–122 (1998)
20. Jacquemard, F.: Decidable approximations of term rewriting systems. In: Ganzinger, H. (ed.) RTA 1996, vol. 1103, pp. 362–376. Springer, Heidelberg (1996)
21. Jacquemard, F., Rusinowitch, M., Vigneron, L.: Tree automata with equality constraints modulo equational theories. IJCAR, 557–571 (2006)
22. Karianto, W., Löding, C.: Unranked tree automata with sibling equalities and disequalities. In: Arge, L., Cachin, C., Jurdziński, T., Tarlecki, A. (eds.) ICALP 2007. LNCS, vol. 4596, pp. 875–887. Springer, Heidelberg (2007)
23. Lamport, L.: A temporal logic of actions. ACM Transactions On Programming Languages And Systems, TOPLAS 16(3), 872–923 (1994)
24. Manna, Z., Pnueli, A.: The Temporal Logic of Reactive and Concurrent Systems: Specification. SV (1992)
25. Meseguer, J.: Conditioned rewriting logic as a united model of concurrency. Theoretical Computer Science 96(1), 73–155 (1992)
26. Meseguer, J.: The temporal logic of rewriting. Technical Report UIDCS-R-2007-2815, Dept. of Computer Science, University of Illinois at Urbana-Champaign (September 2007)
27. Meseguer, J.: The temporal logic of rewriting: A gentle introduction. In: Concurrency, Graphs and Models: Essays Dedicated to Ugo Montanari on the Occasion of His 65th Birthday, pp. 354–382 (2008)
28. Ohsaki, H., Takai, T.: ACTAS: A system design for associative and commutative tree automata theory. Electronic Notes in Theoretical Computer Science 124(1), 97–111 (2005)
29. Pnueli, A.: The temporal logic of programs. In: FOCS 1977, pp. 46–57 (1977)
30. Seidl, H., Schwentick, T., Muscholl, A., Habermehl, P.: Counting in trees for free. In: Díaz, J., Karhumäki, J., Lepistö, A., Sannella, D. (eds.) ICALP 2004. LNCS, vol. 3142, pp. 1136–1149. Springer, Heidelberg (2004)
31. Takai, T., Kaji, Y., Seki, H.: Right-linear finite-path overlapping term rewriting systems effectively preserve recognizability. In: Bachmair, L. (ed.) RTA 2000. LNCS, vol. 1833. Springer, Heidelberg (2000)

Verifying Parallel Programs with Dynamic Communication Structures

Mohamed Faouzi Atig and Tayssir Touili

LIAFA, CNRS & Univ. Paris Diderot, Case 7014, 75205 Paris 13, France
{atig,touili}@liafa.jussieu.fr

Abstract. We address the verification problem of networks of communicating pushdown systems modeling communicating parallel programs with procedure calls. Processes in such networks can read the control state of the other processes according to a given communication structure (specifying the observability rights between processes). The reachability problem of such models is undecidable in general. First, we define a class of networks that effectively preserves recognizability (hence, its reachability problem is decidable). Then, we consider networks where the communication structure can change dynamically during the execution according to a *phase* graph. The reachability problem for these dynamic networks being undecidable in general, we define a subclass for which it becomes decidable. Then, we consider reachability when the switches in the communication structures are bounded. We show that this problem is undecidable even for one switch. Then, we define a natural class of models for which this problem is decidable. This class can be used in the definition of an efficient semi-decision procedure for the analysis of the general model of dynamic networks. Our techniques allowed to find bugs in two versions of a Windows NT Bluetooth driver.

1 Introduction

Verification of concurrent software is a difficult task in the model-checking community. Indeed, concurrent programs include various complex features such as (1) the presence of recursive procedure calls, which can lead to an unbounded number of calls, and (2) concurrency and synchronization between parallel processes. It is well known that checking whether a given control point is reachable is undecidable for programs with recursive procedures and synchronisation statements. During the last few years, several authors have addressed this issue. Different models of these programs have been proposed and analysed.

Pushdown systems have been proposed as an adequate formalism to describe *pure sequential recursive programs* [9,11,19]. This allows to represent the potentially infinite configurations of recursive programs in a symbolic manner using regular languages [2,12,11]. Thus, a natural approach that allows to reason about multitheraded programs is to consider models based on parallel compositions of pushdown systems [4,17,5,3,8]. Unfortunately, such models are undecidable (it suffices to have two communicating pushdown systems to get undecidability).

S. Maneth (Ed.): CIAA 2009, LNCS 5642, pp. 145–154, 2009.
© Springer-Verlag Berlin Heidelberg 2009

Recently, we defined in [1] a new model for multithreaded programs based on networks of pushdown systems. Our model consists of a finite number of parallel processes, each of them corresponding to a pushdown system, and where each process can read the control states of the other ones according to a given *communication structure* specifying the observation rights between processes. Such networks (called PDNs in this paper) are obviously Turing powerful when cyclic communication structures are allowed. We restricted ourselves in [1] to networks with *acyclic* communication structures. In order to represent infinite sets of configurations, we considered symbolic representation structures based on (multidimensional) finite-state automata defining recognizable and rational sets of vectors of words. (Recognizable sets are sets definable as finite unions of products of regular languages). We showed in [1] that reachability is decidable for acyclic networks, that such networks do not preserve recognizability, and we defined a subclass of such networks for which we were able to effectively characterize the reachable configurations by a rational set.

In this work, we go further with this model. First, we define a natural subclass called *stable* acyclic PDNs and prove that it effectively preserves recognizability. Then, we consider networks with dynamic changes in the communication structure according to a *phase graph*, where each phase corresponds to an acyclic PDN. The phase graph specifies the possible switches between a finite number of phases, and the constraints on the configurations under which the system can move from a phase to another. We call this new model MAPN (for Multiphase Acyclic Pushdown Networks). MAPN is a natural model to represent programs where the communication structure between processes can change dynamically.

We show that reachability in MAPN can be reduced to reachability in (possibly cyclic) PDNs, and vice versa. Thus, MAPN has an undecidable reachability problem (even if each communication structure in each phase is acyclic) if we allow cyclic phase graphs. In fact, we prove that the reachability problem is undecidable as soon as we allow one phase switch (and even if communication structures are acyclic).

Then, we define two classes of MAPNs for which reachability becomes decidable. We derive from this a bounded phase-switch analysis procedure for the general MAPN model. For that, we show that it is possible to decompose each given MAPN into an equivalent model where each phase corresponds to a stable acyclic PDN. Finally, we define a semi-algorithm to decide reachability for general PDNs (even cyclic ones) based on the bounded phase-switch analysis for MAPNs. This result generalizes the algorithms proposed in [17,3] for bounded context-switch analysis. Indeed, our notion of phase is more general than the notions of context used in these works in the sense that, if we encode our model in those proposed in [17,3], one single phase according to our definition may correspond to an unbounded number of context switches in their models. Thus, our bounded phase analysis may allow an arbitrary number of context switches (in the sense of [17,3]).

Our MAPN model is a natural model to represent programs where the communication structure between processes can change dynamically. Our PDN model can also be used to describe concurrent programs with synchronisation and procedure calls such as e.g. two versions of a Windows NT Bluetooth driver. Our techniques can be applied to find the bugs of this driver reported in [18,8].

Related work. Recently, several models based on rewriting systems have been considered to model multithreaded programs [15,10,20,16,6,7]. While these models allow to model dynamic thread creation, they do not allow communication between processes.

In [5], we have introduced a model based on networks of pushdown systems called CDPN. While this model allows dynamic creation of processes, it allows only a restricted form of synchronisation where a process has the right to read only the control states of its immediate sons (i.e., the processes it has created).

[21] considers bounded phase reachability in multi-stack systems, where in each phase the system can pop from one stack, and push on some number of stacks. In our model, we allow the manipulation of different stacks in a single phase. However, since the communication relation in the different phases of a MAPN is fixed, our model cannot simulate phase switches in the sense of [21].

Networks of pushdown systems communicating via message passing [4,8], or locks [14,13] have been considered. Pushdown networks with these kinds of communications can also be described in our PDN model.

2   Networks of Communicating Pushdown Systems

A PushDown Network (PDN for short) is given by a tuple $N = (\mathcal{P}_1, \ldots, \mathcal{P}_n, R)$ where $R \subseteq \{(i,j) \mid 1 \leq i,j \leq n, i \neq j\}$ is a binary relation defining the communication structure of the network (R defines a directed graph whose nodes are $1, \ldots, n$), and for every $i \in \{1, \ldots, n\}$, $\mathcal{P}_i = (P_i, \Gamma_i, \Delta_i)$ is a communicating pushdown system such that P_i is a finite set of control states, Γ_i is a finite stack alphabet, and Δ_i is a set of transition rules of the form:

$$\phi \; : \; (p, \gamma) \hookrightarrow (p', w)$$

where $p, p' \in P_i$ are two control states, $\gamma \in \Gamma_i$ is the symbol popped from the stack, $w \in \Gamma_i^*$ is the string pushed in the stack, and $\phi \subseteq \bigcup_{(i,j) \in R} P_j$ is a set of constraints over the current control states of the other observed processes.

A *local configuration* of a process in the network, say $\mathcal{P}_i$, is a word $p_i w_i \in P_i \Gamma_i^*$ where p_i is a state and w_i is a stack content. A *configuration* of the network N is a vector $(p_1 w_1, \ldots, p_n w_n) \in \prod_{i=1}^{n} P_i \Gamma_i^*$, where $p_i w_i$ is the local configuration of $\mathcal{P}_i$.

We define a *transition relation* $\Longrightarrow_N$ between configurations. We have $(p_1 w_1, \ldots, p_n w_n) \Longrightarrow_N (p_1' w_1', \ldots, p_n' w_n')$ if and only if there is an index $i \in \{1, \ldots, n\}$ such that:

- there is a rule $\phi \; : \; (p, \gamma) \hookrightarrow (p', w) \in \Delta_i$ and there exists a word $u \in \Gamma_i^*$ such that $p_i = p$, $p_i' = p'$, $w_i = \gamma u$, $w_i' = wu$, and for every $j \in \{1, \ldots, n\}$, if $(i,j) \in R$, then $p_j \in \phi$.

- $\forall j \in \{1,\ldots,n\}. \; i \neq j. \; p_j = p'_j$ and $w_j = w'_j$.

Let $\Longrightarrow_N^*$ denote the reflexive transitive closure of $\Longrightarrow_N$. Given a configuration c, the set of immediate successors of c is $post_N(c) = \{c' \in \prod_{i=1}^n P_i \Gamma_i^* : c \Longrightarrow_N c'\}$. This notation can be generalized straightforwardly to sets of configurations. Let $post_N^*$ denote the reflexive-transitive closure of $post_N$.

Intuitively, a network $N = (\mathcal{P}_1, \ldots, \mathcal{P}_n, R)$ can be seen as a collection of "standard" pushdown systems that observe each other according to the structure R: $(i,j) \in R$ means that process $\mathcal{P}_i$ observes (reads) the states of process $\mathcal{P}_j$. If a rule $\phi : (p,\gamma) \hookrightarrow (p', w)$ is in Δ_i, then process $\mathcal{P}_i$ can apply the "standard" pushdown rule $(p,\gamma) \hookrightarrow (p', w)$ iff every pushdown system $\mathcal{P}_j$ for j s.t. $(i,j) \in R$ is in a state $p_j \in \phi \cap P_j$. The network is in the configuration $(p_1 w_1, \ldots, p_n w_n)$ means that each pushdown system $\mathcal{P}_i$ is in configuration $p_i w_i$.

A network $N = (\mathcal{P}_1, \ldots, \mathcal{P}_n, R)$ is *acyclic* (resp. *cyclic*) if the graph of its relation R is acyclic (resp. cyclic). A network consisting of a single process $N = (\mathcal{P}, \emptyset)$ will simply be denoted by $\mathcal{P}$ and corresponds to the standard pushdown system $\mathcal{P}$.

3   Symbolic Representation of PDN Configurations

Let $N = (\mathcal{P}_1, \ldots, \mathcal{P}_n, R)$ be a PDN where $\mathcal{P}_i = (P_i, \Gamma_i, \Delta_i)$. Since a configuration of N can be seen as a word of dimension n in $P_1 \Gamma_1^* \times \cdots \times P_n \Gamma_n^*$, a natural way to represent *infinite* sets of PDN configurations is to consider *recognizable* languages. Let $\Sigma_1, \ldots, \Sigma_n$ be n finite alphabets. A n-dim word over $\Sigma_1, \ldots, \Sigma_n$ is an element of $\Sigma_1^* \times \cdots \times \Sigma_n^*$. A n-dim language is a (possibly infinite) set of n-dim words. A n-dim language L is *recognizable* if it is a finite union of products of n regular languages (i.e. $L = \bigcup_{j=1}^m L(A_1^j) \times \cdots \times L(A_n^j)$ for some $m \in \mathbb{N}$, where A_i^j is a finite state automaton over Σ_i). Notice that for $n = 1$, recognizable languages correspond precisely to regular languages.

It is well known that for any dimension $n \geq 1$, the class of recognizable languages is closed under boolean operations and that the emptiness problem of recognizable languages is decidable.

4   Reachability Analysis of PDNs

The reachability problem between sets of configurations C_1 and C_2 for a PDN N is to determine whether there are two configurations $c_1 \in C_1$ and $c_2 \in C_2$ such that $c_1 \Longrightarrow_N^* c_2$. It is easy to see that a PDN with two processes and a cyclic communication structure is Turing prowerful:

Proposition 1. *The reachability problem of PDNs is undecidable.*

Hence, we restrict ourselves to acyclic PDNs. We showed in [1] that acyclic PDNs do not preserve recognizability. In this section, we go further and define conditions under which acyclic PDNs preserve recognizability.

Definition 1. *Let* $N = (\mathcal{P}_1, \ldots, \mathcal{P}_n, R)$ *be an acyclic PDN where for every* $i \in \{1, \ldots, n\}$, $\mathcal{P}_i = (P_i, \Gamma_i, \Delta_i)$. *For* $i \in \{1, \ldots, n\}$, *let* ρ_i *be a binary relation in* $P_i \times P_i$ *defined by* $(p, p') \in \rho_i$ *iff there exists in* Δ_i *a rule of the form* ϕ : $(p, \gamma) \hookrightarrow (p', w)$. *Let* ρ_i^* *be the reflexive-transitive closure of* ρ_i.

N is stable *iff whenever* $(i, j) \in R$, *then for every* $p, p' \in P_j$, *if* $(p, p') \in \rho_j^*$ *and* $(p', p) \in \rho_j^*$, *then for every rule* ϕ : $(q, \gamma) \hookrightarrow (q', w)$ *in* Δ_i, $p \in \phi$ *iff* $p' \in \phi$.

Intuitively, N is *stable* iff if $\mathcal{P}_j$ can go from a state p to a state p' and then back to p, for some index $j \in \{1, \ldots, n\}$; then if $(i, j) \in R$, the rules of Δ_i do not distinguish between the states p and p'.

We show the first main result of our paper: stable acyclic networks effectively preserve recognizability.

Theorem 1. *Let* $N = (\mathcal{P}_1, \ldots, \mathcal{P}_n, R)$ *be a stable acyclic PDN and C be a recognizable set of configurations. Then,* $post_N^*(C)$ *is an effectively recognizable set.*

The construction underlying this theorem is based on the iterative applications of the standard *post** algorithm for standard pushdown systems [2,11] for each pushdown component in the network. The stability of the network guarantees the termination of the iterative procedure.

5   Multiphase Acyclic Pushdown Networks

In this work, we go further and extend the model of acyclic PDNs by allowing dynamic changes in the definition of the network. This section is devoted to the definition of this new model.

A *Multiphase* Acyclic Pushdown Network (MAPN) is given by a tuple $M = (N_1, \ldots, N_m, T)$ where for every $j \in \{1, \ldots, m\}$, $N_j = (\mathcal{P}_1^j, \ldots, \mathcal{P}_n^j, R_j)$ is an acyclic PDN where for $i \in \{1, \ldots, n\}$, $\mathcal{P}_i^j = (P_i, \Gamma_i, \Delta_i^j)$. T is a set of transitions of the form (N_i, Φ, N_j) where $i, j \in \{1, \ldots, m\}$ and $\Phi \subseteq \prod_{k \leq n} P_k \Gamma_k^*$ is a recognizable set of configurations.

We can think of the network N_j as an acyclic network over the processes $(\mathcal{P}_1, \ldots, \mathcal{P}_n)$, where each process $\mathcal{P}_i$ ($i \in \{1, \ldots, n\}$) executes only the rules Δ_i^j, and where these processes observe each other according to the structure R_j. T is a *phase graph*: a transition $(N_i, \Phi, N_j) \in T$ means that if the acyclic PDN N_i is in a configuration $(p_1 w_1, \ldots, p_n w_n) \in \Phi$, then the network can move from a phase where the processes behave according to the network N_i to a phase where they behave according to N_j, i.e., from N_i to N_j.

Let $\mathcal{G}$ be the underlying graph of T, i.e., $(i, j) \in \mathcal{G}$ iff there exists in T a transition of the form (N_i, Φ, N_j). We say that T is cyclic (resp. acyclic) iff $\mathcal{G}$ is cyclic (resp. acyclic). The network M is said to be cyclic (resp. acyclic) iff T is cyclic (resp. acyclic).

An *indexed configuration* of the MAPN is a pair $\langle (p_1 w_1, \ldots, p_n w_n), i \rangle$ where $(p_1 w_1, \ldots, p_n w_n) \in \prod_{k=1}^n P_k \Gamma_k^*$, and $i \in \{1, \ldots, m\}$. The index i records the current phase of the network. A *configuration* of the MAPN is a tuple $(p_1 w_1, \ldots, p_n w_n) \in \prod_{k=1}^n P_k \Gamma_k^*$.

We define a *transition relation* $\Rightarrow_M$ between indexed configurations as follows: $\langle (p_1 w_1, \ldots, p_n w_n), i \rangle \Rightarrow_M \langle (p'_1 w'_1, \ldots, p'_n w'_n), j \rangle$ if and only if:

- $(p_1 w_1, \ldots, p_n w_n) = (p'_1 w'_1, \ldots, p'_n w'_n)$, and there is $(N_i, \Phi, N_j) \in T$ such that $(p_1 w_1, \ldots, p_n w_n) \in \Phi$,
- $(p_1 w_1, \ldots, p_n w_n) \Longrightarrow_{N_j} (p'_1 w'_1, \ldots, p'_n w'_n)$ and $i = j$.

We extend $\Rightarrow_M$ to configurations in $\prod_{k=1}^{n} P_k \Gamma_k^*$ as follows: $(p_1 w_1, \ldots, p_n w_n) \Rightarrow_M$ $(p'_1 w'_1, \ldots, p'_n w'_n)$ iff there exist two phase indices i and j in $\{1, \ldots, m\}$ such that $\langle (p_1 w_1, \ldots, p_n w_n), i \rangle \Rightarrow_M \langle (p'_1 w'_1, \ldots, p'_n w'_n), j \rangle$. Let $\Rightarrow_M^*$ denote the reflexive transitive closure of $\Rightarrow_M$. Let C be a set of (indexed) configurations. We define $post_M(C)$ and $post_M^*(C)$ in the usual manner. Let C be a set of indexed configurations. C is said to be recognizable if and only if the set $C_j = \{(p_1 w_1, \ldots, p_n w_n) | \langle (p_1 w_1, \ldots, p_n w_n), j \rangle \in C\}$ is recognizable for every $j, 1 \leq j \leq m$. As usual, the reachability problem between two sets of (indexed) configurations C_1 and C_2, for a MAPN M, is to determine whether there are two (indexed) configurations $c_1 \in C_1$ and $c_2 \in C_2$ such that $c_1 \Rightarrow_M^* c_2$.

6   The Reachability Problem for MAPNs

In this section, we study the reachability problem for the model MAPN. First, we show that this problem is reducible to its corresponding problem for PDNs and vice-versa. Thus, reachability is undecidable in general for MAPNs. Then, we define two subclasses for which reachability becomes decidable.

Theorem 2. *The reachability problem for PDNs is reducible to its corresponding problem for MAPNs and vice-versa.*

As an immediate consequence of Theorem 2 and Proposition 1 we have:

Proposition 2. *The reachability problem is undecidable for MAPNs.*

Unfortunately, we can show that this undecidability holds even for acyclic MAPNs. We show that solving this problem would imply a decision procedure for the Post's Correspondence Problem (PCP).

Theorem 3. *The reachability problem between two (indexed) configurations is undecidable for acyclic MAPNs. This holds even if the phase graph has a single transition.*

6.1   Reachability for Finitely-Constrained MAPNs

Fortunately, we can show that reachability becomes decidable for MAPNs when the constraints in the phase graph are finite sets of configurations.

Definition 2. *A MAPN* $M = (N_1, \ldots, N_m, T)$ *is called* finitely-constrained *if T is a set of transitions of the form* (N_i, Φ, N_j) *where* $i, j \in \{1, \ldots, m\}$ *and* $\Phi \subseteq \prod_{k \leq n} P_k \Gamma_k^*$ *is a finite set of configurations.*

In [1], we showed that the reachability problem between two recognizable sets of configurations for acyclic PDNs is decidable. Thanks to this result, it is easy to see that in finitely-constrained MAPNs, reachability can be reduced to reachability in a finite graph:

Proposition 3. *The reachability problem between recognizable sets of (indexed) configurations is decidable for finitely-constrained MAPNs.*   ∎

6.2 Reachability for Stable Acyclic MAPNs

We give in this section the second main result of this paper: we define the class of *stable* acyclic MAPNs and show that it effectively preserves recognizability. Hence, its reachability problem is decidable.

Definition 3. *An MAPN $M = (N_1, \ldots, N_m, T)$ is* stable *if for every $j \in \{1, \ldots, m\}$, $N_j = (\mathcal{P}_1^j, \ldots, \mathcal{P}_n^j, R_j)$ is a stable acyclic PDN.*

We show that *stable* acyclic MAPNs effectively preserve recognizability. This is due to the fact that (1) stable acyclic PDNs effectively preserve recognizability, and (2) the phase graphs for acyclic MAPNs are acyclic. This allows to obtain the reachability set for *stable* acyclic MAPNs by successively applying the algorithm underlying Theorem 1 a finite number of times.

Theorem 4. *Let $M = (N_1, \ldots, N_m, T)$ be a stable acyclic MAPN and let C be a recognizable set of (indexed) configurations of M. Then $post_M^*(C)$ is effectively recognizable.*

Since recognizable sets are effectively closed under intersection, we get:

Corollary 1. *The reachability problem between recognizable sets of (indexed) configurations is decidable for stable acyclic MAPNs.*

7   Bounded Phase Switch Reachability for MAPNs

We consider in this section the reachability problem for *general* MAPNs. Since this problem is undecidable, we consider *bounded switch* reachability, where the number of switches between the different phases (the different networks N_i's) is bounded.

Definition 4. *Let $M = (N_1, \ldots, N_m, T)$ be a MAPN where for every $j \in \{1, \ldots, m\}$, $N_j = (\mathcal{P}_1^j, \ldots, \mathcal{P}_n^j, R_j)$ is an acyclic PDN. We define the k-switch transition relation between indexed configurations inductively as follows:*

- $\langle (p_1 w_1, \ldots, p_n w_n), i \rangle \overset{0}{\Longrightarrow}_M \langle (p_1' w_1', \ldots, p_n' w_n'), j \rangle$ *if and only if $i = j$ and $(p_1 w_1, \ldots, p_n w_n) \Longrightarrow_{N_i}^* (p_1' w_1', \ldots, p_n' w_n')$.*
- $\langle (p_1 w_1, \ldots, p_n w_n), i \rangle \overset{k+1}{\Longrightarrow}_M \langle (p_1' w_1', \ldots, p_n' w_n'), j \rangle$ *if and only if there is an indexed configuration $\langle (p_1'' w_1'', \ldots, p_n'' w_n''), l \rangle$ such that: $\langle (p_1 w_1, \ldots, p_n w_n), i \rangle \overset{k}{\Longrightarrow}_M \langle (p_1'' w_1'', \ldots, p_n'' w_n''), l \rangle$; $\langle (p_1'' w_1'', \ldots, p_n'' w_n''), l \rangle \Rightarrow_M \langle (p_1'' w_1'', \ldots, p_n'' w_n''), j \rangle$; and $(p_1'' w_1'', \ldots, p_n'' w_n'') \Longrightarrow_{N_j}^* (p_1' w_1', \ldots, p_n' w_n')$.*

$\xrightarrow{k}_M$ is extended to configurations as follows: $(p_1w_1, \ldots, p_nw_n) \xrightarrow{k}_M$ $(p'_1w'_1, \ldots, p'_nw'_n)$ iff there exist two phase indices i and j such that $\langle(p_1w_1, \ldots, p_nw_n), i\rangle \xrightarrow{k}_M \langle(p'_1w'_1, \ldots, p'_nw'_n), j\rangle$.

The k-bounded switch reachability problem for MAPNs between two sets of (indexed) configurations C and C' consists in determining whether there are $c \in C$ and $c' \in C'$ such that $c \xrightarrow{k}_M c'$. Intuitively, this means that $c \xrightarrow{k}_M c'$ iff the (indexed) configuration c' can be reached from c after switching at most k times the phase of the network according to the phase graph T. In this case, we say that c' is k-bounded reachable from c.

Unfortunately, even k-bounded switch reachability is undecidable for cyclic as well as acyclic MAPNs. Indeed, it is easy to see that performing k-bounded reachability in M amounts to performing "unrestricted" reachability in the acyclic network defined by $(N_1, \ldots, N_m, T_k)$, where T_k is obtained by considering all the possible paths of T having at most k transitions. Therefore, it follows from Theorem 3 that:

Corollary 2. *The k-bounded reachability problem between recognizable sets of (indexed) configurations is undecidable for MAPNs. This holds even for $k = 1$.*

However, it follows from Corollary 1 and the observation above that:

Corollary 3. *The k-bounded switch reachability problem between recognizable sets of (indexed) configurations is decidable for stable MAPNs.*

7.1   A Semi-algorithm for k-Bounded Reachability for MAPNs

The result above can be used to construct a semi-decision procedure for the k-bounded switch reachability problem for *general* MAPNs. Let $M = (N_1, \ldots, N_m, T)$ be a MAPN, the idea consists in taking advantage of the fact that k-bounded switch reachability is decidable for *stable* networks. To do so, we compute a stable network $M' = (N'_1, \ldots, N'_{m'}, T')$ s.t. the processes in M' have the same behaviors as those in M but can perform more phase switches. This ensures that given two configurations c and c', $c \xrightarrow{k}_{M'} c'$ infers that there exists k' such that $c \xrightarrow{k'}_M c'$. This gives the semi-decision procedure since we can decide k-bounded reachability for M' thanks to its stability.

To compute the stable network M', the idea consists in decomposing every acyclic PDN N_j ($j \leq m$) into stable subnetworks $N_j^1, \ldots, N_j^{i_j}$ such that the behavior of each subnetwork N_j^l is also a behavior of N_j, and such that any behavior of N_j can be obtained by performing a number of switches between the different N_j^l's. The computed network satisfies the following:

Theorem 5. *Let C and C' be two recognizable sets of (indexed) configurations. Then if C' is k-bounded reachable from C by M, there exists $k' \geq k$ such that C' is k'-bounded reachable from C by M'.*

7.2 A Semi-algorithm for the Reachability Problem for General PDNs

We show in this section how we can use the previous results on bounded phase switch reachability for MAPNs to derive a semi-algorithm to check reachability for general PDNs (even cyclic ones). Let $N = (\mathcal{P}_1, \ldots, \mathcal{P}_n, R)$ be a PDN, where for i, $1 \leq i \leq n$, $\mathcal{P}_i = (P_i, \Gamma_i, \Delta_i)$ is a communicating pushdown system. The construction underlying Theorem 2 produces a MAPN M such that reachability in N can be reduced to reachability in M. Let C and C' be two recognizable sets of configurations of N. We can show that if C' is reachable from C in N, then there exists an index k such that C' is k-bounded reachable from C in M. Thus, the semi-algorithm given in the previous section can be used to check reachability in N, and thus in PDNs.

This technique generalizes the algorithms proposed in [17,3] for bounded context-switch analysis. Indeed, our notion of phase is more general than the notions of context used in these works in the sense that, if we encode our model in those proposed in [17,3], one single phase according to our definition may correspond to an unbounded number of context switches in their models. Thus, our bounded phase analysis may allow an unbounded number of context switches (in the sense of [17,3]).

8 Conclusion and Applications

In this paper, we consider networks of communicating pushdown systems where the processes can read the control states of the other ones according to a given communication structure. Reachability in such a model being undecidable, we consider networks with *acyclic* communication graphs. We define the class of *stable* acyclic PDNs and show that it effectively preserves recognizability. Then, we consider networks with *dynamic* changes of the communication structures (MAPNs). This model being Turing powerful, we give conditions under which reachability or bounded-phase reachability become decidable for MAPNs, and give a semi-algorithm to decide bounded-phase reachability for general MAPNs and PDNs. Our MAPN and PDN models can be used to describe concurrent programs. For example, it can model two versions of a Windows NT Bluetooth driver. Our techniques can be applied to find the bugs of these drivers reported in [18,8].

References

1. Atig, M.F., Bouajjani, A., Touili, T.: On the reachability analysis of acyclic networks of pushdown systems. In: van Breugel, F., Chechik, M. (eds.) CONCUR 2008. LNCS, vol. 5201, pp. 356–371. Springer, Heidelberg (2008)
2. Bouajjani, A., Esparza, J., Maler, O.: Reachability analysis of pushdown automata: Application to model-checking. In: Mazurkiewicz, A., Winkowski, J. (eds.) CONCUR 1997. LNCS, vol. 1243, pp. 135–150. Springer, Heidelberg (1997)
3. Bouajjani, A., Esparza, J., Schwoon, S., Strejcek, J.: Reachability analysis of multithreaded software with asynchronous communication. In: Sarukkai, S., Sen, S. (eds.) FSTTCS 2005. LNCS, vol. 3821, pp. 348–359. Springer, Heidelberg (2005)

4. Bouajjani, A., Esparza, J., Touili, T.: A generic approach to the static analysis of concurrent programs with procedures. In: POPL, pp. 62–73. ACM, New York (2003)
5. Bouajjani, A., Müller-Olm, M., Touili, T.: Regular symbolic analysis of dynamic networks of pushdown systems. In: Abadi, M., de Alfaro, L. (eds.) CONCUR 2005. LNCS, vol. 3653, pp. 473–487. Springer, Heidelberg (2005)
6. Bouajjani, A., Touili, T.: Reachability analysis of process rewrite systems. In: Pandya, P.K., Radhakrishnan, J. (eds.) FSTTCS 2003. LNCS, vol. 2914, pp. 74–87. Springer, Heidelberg (2003)
7. Bouajjani, A., Touili, T.: On computing reachability sets of process rewrite systems. In: Giesl, J. (ed.) RTA 2005. LNCS, vol. 3467, pp. 484–499. Springer, Heidelberg (2005)
8. Chaki, S., Clarke, E.M., Kidd, N., Reps, T.W., Touili, T.: Verifying concurrent message-passing c programs with recursive calls. In: Hermanns, H., Palsberg, J. (eds.) TACAS 2006. LNCS, vol. 3920, pp. 334–349. Springer, Heidelberg (2006)
9. Esparza, J., Knoop, J.: An automata-theoretic approach to interprocedural data-flow analysis. In: Thomas, W. (ed.) FOSSACS 1999. LNCS, vol. 1578, pp. 14–30. Springer, Heidelberg (1999)
10. Esparza, J., Podelski, A.: Efficient algorithms for pre* and post* on interprocedural parallel flow graphs. In: POPL, pp. 1–11. ACM, New York (2000)
11. Esparza, J., Schwoon, S.: A bdd-based model checker for recursive programs. In: Berry, G., Comon, H., Finkel, A. (eds.) CAV 2001. LNCS, vol. 2102, pp. 324–336. Springer, Heidelberg (2001)
12. Finkel, A., Willems, B., Wolper, P.: A direct symbolic approach to model checking pushdown systems. Electr. Notes Theor. Comput. Sci. 9 (1997)
13. Kahlon, V., Gupta, A.: On the analysis of interacting pushdown systems. In: POPL, pp. 303–314. ACM, New York (2007)
14. Kahlon, V., Ivancic, F., Gupta, A.: Reasoning about threads communicating via locks. In: Etessami, K., Rajamani, S.K. (eds.) CAV 2005. LNCS, vol. 3576, pp. 505–518. Springer, Heidelberg (2005)
15. Lugiez, D., Schnoebelen, P.: The regular viewpoint on pa-processes. In: Sangiorgi, D., de Simone, R. (eds.) CONCUR 1998. LNCS, vol. 1466, pp. 50–66. Springer, Heidelberg (1998)
16. Müller-olm, M.: Variations on constants. Habilitation thesis, Dortmund University (2002)
17. Qadeer, S., Rehof, J.: Context-bounded model checking of concurrent software. In: Halbwachs, N., Zuck, L.D. (eds.) TACAS 2005. LNCS, vol. 3440, pp. 93–107. Springer, Heidelberg (2005)
18. Qadeer, S., Wu, D.: Kiss: keep it simple and sequential. In: PLDI, pp. 14–24. ACM, New York (2004)
19. Reps, T.W., Schwoon, S., Jha, S.: Weighted pushdown systems and their application to interprocedural dataflow analysis. In: Cousot, R. (ed.) SAS 2003. LNCS, vol. 2694, pp. 189–213. Springer, Heidelberg (2003)
20. Seidl, H., Steffen, B.: Constraint-based inter-procedural analysis of parallel programs. In: Smolka, G. (ed.) ESOP 2000. LNCS, vol. 1782, pp. 351–365. Springer, Heidelberg (2000)
21. La Torre, S., Madhusudan, P., Parlato, G.: A robust class of context-sensitive languages. In: LICS, pp. 161–170. IEEE Computer Society, Los Alamitos (2007)

Fixpoint Guided Abstraction Refinement
for Alternating Automata*

Pierre Ganty[1], Nicolas Maquet[2,**], and Jean-François Raskin[2]

[1] University of California, Los Angeles, USA
[2] Université Libre de Bruxelles (ULB), Belgium

Abstract. In this paper, we develop and evaluate two new algorithms for checking emptiness of alternating automata. These algorithms build on previous works. First, they rely on antichains to efficiently manipulate the state-spaces underlying the analysis of alternating automata. Second, they are abstract algorithms with built-in refinement operators based on techniques that exploit information computed by abstract fixed points (and not counter-examples as it is usually the case). The efficiency of our new algorithms is illustrated by experimental results.

1 Introduction

Alternating automata are a generalization of both nondeterministic and universal automata. In an alternating automaton, the transition relation is defined using positive Boolean formulas: disjunctions allow for the expression of nondeterministic transitions and conjunctions allow for the expression of universal transitions. The emptiness problem for alternating automata being PSPACE-COMPLETE [3], several computationally-hard automata-theoretic and model-checking problems can be reduced in polynomial time to the emptiness problem for those automata. It is thus very desirable to design efficient algorithms for checking emptiness of those automata. In this paper, we propose new algorithms for efficiently checking the emptiness problem for alternating automata over finite words. Those new algorithms combine two recent lines of research.

First, we use efficient techniques based on *antichains*, initially introduced in [6], to symbolically manipulate the state-spaces underlying the analysis of alternating automata. Antichain-based techniques have been applied to several problems in automata theory [6,8,9,1] and for solving games of imperfect information [12]. Those techniques have also been applied with success to the satisfiability and model-checking of LTL specifications [8]. Our team has implemented these algorithms in a tool called ALASKA [7], which is available for download[1].

Second, to apply this antichain technique to even larger instances of alternating automata, we instantiate a generic abstract-refinement method that we have proposed

---

* Work supported by the projects: (*i*) Quasimodo: "Quantitative System Properties in Model-Driven-Design of Embedded", http://www.quasimodo.aau.dk/, (*ii*) Gasics: "Games for Analysis and Synthesis of Interactive Computational Systems", http://www.ulb.ac.be/di/gasics/, (*iii*) Moves: "Fundamental Issues in Modelling, Verification and Evolution of Software", http://moves.ulb.ac.be, a PAI program funded by the Federal Belgian Gouvernment, (*iv*) CFV (Federated Center in Verification) funded by the FNRS http://www.ulb.ac.be/di/ssd/cfv/
** This author is supported by an FNRS-FRIA grant.
[1] See http://www.antichains.be

in [5] and further developed in [10,11]. This abstract-refinement method does not use counter-examples to refine inconclusive abstractions contrary to most of the methods presented and implemented in the literature, see for example [4]. Instead, our algorithm uses the entire information computed by the abstract analysis and combines it with information obtained by one application of a concrete predicate transformer. The algorithm presented in [5] is a generic solution that does not lead directly to efficient implementations. In particular, as shown in [10], in order to obtain an efficient implementation of this algorithm, we need to define a family of abstract domains on which abstract analysis can be effectively computed, as well as practical operators to refine the elements of this family of abstract domains. In this paper, we use the set of *partitions* of the locations of an alternating automaton to define the family of abstract domains. Those abstract domains and their refinement operators can be used both in *forward* and *backward* algorithms for checking emptiness of alternating automata.

To show the practical interest of these new algorithms, we have implemented them into the ALASKA tool. We illustrate the efficiency of our new algorithms on examples of alternating automata constructed from LTL specifications interpreted over finite words. With the help of those examples, we show that our algorithms are able to concentrate the analysis on important parts of the state-space and abstract away the less interesting parts *automatically*. This allows us to treat much larger instances than with the concrete forward or backward algorithms. We are confident that those new algorithms will allow us to solve problems of practical relevance that are currently out of reach of automatic methods.

2 Preliminaries

Alternating Automata. Let S be a set. We denote $\mathcal{B}^+(S)$ the set of *positive Boolean formulas* over S. Formally, $\mathcal{B}^+(S) ::= s \mid \phi_1 \vee \phi_2 \mid \phi_1 \wedge \phi_2$, where $s \in S$. A valuation for a set of proposition S is encoded as a subset of S. For each formula $\phi \in \mathcal{B}^+(S)$ we write $[\![\phi]\!] \subseteq 2^S$ the set of valuations that satisfy ϕ; as usual, $c \in [\![\phi]\!]$ is interpreted as the valuation that assigns "true" only to the variables in c. Let Σ be a finite alphabet. A finite word w is a finite sequence $w = \sigma_0\sigma_1\ldots\sigma_{n-1}$ of letters from Σ. We write Σ^* the set of finite words over Σ. We now recall the definition of *alternating automata over finite words* (AFA for short).

Definition 1. *An* alternating finite automaton *is a tuple* $\langle \mathsf{Loc}, \Sigma, q_0, \delta, F \rangle$ *where :* $\mathsf{Loc} = \{l_1, \ldots, l_n\}$ *is the set of locations;* $\Sigma = \{\sigma_1, \ldots, \sigma_m\}$ *is the set of alphabet symbols;* $q_0 \in \mathsf{Loc}$ *is the initial location;* $\delta \colon \mathsf{Loc} \times \Sigma \to \mathcal{B}^+(\mathsf{Loc})$ *is the transition function; and* $F \subseteq \mathsf{Loc}$ *is the set of accepting locations.*

As we will often manipulate sets of sets of locations in the sequel, we will refer to the inner sets as *cells*. Let $\mathsf{Cells}(S) = 2^S$. A *cell* of an AFA with locations Loc is an element of $\mathsf{Cells}(\mathsf{Loc})$. A set of cells X is $\subseteq$-*upward-closed* (resp. $\subseteq$-*downward-closed*) if for all $c \in X$ and for all $c' \in \mathsf{Cells}(\mathsf{Loc})$ s.t. $c \subseteq c'$ (resp. $c' \subseteq c$), we have $c' \in X$. Instead of defining the traditional notion of runs for AFA, we define their semantics as a *directed graph*, the nodes of which are cells. Each edge in the cell graph is labeled by an alphabet symbol.

Definition 2. *Let* $A = \langle \mathsf{Loc}, \Sigma, q_0, \delta, F \rangle$, $[\![A]\!] = \langle V, E \rangle$ *where:* $V = \mathsf{Cells}(\mathsf{Loc})$ *and* $\langle c, \sigma, c' \rangle \in E$ *iff* $c' \in [\![\bigwedge_{l \in c} \delta(l, \sigma)]\!]$. *A word* $w = \sigma_1, \ldots, \sigma_p$ *is accepted by the automaton* A *iff there exists a path* $c_0, c_1, \ldots, c_p$ *of cells of* V *such that* $q_0 \in c_0$, $c_p \in \mathsf{Cells}(F)$ *(the set of accepting cells), and* $\forall i \in [1, \ldots, p] : \langle c_{i-1}, \sigma_i, c_i \rangle \in E$.

In the sequel, we will consider $[\![A]\!]$ simply as the set of edges E of the cell graph and leave the set of vertices V implicit.

Predicate Transformers. We have defined the semantics of alternating automata as a directed graph of cells. To explore this graph, we use *predicate transformers.*

Definition 3. *We consider the following* predicate transformers *(A is an* **AFA***):*

$$post_\sigma[A](X) = \{c_2 \mid \exists \langle c_1, \sigma, c_2 \rangle \in [\![A]\!] : c_1 \in X\} \quad post[A](X) = \bigcup_{\sigma \in \Sigma} post_\sigma[A](X)$$
$$\widetilde{post}_\sigma[A](X) = \{c_2 \mid \forall \langle c_1, \sigma, c_2 \rangle \in [\![A]\!] : c_1 \in X\} \quad \widetilde{post}[A](X) = \bigcap_{\sigma \in \Sigma} \widetilde{post}_\sigma[A](X)$$
$$pre_\sigma[A](X) = \{c_1 \mid \exists \langle c_1, \sigma, c_2 \rangle \in [\![A]\!] : c_2 \in X\} \quad pre[A](X) = \bigcup_{\sigma \in \Sigma} pre_\sigma[A](X)$$
$$\widetilde{pre}_\sigma[A](X) = \{c_1 \mid \forall \langle c_1, \sigma, c_2 \rangle \in [\![A]\!] : c_2 \in X\} \quad \widetilde{pre}[A](X) = \bigcap_{\sigma \in \Sigma} \widetilde{pre}_\sigma[A](X)$$

Theorem 1. *Let* $A = \langle \mathsf{Loc}, \Sigma, q_0, \delta, F \rangle$ *an* **AFA**, $\overline{X} \equiv \mathsf{Cells}(\mathsf{Loc}) \setminus X$, $\mathcal{F} = \mathsf{Cells}(F)$.
$L(A) = \emptyset$ *iff* $(\mu x \cdot post[A](x) \cup [\![q_0]\!]) \subseteq \overline{\mathcal{F}}$ *iff* $(\mu x \cdot pre[A](x) \cup \mathcal{F}) \subseteq \overline{[\![q_0]\!]}$.

The lattice of partitions. The heart of our abstraction scheme is to *partition* the set of locations Loc of an **AFA**, in order to build a smaller (hopefully more manageable) automaton. We recall the notion of partitions and some of their properties. Let $\mathcal{P}$ be a partition of the set $S = \{l_1, \ldots, l_n\}$ into k *classes* (called *blocks* in the sequel) $\mathcal{P} = \{b_1, \ldots, b_k\}$. Partitions are classically ordered as follows: $\mathcal{P}_1 \preceq \mathcal{P}_2$ iff $\forall\, b_1 \in \mathcal{P}_1, \exists\, b_2 \in \mathcal{P}_2 : b_1 \subseteq b_2$. It is well known, see [2], that the set of partitions together with $\preceq$ form a complete lattice where $\{\{l_1\}, \ldots, \{l_n\}\}$ is the $\preceq$-minimal element, $\{\{l_1, \ldots, l_n\}\}$ is the $\preceq$-maximal element and the greatest lower bound of two partitions $\mathcal{P}_1$ and $\mathcal{P}_2$, noted $\mathcal{P}_1 \curlywedge \mathcal{P}_2$, is the partition given by $\{b \neq \emptyset \mid \exists\, b_1 \in \mathcal{P}_1, \exists\, b_2 \in \mathcal{P}_2 : b = b_1 \cap b_2\}$. The least upper bound of two partitions $\mathcal{P}_1$ and $\mathcal{P}_2$, noted $\mathcal{P}_1 \curlyvee \mathcal{P}_2$, is the finest partition such that given $b \in \mathcal{P}_1 \cup \mathcal{P}_2$, for all $l_i \neq l_j : l_i \in b$ and $l_j \in b$ we have: $\exists\, b' \in \mathcal{P}_1 \curlyvee \mathcal{P}_2 : l_i \in b'$ and $l_j \in b'$. Also, we shall use $\mathcal{P}$ as a function such that $\mathcal{P}(l)$ simply returns the block b to which l belongs in $\mathcal{P}$.

3   Deciding AFA Emptiness Using Antichains

A fundamental problem regarding **AFA** is the *emptiness problem*; i.e., to decide if there exists at least one word accepted by an **AFA**. Since nondeterministic automata (NFA, for short) emptiness can be solved in linear-time, a natural solution is to first perform an **AFA** → **NFA** translation and then check for emptiness. The translation is simple (albeit computationally difficult), as it amounts to a subset construction, similar to that of **NFA** determinization. Notice that the cell-graph semantics of **AFA** defined in the previous section is essentially an **NFA** obtained by subset construction. In earlier works [6,8,9], we have designed new efficient algorithms for **AFA** emptiness. Those algorithms are based on efficient manipulations of $\subseteq$-upward- or downward-closed sets of cells using *antichains*. In our context, an antichain is the unique set of $\subseteq$-minimal (resp. $\subseteq$-maximal) cells of an upward-closed (resp. downward-closed) set of cells X, which we denote by $\lfloor X \rfloor$ (resp. $\lceil X \rceil$). The crucial properties of antichains are that (i) they are canonical representations of $\subseteq$-closed sets of cells, (ii) the predicate transformers on **AFA** evaluate to $\subseteq$-closed sets (they can thus be canonically represented with antichains) and, (iii) evaluating a predicate transformer on any set of cells is equivalent to evaluating it on the $\subseteq$-closure of that set (we can thus evaluate predicate transformers *directly* on antichains, without losing any information). Due to lack of space, we do not recall the framework of antichains in this work (it can be found in [6]). In the sequel, we will assume that all the computations on sets of cells are performed using antichains.

4   Abstraction of Alternating Automata

4.1   Abstract Domain

In this section, we present an original algorithmic framework for the analysis of AFA, using antichains along with abstract interpretation. Given an AFA with locations Loc, our algorithm will use a family of abstract domains defined by the set of partitions $\mathcal{P}$ of Loc. The concrete domain is the complete lattice $2^{\mathsf{Cells(Loc)}}$, and each partition $\mathcal{P}$ defines the abstract domain as $2^{\mathsf{Cells}(\mathcal{P})}$. We refer to elements of $\mathsf{Cells(Loc)}$ as *concrete cells* and elements of $\mathsf{Cells}(\mathcal{P})$ as *abstract cells*. An abstract cell is thus a set of blocks of the partition $\mathcal{P}$ and it represents all the concrete cells which can be constructed by choosing at least one location from each block. To capture this representation role of abstract cells, we define the following predicate.

Definition 4. *The predicate* $\mathsf{Covers} : \mathsf{Cells}(\mathcal{P}) \times \mathsf{Cells(Loc)} \rightarrow \{\top, \bot\}$ *is defined as follows:* $\mathsf{Covers}(c^\alpha, c)$ *iff* $c^\alpha = \{\mathcal{P}(l) \mid l \in c\}$.

Example 1. Let $\mathsf{Loc} = \{1, \ldots, 5\}$, $\mathcal{P} = \{a : \{1\}, b : \{2, 3\}, c : \{4, 5\}\}$. We have that $\mathsf{Covers}(\{a, c\}, \{1, 3\}) = \bot$, $\mathsf{Covers}(\{a, c\}, \{1, 4\}) = \top$, and $\mathsf{Covers}(\{a, c\}, \{1\}) = \bot$.

To make proper use of the theory of abstract interpretation, we define an *abstraction* and a *concretization* functions, and show that they form a *Galois connection* between the concrete domain and each of our abstract domains.

Definition 5. *Let* $\mathcal{P}$ *be a partition of the set* Loc, *we define the functions* $\alpha_{\mathcal{P}} : 2^{\mathsf{Cells(Loc)}} \rightarrow 2^{\mathsf{Cells}(\mathcal{P})}$ *and* $\gamma_{\mathcal{P}} : 2^{\mathsf{Cells}(\mathcal{P})} \rightarrow 2^{\mathsf{Cells(Loc)}}$ *as follows :* $\alpha_{\mathcal{P}}(X) = \{c^\alpha \mid \exists\, c \in X : \mathsf{Covers}(c^\alpha, c)\}$, $\gamma_{\mathcal{P}}(X) = \{c \mid \exists\, c^\alpha \in X : \mathsf{Covers}(c^\alpha, c)\}$.

Lemma 1. *For any partition* $\mathcal{P}$ *of* Loc : $(2^{\mathsf{Cells(Loc)}}, \subseteq) \xleftrightarrow[\alpha]{\gamma} (2^{\mathsf{Cells}(\mathcal{P})}, \subseteq)$.

In the sequel, we will omit the $\mathcal{P}$ subscript of α and γ when the partition is clear from the context. Additionaly, we define $\mu_{\mathcal{P}} = \gamma_{\mathcal{P}} \circ \alpha_{\mathcal{P}}$.

4.2   Efficient Abstract Analysis

In the sequel, we will need to evaluate fixpoint-expressions over the abstract domain. In theory, we could simply surround every predicate transformer occuring in the fixpoint-expressions by $\alpha \circ \cdot \circ \gamma$ to obtain an abstract fixpoint. However, for obvious performance concerns, we want to avoid as many concretization and abstraction steps as possible, and ideally make all the computations *directly over the abstract domain*. Furthermore, we would like that these *abstract predicate transformers* enjoy the same useful properties w.r.t. antichains so that we can reuse the results of the previous section. To achieve this goal, we proceed as follows. Given a partition $\mathcal{P}$ of the set of locations of an alternating automaton, we use a *syntactic transformation* θ that builds an *abstract* AFA which over-approximates the behavior of the original automaton. Later in this section we will show that the *pre* and *post* predicate transformers can be directly evaluated on this abstract automaton to obtain the same result (but much faster) than the $\alpha \circ \cdot \circ \gamma$ computation on the original automaton. To express this syntactic transformation, we define *syntactic variants* of the abstraction and concretization functions.

Definition 6. *Let $\mathcal{P}$ be a partition of the set* Loc. *We define the following syntactic abstraction and concretization functions over positive Boolean formulas:* $\hat{\alpha} : \mathcal{B}^+(\text{Loc}) \rightarrow \mathcal{B}^+(\mathcal{P})$ *and* $\hat{\gamma} : \mathcal{B}^+(\mathcal{P}) \rightarrow \mathcal{B}^+(\text{Loc})$, *such that* $\hat{\alpha}(l) = \mathcal{P}(l)$, $\hat{\alpha}(\phi_1 \vee \phi_2) = \hat{\alpha}(\phi_1) \vee \hat{\alpha}(\phi_2)$, *and* $\hat{\alpha}(\phi_1 \wedge \phi_2) = \hat{\alpha}(\phi_1) \wedge \hat{\alpha}(\phi_2)$. *Likewise,* $\hat{\gamma}(b) = \bigvee_{l \in b} l$, $\hat{\gamma}(\phi_1 \vee \phi_2) = \hat{\gamma}(\phi_1) \vee \hat{\gamma}(\phi_2)$, *and* $\hat{\gamma}(\phi_1 \wedge \phi_2) = \hat{\gamma}(\phi_1) \wedge \hat{\gamma}(\phi_2)$.

Lemma 2. *For every* $\phi \in \mathcal{B}^+(\text{Loc})$ *we have that* $[\![\hat{\alpha}(\phi)]\!] = \alpha([\![\phi]\!])$, *and for every* $\phi \in \mathcal{B}^+(\mathcal{P})$ *we have that* $[\![\hat{\gamma}(\phi)]\!] = \gamma([\![\phi]\!])$.

Definition 7. *Let* $A = \langle \text{Loc}, \Sigma, q_0, \delta, F \rangle$ *and* $\mathcal{P}$ *a partition of* Loc. $\theta(A, \mathcal{P}) = \langle \text{Loc}^{\alpha}, \Sigma, b_0, \delta^{\alpha}, F^{\alpha} \rangle$ *where:* $\text{Loc}^{\alpha} = \mathcal{P}$, $b_0 = \mathcal{P}(q_0)$, $\delta^{\alpha}(b, \sigma) = \hat{\alpha}(\bigvee_{l \in b} \delta(l, \sigma))$, *and* $F^{\alpha} = \{b \in \mathcal{P} \mid b \cap F \neq \emptyset\}$.

Theorem 2. *Let* A *be an* AFA, $\mathcal{P}$ *a partition of its locations and* $A^{\alpha} = \theta(A, \mathcal{P})$, $\alpha \circ \text{post}[A] \circ \gamma = \text{post}[A^{\alpha}]$ *and* $\alpha \circ \text{pre}[A] \circ \gamma = \text{pre}[A^{\alpha}]$.

This theorem is crucial for the practical efficiency of our algorithms. In our framework, the evaluation of an abstract fixpoint on a large automaton amounts to compute a concrete fixpoint on a smaller automaton that is easy to obtain (the θ transformation can be done in linear time).

4.3   Precision of the Abstract Domain

We now present some results about precision and representability in our family of abstract domains. In particular, for the automatic refinement of abstract domains, we will need an effective way of computing the *coarsest partition* which can represent an upward- or downward closed set of cells without loss of precision.

Definition 8. *A set of cells* $X \subseteq \text{Cells}(\text{Loc})$ *is representable in the abstract domain* $2^{\text{Cells}(\mathcal{P})}$ *iff* $\mu_{\mathcal{P}}(X) = X$ *(recall that* $\mu_{\mathcal{P}} = \gamma_{\mathcal{P}} \circ \alpha_{\mathcal{P}})$.

Lemma 3. *Let* $X \subseteq \text{Cells}(\text{Loc})$, *let* $\mathcal{P}_1$ *and* $\mathcal{P}_2$ *be two partitions of* Loc. *If* X *is representable with* $\mathcal{P}_1$ *and representable with* $\mathcal{P}_2$, *then* X *is representable with* $\mathcal{P}_1 \curlyvee \mathcal{P}_2$.

As the lattice of partition is a complete lattice, we have the following corollary.

Corollary 1. *For all* $X \subseteq \text{Cells}(\text{Loc})$, *there exists a coarsest partition* $\mathcal{P} = \curlyvee \{\mathcal{P}' \mid \mu_{\mathcal{P}'}(X) = X\}$ *such that* $\mu_{\mathcal{P}}(X) = X$.

For upward- and downward-closed sets, we have an efficient way to compute this coarsest partition which uses the notion of *neighbour list*. The neighbour list of a location l w.r.t. an upward-closed set X, denoted $\mathcal{N}_X(l)$, is defined as follows:

Definition 9. *Let* $X \subseteq \text{Cells}(\text{Loc})$ *be an upward-closed set. The* neighbour list *of a location* $l \in \text{Loc}$ *w.r.t.* X *is the set* $\mathcal{N}_X(l) = \{c \setminus \{l\} \mid c \in \lfloor X \rfloor, l \in c\}$.

The following lemma states that if two locations share the same neighbour lists w.r.t. an upward-closed set X, then they can be put in the same partition block and preserve the representability of X. Conversely, X cannot be exactly represented by any partition which puts into the same block two locations that have different neighbour lists.

Lemma 4. *For any partition* $\mathcal{P}$ *of* Loc, *for any upward-closed set* X, *the set* X *is representable in* $2^{\text{Cells}(\mathcal{P})}$ *iff* $\forall l, l' \in \text{Loc} \cdot \mathcal{P}(l) = \mathcal{P}(l') \rightarrow \mathcal{N}_X(l) = \mathcal{N}_X(l')$.

Corollary 2. *For all upward-closed sets $X \subseteq \mathsf{Cells}(\mathsf{Loc})$, the partition $\mathcal{P}$ induced by the equivalence relation $l \sim l'$ iff $\mathcal{N}_X(l) = \mathcal{N}_X(l')$ is the coarsest partition that is able to represent X. Assuming that $\lfloor X \rfloor$ has been computed, this partition is computable in $O(n \log n)$ set comparisons, where n is the size of $\lfloor X \rfloor$.*

The representability of downward-closed sets is immediate with the following lemma. In practice, we compute the coarsest partition for the complement upward-closed set.

Lemma 5. *Let $X \subseteq \mathsf{Cells}(\mathsf{Loc})$, $\mathcal{P}$ a partition of Loc. $\mu_P(X) = X$ iff $\mu_P(\overline{X}) = \overline{X}$.*

5 Abstraction Refinement Algorithm

This section presents two fixpoint-guided abstraction refinement algorithms for AFA. These algorithms share several ideas with the generic algorithm presented in [5] but they are formally different, so we provide arguments showing their correctness. We concentrate here on explanations related to the abstract forward algorithm. The abstract backward algorithm is the dual of this algorithm and its correctness can be established in a very similar way. We first give an informal presentation of the ideas underlying the algorithm and then we expose formal arguments for its soundness and completeness.

Description of the forward abstract algorithm. The most important information computed in the algorithm is Z_i, which is an over-approximation of the set of reachable cells which cannot reach an accepting cell in i steps or less. In other words, all the cells outside Z_i are either unreachable, or can lead to an accepting cell in i steps or less (or both). Our algorithm always uses the coarsest partition $\mathcal{P}_i$ that allows Z_i to be represented in the corresponding abstract domain. The algorithm begins by initializing Z_0 with the set of non-accepting cells and by initializing $\mathcal{P}_0$ accordingly (lines 1 and 2). The main loop proceeds as follows. First, we compute the abstract reachable cells R_i which are within Z_i, which is done by applying the θ transformation using $\mathcal{P}_i$ (line 4), and by computing a forward abstract fixpoint (line 7). If R_i does not contain a cell

Input: $A = \langle \mathsf{Loc}, \Sigma, q_0, \delta, F \rangle$		**Input:** $A = \langle \mathsf{Loc}, \Sigma, q_0, \delta, F \rangle$
Output: True iff $L(A) = \emptyset$		**Output:** True iff $L(A) = \emptyset$

1	$\mathcal{P}_0 \leftarrow \{F, \mathsf{Loc} \setminus F\}$		1	$\mathcal{P}_0 \leftarrow \{\{q_0\}, \mathsf{Loc} \setminus \{q_0\}\}$
2	$Z_0 \leftarrow \overline{\mathsf{Cells}(F)}$		2	$Z_0 \leftarrow \overline{[\![q_0]\!]}$
3	**for** i **in** $0, 1, 2, \ldots$ **do**		3	**for** i **in** $0, 1, 2, \ldots$ **do**
4	$\quad A_i^\alpha \leftarrow \theta(A, \mathcal{P}_i)$		4	$\quad A_i^\alpha \leftarrow \theta(A, \mathcal{P}_i)$
5	$\quad A_i^\alpha = \langle \mathsf{Loc}^\alpha, \Sigma, b_0, \delta^\alpha, F^\alpha \rangle$		5	$\quad A_i^\alpha = \langle \mathsf{Loc}^\alpha, \Sigma, b_0, \delta^\alpha, F^\alpha \rangle$
6	$\quad I_i \leftarrow [\![b_0]\!]$		6	$\quad B_i \leftarrow \mathsf{Cells}(F^\alpha)$
7	$\quad R_i \leftarrow \mu x \cdot (I_i \cup post[A_i^\alpha](x)) \cap \alpha_{\mathcal{P}_i}(Z_i)$		7	$\quad R_i \leftarrow \mu x \cdot (B_i \cup pre[A_i^\alpha](x)) \cap \alpha_{\mathcal{P}_i}(Z_i)$
8	$\quad$ **if** $post[A_i^\alpha](R_i) \subseteq \alpha_{\mathcal{P}_i}(Z_i)$ **then**		8	$\quad$ **if** $pre[A_i^\alpha](R_i) \subseteq \alpha_{\mathcal{P}_i}(Z_i)$ **then**
9	$\quad\quad$ **return** True		9	$\quad\quad$ **return** True
10	$\quad$ **if** $[\![q_0]\!] \not\subseteq Z_i$ **then**		10	$\quad$ **if** $\mathsf{Cells}(F) \not\subseteq Z_i$ **then**
11	$\quad\quad$ **return** False		11	$\quad\quad$ **return** False
12	$\quad Z_{i+1} \leftarrow \gamma_{\mathcal{P}_i}(R_i) \cap \widetilde{pre}[A](\gamma_{\mathcal{P}_i}(R_i))$		12	$\quad Z_{i+1} \leftarrow \gamma_{\mathcal{P}_i}(R_i) \cap \widetilde{post}[A](\gamma_{\mathcal{P}_i}(R_i))$
13	$\quad \mathcal{P}_{i+1} \leftarrow \curlyvee \{\mathcal{P} \mid \mu_P(Z_{i+1}) = Z_{i+1}\}$		13	$\quad \mathcal{P}_{i+1} \leftarrow \curlyvee \{\mathcal{P} \mid \mu_P(Z_{i+1}) = Z_{i+1}\}$

Fig. 1. The *abstract-forward* (left) and *abstract-backward* (right) FGAR algorithms

which can leave Z_i, we know (see Lemma 6) that the automaton is empty (line 8). If on the other hand, an initial cell (i.e., a cell containing q_0) is no longer in Z_i then we know that it can lead to an accepting cell in i steps or less (as it is obviously reachable) and we conclude that the automaton is non-empty (line 11). In the case where both tests failed, we *refine* the information contained in Z_i by removing all the cells which can leave R_i in one step, as we know that these cells are either surely unreachable or can lead to an accepting cell in $i+1$ steps or less. Finally, the current abstract domain is changed to be able to represent the new Z_i (line 13), using the neighbour list algorithm of Corollary 2. It is important to note that this refinement operation is not the traditional refinement used in counter-example guided abstraction refinement. Note also that our algorithm does not necessarily choose a new abstract domain that is strictly more precise than the previous one as in [5]. Instead, the algorithm uses the most abstract domain possible at all times.

Completeness and correctness of the forward abstract algorithm. Correctness and completeness relies on the properties formalized in the following lemma. The proofs are omitted due to lack of space.

Lemma 6. *Let* $\mathsf{Reach} = \mu x \cdot [\![q_0]\!] \cup post[A](x)$ *be the reachable cells of A, let* $\mathsf{Bad}^k = \cup_{j=0}^{j=k} pre^j[A](\mathsf{Cells}(F))$ *be the cells that can reach an accepting cell in k steps or less, and let us note* $\mathsf{Safe}^k = \mathsf{Cells}(\mathsf{Loc}) \setminus \mathsf{Bad}^k$, *i.e. the set of cells that cannot reach an accepting cell in k steps or less. The following four properties hold:*

1. $\forall i \geq 0$: $\mu_{\mathcal{P}_i}(Z_i) = Z_i$, *i.e.* Z_i *is representable in the successive abstract domains;*
2. $\forall i \geq 0$: $Z_{i+1} \subseteq Z_i$, *i.e. the sets* Z_i *are decreasing;*
3. $\forall i \geq 0$: $\mathsf{Reach} \cap \mathsf{Safe}^i \subseteq Z_i$, *i.e.* Z_i *over-approximates the reachable cells that cannot reach an accepting cell in i steps or less;*
4. *if* $Z_i = Z_{i+1}$ *then* $post[A_i^\alpha](R_i) \subseteq \alpha_{\mathcal{P}_i}(Z_i)$.

Theorem 3. *The forward abstract algorithm with refinement is sound and complete to decide the emptiness of* AFA.

6 Experimental Evaluation

In this section, we evaluate the practical performance of our techniques with three series of benchmarks. Each benchmark is composed of a pair of LTL formulas $\langle \psi, \phi \rangle$ interpreted on finite words, and for which we want to know if ϕ is a logical consequence of ψ, i.e. if $\psi \models \phi$ holds. To solve this problem, we translate the formula $\psi \wedge \neg \phi$ into an AFA and check that the language of the AFA is empty. This translation is linear in the size of the formula (except for the alphabet which is of exponential size) and creates a location in the AFA for each subformula. As we will see, our ψ formulas are constructed as large conjunctions of constraints and model the behavior of finite-state systems, while the ϕ formulas model properties of those systems. We defined properties with varying degrees of *locality*. Intuitively, a property ϕ is local when only a small number of subformulas of ψ are needed to establish $\psi \models \phi$. This is not a formal notion but it will be clear from the examples. We will show in this section that our abstract algorithms are able to automatically identify subformulas which are not needed to establish the property. Due to lack of space, we only report results where $\psi \models \phi$ holds. We now present each benchmark in turn.

Benchmark 1. The first benchmark takes 2 parameters $n > 0$ and $0 < k \leq n$: $\mathsf{Bench1}(n, k) = \langle \bigwedge_{i=0}^{n-1} G(p_i \rightarrow (F(\neg p_i) \wedge F(p_{i+1}))), Fp_0 \rightarrow Fp_k \rangle$. Clearly we have that $\psi \models \phi$ holds for all values of k and also that the subformulas of ψ for $i > k$ are not needed to establish $\psi \models \phi$.

Benchmark 2. This second benchmark is used to demonstrate how our algorithms can automatically detect less obvious versions of locality than for Bench1. It uses 2 parameters k and n with $0 < k \leq n$ and is built using the following recursive nesting definition: $\mathsf{Sub}(n, 1) = Fp_n$; for odd values of $k > 1$ $\mathsf{Sub}(n, k) = F(p_n \wedge X(\mathsf{Sub}(n, k-1)))$; and for even values of $k > 1$ $\mathsf{Sub}(n, k) = F(\neg p_n \wedge X(\mathsf{Sub}(n, k-1)))$. Our second benchmark is : $\mathsf{Bench2}(n, k) = \langle \bigwedge_{i=0}^{n-1} G(p_i \rightarrow \mathsf{Sub}(i+1, k)), Fp_0 \rightarrow Fp_n \rangle$. It is relatively easy to see that $\psi \models \phi$ holds for any value of k, and that for odd values of k, the nested subformulas beyond the first level are not needed to establish the property.

Benchmark 3. This third and final benchmark aims to demonstrate the usefulness of our abstraction algorithms in a more realistic setting. We specified the behavior of a lift with n floors with a parametric **LTL** formula.For n floors, Prop = $\{f_1, \ldots, f_n, b_1, \ldots, b_n, open\}$. The f_i propositions represent the current floor. Only one of the f_i's can be true at any time, which is initially f_1. The b_i propositions represent the state (lit or unlit) of the call-buttons of each floor and there is only one button per floor. The additional *open* proposition is true when the doors of the lift are open. The constraints on the dynamics of this system are as follows : (i) initially the lift is at the first floor and the doors are open, (ii) the lift must close its doors when changing floors, (iii) the lift must go through floors in the correct order, (iv) when a button is lit, the lift eventually reaches the corresponding floor and opens its doors, and finally (v) when the lift reaches a floor, the corresponding button becomes unlit. Let n be the number of floors. We apply our algorithms to check two properties which depend on a parameter k with $1 < k \leq n$, namely $\mathsf{Spec1}(k) = G((f_1 \wedge b_k) \rightarrow (\neg f_k U f_{k-1}))$, and $\mathsf{Spec2}(k) = G((f_1 \wedge b_k \wedge b_{k-1}) \rightarrow (b_k U \neg b_{k-1}))$.

Experimental results. All the results of our experiments are found in Fig. 2, and were performed on a quad-core 3,2 Ghz Intel CPU with 12 Gb of memory. Due to lack of space, we only report results for the concrete forward and abstract backward algorithms which were the fastest (by a large factor) in all our experiments. The columns of the table are as follows. *ATC* is the size of the largest antichain encountered, *iters* is the number of iterations of the fixpoint in the concrete case and the maximal number of iterations of all the abstract fixpoints in the abstract case, ATC^α and ATC^γ are respectively the sizes of the largest abstract and concrete antichains encountered, *steps* is the number of execution of the refinement steps and $|\mathcal{P}|$ is the maximum number of blocks in the partitions.

Benchmark 1. The partition sizes of the first benchmark illustrate how our algorithm exploits the locality of the property to abstract away the irrelevant parts of the system. For local properties, i.e. for small values of k, $|\mathcal{P}|$ is small compared to $|\mathsf{Loc}|$ meaning that the algorithm automatically ignores many subformulas which are irrelevant to the property. For larger values of k, the abstraction overhead becomes larger, but that overhead becomes less important as the system grows.

Benchmark 2. On the second benchmark, our abstract algorithm largely outperforms the concrete algorithm. Notice how for $k \geq 3$ the partition sizes do not continue to grow (it also holds for values of k beyond 5). This means that contrary to the concrete algorithm, FGAR does not get trapped in the intricate nesting of the F modalities (which are not

	n	k	‖Loc‖	‖Prop‖	concrete forward			abstract backward					
					time	ATC	iters	time	ATC^α	ATC^γ	iters	steps	‖$\mathcal{P}$‖
Bench1	11	5	50	12	0,10	6	3	0,23	55	2	5	3	27
	15	5	66	16	1,60	6	3	0,56	55	2	5	3	31
	19	5	82	20	76,62	6	3	8,64	55	2	5	3	35
	11	7	50	12	0,13	8	3	0,87	201	2	5	3	31
	15	7	66	16	2,04	8	3	1,21	201	2	5	3	35
	19	7	82	20	95,79	8	3	9,99	201	2	5	3	39
	11	9	50	12	0,16	10	3	12,60	779	2	5	3	35
	15	9	66	16	2,69	10	3	13,42	779	2	5	3	39
	19	9	82	20	125,85	10	3	46,47	779	2	5	3	43
Bench2	7	1	19	8	0,06	8	2	0,10	11	2	4	3	14
	10	1	25	11	0,06	10	2	0,10	14	2	4	3	17
	13	1	31	14	0,08	14	2	0,12	17	2	4	3	20
	7	3	33	8	0,78	201	14	0,13	11	2	4	3	26
	10	3	45	11	802,17	4339	20	0,30	14	2	4	3	35
	13	3	57	14	> 1000	-	-	1,26	17	2	4	3	44
	7	5	47	8	88,15	2122	26	0,14	11	2	4	3	26
	10	5	65	11	> 1000	-	-	0,37	14	2	4	3	35
	13	5	83	14	> 1000	-	-	1,47	17	2	4	3	44
Lift : Spec1	8	3	84	17	0,30	10	17	0,51	23	40	7	4	21
	12	3	116	25	17,45	10	25	1,63	23	40	7	4	21
	16	3	148	33	498,65	10	33	26,65	23	40	7	4	21
	8	4	84	17	0,26	10	17	1,29	37	72	10	6	24
	12	4	116	25	17,81	10	25	5,02	37	72	10	6	24
	16	4	148	33	555,44	10	33	78,75	37	72	10	6	24
	8	5	84	17	0,32	10	17	3,70	42	141	12	8	27
	12	5	116	25	20,24	10	25	47,45	42	141	12	8	27
	16	5	148	33	543,27	10	33	> 1000	-	-	-	-	-
Lift : Spec2	8	3	84	17	0,46	10	17	1,18	58	72	8	4	22
	12	3	116	25	17,98	10	25	3,64	58	72	8	4	22
	16	3	148	33	557,75	10	33	48,90	58	72	8	4	22
	8	4	84	17	0,29	10	17	3,04	124	126	11	6	25
	12	4	116	25	19,29	10	25	10,63	124	126	11	6	25
	16	4	148	33	576,56	10	33	128,40	124	126	11	6	25
	8	5	84	17	0,31	10	17	15,88	131	266	14	8	28
	12	5	116	25	19,47	10	25	283,90	131	266	14	8	28
	16	5	148	33	568,83	10	33	> 1000	-	-	-	-	-

Fig. 2. Experimental results. Times are in seconds.

necessary to prove the property) and abstracts it completely with a constant number of partition blocks. The speed improvement is considerable.

Benchmark 3. On this final benchmark, the abstract algorithm outperforms the concrete algorithm when the locality of the property spans less than 5 floors. Beyond that value, the abstract algorithm starts to take longer than the concrete version. From the *ATC* column, the antichain sizes remain constant in the concrete algorithm, when the number of floors increases. This indicates that the difficulty of this benchmark comes mainly from the exponential size of the alphabet rather than the state-space itself. As our algorithms only abstracts the locations and not the alphabet, these results are not surprising.

7 Discussion

We have proposed in this paper two new abstract algorithms with refinement for deciding language emptiness for AFA. Our algorithm is based on an abstraction-refinement scheme inspired from [5], which is different from the usual refinement techniques based on counter-example elimination [4]. Our algorithm also builds on the successful technique of antichains, that we have introduced in [6], to symbolically manipulate closed sets of cells (sets of sets of locations). We have demonstrated with a set of benchmarks that our algorithm is able to find coarse abstractions for complex automata constructed from large LTL formulas. For a large number of instances of those benchmarks, the abstract algorithms outperform by several order of magnitude the concrete algorithms. We believe that this clearly shows the interest of our new algorithms and their potential future developments.

Acknowledgments. The authors would like to thank Gilles Geeraerts for some fruitful discussions on the abstraction scheme.

References

1. Bouajjani, A., Habermehl, P., Holík, L., Touili, T., Vojnar, T.: Antichain-based universality and inclusion testing over nondeterministic finite tree automata. In: Ibarra, O.H., Ravikumar, B. (eds.) CIAA 2008. LNCS, vol. 5148, pp. 57–67. Springer, Heidelberg (2008)
2. Burris, S., Sankappanavar, H.P.: A Course in Universal Algebra. Springer, Heidelberg (1981)
3. Chandra, A.K., Kozen, D., Stockmeyer, L.J.: Alternation. J. ACM 28(1), 114–133 (1981)
4. Clarke, E.M., Grumberg, O., Jha, S., Lu, Y., Veith, H.: Counterexample-guided abstraction refinement for symbolic model checking. J. ACM 50(5), 752–794 (2003)
5. Cousot, P., Ganty, P., Raskin, J.-F.: Fixpoint-guided abstraction refinements. In: Riis Nielson, H., Filé, G. (eds.) SAS 2007. LNCS, vol. 4634, pp. 333–348. Springer, Heidelberg (2007)
6. De Wulf, M., Doyen, L., Henzinger, T.A., Raskin, J.-F.: Antichains: A new algorithm for checking universality of finite automata. In: Ball, T., Jones, R.B. (eds.) CAV 2006. LNCS, vol. 4144, pp. 17–30. Springer, Heidelberg (2006)
7. De Wulf, M., Doyen, L., Maquet, N., Raskin, J.-F.: Alaska. In: Cha, S(S.), Choi, J.-Y., Kim, M., Lee, I., Viswanathan, M. (eds.) ATVA 2008. LNCS, vol. 5311, pp. 240–245. Springer, Heidelberg (2008)
8. De Wulf, M., Doyen, L., Maquet, N., Raskin, J.-F.: Antichains: Alternative algorithms for LTL satisfiability and model-checking. In: Ramakrishnan, C.R., Rehof, J. (eds.) TACAS 2008. LNCS, vol. 4963, pp. 63–77. Springer, Heidelberg (2008)
9. Doyen, L., Raskin, J.-F.: Improved algorithms for the automata-based approach to model-checking. In: Grumberg, O., Huth, M. (eds.) TACAS 2007. LNCS, vol. 4424, pp. 451–465. Springer, Heidelberg (2007)
10. Ganty, P.: The Fixpoint Checking Problem: An Abstraction Refinement Perspective. PhD thesis, Université Libre de Bruxelles (2007)
11. Ganty, P., Raskin, J.-F., Van Begin, L.: From many places to few: automatic abstraction refinement for petri nets. Fundamenta Informaticae 88(3), 275–305 (2008)
12. Raskin, J.-F., Chatterjee, K., Doyen, L., Henzinger, T.A.: Algorithms for omega-regular games with imperfect information. Logical Methods in Computer Science 3(3) (2007)

Automata-Based Termination Proofs

Radu Iosif[1] and Adam Rogalewicz[2]

[1] VERIMAG, CNRS, 2 av. de Vignate, F-38610 Gières
iosif@imag.fr
[2] FIT, BUT, Božetěchova 2, CZ-61266 Brno
rogalew@fit.vutbr.cz

Abstract. This paper proposes a framework for detecting termination of programs handling infinite and complex data domains, such as pointer structures. In this framework, the user has to specify a finite number of well-founded relations on the data domain manipulated by these programs. Our tool then builds an initial abstraction of the program, which is checked for existence of potential infinite runs, by testing emptiness of its intersection with a predefined Büchi automaton. If the intersection is non-empty, a lasso-shaped counterexample is found. This counterexample is checked for spuriousness by a domain-specific procedure, and in case it is found to be spurious, the abstraction is refined, again by intersection with the complement of the Büchi automaton representing the lasso. We have instantiated the framework for programs handling tree-like data structures, which allowed us to prove termination of programs such as the depth-first tree traversal, the Deutsch-Schorr-Waite tree traversal, or the linking leaves algorithm.

1 Introduction

Proving termination is an important challenge for the existing software verification tools, requiring specific analysis techniques [18,6,21]. The basic principle underlying these methods is proving that, in every infinite computation of the program, a certain measure, pertaining to a well-founded domain, decreases infinitely often.

We propose here a new termination analysis, based on the following principles:

1. We consider programs working on infinite data domains $\langle D, \preceq_1, \ldots, \preceq_n \rangle$ equipped with an arbitrary number of well-founded partial orders.
2. If $\Rightarrow \subseteq D \times D$ is any transformation induced by a program statement, and $\preceq_i$, $1 \leq i \leq n$ is any partial order on D, i.e. we assume that the problem $\Rightarrow \cap \preceq_i \overset{?}{=} \emptyset$ is decidable algorithmically.
3. An abstraction of the program is built automatically and checked for the existence of potential non-terminating execution paths. If such a path exists, then an infinite path of the form $\sigma\lambda^\omega$ (called *lasso*) is exhibited.
4. Due to the over-approximation involved in the construction of the abstraction, the lasso found may be *spurious* i.e. it may not correspond to a real execution of the program. In this case we use domain-specific procedures to detect spuriousness, and, if the lasso is found to be spurious, the abstraction is refined by eliminating it.

The framework described here needs to be instantiated for particular classes of programs, by providing the following ingredients:

S. Maneth (Ed.): CIAA 2009, LNCS 5642, pp. 165–177, 2009.
© Springer-Verlag Berlin Heidelberg 2009

- well-founded relations $\preceq_1, \ldots, \preceq_n$ on the working domain D. (In principle, their choice is naturally determined by the working domain.)
- a decision procedure for the problems $\Rightarrow \cap \preceq_i \overset{?}{=} \emptyset$, $1 \leq i \leq n$, where $\Rightarrow$ is any transition relation induced by a program statement.
- a decision procedure for the spuriousness problem: given a lasso $\sigma\lambda^\omega$, where σ and λ are finite sequences of program statements, does there exists an infinite execution of the program along the path $\sigma\lambda^\omega$?

The main reason for which we currently ask the user to provide the relations is that our technique is geared towards data domains which cannot be encoded by a finite number of descriptors, such as tree-structured domains, and more complex pointer structures. Well-founded relations for classical such domains (e.g. terms over a ranked alphabet) are provided in the literature. Moreover, we are not aware of efficient techniques for automatic discovery of well-founded relations on such domains, which is an interesting topic for future research.

Providing suitable representations for the well-founded relations, as well as for the program transitions enables the framework to compute an initial abstraction of the program. The initial abstraction is an automaton which has the same control states as the program, and each edge in the control flow graph of the program is covered by one or more transitions labeled with relational symbols.

The abstraction is next checked for the existence of potentially non-terminating executions. This check uses the information provided by the well-founded relations, and excludes all lassos for which there exists a strictly decreasing well-founded relation $\succ_i$, $1 \leq i \leq n$ that holds between the entry and exit of the loop body. This step amounts to checking non-emptiness of the intersection between the abstraction and a predefined Büchi automaton. If the intersection is empty, the original program terminates, otherwise a lasso-shaped counterexample of the form $\sigma\lambda^\omega$ is exhibited.

Deciding spuriousness of lassos is also a domain-dependent problem. For integer domains, techniques exist in cases where the transition relation of the loop is a difference bound matrix (DBM) [5] or an affine transformation with the finite monoid property [13]. For tree-structured data domains, we have shown decidability of spuriousness, in cases where the loop does not modify the structure of trees [14].

If a lasso is found to be spurious, the program model is refined by excluding the lasso from the abstraction automaton. In our framework based on Büchi Automata, this amounts to intersecting the abstraction automaton with the complement of the Büchi Automaton representing the lasso. Since a lasso is trivially a Weak Deterministic Büchi Automaton (WDBA), complementation increases the size of the automaton by at most one state, and is done in constant time. This refinement scheme can be extended to exclude entire families of spurious lassos, also described by WDBA.

We have instantiated the framework to the verification of programs handling trees and more complex data structures with a tree-like backbone, e.g. doubly-linked lists, trees with parent pointers, or trees with linked leaves. We provide two families of well-founded relations on trees, (i) a lexicographical ordering on positions of program variables and (ii) a subset relation on nodes labeled with a given data element (from a finite domain). Program statements as well as the well-founded relations are encoded using tree automata [8], which provide an effective method for checking emptiness of intersections between relations. A prototype tool has been implemented on top of the ARTMC [4] invariant generator for programs with dynamic linked data structures. Experimental results include push-button termination proofs for the Deutsch-Schorr-Waite tree traversal, deleting nodes in red-black trees, as well as for the Linking Leaves procedures. Most of these programs could not be verified by existing approaches.

Related Work. Efficient techniques have been developed in the past for proving termination of programs with integer variables [18,6]. This remains probably the most extensively explored class of programs, concerning termination.

Recently, techniques for programs with singly-linked lists have been developed in [2,12,16]. These techniques rely on tracking numeric information related to the sizes of the list segments. An extension of this method to tackle programs handling trees has been given in our previous work [14]. Unlike the works on singly-linked lists from [2,12], where refinement (of the counter model) is typically not needed, in [14] we considered a basic form of counterexample-driven refinement.

Abstraction refinement for termination has been first considered in [9], where the refinement consists in discovering and adding new well-founded relations to the set of relations used by the analysis. Since techniques for the discovery of well-founded relations (based on e.g., spurious program loops) are available only for integer domains, it is not clear for the time being whether the algorithm proposed in [9] can be also applied to programs handling pointer structures.

Several ideas in this paper can be also found elsewhere. Namely, (1) using Büchi automata to encode the non-termination condition of the program was introduced by [21], and (2) proving termination for programs handling tree-like data structures was also considered in [14]. On one hand, the *size-change* termination approach from [21] does not typically come with a refinement procedure. On the other hand, the method presented here is more general and its refinement schema is more efficient then the one presented in [14]. In particular, the *Red-Black Delete* example (presented in Section 4) could not be shown to terminate using the refinement method from [14].

Automated checking of termination of programs manipulating trees has been also considered in [17], where the Deutsch-Schorr-Waite tree traversal algorithm was proved to terminate using a manually created progress monitor. In our approach, this example could be verified using the common well-founded relations on trees.

2 The Termination Analysis Framework

We first explain the approach informally, with the aid of an example. Let us consider the program in Fig. 1 (a), working on a binary tree data structure, in which each node has two pointers to its left- and right-sons and one pointer up to its parent. We assume that leaves have null left and right pointers, and the root has a null up pointer.

The first loop (lines 2,3) terminates because the variable x is bound to reach a node with x.left = null (or x.left.right = null), since the tree is finite and no new nodes are created. The second loop (lines 4,5) terminates because no matter where x points to in the beginning, by going up, it will reach the root and then become null.

Let us suppose that the only well-founded ordering considered is the following: for any two trees t_1 and t_2, we have $t_1 \geq_x t_2$ if and only if the position of x in t_2 is a prefix

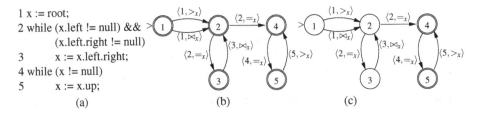

```
1 x := root;
2 while (x.left != null) &&
       (x.left.right != null)
3      x := x.left.right;
4 while (x != null)
5      x := x.up;
```

(a)   (b)   (c)

Fig. 1.

of the position of x in t_1. Then we build the abstraction of the program given in Fig. 1 (b), where $=_x$ holds if both $\leq_x$ and $\geq_x$ hold, and $\bowtie_x$ stands for $\not\geq_x$.

The states in the abstract model correspond to line numbers in the original program, and every state is considered to be accepting, initially. Checking non-termination of the abstract model amounts to checking the existence of an infinite run that *does not* have a suffix of the form $(=_x^* >_x)^\omega$, for otherwise, the well-foundedness of $\geq_x$ would prevent this execution from occurring in reality. Checking non-termination is done by checking emptiness of the intersection between the abstraction and the complement of the Büchi automaton recognizing the language $(\langle \_, =_x \rangle^* \langle \_, >_x \rangle)^\omega$ (cf. Fig. 2). For technical reasons that will become clear in the sequel we label the edges of the automaton with the identifier of the source states, which correspond to program lines. In our case, the intersection is not empty, counterexamples being $\langle 1, >_x \rangle (\langle 2, =_x \rangle \langle 3, \bowtie_x \rangle)^\omega$ and $\langle 1, \bowtie_x \rangle (\langle 2, =_x \rangle \langle 3, \bowtie_x \rangle)^\omega$, which both correspond to the infinite execution of the first loop, i.e. lines $1(23)^\omega$.

This execution is found to be spurious by a specialized procedure that checks whether a given program lasso can be fired infinitely often. For this purpose, the method given in [14] could be used here. The refinement of the abstraction consists in eliminating the infinite path $1(23)^\omega$ from the model. This is done by intersecting the model with the automaton that recognizes the *complement* of the language $\{\langle 1, \geq_x \rangle, \langle 1, \bowtie_x \rangle\}$ $(\langle 2, =_x \rangle \langle 3, \bowtie_x \rangle)^\omega$, which corresponds to the program path $1(23)^\omega$. The result of this intersection is shown Fig. 1 (c). Notice that, in this case, the refinement does not increase the size of the abstraction. Since now, only 4 and 5 are accepting states, another intersection with the automaton in Fig. 2 will establish that the refined abstraction does not have further non-terminating executions, proving thus termination of the original program.

2.1   Büchi Automata

This section introduces the necessary notions related to the theory of Büchi automata. Let $\Sigma = \{a, b, \ldots\}$ be a finite alphabet. We denote by Σ^* the set of finite words over Σ, and by Σ^ω we denote the set of all infinite words over Σ. For an infinite word $w \in \Sigma^\omega$, let $\inf(w)$ be the set of symbols occurring infinitely often on w. If $u, v \in \Sigma^*$ are finite words, uv^ω denotes the infinite word $uvvv\ldots$.

A *Büchi automaton* (BA) over Σ is a tuple $A = \langle S, I, \rightarrow, F \rangle$, where: S is a finite set of states, $I \subseteq S$ is a set of *initial states*, $\rightarrow \subseteq S \times \Sigma \times S$ is a *transition relation* – we denote $(s, a, s') \in \rightarrow$ by $s \xrightarrow{a} s'$, and $F \subseteq S$ is a set of *final states*.

A run of A over an infinite word $a_0 a_1 a_2 \ldots \in \Sigma^\omega$ is an infinite sequence of states $s_0 s_1 s_2 \ldots$ such that $s_0 \in I$ and for all $i \geq 0$ we have $s_i \xrightarrow{a_i} s_{i+1}$. A run π of A is said to be *accepting* iff $\inf(\pi) \cap F \neq \emptyset$. An infinite word w is *accepted* by a Büchi automaton A iff A has an accepting run on w. The *language* of A, denoted by $\mathcal{L}(A)$, is the set of all words accepted by A.

It is well-known that Büchi-recognizable languages are closed under union, intersection and complement. For two Büchi automata A and B, let $A \otimes B$ be the automaton recognizing the language $\mathcal{L}(A) \cap \mathcal{L}(B)$. If $\|A\|$ denotes the number of states (size) of A, it can be shown that $\|A \otimes B\| \leq 3 \cdot \|A\| \cdot \|B\|$.

A Büchi automaton $A = \langle S, I, \rightarrow, F \rangle$ is said to be *complete* if for every $s \in S$ and $a \in \Sigma$ there exists $s' \in S$ such that $s \xrightarrow{a} s'$. A is said to be *deterministic* (DBA) if I is a singleton, and for each $s \in S$ and $a \in \Sigma$, there exists at most one state $s' \in S$ such that $s \xrightarrow{a} s'$. A is moreover said to be *weak* if, for each strongly connected component $C \subseteq S$, either $C \subseteq F$ or $C \cap F = \emptyset$. It is well-known that complete weak deterministic Büchi automata can be complemented by simply reverting accepting and non-accepting states. Then, for any Weak Deterministic Büchi automaton (WDBA), we have that $\|\overline{A}\| \leq \|A\| + 1$, where $\overline{A}$ is the automaton accepting the language $\Sigma^\omega \setminus \mathcal{L}(A)$—i.e. the *complement* of A.

2.2 Programs and Abstractions

In this section we introduce a model for programs handling data from a possibly infinite domain D, and define program abstractions as Büchi automata. Let $\mathfrak{I}$ be a finite set of *instructions* over a data domain $\langle D, \preceq_1, \ldots, \preceq_n \rangle$, where $\preceq_i \subseteq D \times D$ is a partial order, for $1 \leq i \leq n$. An instruction $i \in \mathfrak{I}$ is a pair $\langle g, a \rangle$ where $g \subseteq D$ is called the *guard* and $a : D \rightarrow D$ is called the *action*. An unspecified guard is assumed to be the entire domain.

A *program* over $\mathfrak{I}$ is a graph $P = \langle \mathfrak{I}, L, l_0, \Rightarrow \rangle$, where L is the set of *control locations*, $l_0 \in L$ is the *initial location*, and $\Rightarrow \subseteq L \times \mathfrak{I} \times L$ is the *edge relation* denoted as $l \xRightarrow{g:a} l'$. We assume furthermore, that there is at most one instruction in between any two control locations, i.e. if $l \xRightarrow{g_1:a_1} l'$ and $l \xRightarrow{g_2:a_2} l'$ then $g_1 = g_2$ and $a_1 = a_2$.

A *program configuration* is a pair $\langle l, d \rangle \in L \times D$, where l is a control location and d is a data value. An *execution* is a (possibly infinite) sequence of program configurations $\langle l_0, d_0 \rangle, \langle l_1, d_1 \rangle, \langle l_2, d_2 \rangle, \ldots$ starting with the initial program location l_0 and some configuration $d_0 \in D$ such that, for all $i \geq 0$ there exists an edge $l_i \xRightarrow{g:a} l_{i+1}$ in the program, such that $d_i \in g$ and $d_{i+1} = a(d_i)$.

Let $D_0 \subseteq D$ be a set of initial data values. Then a configuration $\langle l, d \rangle$ is said to be *reachable* if there exists $d_0 \in D_0$, and the program has an execution from $\langle l_0, d_0 \rangle$ to $\langle l, d \rangle$. An *invariant* of the program (with respect to the set D_0) is a function $\iota : L \rightarrow 2^D$ such that, for each $l \in L$, if $\langle l, d \rangle$ is reachable, then $d \in \iota(l)$.

Given a program $P = \langle \mathfrak{I}, L, l_0, \Rightarrow \rangle$ working over a domain $\langle D, \preceq_1, \ldots, \preceq_n \rangle$ we define the alphabet $\Sigma_{(P,D)} = L \times \{>, \bowtie, =\}^n$. For a tuple $\rho \in \{>, \bowtie, =\}^n$, we define $[\rho] \in D \times D$ as $: d [\langle r_1, \ldots, r_n \rangle] d'$ if and only if, for all $1 \leq i \leq n$: (i) $d \succ_i d'$ iff r_i is $>$, (ii) $d \not\preceq_i d'$ iff r_i is $\bowtie$, and (iii) $d \approx_i d'$ iff r_i is $=$.

Definition 1. *Let $P = \langle \mathfrak{I}, L, l_0, \Rightarrow \rangle$ be a program, and $\langle D, \preceq_1, \ldots, \preceq_n \rangle$ be a domain. A Büchi automaton $A = \langle S, I, \rightarrow, F \rangle$ over $\Sigma_{(P,D)}$ is said to be an abstraction of P if and* *only if, for every infinite execution of P :* $\langle l_0, d_0 \rangle \langle l_1, d_1 \rangle \langle l_2, d_2 \rangle \ldots$, *there exists an infinite word* $\langle l_0, \rho_0 \rangle \langle l_1, \rho_1 \rangle \langle l_2, \rho_2 \rangle \ldots \in L(A)$ *such that* $d_i [\rho_i] d_{i+1}$, *for all* $i \geq 0$.

Consequently, if P has a non-terminating execution, then its abstraction A will be non-empty. However, for reasons related to the complexity of the universal termination problem, one cannot in general build an abstraction of a program that will be empty if and only if the program terminates.

2.3   Building Abstractions Automatically

A first question is how to build abstractions of programs effectively. We propose a method that performs under the assumption that program instructions, as well as the relations of the working domain can be symbolically represented by structures that are closed under projection, intersection and complement, and which, moreover, have a decidable emptiness problem.

Given a program $P = \langle \mathfrak{I}, L, l_0, \Rightarrow \rangle$ working over the domain $\langle D, \preceq_1, \ldots, \preceq_n \rangle$, and an invariant $\iota : L \to 2^D$, with respect to a set of initial data values D_0, the *initial abstraction* is the Büchi automaton $A_P^\iota = \langle L, \{l_0\}, \to, L \rangle$, where, for all $l, l' \in L$ and $\rho \in \{>, \bowtie, =\}^n$, we have :

$$l \xrightarrow{\langle l, \rho \rangle} l' \iff l \xrightarrow{g:a} l' \text{ and } pr_1(R_{\langle g, a \rangle} \cap [\rho]) \cap \iota(l) \neq \emptyset \tag{1}$$

where $R_{\langle g, a \rangle} = \{(d, d') \in D \mid d \in g, \, d' = a(d)\}$ and, for a relation $R \subseteq D \times D$, we denote by $pr_1(R) = \{x \mid \exists y \in D . \langle x, y \rangle \in R\}$.

Intuitively, a transition between l and l' is labeled with a tuple of relational symbols ρ if and only if there exists a program instruction between l and l' and a pair of reachable configurations $\langle l, d \rangle, \langle l', d' \rangle \in L \times D$ such that $d[\rho]d'$ and the program can move from $\langle l, d \rangle$ to $\langle l', d' \rangle$ by executing the instruction $\langle g, a \rangle$. The intuition is that every transition relation induced by the program is "covered" by all partial orderings that have a non-empty intersection with it. For reasons related to abstraction refinement, that will be made clear in the following, the transition in the Büchi automaton A_P^ι is also labeled with the source program location l. As an example, Fig. 1 (b) gives the initial abstraction for the program in Fig. 1 (a).

The program invariant $\iota(l)$ from (1) is needed in order to limit the coverage only to the relations involving configurations reachable at line l. In principle, we can compute a very coarse initial abstraction by considering that $\iota(l) = D$ at each program line. However, using stronger invariants enables us to compute more precise program abstractions. The following lemma proves that the initial abstraction respects Def. 1. For space reasons, all proofs have been deferred to technical report [22].

Lemma 1. *Given a program P working over the domain* $\langle D, \preceq_1, \ldots, \preceq_n \rangle$, $D_0 \subseteq D$ *an initial set, and* $\iota : L \to 2^D$ *an invariant with respect to the initial set* D_0, *the Büchi automaton* A_P^ι *is an abstraction of P.*

2.4   Checking Termination on Program Abstractions

In light of Def. 1, if a Büchi automaton A is an abstraction of a program P, then each accepting run of A reveals a *potentially* infinite execution of P. However, the set of accepting runs of a Büchi automaton is, in general not enumerable, therefore an effective termination analysis cannot attempt to check whether each run of A corresponds to a real computation of P. We propose an effective technique, based on the following:

Hypothesis 1. *The given domain is $\langle D, \preceq_1, \ldots, \preceq_n \rangle$ for a fixed $n > 0$, and the partial orders $\preceq_i$ are well-founded, for all $i = 1, \ldots, n$.*

Consequently, any infinite word $\langle l_0, \rho_0 \rangle \langle l_1, \rho_1 \rangle \langle l_2, \rho_2 \rangle \ldots \in L(A)$ from which we can extract a sequence $(\rho_0)_i (\rho_1)_i (\rho_2)_i \ldots \in (=^*>)^\omega$, for some $1 \leq i \leq n$, cannot correspond to a real execution of the program, in the sense of Definition 1. Therefore, we must consider only the words for which, for all $1 \leq i \leq n$, either:

1. there exists $K \in \mathbb{N}$ such that, $(\rho_k)_i$ is $=$, for all $k \geq K$, or
2. for infinitely many $k \in \mathbb{N}$, $(\rho_k)_i$ is $\bowtie$.

The condition above can be encoded by a Büchi automaton defined as follows. Consider that $\Sigma_{(P,D)} = L \times \{>, \bowtie, =\}^n$ is fixed. Let $S_i = \{\langle l, (r_1, \ldots, r_n) \rangle \in \Sigma_{(P,D)} \mid r_i \text{ is } \bowtie\}$ and $E_i = \{\langle l, (r_1, \ldots, r_n) \rangle \in \Sigma_{(P,D)} \mid r_i \text{ is } =\}$, for $1 \leq i \leq n$. With this notation, let B_i be the Büchi automaton recognizing the ω-regular language $\Sigma^* (S_i \Sigma^*)^\omega \cup \Sigma^* E_i^\omega$. This automaton is depicted in Fig. 2. Since the above condition holds for all $1 \leq i \leq n$, we need to compute $B = \bigotimes_{i=1}^n B_i$.

If A is an abstraction of P and $L(A \otimes B) = L(A) \cap L(B) = \emptyset$, we can infer that P has no infinite runs. Otherwise, it is possible to exhibit a lasso-shaped non-termination witness of the form $\sigma \lambda^\omega \in L(A \otimes B)$, where $\sigma, \lambda \in \Sigma^*$ are finite words labeling finite paths in $A \otimes B$. The following lemma proves the existence of lasso-shaped counterexamples.

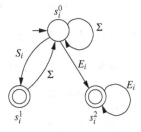

Fig. 2.

Lemma 2. *Given a well-founded domain $\langle D, \preceq_1, \ldots, \preceq_n \rangle$, A and $B = \bigotimes_{i=1}^n B_i$ Büchi automata over the alphabet $\Sigma_{(P,D)}$, if $L(A \otimes B) \neq \emptyset$ then $\sigma \lambda^\omega \in L(A \otimes B)$ for some $\sigma, \lambda \in \Sigma_{(P,D)}^*$, where $|\sigma|, |\lambda| \leq \|A\| \cdot (n+1) \cdot 2^n$.*

Despite the exponential bound on the size of the counterexamples, in practice it is possible to use efficient algorithms for finding lassos in Büchi automata on-the-fly, such as for instance the Nested Depth First Search algorithm [11].

2.5 Counterexample-Based Abstraction Refinement

If a Büchi automaton A is an abstraction of a program $P = \langle \mathfrak{I}, L, l_0, \Rightarrow \rangle$ (cf. Def. 1), $D_0 \in D$ is a set of initial values, and $\sigma \lambda^\omega \in L(A)$ is a lasso, where $\sigma = \langle l_0, \rho_0 \rangle \ldots \langle l_{|\sigma|-1}, \rho_{|\sigma|-1} \rangle$ and $\lambda = \langle l_{|\sigma|}, \rho_{|\sigma|} \rangle \ldots \langle l_{|\sigma|+|\lambda|-1}, \rho_{|\sigma|+|\lambda|-1} \rangle$, the *spuriousness problem* asks whether P has an execution along the infinite path $(l_0 \ldots l_{|\sigma|-1})(l_{|\sigma|} \ldots l_{|\sigma|+|\lambda|-1})^\omega$ starting with some value $d_0 \in D_0$. Notice that each pair of control locations corresponds to exactly one program instruction, therefore the sequence of instructions corresponding to the infinite unfolding of the lasso is uniquely identified by the sequences of locations $l_0, \ldots, l_{|\sigma|-1}$ and $l_{|\sigma|}, \ldots, l_{|\sigma|+|\lambda|-1}$.

Algorithms for solving the spuriousness problem exist, depending on the structure of the domain D and on the semantics of the program instructions. Details regarding spuriousness problems for integer and tree-manipulating lassos can be found in [14].

Given a lasso $\sigma\lambda^\omega \in L(A)$, the refinement builds another abstraction A' of P such that $\sigma\lambda^\omega \notin L(A')$. Having established that the program path $(l_0 \ldots l_{|\sigma|-1})(l_{|\sigma|} \cdots l_{|\sigma|+|\lambda|-1})^\omega$, corresponding to $\sigma\lambda^\omega$, cannot be executed for any value from the initial set, allows us to refine by excluding potentially more spurious witnesses, than just $\sigma\lambda^\omega$. Let C be the Büchi automaton recognizing the language $L_\sigma L_\lambda^\omega$, where:

$$L_\sigma = \{\langle l_0, \rho_0 \rangle \ldots \langle l_{|\sigma|-1}, \rho_{|\sigma|-1} \rangle \mid \rho_i \in \{>, \bowtie, =\}^n, \ 0 \le i < |\sigma|\}$$
$$L_\lambda = \{\langle l_{|\sigma|}, \rho_0 \rangle \ldots \langle l_{|\sigma|+|\lambda|-1}, \rho_{|\lambda|-1} \rangle \mid \rho_i \in \{>, \bowtie, =\}^n, \ 0 \le i < |\lambda|\}$$

Then $A' = A \otimes \overline{C}$, where $\overline{C}$ is the complement of C, is the refinement of A that excludes the lasso $\sigma\lambda^\omega$, and all other lassos corresponding to the program path $(l_0 \ldots l_{|\sigma|-1})(l_{|\sigma|} \cdots l_{|\sigma|+|\lambda|-1})^\omega$.

On the down side, complementation of Büchi automata is, in general, a costly operation: the size of the complement is bounded by $2^{O(n \log n)}$, where n is the size of the automaton, and this is also a lower bound [20]. However, the particular structure of the automata considered here comes to rescue. It can be seen that $L_\sigma L_\lambda^\omega$ can be recognized by a WDBA, hence complementation is done in constant time, and $\|A'\| \le 3 \cdot (|\sigma| + |\lambda| + 1) \cdot \|A\|$.

Lemma 3. *Let A be a Büchi automaton that is an abstraction of a program P, and $\sigma\lambda^\omega \in L(A)$ be a spurious counterexample. Then the Büchi automaton recognizing the language $L(A) \setminus L_\sigma \cdot L_\lambda^\omega$ is an abstraction of P.*

This refinement technique, based on the closure of ω-regular languages, can be generalized to exclude an entire family of counterexamples, described as an ω-regular language, all at once. In the following we provide such a refinement heuristics. The interested reader is pointed to [22] for another refinement heuristic.

Infeasible Elementary Loop Refinement. We suppose that there exists an upper bound $B > 0$ on the number of times λ can be iterated, starting with any data value from $\iota(l_{|\sigma|})$. The existence of such a bound can be discovered by e.g. a symbolic execution of the loop. In case such a bound exists, the language $\Sigma^*_{(P,D)} \cdot L_\lambda^B \cdot \Sigma^\omega_{(P,D)}$ is easily shown to be recognizable by a WDBA C, and the Büchi automaton $A \otimes \overline{C}$ is an abstraction of P, which excludes the spurious trace $\sigma\lambda^\omega$, as shown by the following Lemma:

Lemma 4. *Given a program $P = \langle \mathfrak{I}, L, l_0, \Rightarrow \rangle$, $\iota : L \to 2^D$ and invariant of P, A an abstraction of P, and $\lambda \in \Sigma^*_{(P,D)}$ a lasso starting and ending with $\ell \in L$. If there exists $B > 0$ such that λ^B is infeasible, for any $d \in \iota(\ell)$, then the Büchi automaton recognizing the language $L(A) \setminus \Sigma^*_{(P,D)} \cdot L_\lambda^B \cdot \Sigma^\omega_{(P,D)}$ is an abstraction of P.*

This heuristic was used to prove termination of the *Red-black delete* algorithm, reported in Section 4. Interestingly, this algorithm could not be proved to terminate using standard refinement (cf. Lemma 3).

3   Proving Termination of Programs with Trees

In this section we instantiate our termination verification framework for programs manipulating tree-like data structures. We consider sequential, non-recursive C-like programs working over tree-shaped data structures with a finite set of pointer variables *PVar*. Each node in a tree contains a data value field, ranging over a finite set *Data* and three selector fields, denoted left, right, and up. For $x, y \in PVar$ and $d \in Data$, we consider the programs over the set of instructions $\mathfrak{I}_T$ composed of the following :

- **guards** : $x == \texttt{null}, x == y, x.\texttt{data} == d$, and boolean combinations of the above,
- **actions** : $x = \texttt{null}, x = y, x = y.\{\texttt{left}|\texttt{right}|\texttt{up}\}, x.\texttt{data} = d, x.\{\texttt{left}|\texttt{right}\} = \texttt{new}$ and $x.\{\texttt{left}|\texttt{right}\} = \texttt{null}$.

This set of instructions covers a large class of practical tree-manipulating procedures. For instance, Fig. 3 shows a depth-first tree traversal procedure, commonly used in real-life programs. In particular, here $PVar = \{x\}$ and $Data = \{marked, unmarked\}$.

In order to use our framework for analyzing termination of programs with trees, we need to provide (1) well-founded partial orderings on the tree domain, (2) symbolic encodings for the partial orderings as well as for the program semantics and (3) a decision procedure for the spuriousness problem. The last point was tackled in our previous work [14], for lassos without destructive updates (i.e. instructions x.left|right := new|null). Recently, we have developed a spuriousness detection method that works also these destructive updates [15].

3.1   Trees and Tree Automata

For a partial mapping $f : A \rightarrow B$ we denote $f(x) = \bot$ the fact that f is undefined at some point $x \in A$. The domain of f is denoted $dom(f) = \{x \in A \mid f(x) \neq \bot\}$.

Given a finite set of *colors* C, we define the *binary alphabet* $\Sigma_C = C \cup \{\Box\}$, where the *arity* function is $\#(c) = 2$ and $\#(\Box) = 0$. Π denotes the set of tree positions $\{0, 1\}^*$. Let $\varepsilon \in \Pi$ denote the empty sequence, and $p.q$ denote the concatenation of sequences $p, q \in \Pi$. $p \leq_{pre} q$ denotes the fact that p is a prefix of q and $p \leq_{lex} q$ is used to denote the fact that p is less than q in the lexicographical order. We denote by $p \simeq_{pre} q$ the fact that either $p \leq_{pre} q$, or $p \geq_{pre} q$. A *tree* t over C is a partial mapping $t : \Pi \rightarrow \Sigma_C$ such that $dom(t)$ is a finite prefix-closed subset of Π, and for each $p \in dom(t)$:

```
0   x := root;
1   while (x!=null)
2       if (x.left!=null) and
            (x.left.data!=mark)
3           x:=x.left;
4       else if (x.right!=null) and
            (x.right.data!=mark)
5           x:=x.right;
        else
6           x.data:=marked;
7           x:=x.up;
```

Fig. 3. Depth-first tree traversal

- if $\#(t(p)) = 0$, then $t(p.0) = t(p.1) = \bot$,
- otherwise, if $\#(t(p)) = 2$, then $p.0, p.1 \in dom(t)$.

When writing $t(p) = \bot$, we mean that t is undefined at position p. We denote by $\mathcal{T}(C)$ the set of all trees over the alphabet Σ_C.

A pair of trees $(t_1, t_2) \in \mathcal{T}(C_1) \times \mathcal{T}(C_2)$ can be encoded by a tree over the alphabet $(C_1 \cup \{\Box, \bot\}) \times (C_2 \cup \{\Box, \bot\})$, where $\#(\langle \bot, \bot \rangle) = 0$, $\#(\langle \alpha, \bot \rangle) = \#(\langle \bot, \alpha \rangle) = \#(\alpha)$ if $\alpha \neq \bot$, and $\#(\langle \alpha_1, \alpha_2 \rangle) = \max(\#(\alpha_1), \#(\alpha_2))$. The projection functions are defined as usual i.e., for all $p \in dom(t)$ we have $pr_1(t)(p) = c_1$ if $t(p) = \langle c_1, c_2 \rangle$ and $pr_2(t)(p) = c_2$ if $t(p) = \langle c_1, c_2 \rangle$. Finally, let $\mathcal{T}(C_1 \times C_2) = \{t \mid pr_1(t) \in \mathcal{T}(C_1) \text{ and } pr_2(t) \in \mathcal{T}(C_2)\}$.

A *tree automaton* [8] over an alphabet Σ_C is a tuple $A = (Q, F, \Delta)$ where Q is a set of states, $F \subseteq Q$ is a set of final states, and Δ is a set of transition rules of the form: (i) $\Box \to q$ or (ii) $c(q_1, q_2) \to q$, $c \in C$.

A *run* of A over a tree $t : \Pi \to \Sigma_C$ is a mapping $\pi : dom(t) \to Q$ such that for each position $p \in dom(t)$, where $q = \pi(p)$, we have:

- if $\#(t(p)) = 0$ (i.e., if $t(p) = \Box$), then $\Box \to q \in \Delta$,
- otherwise, if $\#(t(p)) = 2$ and $q_i = \pi(p.i)$ for $i \in \{0, 1\}$, then $t(p)(q_0, q_1) \to q \in \Delta$.

A run π is said to be *accepting* if and only if $\pi(\varepsilon) \in F$. The *language* of A, denoted as $\mathcal{L}(A)$, is the set of all trees over which A has an accepting run. A set of trees $T \subseteq \mathcal{T}(C)$ (a tree relation $R \subseteq \mathcal{T}(C_1 \times C_2)$) is said to be *rational* if there exists a tree automaton A such that $\mathcal{L}(A) = T$ (respectively, $\mathcal{L}(A) = R$).

For two relations $R' \subseteq \mathcal{T}(C \times C')$ and $R'' \subseteq \mathcal{T}(C' \times C'')$ we define the composition $R' \circ R'' = \{\langle pr_1(t'), pr_2(t'') \rangle \mid t' \in R', t'' \in R'', pr_2(t') = pr_1(t'')\}$. It is well-known that rational tree languages are closed under union, intersection, complement and projection.

3.2   Abstracting Programs with Trees into Büchi Automata

A memory configuration is a binary tree with nodes labeled by elements of the set $C = Data \times 2^{PVar} \cup \{\Box\}$ i.e., a node is either null ($\Box$) or it contains a data value and a set of pointer variables pointing to it ($\langle d, V \rangle \in D \times 2^{PVar}$). Each pointer variable can point to at most one tree node (if it is null, it does not appear in the tree). For a tree $t \in \mathcal{T}(C)$ and a position $p \in dom(t)$ such that $t(p) = \langle d, V \rangle$, we denote $\delta_t(p) = d$ and $v_t(p) = V$. First we show that all program actions considered here can be encoded as rational tree relations[1].

Lemma 5. *For any program instruction* $i = \langle g, a \rangle \in \mathfrak{I}_T$, *the tree relation* $R_i = \{\langle t, t' \rangle \mid t \in g, t' = a(t)\}$ *is rational.*

In order to abstract programs with trees as Büchi automata (cf. Def. 1), we must introduce the well-founded partial orders on the working domain. Let $D_T = \langle \mathcal{T}(C), \{\preceq_x, \preceq_x^r\}_{x \in PVar}, \{\preceq_d, \preceq_d^r\}_{d \in Data} \rangle$, where:

- $t_1 \preceq_x t_2$, for some $x \in PVar$ iff there exists positions $p_1 \in dom(t_1)$, $p_2 \in dom(t_2)$ such that $x \in v_{t_1}(p_1)$, $x \in v_{t_2}(p_2)$ and $p_1 \leq_{lex} p_2$.
- $t_1 \preceq_x^r t_2$, for some $x \in PVar$ iff (i) $dom(t_1) \subseteq dom(t_2)$, and (ii) there exists positions $p_1 \in dom(t_1)$, $p_2 \in dom(t_2)$ such that $x \in v_{t_1}(p_1)$, $x \in v_{t_2}(p_2)$ and $p_1 \geq_{lex} p_2$.
- $t_1 \preceq_d t_2$, for some $d \in Data$ iff for any position $p \in dom(t_1)$ such that $\delta_{t_1}(p) = d$ we have $p \in dom(t_2)$ and $\delta_{t_2}(p) = d$.
- $t_1 \preceq_d^r t_2$, for some $d \in Data$ iff (i) $dom(t_1) \subseteq dom(t_2)$, and (ii) for any position $p \in dom(t_2)$ such that $\delta_{t_2}(p) = d$ we have $p \in dom(t_1)$ and $\delta_{t_1}(p) = d$.

---

[1] The semantics of the program instructions considered is given in technical report [22].

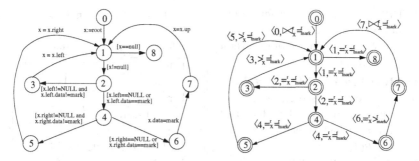

Fig. 4. The Depth-first tree traversal procedure and its initial abstraction

It can easily be shown that all relations of the form $\preceq_x$, $\preceq_x^r$, $\preceq_d$ and $\preceq_d^r$ are well-founded. Therefore the Hypothesis 1 is true for the working domain $D_T = \langle \mathcal{T}(C), \{\preceq_x, \preceq_x^r\}_{x \in PVar}, \{\preceq_d, \preceq_d^r\}_{d \in Data}\rangle$, and hence the whole termination analysis framework presented in the section 2 can be employed.

Lemma 6. *The relations $\preceq_x$, $\preceq_x^r$, $x \in PVar$ and $\preceq_d, \preceq_d^r$, $d \in Data$ are rational.*

The Büchi automaton representing the initial abstraction of the depth-first tree traversal procedure is depicted in Fig. 4. To simplify the figure, we use only the orders $\preceq_x^r$ and $\preceq_{mark}^r$. Thanks to these orders, there is no potential infinite run in the abstraction.

Extensions. In order to cover larger classes of programs, we extended our framework in two ways. On one hand, we handle data structures more general than trees, using the invariant generation method from [4]. Here we encode graphs as trees with extra edges. The basic idea is that each structure has an underlying tree (called a *backbone*), which stays unchanged during the whole computation. The set of extra edges is specified by *pointer descriptors*, which are references to regular expressions to the set of directions in the tree (left, right, left-up, right-up). We check termination using the existing relations $\preceq_x$, $\preceq_x^r$, $x \in PVar$ and $\preceq_d, \preceq_d^r$, $d \in Data$ on the backbone, as well as two new ones $\preceq_{i:s}$ and $\preceq_{i:s}^r$. Intuitively, $t_1 \preceq_{i:s} t_2$ if the set of positions of t_1 whose i-th descriptor is set to s is a subset of the set of positions of t_2 with the same property.

A second extension is allowing tree left- and right-rotations as program statements. Since rotations cannot be described by rational tree relations, we cannot check whether $\preceq_x, \preceq_x^r, \preceq_d$ and $\preceq_d^r$ hold, simply by intersection. However we know that rotations do not change the number of nodes in the tree, therefore we can label them a-posteriori with $=_d, =_d^r$, $d \in Data$, and $\bowtie_x, \bowtie_x^r$, $x \in PVar$, since the relative positions of the variables after the rotations are not known.

4   Implementation and Experimental Results

We have implemented a prototype tool that uses this framework to detect termination of programs with trees and trees with extra edges. The tool was built as an extension of

the ARTMC [4] verifier for safety properties (null-pointer dereferences, memory
leaks, etc.). We applied our tool to several
programs that manipulate:

- **doubly-linked lists:** *DLL-insert* (*DLL-delete*) which inserts (deletes) a node
  in (from) a doubly-linked list, and
  DLL-reverse which is the list reversal.
- **trees:** *Depth-first search* and *Deutsch-Schorr-Waite* which are tree traversals,
  Red-black delete (*insert*) which rebalances a red-black tree after the deletion
  (insertion) of a node.
- **tree with extra edges:** *Linking leaves*
  (*Linking nodes*) which insert all leaves
  (nodes) of a tree in a singly-linked list.

Table 1. Experimental results

Example	Time	N_{refs}
DLL-insert	2s	0
DLL-delete	1s	0
DLL-reverse	2s	0
Depth-first search	17s	0
Linking leaves in trees	14s	0
Deutsch-Schorr-Waite	1m 24s	0
Linking Nodes	5m 47s	0
Red-black delete	4m 54s	2
Red-black insert	29s	0

The results obtained on a Intel Core 2 PC with 2.4 GHz CPU and 2 GB RAM memory
are given in the table 1. The field *time* represents the time necessary to generate invariants and build the initial abstraction. The field N_{refs} represents number of refinements.
The only case in which refinement was needed is the *Red-black delete* example, which
was verified using the *Infeasible Elementary Loop* refinement heuristic (Section 2.5).

5 Conclusions

We proposed a new generic termination-analysis framework. In this framework, infinite
runs of a program are abstracted by Büchi automata. This abstraction is then intersected with a predefined automaton representing potentially infinite runs. In case of
non-empty intersection, a counterexample is exhibited. We instantiated the framework
for programs manipulating tree-like data structures and we experimented with a prototype implementation, on top of the ARTMC invariant generator. Test cases include a
number of classical algorithms that manipulate tree-like data structures.

Future work includes instantiation of the method for other classes of the programs.
Using the proposed method, we would like also to tackle the termination analysis for
concurrent programs. Moreover, we would like to investigate methods for automated
discovery of well-founded orderings on the complex data domains as trees and graphs.

Acknowledgement. This work was supported by the French project RNTL AVERILES,
the Czech Science Foundation (projects 102/07/0322, 201/09P531), and the Czech Ministry of Education by the project MSM 0021630528.

References

1. Berdine, J., Chawdhary, A., Cook, B., Distefano, D., O'Hearn, P.: Variance Analyses from
   Invariance Analyses. In: Proc. of POPL 2007. ACM Press, New York (2007)
2. Bouajjani, A., Bozga, M., Habermehl, P., Iosif, R., Moro, P., Vojnar, T.: Programs with Lists
   are Counter Automata. In: Ball, T., Jones, R.B. (eds.) CAV 2006. LNCS, vol. 4144, pp. 517–
   531. Springer, Heidelberg (2006)

3. Bouajjani, A., Habermehl, P., Rogalewicz, A., Vojnar, T.: Abstract Regular Tree Model Checking. ENTCS 149, 37–48 (2006); A preliminary version was presented at Infinity (2005)

4. Bouajjani, A., Habermehl, P., Rogalewicz, A., Vojnar, T.: Abstract Regular Tree Model Checking of Complex Dynamic Data Structures. In: Yi, K. (ed.) SAS 2006. LNCS, vol. 4134, pp. 52–70. Springer, Heidelberg (2006)

5. Bozga, M., Iosif, R., Lakhnech, Y.: Flat Parametric Counter Automata. In: Bugliesi, M., Preneel, B., Sassone, V., Wegener, I. (eds.) ICALP 2006. LNCS, vol. 4052, pp. 577–588. Springer, Heidelberg (2006)

6. Bradley, A.R., Manna, Z., Sipma, H.B.: Termination of Polynomial Programs. In: Cousot, R. (ed.) VMCAI 2005. LNCS, vol. 3385, pp. 113–129. Springer, Heidelberg (2005)

7. Colón, M.A., Sipma, H.B.: Synthesis of linear ranking functions. In: Margaria, T., Yi, W. (eds.) TACAS 2001. LNCS, vol. 2031, p. 67. Springer, Heidelberg (2001)

8. Comon, H., Dauchet, M., Gilleron, R., Jacquemard, F., Lugiez, D., Tison, S., Tommasi, M.: Tree Automata Techniques and Applications (2005), www.grappa.univ-lille3.fr/tata

9. Cook, B., Podelski, A., Rybalchenko, A.: Abstraction Refinement for Termination. In: Hankin, C., Siveroni, I. (eds.) SAS 2005. LNCS, vol. 3672, pp. 87–101. Springer, Heidelberg (2005)

10. Cook, B., Podelski, A., Rybalchenko, A.: Terminator: Beyond Safety. In: Ball, T., Jones, R.B. (eds.) CAV 2006. LNCS, vol. 4144, pp. 415–418. Springer, Heidelberg (2006)

11. Courcoubetis, C., Vardi, M.Y., Wolper, P., Yannakakis, M.: Memory Efficient Algorithms for the Verification of Temporal Properties. In: Clarke, E., Kurshan, R.P. (eds.) CAV 1990. LNCS, vol. 531. Springer, Heidelberg (1991)

12. Distefano, D., Berdine, J., Cook, B., O'Hearn, P.W.: Automatic termination proofs for programs with shape-shifting heaps. In: Ball, T., Jones, R.B. (eds.) CAV 2006. LNCS, vol. 4144, pp. 386–400. Springer, Heidelberg (2006)

13. Finkel, A., Leroux, J.: How to compose presburger-accelerations: Applications to broadcast protocols. In: Agrawal, M., Seth, A.K. (eds.) FSTTCS 2002. LNCS, vol. 2556, pp. 145–156. Springer, Heidelberg (2002)

14. Habermehl, P., Iosif, R., Rogalewicz, A., Vojnar, T.: Proving termination of tree manipulating programs. In: Namjoshi, K.S., Yoneda, T., Higashino, T., Okamura, Y. (eds.) ATVA 2007. LNCS, vol. 4762, pp. 145–161. Springer, Heidelberg (2007)

15. Iosif, R., Rogalewicz, A.: On the Spuriousness Problem for Tree Manipulating Lassos. Technical Report TR-2008-12, Verimag (2008)

16. Lahiri, S.K., Qadeer, S.: Verifying Properties of Well-Founded Linked Lists. In: Proc. of POPL 2006. ACM Press, New York (2006)

17. Loginov, A., Reps, T.W., Sagiv, M.: Automated Verification of the Deutsch-Schorr-Waite Tree-Traversal Algorithm. In: Yi, K. (ed.) SAS 2006. LNCS, vol. 4134, pp. 261–279. Springer, Heidelberg (2006)

18. Podelski, A., Rybalchenko, A.: Transition Invariants. In: Proc. of LICS 2004. IEEE, Los Alamitos (2004)

19. Rybalchenko, A.: The ARMC tool, http://www.mpi-inf.mpg.de/~rybal/armc/

20. Vardi, M.Y.: The büchi complementation saga. In: Thomas, W., Weil, P. (eds.) STACS 2007. LNCS, vol. 4393, pp. 12–22. Springer, Heidelberg (2007)

21. Lee, C.S., Jones, N.D., Ben-Amram, A.M.: The Size-Change Principle for Program Termination. In: Proc of POPL 2001. ACM Press, New York (2001)

22. Iosif, R., Rogalewicz, A.: Automata-based Termination Proofs. Technical Report TR-2008-17. Verimag (2008)

Implementation of State Elimination Using Heuristics

Jae-Hee Ahn[1] and Yo-Sub Han[2]

[1] NHN Corporation, Korea
jaehee.ahn@nhncorp.com
[2] Department of Computer Science, Yonsei University, Korea
emmous@cs.yonsei.ac.kr

Abstract. State elimination is an intuitive and easy-to-implement algorithm that computes a regular expression from a finite-state automaton (FA). The size of a regular expression from state elimination depends on the state removal sequence. Note that it is very hard to compute the shortest regular expression for a given FA in general and we cannot avoid the exponential blow-up from state elimination. Nevertheless, we notice that we may have a shorter regular expression if we choose a good removal sequence. This observation motivates us to examine heuristics based on the structural properties of an FA and implement state elimination using the heuristics that run in polynomial time. We demonstrate the effectiveness of our algorithm by experiments.

1 Introduction

It is well known that finite-state automata (FAs) have the same expressive power as regular expressions [11]. This well-known statement is proved by showing that we can construct FAs from regular expressions and that we can compute regular expressions from FAs. There are many algorithms for constructing FAs and obtaining regular expressions [5,12,16]. Note that we construct a linear-size nondeterministic finite-state automaton (NFA) from a regular expression [16]. On the other hand, we often have an exponential-size regular expression from an FA: For example, given an FA A with n states over k letter alphabet, the size of a corresponding regular expression can be $O(nk4^n)$ in the worst-case [4,9].

Jiang and Ravikumar [10] proved that it is PSPACE-complete to compute a minimal regular expression and NP-complete to find a minimal regular expression for an acyclic FA. Note that the regular expression minimization problem in general is PSPACE-complete [13]. Ellul et al. [4] showed that if A is a planar graph, then we can obtain a regular expression whose size is less than $e^{O(\sqrt{n})}$. Recently, based on this work, Gruber and Holzer [6] demonstrated that we can compute a regular expression whose size is $O(1.742^n)$ for an n-state deterministic FA. However, the running time for these algorithms are exponential and, therefore, are not suitable for implementation. We examine some known heuristics that may lead to shorter regular expressions and design a new state elimination algorithm using heuristics.

S. Maneth (Ed.): CIAA 2009, LNCS 5642, pp. 178–187, 2009.

In Section 2, we define some basic notions. In Section 3, we briefly describe state elimination and demonstrate the importance of state removal sequence. Then, we revisit known heuristics and related issues in Section 4. Based on these heuristics, we design a new state elimination algorithm, implement the algorithm in Grail+[1] and show experimental results in Section 5.

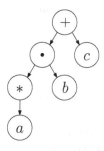

Fig. 1. The syntax tree representation for a regular expression $E = a^*b + c$. We define the size $|E|$ of E to be the number of nodes in the corresponding syntax tree. For instance, $|E| = 6$.

2   Preliminaries

Let Σ denote a finite alphabet of characters and Σ^* denote the set of all strings over Σ. The size $|\Sigma|$ of Σ is the number of characters in Σ. A language over Σ is any subset of Σ^*. The symbol $\emptyset$ denotes the empty language and the symbol λ denotes the null string.

An FA A is specified by a tuple $(Q, \Sigma, \delta, s, F)$, where Q is a finite set of states, Σ is an input alphabet, $\delta : Q \times \Sigma \to 2^Q$ is a transition function, $s \in Q$ is the start state and $F \subseteq Q$ is a set of final states. If F consists of a single state f, then we use f instead of $\{f\}$ for simplicity. Let $|Q|$ be the number of states in Q and $|\delta|$ be the number of transitions in δ. Then, the size of A is $|A| = |Q| + |\delta|$. For a transition $\delta(p, a) = q$ in A, we say p has an *out-transition* and q has an *in-transition*. Furthermore, we say that A is *non-returning* if the start state of A does not have any in-transitions and A is *non-exiting* if all final states of A do not have any out-transitions. If $\delta(q, a)$ has a single element q', then we denote $\delta(q, a) = q'$ instead of $\delta(q, a) = \{q'\}$ for simplicity.

A string x over Σ is accepted by A if there is a labeled path from s to a final state such that this path spells out x. We call this path an *accepting path*. Then, the language $L(A)$ of A is the set of all strings spelled out by accepting paths in A. We say that a state of A is *useful* if it appears in an accepting path in A; otherwise, it is *useless*. Unless otherwise mentioned, in the following we assume that all states of an FA are useful.

---

[1] Grail+ is a symbolic computation environment for finite-state FAs, regular expressions and finite languages. Homepage: http://www.csd.uwo.ca/Research/grail/

We define the size of a regular expression E to be the number of characters of Σ and the number of operations[2]. Note that we often omit the catenation symbol in a regular expression. For instance, we write ab instead of $a \cdot b$ and the sizes of both regular expressions are 3. For the precise definition, we can think of the size of E as the number of nodes in the corresponding syntax tree. Fig. 1 gives an example.

For complete background knowledge in automata theory, the reader may refer to textbooks [9,17].

3   State Elimination

We define the *state elimination* of $q \in Q \setminus \{s, f\}$ in A to be the bypassing of state q, q's in-transitions, q's out-transitions and q's self-looping transition with equivalent expression transition sequences. For each in-transition (p_i, α_i, q), $1 \le i \le m$, for some $m \ge 1$, for each out-transition (q, γ, r_j), $1 \le j \le n$, for some $n \ge 1$, and for the self-looping transition (q, β, q) in δ, construct a new transition $(p_i, \alpha_i \cdot \beta^* \cdot \gamma_j, r_j)$. If there exists transition (p, ν, r) in δ for some expression ν, then we merge two transitions to give the bypass transition $(p, (\alpha_i \cdot \beta^* \cdot \gamma_j) + \nu, r)$. We then remove q and all transitions into and out of q in δ. For more details on state elimination, refer to the literature [2,17].

One interesting property in state elimination is that the resulting regular expression from state elimination depends on the removal sequence. Therefore, depending on which removal sequence we choose, we may have a shorter regular expression for the same FA. Fig. 2 illustrates this idea.

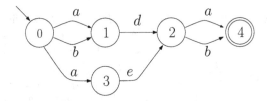

Fig. 2. An example of different regular expressions by different removal sequences for a given FA. $E_1 = ae(a + b) + (a + b)d(a + b)$ is the output of state elimination in $1 \rightarrow 2 \rightarrow 3$ order and $E_2 = ((a + b)d + ae)(a + b)$ is the output of state elimination in $1 \rightarrow 3 \rightarrow 2$ order, where $L(E_1) = L(E_2)$.

For an n-state FA A, there are $n!$ removal sequences. It is undesirable to try all possible sequences for shorter regular expressions. Instead, we use the structural properties of A and design a fast heuristic for state elimination that can give a shorter regular expression.

---

[2] Grail+ also defines the size of regular expression in this way.

4   Heuristics for State Elimination

There are several heuristics for finding a removal sequence for state elimination. For example, Gruber and Holzer [6] suggested graph separator techniques and Delgado and Morais [3] relied on state weight. Recently, Moreira and Reis [14] presented an $O(n^2 \log n)$ time algorithm that obtains an $O(n)$ size regular expressions from an n-state acyclic FA A. Gulan and Fernau [7] proposed a construction of regular expression from a restricted NFA via extended automata. Note that some heuristics for state elimination run in exponential time. Since we intend to compute a shorter regular expression from an FA quickly, we only consider polynomial running time heuristics for our implementation. We use the decomposition heuristic by Han and Wood [8] and the state weight approach by Delgado and Morais [3]. Both approaches run in polynomial time.

4.1   The Decomposition Heuristic

Han and Wood [8] suggested two decomposition approaches, one is a horizontal decomposition and the other is a vertical decomposition, based on the structural properties of a given FA.

First, we use the vertical decomposition since it always guarantees the shortest regular expression by state elimination. For the vertical decomposition, we first identify bridge states.

Definition 1. *We define a state q in an FA A to be a* bridge state *if it satisfies the following conditions:*

1. *State q is neither a start nor a final state.*
2. *For each string $w \in L(A)$, its path in A must pass through q at least once.*
3. *State q is not in any cycle except for the self-loop.*

Note that the bridge state condition is more restricted than the original condition proposed by Han and Wood [8][3]. This is because we find a counter example that does not guarantee an optimal solution under the original conditions. In Fig. 3, the removal sequence $1 \rightarrow 2$ gives $E_1 = cd(b + ad)^*a$ whereas the removal sequence $2 \rightarrow 1$ gives $E_2 = c(db^*a)^*(db^*a)$. Note that $|E_1| < |E_2|$.

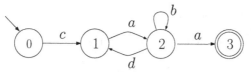

Fig. 3. State 1 satisfies the bridge conditions by Han and Wood [8]. However, it is not a bridge state according to Definition 1.

Han and Wood [8] presented an algorithm that finds bridge states in linear time in the size of a given FA based on the DFS algorithm. We can slightly modify the algorithm and find all bridge states in Definition 1 in linear time as well.

---

[3] The original condition allows q to be in a cycle.

Proposition 1. *Given an FA $A = (Q, \Sigma, \delta, s, f)$ and a set B of bridge states of A, the optimal removal sequence must eliminate all states in $Q \setminus B \cup \{s, f\}$ before eliminating any bridge states.*

Given an FA A, we find bridge states in liner time and apply the vertical decomposition. Once we obtain several decomposed subautomata for A, we try the horizontal decomposition before computing a regular expression for each subautomaton.

Proposition 2 (Han and Wood [8]). *Given a finite-state automaton $A = (Q, \Sigma, \delta, s, f)$, we can discover all subautomata that are disjoint from each other except s and f in $O(|Q| + |\delta|)$ time using DFS.*

Fig. 4 gives an example of a horizontal decomposition. We notice that the horizontal decomposition is a good heuristic for state elimination since the removal sequence for each separated subautomaton does not influence any other removal sequence for other subautomata. For example, in Fig. 4, the removal sequence $2 \rightarrow 5 \rightarrow 3 \rightarrow 4 \rightarrow 6$ and the removal sequence $2 \rightarrow 3 \rightarrow 4 \rightarrow 6 \rightarrow 5$ give the same regular expressions. Namely, we only look at each subautomaton to find a proper removal sequence and merge the resulting regular expressions using unions. Therefore, if possible, we always decompose a given FA into several horizontally disjoint subautomata, and compute the corresponding regular expressions for subautomata and merge them.

Proposition 3. *We can use the horizontal decomposition for finding a short regular expression using state elimination. Note that the horizontal decomposition does not affect the optimal removal sequence.*

Moreover, as shown in Fig. 4, states 3, 4 and 5 become bridge states in A_l that are not bridge states in A. In other words, we can repeat the vertical decomposition, if possible, and the horizontal decomposition again. Since there

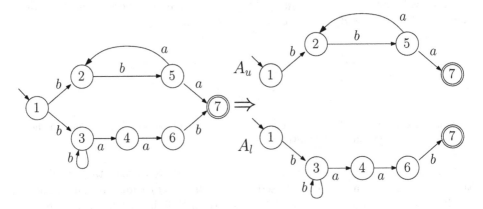

Fig. 4. An example of a horizontal decomposition for a given FA without bridge states

are only finite number of states, this process runs in polynomial time. Overall, the decomposition heuristic is a classical divide-and-conquer approach for state elimination.

Proposition 4. *Given an FA A, we can decompose A, if possible, into several subautomata in which both horizontal and vertical decomposition are not feasible in $O(|A|^2)$ worst-case time.*

4.2   The State Weight Heuristic

Delgado and Morais [3] proposed the sate weight heuristic. They defined a state weight be the the size of new transition labels that are created by eliminating the state. We borrow their notion and define the weight of a state q in an FA $A = (Q, \Sigma, \delta, s, f)$ as follows:

$$\sum_{i=1}^{In}(W_{in}(i) \times Out) + \sum_{i=1}^{Out}(W_{out}(i) \times In) + W_{loop} \times (In \times Out), \qquad (1)$$

where In is the number of in-transitions excluding self-loop, Out is the number of out-transitions excluding self-loop, $W_{in}(i)$ is the size of the transition label on the ith in-transition, $W_{out}(i)$ is the size of the transition label on the ith out-transition and W_{loop} is the self-loop label size for q. Note that our weight definition is slightly different from Delgado and Morais [3]: We define the weight be to the total size of transition labels after eliminating q. We can compute the weight of all states in A in polynomial time.

Delgado and Morais [3] noticed that the state weight heuristic does not guarantee the shortest regular expression. For instance, in Fig. 5, the state weight heuristic suggests $1 \rightarrow 3 \rightarrow 2$ removal sequence, which gives $E_1 = abc(((a + b + c) + (b + bb)c))^*(b + bb)a$ whereas the removal sequence $1 \rightarrow 2 \rightarrow 3$ gives $E_2 = ab(c(a + b + c)^*(b + bb))^*a$. Note that we can select a least weight state and remove it, and recompute the state weight and choose a new least weight state in the resulting FA. This approach does not guarantee the shortest regular expression either but it often gives shorter regular expressions compared

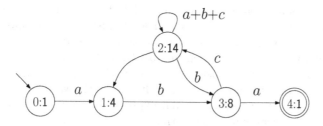

Fig. 5. Each state has a state index and the state weight by Equation (1). In this FA, the state weight heuristic suggests $1 \rightarrow 3 \rightarrow 2$ removal sequence but it is not the best removal sequence.

with the one-time state weight heuristic. On the other hand, since we calculate state weight every step, it may take more time than the one-time state weight heuristic. We implement both approaches and analyze the experimental results in Section 5.

5   Implementation and Experimental Results

Given an FA $A = (Q, \Sigma, \delta, s, F)$, we first remove all unreachable states, merge multiple transitions between two states into a single transition and make A to have a single final state using λ-transitions. This preprocessing takes $O(|A|)$ time. We use combinations of heuristics in Section 4 for state removal sequences as follows.

1. We eliminate states in state order without any heuristics. Let C-I denote this case.
2. We use both the vertical decomposition and the horizontal decomposition until both decompositions are not feasible. Once the decomposition step is over, we eliminate states in order. Let C-II denote this case.
3. We compute the state weight of all states and eliminate a state with less weight. Note that we compute the state weight only once. Let C-III denote this case.
4. We first use the vertical and horizontal decompositions and decide the removal sequence for each decomposed subautomaton using the state weight heuristic as C-III. Let C-IV denote this case.
5. We select a least weight state and eliminate it. Then, we compute the state weight again for the resulting FA and eliminate the new least weight state. We repeat this until there is no more state to remove. Namely, we have to compute the state weight roughly $|Q|$ times, where $|Q|$ is the number of states in an input FA. Let C-V denote this case. Note that C-V is different from C-III.
6. We use the vertical and horizontal decompositions. Then, for each decomposed subautomaton, we use the repeated state weight heuristics to decide the removal order as C-V. Let C-VI denote this case.

Our implementation is based on Grail+. C-I is the current state elimination algorithm implemented in Grail+ as well as JFLAP [15]. We implement the other 5 heuristics in Grail+. We randomly generate FAs and run the 6 different algorithms for each of FAs on a Pentium-5 PC. Table 1 shows some of the experimental results. (We omit most cases because of the space limit.) Notice that if the number of transitions is large, then the straightforward state elimination approach (C-I) cannot compute a regular expression because of the exponential blow-up. (Our empirical experience is that if the number of transitions is more than 200, then C-I often fails.)

Fig. 6 shows the relation graph between the number of states and the size of regular expressions. This shows that C-VI is best followed by C-IV $\rightarrow$ C-V $\rightarrow$ C-II $\rightarrow$ C-III $\rightarrow$ C-I.

Table 1. Experimental results

$|\delta|$	$|Q|$	C-I	C-II	C-III	C-IV	C-V	C-VI
		the size of resulting regular expression for each case					
		the real running time in second					
43	10	1773	779	644	399	504	399
		0.079	0.031	0.015	0.016	0.016	0.015
48	10	2605	687	1119	468	427	427
		0.125	0.032	0.046	0.016	0.016	0.015
59	12	1654	1148	1186	899	722	599
		0.078	0.047	0.062	0.031	0.032	0.015
65	14	1072	300	969	300	311	300
		0.047	0.016	0.031	0.016	0.015	0.016
67	15	16048	9609	1572	711	699	699
		0.906	0.5	0.078	0.016	0.031	0.031
99	17	15268	717	964	469	475	469
		0.937	0.047	0.047	0.015	0.032	0.015
157	24	826669	5664	15867	3104	9425	2892
		70.141	0.25	1.141	0.14	0.609	0.109
175	23	2007485	28855	25472	21566	16430	13940
		169.984	1.609	2.125	1.203	1.078	0.625
265	35	-	2022	47007	1614	7614	1592
		-	0.078	4.781	0.062	0.532	0.047
296	40	-	1797	46803	1508	1853	1448
		-	0.063	4.875	0.063	0.219	0.062
673	56	-	-	-	38117	36090	27920
		-	-	-	2.078	4.563	1.25

Proposition 5. *We propose the following suggestions for the state elimination implementation based on our experimental results:*

1. *It is better to apply the decomposition heuristic first and the state weight heuristic later for each decomposed subautomaton.*
2. *Heuristics for state elimination enable to obtain a regular expression faster compared with state elimination without heuristics although they require additional processing time. This is because heuristics help to have smaller transition labels while running state elimination.*
3. *The number of transitions is more closely related to the size of regular expressions than the number of states. (The correlation between the size of regular expressions by C-VI and the number of states is 0.66 whereas the correlation between the size of regular expressions by C-VI and the number of transitions is 0.79.)*

Proposition 5 suggests to investigate the relation between the number of transitions and the number of states. Thus, it is natural future work to examine a tight bound for the size of a regular expression from an n-transition FA. Moreover, we can use some other heuristics that run in polynomial time. For example, we

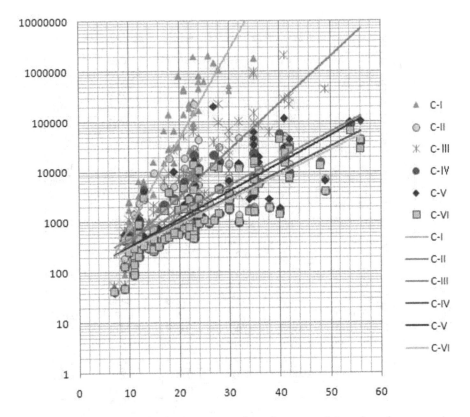

Fig. 6. Experimental results for 6 cases: number of states and size of regular expressions

can use the orbit property established by Brüggemann-Klein and Wood [1] that gives a certain removal order and the Kleene star operation.

Acknowledgment

We wish to thank the referees for the care they put into reading the previous version of this manuscript.

References

1. Brüggemann-Klein, A., Wood, D.: One-unambiguous regular languages. Information and Computation 140, 229–253 (1998)
2. Brzozowski, J., McCluskey Jr., E.: Signal flow graph techniques for sequential circuit state diagrams. IEEE Transactions on Electronic Computers EC-12, 67–76 (1963)
3. Delgado, M., Morais, J.: Approximation to the smallest regular expression for a given regular language. In: Domaratzki, M., Okhotin, A., Salomaa, K., Yu, S. (eds.) CIAA 2004. LNCS, vol. 3317, pp. 312–314. Springer, Heidelberg (2005)

4. Ellul, K., Krawetz, B., Shallit, J., Wang, M.-W.: Regular expressions: New results and open problems. Journal of Automata, Languages and Combinatorics 9, 233–256 (2004)
5. Glushkov, V.: The abstract theory of automata. Russian Mathematical Surveys 16, 1–53 (1961)
6. Gruber, H., Holzer, M.: Provably shorter regular expressions from deterministic finite automata. In: Ito, M., Toyama, M. (eds.) DLT 2008. LNCS, vol. 5257, pp. 383–395. Springer, Heidelberg (2008)
7. Gulan, S., Fernau, H.: Local elimination-strategies in automata for shorter regular expressions. In: Proceedings of SOFSEM 2008, pp. 46–57 (2008)
8. Han, Y.-S., Wood, D.: Obtaining shorter regular expressions from finite-state automata. Theoretical Computer Science 370(1-3), 110–120 (2007)
9. Hopcroft, J., Ullman, J.: Introduction to Automata Theory, Languages, and Computation, 2nd edn. Addison-Wesley, Reading (1979)
10. Jiang, T., Ravikumar, B.: Minimal NFA problems are hard. SIAM Journal on Computing 22(6), 1117–1141 (1993)
11. Kleene, S.: Representation of events in nerve nets and finite automata. In: Shannon, C., McCarthy, J. (eds.) Automata Studies, pp. 3–42. Princeton University Press, Princeton (1956)
12. McNaughton, R., Yamada, H.: Regular expressions and state graphs for automata. IEEE Transactions on Electronic Computers 9, 39–47 (1960)
13. Meyer, A., Stockmeyer, L.: The equivalence problem for regular expressions with squaring requires exponential time. In: Proceedings of the Thirteenth Annual IEEE Symposium on Switching and Automata Theory, pp. 125–129 (1972)
14. Moreira, N., Reis, R.: Series-parallel automata and short regular expressions. Fundamenta Informaticae (accepted for publication, 2009)
15. Rodger, S.H., Finley, T.W.: JFLAP: An Interactive Formal Languages and Automata Package. Jones & Bartlett Pub. (2006)
16. Thompson, K.: Regular expression search algorithm. Communications of the ACM 11, 419–422 (1968)
17. Wood, D.: Theory of Computation. John Wiley & Sons, Inc., New York (1987)

Short Regular Expressions from Finite Automata: Empirical Results

Hermann Gruber[1], Markus Holzer[1], and Michael Tautschnig[2]

[1] Institut für Informatik, Universität Giessen
Arndtstraße 2, D-35392 Giessen, Germany
{hermann.gruber,holzer}@informatik.uni-giessen.de
[2] Fachbereich Informatik, Technische Universität Darmstadt,
Hochschulstraße 10, D-64289 Darmstadt, Germany
tautschnig@forsyte.cs.tu-darmstadt.de

Abstract. We continue our work [H. Gruber, M. Holzer: Provably shorter regular expressions from deterministic finite automata (extended abstract). In *Proc. DLT*, LNCS 5257, 2008] on the problem of finding good elimination orderings for the state elimination algorithm, one of the most popular algorithms for the conversion of finite automata into equivalent regular expressions. Here we tackle this problem both from the theoretical and from the practical side. First we show that the problem of finding optimal elimination orderings can be used to estimate the cycle rank of the underlying automata. This gives good evidence that the problem under consideration is difficult, to a certain extent. Moreover, we conduct experiments on a large set of carefully chosen instances for five different strategies to choose elimination orderings, which are known from the literature. Perhaps the most surprising result is that a simple greedy heuristic by [M. Delgado, J. Morais: Approximation to the smallest regular expression for a given regular language. In *Proc. CIAA*, LNCS 3317, 2004] almost always outperforms all other strategies, including those with a provable performance guarantee.

1 Introduction

The classical theorem of Kleene [15] implies that every n-state finite automaton over alphabet Σ admits an equivalent regular expression. This conversion problem has received quite some attention recently, see, e.g., [9,10,11,12,13]. One of the most popular algorithms for this conversion is the so called *state elimination* algorithm. There, states from the automaton are successively eliminated by re-routing the in- and out-going transitions, which leads to an automaton with transitions labeled by regular expressions. The sequence of states eliminated thereby is called an *elimination ordering* or *elimination sequence*. If state elimination is applied to an n-state finite automaton, the resulting expression is of size at most $|\Sigma| \cdot 4^n$. While this bound appears large, it is known that an exponential blowup is necessary in the worst case [5,10].

These theoretical results pushed the on-going quest for heuristics finding good elimination orderings leading to short regular expressions [2,11,13]. Recently

S. Maneth (Ed.): CIAA 2009, LNCS 5642, pp. 188–197, 2009.

improved upper bounds on the size of the regular expressions resulting from deterministic finite automata (DFA) over small alphabets were obtained [11]. The latter are based on algorithms with a combinatorial flavor, and the analysis is facilitated by results from extremal graph theory. Although all of the heuristics choose an ordering for state elimination, only the algorithms from [11] lend themselves to a theoretical analysis at all. Thus a theoretical comparison of the different approaches would appear rather difficult.

In the present paper we continue our research on good elimination orderings for the state elimination algorithm from the theoretical as well as the practical side by doing experiments on a large dataset. On the theoretical side, we investigated the possibility whether designing an efficient approximation algorithm would be within reach, but our theoretical results are somewhat negative. Already weak approximation algorithms for the elimination orderings would constitute a major step towards a resolving the approximability of the undirected cycle rank problem, which is not completely understood yet [7]. Therefore we implemented some of the heuristics and compared their performance on a large but carefully chosen set of test instances. In short, the main empirical observations are the following: (1) Even the easiest heuristics provide a huge advantage over randomly chosen elimination orderings, thus substantiating an observation made earlier in [2] on very few instances. (2) Larger alphabets, and hence more transitions, in the given DFAs result in larger regular expressions. (3) For ε-NFAs obtained from regular expressions using the standard construction [14], the transformation back into regular expressions is much easier than for random DFAs. (4) Simplifying intermediate regular expressions on-the-fly as they appear during the conversion appears not to have a striking effect on the result on the average. Perhaps most surprisingly, it turned out that the simple greedy heuristic by Delgado and Morais [2] almost always outperforms the algorithms with provable performance guarantee from [11].

2   Definitions

We assume the reader to be familiar with basic notions in formal language theory, in particular with those of ε-NFAs, NFAs, DFAs, regular expressions, and the languages they denote. Here we follow exactly the notational conventions from [14], with the following additions: The *size* or *alphabetic width* of a regular expression r over the alphabet Σ, denoted by alph(r), is defined as the total number of occurrences of letters of Σ in r. For a regular language L, we define its alphabetic width, alph(L), as the minimum alphabetic width among all regular expressions describing L. When working with ε-NFAs, we will often assume that the given automaton A is *normalized* in the sense that A has the state set $Q \cup \{s, t\}$ where s is the start state and has no incoming transitions, and t is the sole accepting state and has no outgoing transitions. This can be achieved by a simple construction if needed. As usual, two finite automata are called *equivalent* if they accept the same language.

Now we present an algorithm scheme that became known as *state elimination*, cf. [19]. Let Q be the state set of a finite automaton A. For a subset U of Q and an input word $w \in \Sigma^*$, we say that A can go on input w from state j through U to state k, if it has a computation on input w taking A from state j to k without going through any state outside U. Here, by "going through a state," we mean both entering and leaving. Now let L_{jk}^U be the set of words on which A can go from state j to state k through U. Observe that in particular for a normalized finite automaton A then holds $L_{st}^Q = L(A)$. The state elimination algorithm scheme proceeds as follows: We maintain a working set U and a matrix the entries of which are regular expressions r_{jk}^U denoting the languages L_{jk}^U. The algorithm proceeds in rounds: Beginning with $U = \emptyset$, we enlarge the set U by adding a new state $i \in Q \setminus U$ in each round. The round consists of computing the new entries denoting the languages $L_{jk}^{U \cup \{i\}}$, for each j, k satisfying $j, k \notin U \cup \{i\}$, by letting $r_{jk}^{U \cdot i} = r_{ji}^U \cdot (r_{ii}^U)^* \cdot r_{ik}^U$, where $U \cdot i$ denotes the ordering induced by U followed by i (cf. [11]). Here it is understood that the resulting expression on the left-hand side equals $\emptyset$ if r_{ji}^U or r_{ik}^U denotes the empty set. If the given automaton was normalized, we finally end up with a regular expression describing L_{st}^Q, a set equal to $L(A)$. Observe that the above algorithm requires an ordering in which the states i are to be processed one after another; such an ordering on Q is called an *elimination ordering*. It is well known that the choice of ordering can greatly influence the size of the resulting regular expressions, cf. [2,19].

3   A Theoretical Result on Elimination Orderings

This section is devoted to the question whether we can find an optimum, or at least an approximately optimum elimination ordering in polynomial time. Sakarovitch stated that this is probably a hard combinatorial problem [19]. Although we cannot provide proper evidence that this problem is algorithmically intractable (such as **NP**-hardness), our result indicates that even designing an approximation algorithm with a reasonable performance guarantee is a challenging research problem.

Definition 1. *The* cycle rank *of a digraph* $G = (V, E)$*, denoted by* $cr(G)$*, is inductively defined as follows: (1) If* G *is acyclic, then* $cr(G) = 0$*. (2) If* G *is strongly connected and not acyclic, then* $cr(G) = 1 + \min_{v \in V} \{cr(G - v)\}$*. (3) If* G *is not strongly connected, then* $cr(G)$ *equals the maximum cycle rank among all strongly connected components of* G*. The* undirected cycle rank *of* G *is defined as the cycle rank of its symmetric closure.*

We will relate the undirected cycle rank to elimination orderings in the following. To this end, recall the following lemma from [11]:

Lemma 2. *Let* A *be a normalized* ε*-NFA with state set* $\{s, t\} \cup Q$*, and let* G *be the digraph underlying the transition structure of* A*. Assume* $U \subseteq Q$ *can be partitioned into two sets* T_1 *and* T_2 *such that the induced subdigraph* $G[U]$ *falls apart into mutually disconnected components* $G[T_1]$ *and* $G[T_2]$*. Then for* the expression $r_{jk}^{T_1 \cdot T_2}$ obtained by elimination of the the vertices in T_1 followed by elimination of the vertices in T_2 it holds $r_{jk}^{T_1 \cdot T_2} \cong r_{jk}^{T_1} + r_{jk}^{T_2}$, for all states $j, k \in Q \setminus U$.

Using this lemma, we can prove that the undirected cycle rank of the underlying graph is a parameter that renders the problem of converting ε-NFAs into regular expressions fixed-parameter tractable—not in the usual sense of *computational*, but rather of *descriptional* complexity. We omit the proof of the next two statements due to space constraints.

Theorem 3. *Let A be a normalized ε-NFA with state set $\{s, t\} \cup Q$, let c be a positive integer, and let G be its underlying (di)graph. If $U \subseteq Q$ is such that $G[U]$ has undirected cycle rank at most c, then there is an elimination ordering for U which yields, for all states j, k in $Q \setminus U$, regular expressions r_{jk}^U of size at most $|\Sigma| \cdot 4^c \cdot |U|$.*

The problem in transforming the above result into an algorithm is that determining the undirected cycle rank of a graph or digraph is **NP**-complete and the best known approximation algorithm has, for a given graph with n vertices and (unknown) undirected cycle rank c, a performance ratio of $O(\sqrt{\log c} \cdot \log n)$, see [7]. It turns out that merely estimating the *order of magnitude* of the expression size resulting from an optimum ordering is by no means easier:

Lemma 4. *Given an undirected graph G on n vertices and of (unknown) cycle rank c, we can construct in polynomial time a DFA A such that the optimum elimination ordering for A yields an equivalent regular expression r with*

$$\frac{1}{3} \cdot c - 2 \leq \log \text{alph}(r) \leq 2 \cdot c + \log n.$$

This shows that the optimum ordering expression size can be used as a pretty good estimate for the cycle rank, and already weak approximation algorithms for the former problem would constitute a major step towards a more complete understanding of the approximability of the undirected cycle rank problem, compare [7].

4   Algorithms for Choosing Elimination Orderings

When eliminating a state with m entering and n exiting transitions, the resulting digraph has up to $(m-1) \cdot (n-1)$ newly added edges. Intuitively, we want to keep the intermediate digraphs produced by the elimination process as sparse as possible. Thus it may be advisable to delay the elimination of heavily trafficked states as long as possible, as noted already by different authors [2,13,19]. An extremely simple strategy is to order the states by a measure that is defined as the number of ingoing edges times the number of outgoing edges (Algorithm **0A**). An easy observation is that this measure can of course change as the elimination proceeds, and a refined strategy recomputes these measures on the intermediate digraphs after each elimination round (Algorithm **0B**). A further refinement devised in [2] works with a measure function, which also takes the size of the intermediate regular expressions into account (Algorithm **DM**)—we refer to [2] for details.

Recently, two new ordering algorithms were discovered in [11], which were also the first ones to come with a provably better performance guarantee on the resulting regular expressions, at least in case the given automata are deterministic and over not too large alphabets. Turán's Theorem in extremal graph theory states that sparse (di)graphs have independent sets of linear size, and that these can be eliminated at low cost and can be found by a simple greedy algorithm. This gives rise to the following algorithm (Algorithm **IS**): First, we find a huge independent set S in the graph underlying the automaton. Then we order the states in S arbitrarily, and eliminate them. For any remaining states we again find a huge independent set in the resulting digraph, and so on. It is shown in [11] that this algorithm is guaranteed to produce regular expressions of size at most $O(2.602^n)$, when given a DFA over binary alphabet.

A recent generalization of Turán's theorem by Edwards and Farr [3] concerns induced subgraphs of (undirected) treewidth at most 2 instead of independent sets. There the guaranteed size is three times larger, and again these can be eliminated at low cost and can be found by a simple greedy algorithm. Large induced subgraphs of low treewidth are useful, because it was proved in that these admit orderings, similar to independent set, such that eliminating them in the beginning can incur an increase in intermediate expression size bounded by a polynomial factor. The proof of that fact does not rely directly on tree decompositions, but proceeds by finding small balanced separators, and then recurring on the separated subgraphs. Following [11], this suggests the following algorithm (Algorithm **B3S**): First, we find a huge induced subgraph S of treewidth at most 2 in the graph underlying the automaton. Then we order the set S by finding a balanced 3-way separator X for S. If C_1, C_2 and C_3 are the parts of S separated by X, the resulting ordering is of the form C_1, C_2, C_3, X, where the ordering for the component C_i is found recursively, by finding a balanced 3-separator for C_i, and so on. Then we eliminate S. Finally, we eliminate $Q \setminus S$ with an "arbitrary" ordering; to optimize the latter, we used the heuristic **DM** on $Q \setminus S$. For finding huge independent sets and induced subgraphs of treewidth 2, we used a software library developed by Kerri Morgan [17]. It was shown in [11] that this approach allows for a guaranteed performance of $O(1.742^n)$ on DFAs over binary alphabet. We also note that all of the algorithms run in output polynomial time. In particular, they run in polynomial time provided they produce a regular expression of polynomial size.

5   Experiments

We have conducted experiments with the algorithms described in the previous section plus an additional random elimination ordering (**RA**). We have implemented the algorithms in C++, using the Automata Standard Template Library (ASTL) [16] for representation and manipulation of automata. We have chosen the library ASTL to represent the NFAs and the intermediate results during state-elimination mainly because of the cursor concept and because it allows arbitrary input alphabets. This facilitates a direct implementation of the algorithms by programming appropriate iterators (*cursors*) over the state set. To gain performance, regular expressions are not stored as syntax trees, but as directed acyclic graphs, allowing for sharing common subexpressions. Similar ideas were used in [8]. Tests have shown that this allows us to compute regular expressions of very large alphabetic width—up to 10^{20}—while still having small memory footprint. The front end for reading the input NFAs or regular expressions is a `lex` and `yacc` generated parser. This resulted in an overall size of roughly 4000 lines of code. The tests are performed on a quad core Intel Xeon CPU E5345 with 2.33 GHz equipped with 16 GB RAM running Linux as an operating system. To limit the number of bugs in our program, unit-tests were performed with the help of the *Diagnostics* framework.[1]

Moreover, simplification of the regular expressions constructed during state elimination can be en- or disabled. Unless stated otherwise, all tests were run with simplification turned on. The simplification process is described by a term rewriting system (TRS) which works modulo ACIZ-identities[2] and some further identities, namely $r \cdot \varepsilon = \varepsilon \cdot r = r$, $a \cdot \emptyset = \emptyset \cdot r = \emptyset$, plus identities that deal with the Kleene star, which are $\emptyset^* = \varepsilon$, $\varepsilon^* = \varepsilon$, $(r^*)^* = r^*$, $(r + \varepsilon)^* = r^*$, $(r + s^*)^* = (r + s)^*$, and $(r^* s^*)^* = (r+s)^*$. They are similar to those used in [8]. Notice that the associativity laws can be built into the data structure by using list data types. For implementing commutativity we defined, apart from the above notion of equivalence, also an appropriate order on the subsorts of expressions.

Our test instances are chosen as follows: We used randomly generated DFAs for different numbers of states and alphabet sizes and regular expressions of varying alphabetic width. Moreover, we have also performed tests on special automata instances that appeared in the literature—we will discuss this issue in more detail below. To randomly generate DFAs (more precisely initially connected DFAs) we used the FAdo toolkit [1], while the random generation of regular expressions was done by GenRGenS [18]. The latter software was originally designed to randomly generate genome sequences and supports several classes of models, including context-free grammars. Observe that the generation of DFAs is uniformly at random. A running time limit for all tests was not established and all tests were finished after about 30 CPU days. All test instances and the source code are available online at `http://code.forsyte.de/automata` for download. The unambiguous grammar used for generating regular expressions is included with the download.

---

[1] *Diagnostics*, developed by the "Formal Methods in Systems Engineering" group at Technische Universität Darmstadt, is a unified framework for code annotation, logging, program monitoring, and unit-testing. Download and more information is available at `http://code.forsyte.de/diagnostics`

[2] The set of equations $r + (s + t) = (r + s) = t$, $r + s = s + r$, $r + r = r$, and $r + \emptyset = r$ are commonly called ACIZ-identities or -axioms, where letter A is an abbreviation for associativity, C for commutativity, I for idempotency, and Z for zero absorption.

For the DFA samples we used automata with $5 \leq n \leq 50$ states—in steps of 5 states—and input alphabets with $1 \leq k \leq 10$ symbols. We only show the diagrams for $k \in \{2, 3, 5, 10\}$. For each parameter n and k, a sample of 1000 random instances was generated and tested. The results are summarized in Figure 1 and can be interpreted as follows.

At first glance one observes that larger alphabet size, and hence more transitions, in the DFAs result in larger regular expressions. This is of course expected. Taking a closer look, one further observes that the Algorithm **0B** with the simple greedy strategy and the Algorithm **DM** with the more sophisticated measure function of Delgado and Morais [2] almost always outperforms the Algorithms **IS** and **B3S** with provable performance guarantees—indicated by fitted appropriate exponential functions—from [11], on the average. This was a nice surprise and not really expected. Apart from the random ordering **RA**, only Algorithm **0A** is significantly worse than the other tested algorithms, not only on the average, but also on the worst-case behavior. Again, not a real surprise, since this algorithm is too static, by not taking changes of the underlying graph

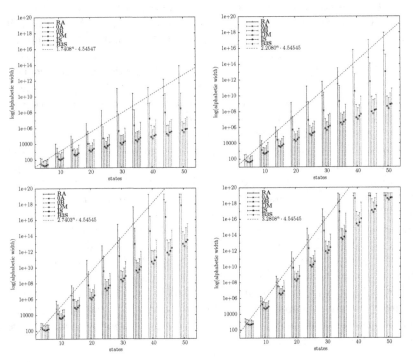

Fig. 1. Alphabetic size (y-axis, logarithmically scaled) in relation to the number of states (x-axis, linearly scaled) for DFAs with $5 \leq n \leq 50$ states—in steps of 5 states— and input alphabet size 2 (upper left), 3 (upper right), 5 (lower left), and 10 (lower right) for the random ordering **RA** and Algorithms **0A**, **0B**, **DM**, **IS**, and **B3S**. Here a vertical bar for an algorithm indicates the maximal occurring alphabetic width by its height. Moreover it also shows the alphabetic width on average indicated by the appropriate mark symbol.

during the elimination process into account. Moreover, another effect, not depicted here, was encountered during our test: Simplifying of intermediate regular expressions does not have any significant effect on the outcome of the conducted experiments. Possible reasons for this may be that we have run our tests on DFAs, not NFAs, and that we have excluded more powerful simplification rules such as $r \cdot s + r \cdot t = r \cdot (s + t)$. We plan to conduct further experiments in this direction.

Next we summarize our results on special instances, which were already discussed in the literature. First we have reproduced the experiments done in [2] on automata with transformation monoids from $\mathcal{POI}_n$ and $\mathcal{POPI}_n$ of all injective order preserving and orientation preserving, respectively, partial transformations on a chain with n elements. Moreover, we have considered DFAs whose transition structure is a $n \times n$ grid graph with a input alphabet of size 4, one letter for each direction. Recently, these automata, referred to as $Grid_n$, were used to prove lower bounds on the alphabetic width for the conversion of planar DFAs to regular expressions [10]. Finally, we also considered DFAs accepting the languages $L_n = \Sigma^* \setminus (\Sigma^* f_n \Sigma^*)$, where $\Sigma = \{a, b\}$ and f_n is the nth finite Fibonacci word defined by $f_0 = a$, $f_1 = ab$, and $f_n = f_{n-1} \cdot f_{n-2}$, for $n \geq 2$. These automata denoted by Fib_n were proposed in [6] as possibly difficult candidates for converting DFAs into regular expressions. Some of the obtained results are summarized in Table 1. Here a similar situation shows up as for random instances. The Algorithm **DM** is superior to the other algorithms. Furthermore, the automata Fib_n don't show the conjectured behavior as difficult candidates for converting DFAs into regular expressions. Here the grid automata $Grid_n$ are much more difficult as indicated by the enormously large alphabetic width of at most $1.1 \cdot 10^{17}$ produced by the Algorithm **IS**.

We also studied the setup when starting with a regular expression instead of a DFA. For the conversion from a regular expression to a finite automaton we have implemented Thompson's algorithm [14]. Again Algorithm **DM** outperforms all the other algorithms; but note that the resulting expressions are much smaller

Table 1. Results on the alphabetic width for some specific DFAs instances that appeared already in the literature [2,6,10]. In particular, (A), (B), (C), (D) denote the automata $Min(\mathcal{POI}_4[1, 20])$, $Min(\mathcal{POI}_5[1, 125])$, $Min(\mathcal{POPI}_4[1, 60])$ and $Min(\mathcal{POPI}_5[1, 70])$ as they appear in [2].

Algorithm	(A)	(B)	(C)	(D)	Instance $Grid_3$	$Grid_{12}$	Fib_3	Fib_{12}
RA	1304	93688	7426	1404252	7516	$\leq 1.3 \cdot 10^{19}$	7	2119
OA	1121	54625	2425	819934	1988	$\leq 4.5 \cdot 10^{18}$	11	70877
OB	634	25816	882	13240	634	$\leq 1.1 \cdot 10^{18}$	5	377
DM	491	8989	704	11528	622	$\leq 7.7 \cdot 10^{17}$	5	377
IS	535	9750	929	14701	634	$\leq 1.1 \cdot 10^{17}$	8	1584
B3S	768	11663	793	13062	958	$\leq 1.2 \cdot 10^{19}$	9	1586

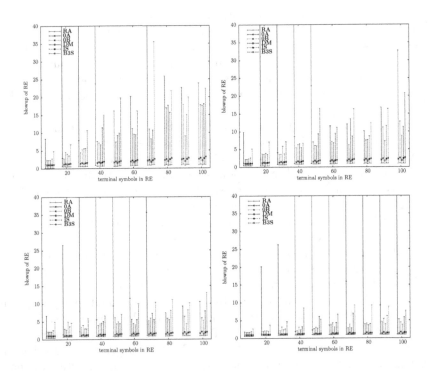

Fig. 2. Blowup (y-axis, linearly scaled) in relation to the length n (x-axis, linearly scaled) of the regular expression (RE) for $10 \leq n \leq 100$ in steps of 10 caused by the transformation RE $\rightarrow$ NFA $\rightarrow$ RE for input alphabet size 2 (upper left), 3 (upper right), 5 (lower left), and 10 (lower right) for the random ordering **RA** and Algorithms **0A**, **0B**, **DM**, **IS**, and **B3S**. The length of a regular expression is defined to be the number of terminal symbols. Here a vertical bar for an algorithm indicates the maximal occurring blowup. Moreover it also shows the average bloat factor indicated by the corresponding mark symbol. Missing lines for **RA** indicate that even the average blowup is greater than 40.

than for random DFAs. For regular expressions of length $10 \leq n \leq 100$ in steps of 10 and input alphabet size $1 \leq k \leq 10$ the size blowup is depicted in Figure 2—again only the diagrams for $k \in \{2, 3, 5, 10\}$ are shown.

Whether using a different conversion algorithm than Thompson's can affect the obtained results is not clear and has to be verified by further experiments. Finally, we mention that we believe that all of the algorithms under consideration would equally benefit from the preprocessing techniques presented in [13]; in particular we do not expect that they have a noticeable effect on random DFA input.

Acknowledgment. We are indebted to Loek Cleophas, Manuel Delgado, Vincent Le Maout, and Kerri Morgan for helping us to effectively build on their previous research.

References

1. Almeida, M., Moreira, N., Reis, R.: Enumeration and generation with a string automata representation. Theor. Comput. Sci. 387(2), 93–102 (2007)
2. Delgado, M., Morais, J.: Approximation to the smallest regular expression for a given regular language. In: Domaratzki, M., Okhotin, A., Salomaa, K., Yu, S. (eds.) CIAA 2004. LNCS, vol. 3317, pp. 312–314. Springer, Heidelberg (2005)
3. Edwards, K., Farr, G.E.: Planarization and fragmentability of some classes of graphs. Discrete Math. 308(12), 2396–2406 (2008)
4. Eggan, L.C.: Transition graphs and the star height of regular events. Mich. Math. J. 10, 385–397 (1963)
5. Ehrenfeucht, A., Zeiger, H.P.: Complexity measures for regular expressions. J. Comput. Syst. Sci. 12(2), 134–146 (1976)
6. Ellul, K., Krawetz, B., Shallit, J., Wang, M.: Regular expressions: New results and open problems. J. Autom. Lang. Comb. 10(4), 407–437 (2005)
7. Feige, U., Hajiaghayi, M., Lee, J.R.: Improved approximation algorithms for minimum weight vertex separators. SIAM J. Comput. 38(2), 629–657 (2008)
8. Frishert, M., Cleophas, L.G., Watson, B.W.: The effect of rewriting regular expressions on their accepting automata. In: Ibarra, O.H., Dang, Z. (eds.) CIAA 2003, vol. 2759, pp. 304–305. Springer, Heidelberg (2003)
9. Gelade, W., Neven, F.: Succinctness of the complement and intersection of regular expressions. In: STACS 2008. Dagstuhl Seminar Proceedings, vol. 08001, pp. 325–336. IBFI Schloss Dagstuhl (2008)
10. Gruber, H., Holzer, M.: Finite automata, digraph connectivity, and regular expression size. In: Aceto, L., Damgård, I., Goldberg, L.A., Halldórsson, M.M., Ingólfsdóttir, A., Walukiewicz, I. (eds.) ICALP 2008, Part II. LNCS, vol. 5126, pp. 39–50. Springer, Heidelberg (2008)
11. Gruber, H., Holzer, M.: Provably shorter regular expressions from deterministic finite automata (extended abstract). In: Ito, M., Toyama, M. (eds.) DLT 2008. LNCS, vol. 5257, pp. 383–395. Springer, Heidelberg (2008)
12. Gruber, H., Johannsen, J.: Optimal lower bounds on regular expression size using communication complexity. In: Amadio, R.M. (ed.) FOSSACS 2008. LNCS, vol. 4962, pp. 273–286. Springer, Heidelberg (2008)
13. Han, Y., Wood, D.: Obtaining shorter regular expressions from finite-state automata. Theor. Comput. Sci. 370(1-3), 110–120 (2007)
14. Hopcroft, J.E., Ullman, J.D.: Introduction to automata theory, languages and computation. Addison-Wesley, Reading (1979)
15. Kleene, S.C.: Representation of events in nerve nets and finite automata. In: Automata studies, pp. 3–42. Princeton University Press, Princeton (1956)
16. Le Maout, V.: Cursors. In: Yu, S., Păun, A. (eds.) CIAA 2000. LNCS, vol. 2088, pp. 195–207. Springer, Heidelberg (2001)
17. Morgan, K.: Approximation algorithms for the maximum induced planar and outerplanar subgraph problems. Bachelor with honors thesis, Monash University, Australia (2005)
18. Ponty, Y., Termier, M., Denise, A.: GenRGenS: software for generating random genomic sequences and structures. Bioinformatics 22(12), 1534–1535 (2006)
19. Sakarovitch, J.: The language, the expression, and the (small) automaton. In: Farré, J., Litovsky, I., Schmitz, S. (eds.) CIAA 2005. LNCS, vol. 3845, pp. 15–30. Springer, Heidelberg (2006)

Small Extended Expressions for Acyclic Automata

Pascal Caron, Jean-Marc Champarnaud, and Ludovic Mignot

LITIS, University of Rouen, France
{pascal.caron,jean-marc.champarnaud}@univ-rouen.fr
ludovic.mignot@etu.univ-rouen.fr

Abstract. A regular expression with n occurrences of symbol can be converted into an equivalent automaton with $n + 1$ states, the so-called Glushkov automaton of the expression. Conversely, it is possible to decide whether a given $(n+1)$-state automaton is a Glushkov one and, if so, to convert it back to an equivalent regular expression of size n. Our goal is to extend the class of automata for which such a linear retranslation is possible. We define new regular operators, called multi-tilde-bars, allowing us to simultaneously apply a multi-tilde operator and a multi-bar one to a list of expressions. The main result is that any acyclic n-state automaton can be turned into an extended expression of size $O(n)$.

1 Introduction

This paper deals with the translation from a finite automaton to a regular expression and more particularly with the efficiency of this translation, as measured by the size of the expression. Polynomial algorithms have been designed for this translation and the inverse one; the first ones are due to McNaughton and Yamada [15] for both constructions, to Glushkov [9] for constructing an automaton, and to Brzozowski and McCluskey [1] for constructing an expression.

It turns out that many efforts have been developed to tackle the problem of constructing a small automaton as efficiently as possible (see for example [5,14]). On the opposite, given an n-state automaton, the size of the expression computed by classical conversion algorithms is exponential with respect to n, and investigations for constructing a small expression [6,12] are not so many. An alternative approach, described in [7], is the study of the descriptional complexity of regular expressions and more precisely the effect of regular operations on this complexity. For example, the operation of removing the empty word has been proved to incur at most a quasilinear increase in regular expressions [17]. Recently, new bounds have been provided for intersection, shuffle and complementation [8,10]. In [11], it is shown that quadratic size expressions can be computed for language quotient operations and cubic size expressions for circular shift operation.

Our project also addresses the problem of computing short expressions, and it focuses on a specific kind of conversion based on Glushkov automata. It is well-known that a regular expression with n occurrences of symbol can be converted into an equivalent automaton with $n + 1$ states, the so-called Glushkov

S. Maneth (Ed.): CIAA 2009, LNCS 5642, pp. 198–207, 2009.
© Springer-Verlag Berlin Heidelberg 2009

automaton of the expression. Conversely, it is possible to decide whether a given $(n + 1)$-state automaton is a Glushkov one [4] and, if so, to convert it back to an equivalent regular expression of size n. Our goal is to find subclasses of the finite automata for which an efficient translation to (extended) regular expressions is possible. This is achieved by designing new regular operators, such as multi-bar operators that delete empty words and multi-tilde operators that add empty words. We have shown in a first step [3,2] that these operators fit with the Glushkov construction and that they lead to extended expressions significantly shorter than equivalent simple regular expressions.

In this paper, we first define new regular operators, called multi-tilde-bars, that allow us to simultaneously apply a multi-tilde operator and a multi-bar operator to a given list of expressions. We then show that any standard and homogeneous acyclic automaton with $n+1$ states can be turned into a multi-tilde-bar expression of size n, which means that any standard and homogeneous acyclic automaton is a Glushkov automaton (in the extended sense). As a corollary, there exists a linear translation to multi-tilde-bar expressions for the subclass of acyclic automata. Quadratic algorithms are provided for converting a standard and homogeneous acyclic automaton (respectively an acyclic automaton) into a multi-tilde-bar expression.

The following section gathers fundamental notions concerning finite automata and regular expressions. We give the definition of the language of a multi-tilde-bar expression in Section 3. Section 4 is devoted to the translation of acyclic automata to multi-tilde-bar expressions.

2   Preliminaries

In this section we recall fundamental notions concerning finite automata and regular expressions (see for example [13,16] for a comprehensive treatment) and we introduce some notation concerning lists of couples of integers.

A *finite automaton* is a 5-tuple $A = (\Sigma, Q, I, F, \delta)$ such that Σ is a finite set of symbols, called the *alphabet*, Q is a finite *set of states*, $I \subset Q$ is the *set of initial states*, $F \subset Q$ is the *set of final states* and $\delta : Q \times \Sigma \to 2^Q$ is the *function of transition*. The domain of the function of transition can be extended to $2^Q \times \Sigma^*$ as follows: $\forall a \in \Sigma, \delta(\emptyset, a) = \emptyset$; $\forall Q' \subset Q \mid Q' \neq \emptyset, \forall a \in \Sigma, \delta(Q', a) = \bigcup_{q \in Q'} \delta(q, a)$; $\forall Q' \subset Q, \delta(Q', \varepsilon) = Q'$; $\forall Q' \subset Q, \forall a \in \Sigma, \forall w \in \Sigma^*, \delta(Q', aw) = \delta(\delta(Q', a), w)$.

A triplet (q, a, q') in $Q \times \Sigma \times Q$ is said to be a *transition* if $q' \in \delta(q, a)$. The function δ can also be viewed as the set of the transitions of the automaton. Let $A = (\Sigma, Q, I, F, \delta)$ be an automaton and $v = (q, a, q')$ be a transition of A. The state q (resp. q') is called the *head* (resp. the *tail*) of v. A *path* of *length* $l > 0$ from p to q is a sequence of l transitions $(v_1, \ldots, v_l)$ such that the head of v_1 is p, the tail of v_l is q and, for all $k < l$, the tail of v_k is the head of v_{k+1}. A path from p to q is said to be *hamiltonian* if and only if every state of the automaton, except for p and q, is the head of exactly one transition of the path and the tail of exactly one transition of the path. The automaton A is said to be *acyclic* if and only if for every couple $(p, q) \in Q \times Q$ such that there exists a path from p

to q, then there exists no path from q to p. Let $A = (\Sigma, Q, I, F, \delta)$ be an acyclic automaton. The automaton A is *homogeneous* if and only if for every couple of transitions (p, a, q) and (p', a', q), it holds $a = a'$. The automaton A is *standard* if and only if it has a unique initial state q_0 and no transition with q_0 as tail. A *topological sort* of A is a bijection $\tau : Q \rightarrow [\![0, \#Q - 1]\!]$ such that for each couple (q, q') of Q^2, $\tau(q) < \tau(q')$ implies that there exists no path from q' to q.

A regular expression E with only $+$, $\cdot$ and $*$ operators is said to be a *simple* one. Two regular expressions are *equivalent* if they denote the same language. The size of E, denoted by $|E|$, is the number of occurrences of symbol in E. A regular expression E is said to be a *minimal* one if there exists no equivalent expression E' defined on the same set of operators and such that $|E'| < |E|$. Let E be a regular expression over the alphabet Σ. The expression E is said to be *linear* if every symbol in Σ occurs at most once in E. The *linearized expression* $E^{\#}$ of E is obtained by replacing each occurrence of symbol in E by its position. For example, if $E = a \cdot b + b$ then $E^{\#} = 1 \cdot 2 + 3$. Let $\Sigma^{\#}$ be the set of positions in E. The alphabetical morphism $h_E()$ from $(\Sigma^{\#})^*$ to Σ^* defined by: for all k in $\Sigma^{\#}$, $h_E(k)$ is the symbol at the position k in E, is called *linearization morphism*.

Let n be a positive integer. The list of expressions $(E_1, \ldots, E_n)$ is denoted by $E_{1,n}$. The expression $E_1 \cdot E_2 \cdots E_n$ is denoted by $E_{1\ldots n}$. In the following, we will consider finite lists of couples (i, f) of integers such that $1 \leq i \leq f \leq n$. Let S be such a list. The size of S is denoted by $\#S$. The set of integers $\{1, \ldots, \#S\}$ is denoted by $[\![1, \#S]\!]$. The set of couples (i, f) in $[\![1, n]\!]^2$ such that $i \leq f$ is denoted by $[\![1, n]\!]^2_{\leq}$. Let $I_S = [\![1, \#S]\!]$ be the set of indices of the list S. Then a list S is defined by $S = ((i_k, f_k)_{k \in I_S})$, with $\forall k \in [\![1, \#S]\!]$, $(i_k, f_k) \in [\![1, n]\!]^2_{\leq}$. The set of all such lists is denoted by $\mathcal{S}_n$. A couple $(i, f) \in S$ is *overlapped* if and only if there exists a couple $(i', f') \in S$ such that $i' < i < f' < f$ (left overlapped) or $i < i' < f < f'$ (right overlapped). A couple $(i, f) \in S$ is *included* if and only if there exists a couple $(i', f') \in S \setminus \{(i, f)\}$ such that $i' \leq i \leq f \leq f'$. A couple is *overhanging* if and only if it is not overlapped. A finite list S of couples is *free* if and only if $\forall (i, f), (i', f') \in S \mid (i, f) \neq (i', f')$, $[\![i, f]\!] \cap [\![i', f']\!] = \emptyset$.

Finally, we introduce the notion of ε-*maximal factor*. Let $w = w_1 \cdots w_n$ be a word such that for all $k \in [\![1, n]\!]$, $w_k \in L(E_k) \cup \{\varepsilon\}$. Let us suppose that there exists a factor $w_i \cdots w_f = \varepsilon$ in w. This factor is said to have a *left* (resp. *right*) ε-*extension* in w if there exists $k = i - 1$ (resp. $k = f + 1$) such that $w_k = \varepsilon$. If there exists no ε-extension, then the factor is said to be ε-*maximal in w*.

3   The Family of Multi-Tilde-Bar Operators

In this paper, we study a new family of operators, called multi-tilde-bar operators. Multi-tilde-bar operators combine multi-tilde operators and multi-bar operators (see [3,2] for a comprehensive treatment). Multi-tilde-bar operators are defined by a list of tildes and a list of bars that can overlap and that are simultaneously applied on a given list of expressions. Thus, a tilde represents a new degree of freedom, the addition of the empty word, while a bar

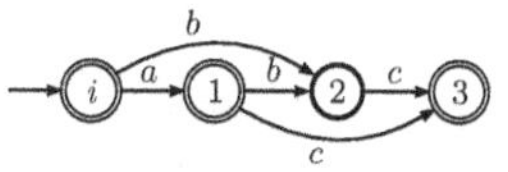

$$E' = \underbrace{(a(b+\varepsilon)+b)c}+a+\varepsilon$$
$$E'' = (\widetilde{a})(\widetilde{b})c + \widetilde{a}$$
$$E = \widetilde{\widetilde{a}\ \widetilde{b}\ c}$$
$$= \overset{\displaystyle\frown\!\!\frown}{}_{(1,1),(2,2),(2,3);(1,2)}(a,b,c)$$

Fig. 1. An example of reduction with a multi-tilde-bar operator

is a constraint, preventing the nullability of a factor. Multi-tilde-bar operators allow us to translate n-state automata that are not Glushkov ones into extended regular expressions with $O(n)$ occurrences of symbol. For example, let us consider the automaton of Figure 1. The simple regular expression E', of size 5, is a minimal one. The expression E'', with multi-tilde and multi-bar operators is of size 4. The expression E, with a multi-tilde-bar operator, is of size 3 only.

More formally, multi-tilde-bar expressions are defined in the following way.

Definition 1. *An* Extended to Multi-tilde-bar Regular Expression *(**EMRE**) is inductively defined by:*

$\mathbf{E} = \emptyset$	$\mathbf{E} = \mathbf{F} + \mathbf{G}$, *with F and G two EMREs*
$\mathbf{E} = \varepsilon$	$\mathbf{E} = \mathbf{F} \cdot \mathbf{G}$, *with F and G two EMREs*
$\mathbf{E} = \mathbf{a}$, *with $a \in \Sigma$*	$\mathbf{E} = \mathbf{F}^*$, *with F an EMRE*

$$\mathbf{E} = \overset{\frown\!\!\frown}{}_{\mathbf{T};\mathbf{B}}(\mathbf{E_{1,n}})\ ,\ \textit{with } T \textit{ and } B \textit{ two disjoint lists of } \mathcal{S}_n$$
$$\textit{and } E_{1,n} \textit{ a list of (different of } \varepsilon\textit{) EMREs}$$

Notice that due to the storage of tildes and bars, the length of a multi-tilde-bar expression is quadratic w.r.t. n. However, there exist families of languages such that the length of the minimal simple expression is exponential. In the following two subsections, we give the definition of the language of a multi-tilde-bar expression. We first consider the case of linear expressions.

3.1   The Language of a Linear Multi-Tilde-Bar EMRE

The language of a linear multi-tilde-bar expression is computed according to formulas that correspond to four different cases, depending on the existence or not of bars and on a possible overlapping of a bar with one or more tildes.

Case of a Unique Bar and No Overlapping with a Tilde. This is the easiest case, where elementary operators (tildes or bars) are independent from each other and can be directly applied to the corresponding factor. There are three subcases, as illustrated by the Table 1: inclusion of one or more tildes (expression E_1), inclusion of a bar (expression E_2) and no inclusion (expression E_3).

Table 1. Examples of basic multi-tilde-bar expressions

$$E_1 = \overline{a\ b\ \widetilde{\overline{c}}\ d}$$
$$= \widetilde{}_{(2,2),(3,3);(2,3)}(a,b,c,d)$$

$$L(E_1) = L(a((b+\varepsilon)(c+\varepsilon)\setminus\varepsilon)d)$$
$$= L(a(b+\varepsilon)cd + ab(c+\varepsilon)d)$$

$$E_2 = \overline{\overset{\widetilde{}}{a(b+\varepsilon)(c+\varepsilon)d}}$$
$$= \widetilde{}_{(1,4);(2,3)}(a,b+\varepsilon,c+\varepsilon,d)$$

$$L(E_2) = L(a((b+\varepsilon)(c+\varepsilon)\setminus\varepsilon)d + \varepsilon)$$
$$= L(a(b+\varepsilon)cd + ab(c+\varepsilon)d + \varepsilon)$$

$$E_3 = \overline{\overline{(a+\varepsilon)(b+\varepsilon)\ \widetilde{c}\ }\ d}$$
$$= \widetilde{}_{(3,3),(4,4);(1,2)}(a+\varepsilon,b+\varepsilon,c,d)$$

$$L(E_3) = L(((a+\varepsilon)(b+\varepsilon)\setminus\varepsilon)(c+\varepsilon)(d+\varepsilon))$$
$$= L(a(b+\varepsilon)(c+\varepsilon)(d+\varepsilon))$$
$$\cup L((a+\varepsilon)b(c+\varepsilon)(d+\varepsilon))$$

Definition 2. *Let $E = \widetilde{}_{T;(i,f)}(E_{1,n})$ be an EMRE such that $E_{1\cdots n}$ is linear, T is a free list and (i,f) is a couple of $[\![1,n]\!]_{\leq}^2$. We assume that (i,f) is not in T and is not overlapped by an element of T. Let L' be the language defined by:*

$$L' = \begin{cases} L(E_i\cdots \overset{\widetilde{}}{E_{i_k\cdots f_k}} \cdots \overset{\widetilde{}}{E_{i_{k'}\cdots f_{k'}}} \cdots E_f) & \text{inclusion of one or more tildes,} \\ L(\ \overline{\overset{\widetilde{}}{E_{i_k}}\cdots E_{i\cdots f}}\cdots E_{f_k}\ ) & \text{inclusion of one bar,} \\ L(\ \overset{\widetilde{}}{E_{i_k\cdots f_k}}\cdots \overline{E_{i\cdots f}}\cdots \overset{\widetilde{}}{E_{i_{k'}\cdots f_{k'}}}\ ) & \text{no inclusion.} \end{cases}$$

The language of the expression $E = \widetilde{}_{T;(i,f)}(E_{1,n})$ is then defined as follows:

$$L(E) = L(E_{1\cdots i_1-1}) \cdot L(\ \overset{\widetilde{}}{E_{i_1\cdots f_1}}\ ) \cdot L(E_{f_1+1\cdots i_2-1}) \cdots$$
$$L' \cdots$$
$$L(E_{f_{\#T}-1+1\cdots i_{\#T}-1}) \cdot L(\ \overset{\widetilde{}}{E_{i_{\#T}\cdots f_{\#T}}}\ ) \cdot L(E_{f_{\#T}+1\cdots n})$$

Case of a Unique Bar Overlapping with Tildes of a Free List. In this case, our choice is the following: applying a tilde to a list of expressions $E_{i,j}$ adds the empty word to the factor $E_{i\cdots j}$ while applying a bar eliminates every occurrence of the empty word that <u>appears on</u> the interval of this bar. For example, for the expression $E = \overset{\widetilde{}}{a\ \overline{(b+\varepsilon)(c+\varepsilon)}\ d}$, the tildes make it possible to substitute ε to the expression $a(b+\varepsilon)$ or to the expression $(c+\varepsilon)d$; on the opposite, the bar prevents to substitute ε to the expression $(b+\varepsilon)(c+\varepsilon)$.

Definition 3. *Let $E = \widetilde{}_{T';(i,f)}(E_{1,n})$ be an EMRE such that $E_{1\cdots n}$ is linear, T' is a free list and (i,f) is a couple of $[\![1,n]\!]_{\leq}^2$ such that $(i,f) \notin T'$. Let T'_+ (resp. T'_-) be the sublist of T' that overlaps (resp. does not overlap) with the bar (i,f). We set $L_+ = \bigcup_{(i',f')\in T'_+} L(\overset{\frown}{}_{T'\setminus(i',f')}(E_1,\ldots,E_{i'-1},\varepsilon,\ldots,\ \varepsilon,E_{f'+1},\ldots,E_n))$ and $L_- = L(\overset{\frown}{}_{T'_-;(i,f)}(E_{1,n}))$. The language of the expression E is defined by:*

$$L(\overset{\frown}{}_{T';(i,f)}(E_{1,n})) = L_- \cup L_+$$

Case of a List of Bars and a Free List of Tildes. In this case, we have to make sure that for all word w in $L(E)$, all the bars are correctly applied. As for multi-tilde expressions, it amounts to check that for all ε-maximal factor of w, there is no bar defined over this factor.

Definition 4. *Let $E = \widetilde{}_{T';B}(E_{1,n})$ be an EMRE such that $E_{1...n}$ is linear and T' is a free sublist. The language of the expression E is defined as follows:*

$$L(\widetilde{}_{T';B}(E_{1,n})) = \begin{cases} \displaystyle\bigcap_{(i_b,f_b)\in B} L(\widetilde{}_{T';(i_b,f_b)}(E_{1,n})) & \text{if } B \neq \emptyset \\ L(\widetilde{}_{T'}(E_{1,n})) & \text{otherwise} \end{cases}$$

Case of Disjoint Lists of Bars and Tildes. As for the language of a multi-tilde expression, we consider the set T of the free sublists of the list of tildes.

Definition 5. *Let $E = \widetilde{}_{T;B}(E_{1,n})$ be an EMRE such that $E_{1...n}$ is linear. The language of the expression E is defined as follows:*

$$L(\widetilde{}_{T;B}(E_{1,n})) = \bigcup_{T'\in T} L(\widetilde{}_{T';B}(E_{1,n}))$$

3.2   The Language of a Multi-Tilde-Bar EMRE

The language of a not necessarily linear EMRE is defined from the language of its linearized expression.

Definition 6. *Let $E = \widetilde{}_{T;B}(E_{1,n})$ be an EMRE and $E^{\#}$ be its linearized expression. Let $h_E()$ be the alphabetical morphism associated with the linearization. By definition, we set $L(E) = h_E(L(E^{\#}))$.*

Lemma 1. *Let $E = \widetilde{}_{T;B}(E_{1,n})$ and $E^{\#}$ its linearized expression. Let w be a word of $(L(E_1)\cup\{\varepsilon\})\cdots(L(E_n)\cup\{\varepsilon\})$. The following four conditions are equivalent: (1) The word w is in $L(E)$; (2) The word w is in $h_E(L(E^{\#}))$; (3) There exists a word w' in $L(E^{\#})$ such that $h_E(w') = w$; (4) There exists a word $w' = w'_1\cdots w'_n$ in $L(E^{\#})$ such that for all $k \in [\![1,n]\!]$, $h_E(w'_k) = w_k$.*

3.3   Properties of EMREs

EMREs have some semantic properties that are useful for conversion of finite automata. For instance, since tildes make it possible for a factor to be substituted by the empty word, EMREs have nice nullability properties. Given an expression $F = E_1 \cdots E_n$ and a word $w \in L(F)$, we say that $w_1 \cdots w_n$ is a decomposition of w if and only if for all $k \in [\![1,n]\!]$, $w_k \neq \varepsilon \Rightarrow w_k \in L(E_k)$. If the expression F is not linear, there may exist several decompositions for a given word. The following lemma addresses the case where F is linear.

Lemma 2. *Let $F = E_{1...n}$ be a linear expression and $w \in L(F)$. There exists a unique decomposition $w = w_1\cdots w_n$ such that $\forall k \in [\![1,n]\!]$, $w_k \in L(E_k)\cup\{\varepsilon\}$.*

Definition 7. *An EMRE $E = \widetilde{}_{T;B}(E_{1,n})$ is said to be total if and only if:*
$$T \uplus B = [\![1,n]\!]^2_{\leq}$$

Lemma 3. *Let $E = \widetilde{}_{T;B}(E_{1,n})$ be a linear total EMRE. Let $w = w_1 \cdots w_n$ be a word of $(L(E_1) \cup \{\varepsilon\}) \cdots (L(E_n) \cup \{\varepsilon\})$. Then the word w is in $L(E)$ if and only if for all ε-maximal factor $w_i \cdots w_f$ of w, the couple (i, f) is in T.*

Lemma 4. *Let $E = \widetilde{}_{T;B}(E_{1,n})$ be a total EMRE. Let w be a word in $(L(E_1) \cup \{\varepsilon\}) \cdots (L(E_n) \cup \{\varepsilon\})$. Then the word w is in $L(E)$ if and only if there exists a decomposition $w_1 \cdots w_n$ of w such that for all ε-maximal factor $w_i \cdots w_f$, the couple (i, f) is in T.*

4   Conversion of Acyclic Automata into Multi-Tilde-Bar Expressions

We show that there exists an efficient conversion into multi-tilde-bar expressions for the class of acyclic automata. We first define the notion of inline automaton and show that any standard and homogeneous inline $(n + 1)$-state automaton can be converted into a multi-tilde-bar expression of size n. We then extend this result to the class of standard and homogeneous acyclic automata.

4.1   Case of Inline Automata

Definition 8. *An acyclic automaton A is* inline *if and only if for every couple (q, q') of states, there exists either a path from q to q' or a path from q' to q.*

An acyclic automaton is inline if and only if it admits a unique hamiltonian path. The transitions of this path induce a total order over the set of states and, as a consequence, an inline automaton admits a unique topological sort.

We now consider the subclass of standard and homogeneous inline $(n + 1)$-state automata. Let $A = (\Sigma, Q, \{q_0\}, F, \delta)$ be such an automaton and τ be its topological sort. Without loss of generality, we suppose that the automaton A is *sorted* with respect to τ, *i.e.* the states are numbered according to their position in the topological sort τ, the unique initial state having position 0; hence we have $Q = [\![0, n]\!]$ and $q_0 = 0$. Since A is standard and homogeneous, it is possible to define a state-labeling via a mapping $h_A()$ from Q to Σ, such that for all $q \in Q \setminus \{q_0\}$, $h_A(q)$ is the symbol of any transition entering the state q. Finally, we consider the *twin automaton* $A' = (\Sigma', Q, \{0\}, F, \delta')$ of A, defined over the alphabet $\Sigma' = [\![1, n]\!]$ and such that δ' is a mapping from $Q \times \Sigma'$ to 2^Q, with $(p, q, q) \in \delta' \Leftrightarrow (p, h_A(q), q) \in \delta$. A twin automaton is obviously a standard, homogeneous, sorted and inline one.

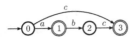

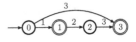

Fig. 2. A standard, homogeneous and sorted inline automaton ...

Fig. 3. ... and its twin automaton

4.2   From a Standard Homogeneous Inline Automaton to an EMRE

We now show that any standard and homogeneous inline $(n+1)$-state automaton can be converted into an EMRE of size n.

Definition 9. *Let $A = (\Sigma, Q, \{0\}, F, \delta)$ be a standard, homogeneous and sorted inline automaton and $A' = (\Sigma', Q, \{0\}, F, \delta')$ be its twin automaton. Let $n = \#Q - 1$. We set $T = (\{(i, f) \mid f + 1 \in \delta'(i-1, f+1)\} \cup \{(i, n) \mid i-1 \in F\}) \cap [\![1, n]\!]^2_{\leq}$ and $B = [\![1, n]\!]^2_{\leq} \setminus T$.*
The expression $E' = \mathbin{\widetilde{}}_{T;B}(1, \ldots, n)$ is the characteristic expression of A'.

The characteristic expression of a twin automaton is obviously total. The EMRE $E = \mathbin{\widetilde{}}_{T;B}(E_{1,n})$ is said to be *flat* if and only if for all $k \in [\![1, n]\!]$, the expression E_k is a symbol. The expression E' is clearly a flat and linear one.

We now study the language of the characteristic expression of a twin automaton. Notice that the mapping $\mathrm{h}_A()$ can be viewed as an alphabetic morphism from Σ'^* to Σ^*. We will say that $\mathrm{h}_A()$ is the morphism *associated* with A.

Lemma 5. *Let A be an automaton and A' be its twin automaton. Let $\mathrm{h}_A()$ be the associated morphism. Then it holds: $\mathrm{h}_A(L(A')) = L(A)$.*

Theorem 1. *Let A' be a twin automaton. The characteristic expression $E' = \mathbin{\widetilde{}}_{T;B}(1, \ldots, n)$ of A', of size n, can be computed in $O(n^2)$ time and is such that $L(A') = L(E')$.*

Lemma 4 allows us to compute an EMRE E such that $L(E) = L(A)$.

Theorem 2. *Let A be a standard and homogeneous inline $(n + 1)$-state automaton. Let $E' = \mathbin{\widetilde{}}_{T;B}(1, \ldots, n)$ be the characteristic expression of the twin automaton of A. The EMRE $E = \mathbin{\widetilde{}}_{T;B}(\mathrm{h}_A(1), \ldots, \mathrm{h}_A(n))$ of size n can be computed in $O(n)$ from E' and is such that $L(E) = L(A)$.*

The expression E is called the *canonical* EMRE of the automaton A.

4.3   From an Acyclic Automaton to an EMRE

We now extend Theorem 2 to acyclic automata. In a first step, we consider acyclic automata that are standard and homogeneous. Given such a $(n+1)$-state automaton A, we construct an inline n'-state automaton A', with $n' \leq 2(n-1)$.

Definition 10. *Let $A = (\Sigma, Q, \{q_0\}, F, \delta)$ be a standard and homogeneous acyclic automaton. Let $\mathrm{h}_A()$ be the mapping from Q to Σ such that for all q in Q, $\mathrm{h}_A(q)$ is the symbol that labels any transition entering in q. Let τ be a topological sort of A. Let $\perp$ be the set $\{\perp_k \mid \tau^{-1}(k+1) \notin \delta(\tau^{-1}(k), \mathrm{h}_A(\tau^{-1}(k+1)))\}$. The automaton $A' = (\Sigma', Q', I', F', \delta')$, called the plump automaton of A according to τ, is defined by: $\Sigma' = \Sigma \cup \perp$, $I' = \{q_0\}$, $Q' = Q \cup \perp$, $F' = F$ and*

$$\forall (p, a) \in Q' \times \Sigma', \ \delta'(p, a) = \begin{cases} \delta(p, a) & \text{if } (p, a) \in Q \times \Sigma \\ \tau^{-1}(k+1) & \text{if } p = \perp_k \text{ and } a = \mathrm{h}_A(\tau^{-1}(k+1)) \\ \perp_k & \text{if } a = \perp_k \text{ and } \tau(p) = k \\ \emptyset & \text{otherwise.} \end{cases}$$

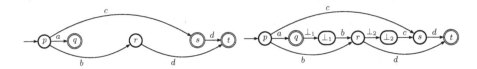

Fig. 4. A standard and homogeneous acyclic automaton ...

Fig. 5. ... and one of its plump automata

Properties of plump automata are gathered in the following lemma.

Lemma 6. *Let* $A = (\Sigma, Q, \{q_0\}, F, \delta)$ *be a standard and homogeneous acyclic* $(n+1)$-*state automaton and* $A' = (\Sigma', Q', I', F', \delta')$ *be one of its plump automata. Then* A' *is a standard and homogeneous inline automaton and it has no more than* $2(n-1)$ *states. Moreover, for all* w *in* Σ^*, $w \in L(A) \Leftrightarrow w \in L(A')$.

Following Theorem 2, we compute an EMRE E' of size n' such that $L(A') = L(E')$ and show how to compute an EMRE E of size n such that $L(E) = L(A)$.

Theorem 3. *Let* A *be a standard and homogeneous acyclic* $(n+1)$-*state automaton. Let* A' *be a plump automaton of* A *and* $E' = \overset{\frown}{\sim}_{T;B}(E'_{1,n'})$ *be its canonical EMRE. Let* $E = \overset{\frown}{\sim}_{T;B}(E_{1,n'})$ *be such that for every* $k \in [\![1, n']\!]$, $E_k = \emptyset$ *if* $E'_k = \perp_{k'}$, $E_k = E'_k$ *otherwise. Then the EMRE* E *of size* n *can be computed in* $O(n')$ *time from* E' *and is such that* $L(E) = L(A)$.

We now consider the class of acyclic automata and we show that any n-state acyclic automaton can be converted into an EMRE of size $O(n)$. This result is based on the following lemma.

Lemma 7. *Let* $A = (\Sigma, Q, I, F, \delta)$ *be an acyclic automaton. Then an equivalent acyclic automaton* $A' = (\Sigma, Q', I', F', \delta')$, *standard, homogeneous and such that* $\#Q' \leq \#\Sigma \times \#Q$ *can be computed in* $O(\#\Sigma^2 \times n^2)$ *time.*

Theorem 4. *Let* A *be an acyclic* n-*state automaton. Then it is possible to construct an EMRE* E *of size* $O(n)$ *such that* $L(E) = L(A)$ *in* $O(n^2)$ *time.*

5   Conclusion

The main result proved in this paper is that any standard and homogeneous acyclic automaton is a Glushkov one, as far as conversion into an extended to multi-tilde-bar expression is concerned. As a corollary, there exists an $O(n)$ conversion into such an expression for the class of acyclic n-state automata. The EMRE that we compute from an acyclic n-state automaton is a total one. It means that $O(n^2)$ couples are necessary to define the multi-tilde-bar operator. We intend to study how to reduce the number of such couples. Finally, notice that although not described in this paper, there exists an $O(n^2)$ time algorithm for converting an EMRE of size n into an $(n+1)$-state automaton.

References

1. Brzozowski, J.A., McCluskey, E.J.: Signal flow graph techniques for sequential circuit state diagrams. IEEE Trans. on Electronic Computers EC-12(2) (1963)
2. Caron, P., Champarnaud, J.-M., Mignot, L.: Multi-tilde operators and their Glushkov automata. In: Dediu, A.H., Ionescu, A.M., Martín-Vide, C. (eds.) LATA 2009. LNCS, vol. 5457. Springer, Heidelberg (2009)
3. Caron, P., Champarnaud, J.-M., Mignot, L.: A new family of regular operators fitting with the position automaton computation. In: Nielsen, M., et al. (eds.) SOFSEM 2009. LNCS, vol. 5404. Springer, Heidelberg (2009)
4. Caron, P., Ziadi, D.: Characterization of Glushkov automata. Theoret. Comput. Sci. 233(1-2), 75–90 (2000)
5. Champarnaud, J.-M., Ziadi, D.: From c-continuations to new quadratic algorithms for automata synthesis. Internat. J. Algebra Comput. 11(6), 707–735 (2001)
6. Delgado, M., Morais, J.: Approximation to the smallest regular expression for a given regular language. In: Domaratzki, M., Okhotin, A., Salomaa, K., Yu, S. (eds.) CIAA 2004. LNCS, vol. 3317, pp. 312–314. Springer, Heidelberg (2005)
7. Ellul, K., Krawetz, B., Shallit, J., Wang, M.: Regular expressions: New results and open problems. Journal of Automata, Languages and Combinatorics 10(4), 407–437 (2005)
8. Gelade, W., Neven, F.: Succinctness of the complement and intersection of regular expressions. In: Albers, S., Weil, P. (eds.) STACS. Dagstuhl Seminar Proceedings, vol. 08001, pp. 325–336 (2008)
9. Glushkov, V.M.: On a synthesis algorithm for abstract automata. Ukr. Matem. Zhurnal 12(2), 147–156 (1960) (in Russian)
10. Gruber, H., Holzer, M.: Finite automata, digraph connectivity, and regular expression size. In: Aceto, L., Damgård, I., Goldberg, L.A., Halldórsson, M.M., Ingólfsdóttir, A., Walukiewicz, I. (eds.) ICALP 2008, Part II. LNCS, vol. 5126, pp. 39–50. Springer, Heidelberg (2008)
11. Gruber, H., Holzer, M.: Language operations with regular expressions of polynomial size. In: Pighizzini, G., Câmpeanu, C. (eds.) 10th International Workshop on Descriptional Complexity of Formal Systems (DCFS 2008), Charlottetown, Canada, pp. 182–193 (2008)
12. Han, Y.-S., Wood, D.: Obtaining shorter regular expressions from finite-state automata. Theor. Comput. Sci. 370(1-3), 110–120 (2007)
13. Hopcroft, J.E., Ullman, J.D.: Introduction to Automata Theory, Languages and Computation. Addison-Wesley, Reading (1979)
14. Ilie, L., Yu, S.: Follow automata. Inf. Comput. 186(1), 140–162 (2003)
15. McNaughton, R.F., Yamada, H.: Regular expressions and state graphs for automata. IEEE Transactions on Electronic Computers 9, 39–57 (1960)
16. Yu, S.: Regular languages. In: Rozenberg, G., Salomaa, A. (eds.) Handbook of Formal Languages. Word, Language, Grammar, vol. I, pp. 41–110. Springer, Berlin (1997)
17. Ziadi, D.: Regular expression for a language without empty word. Theor. Comput. Sci. 63(1,2), 309–315 (1996)

Quantum Queries on Permutations
with a Promise

Rūsiņš Freivalds[1,*] and Kazuo Iwama[2]

[1] Department of Computer Science, University of Latvia, Raiņa bulvāris. 29, Riga,
LV-1459, Latvia
[2] Department of Communications and Computer Engineering, School of Informatics,
Kyoto University, Kyoto 606-8501, Japan

Abstract. This paper studies quantum query complexities for deciding
(exactly or with probability 1.0) the parity of permutations of n numbers,
0 through $n-1$. Our results show quantum mechanism is quite strong for
this non-Boolean problem as it is for several Boolean problems: (i) For
$n = 3$, we need a single query in the quantum case whereas we obviously
need two queries deterministically. (ii) For even n, $n/2$ quantum queries
are sufficient whereas we need $n - 1$ queries deterministically. (iii) Our
third result is for the problem deciding whether the given permutation
is the identical one. For this problem, we show that there is a nontrivial
promise such that if we impose that promise to the input of size $n = 4m$,
then we need only two quantum queries, while at least $2m+2$ $(= n/2+2)$
deterministic queries are necessary.

1 Introduction

Many papers on query algorithms assume that they compute Boolean functions.
The input of the query algorithm is a black box oracle containing the values of
the variables $x_1 = a_1, x_2 = a_2, \cdots, x_n = a_n$ for an explicitly known Boolean
function $f(x_1, \cdots, x_n)$. The result of the query algorithm is to be the value
$f(a_1, \cdots, a_n)$. The query algorithm can ask for the values of the variables. The
queries are asked individually, and the result of any query influences the next
query to be asked or the result to be output.

The complexity of the query algorithm is defined as the number of the queries
asked to the black box oracle. Deterministic query algorithms prescribe the next
query uniquely depending only on the previously received answers from the black
box oracle. Probabilistic query algorithms allow randomization of the process of
computation.

Quantum query algorithms (see a formal definition in [5]) consists of a finite
number of states in each of which they make a query to the black box oracle
and determine how to change states. In fact they alternate *query operations*

---

* The research was performed during the stay of the first author at the University
of Kyoto and partly supported by Grant No. 09.1437 from the Latvian Council of
Science.

S. Maneth (Ed.): CIAA 2009, LNCS 5642, pp. 208–216, 2009.

and *unitary transformations*. In the steps called *query operations* the states of
the algorithm are divided into subsets corresponding to the allowed quantum-
parallel queries. If each of states $q_{i_1}, \cdots, q_{i_m}$ asks a query "$x_i = ?$" then for
every possible answer "$x_i = j$" a unitary operation over the states $q_{i_1}, \cdots, q_{i_m}$
is pre-programmed. In the steps called *unitary transformations* the amplitudes
of all states are transformed according a unitary matrix. All the sequence of the
steps is ended in a special operation called *measurement* in which the amplitudes
(being complex numbers) for all the states are substituted by real numbers called
probabilities by the following rule. The complex number $a + bi$ is substituted by
the real number $a^2 + b^2$. It follows from the unitarity of all the operations that
the total of the probabilities of all states equals 1. Some states are defined to
be accepting, and the other states are defined to be rejecting. This distinction is
not seen before the measurement. After the measurement the probabilities of the
accepting states are totalled and the result is called the accepting probability.
We say that the quantum query algorithm is *exact* if the accepting probability
is always either 1 or 0.

The notion of *promise* for quantum algorithm was introduced by Deutsch
and Jozsa [9], and Simon [10]. In quantum query algorithms for problems under
promise the domain of correctness of the algorithm is explicitly restricted. We are
not interested in behavior of the algorithm outside this restriction. For instance,
in this paper all the query algorithms are considered under a promise that the
target function describes a permutation (in a way precisely stated below).

Recently there have been many papers studying query algorithms computing
Boolean functions. A good reference is the survey by Buhrman and de Wolf [5].

We consider in this paper a more general class of functions $f(x_1, \cdots, x_n)$,
namely, functions $\{0, 1, 2, \cdots, n-1\}^n \rightarrow \{0, 1\}$. The domain $\{0, 1, 2, \cdots, n\}^n$
includes a particularly interesting case - permutations. For instance,

$$x_1 = 4, x_2 = 3, x_3 = 2, x_4 = 1, x_5 = 0$$

can be considered as a permutation of 5 symbols $\{0,1,2,3,4\}$ usually described as
43210. Under such a restriction the functions $f : \{0, 1, 2, \cdots, n-1\}^n \rightarrow \{0, 1\}$
can be considered as properties of permutations. For instance, the function

$$f(0, 1, 2) = 1, f(1, 2, 0) = 1, f(2, 0, 1) = 1, f(0, 2, 1) = 0, f(1, 0, 2) = 0, f(2, 1, 0) = 0$$

describes the property of 3-permutations to be *even* (as opposed to the property
to be *odd*).

The property of a permutation to be even or odd can be defined in many
equivalent ways. One of the most popular definitions used below is as follows.
A permutation $x_1 = a_1, x_2 = a_2, \cdots, x_n = a_n$ is called even (odd) if it can be
obtained from the identical permutation $x_1 = 0, x_2 = 1, \cdots, x_n = n-1$ by an
even (odd) number of transpositions, i.e. mutual changes of exactly two elements
of the permutation: substituting $x_i = a_i$ and $x_j = a_j$ by $x_i = a_j$ and $x_j = a_i$. It
is a well-known fact that the property to be even or odd does not depend on the
particular sequence of transpositions. Deciding whether a given permutation is
even or odd is called deciding the parity of this permutation.

Our Contribution. In this paper, we show that quantum mechanism is quite strong for this non-Boolean problem as it is for several Boolean problems: (i) We first show that for $n = 3$, only a single query is enough in the quantum case whereas we obviously need two queries deterministically. As for $n = 4$, it turns out due to the next result that two quantum queries are enough. Thus it is an interesting open question whether the true complexity is one or two for the case of $n = 4$. (ii) For an even n, $n/2$ quantum queries are sufficient whereas we need $n - 1$ queries deterministically. Since we need $n/2$ queries for determining the parity of n Boolean variables [6], we conjecture this result is somewhat tight. (iii) Our third result is for the problem deciding whether the given permutation is identical. For this problem, we show that there is a promise such that if we impose that promise to the input of size $n = 4m$, then we need only two quantum queries, while $2m + 2$ ($= n/2 + 2$) deterministic queries are necessary (and sufficient).

2   First Example

Theorem 1. *There is an exact quantum query algorithm deciding the parity of 3-permutations with one query.*

Proof. By the way of quantum parallelism, in the state q_1 we ask the query x_1 with an amplitude $\frac{1}{\sqrt{3}}$, in the state q_2 we ask the query x_2 with an amplitude $\frac{1}{\sqrt{3}}$, and in the state q_3 we ask the query x_3 with an amplitude $\frac{1}{\sqrt{3}}$.

If the answer from the black box to the query x_1 is 0, we do not change the amplitude of the state q_1. If the answer is 1, we multiply the existing amplitude to $e^{i\frac{2\pi}{3}}$. If the answer is 2, we multiply the existing amplitude to $e^{i\frac{4\pi}{3}}$.

If the answer from the black box to the query x_2 is 0, we multiply the amplitude of the state q_2 to $e^{i\frac{4\pi}{3}}$. If the answer is 1, we do not change the amplitude. If the answer is 2, we multiply the existing amplitude to $e^{i\frac{2\pi}{3}}$.

If the answer from the black box to the query x_3 is 0, we multiply the amplitude the state q_3 to $e^{i\frac{2\pi}{3}}$. If the answer is 1, we multiply the existing amplitude to $e^{i\frac{4\pi}{3}}$. If the answer is 2, we do not change the amplitude.

We process the obtained amplitudes of the states q_1, q_2, q_3 by a unitary transformation corresponding to the matrix

$$\begin{pmatrix} (\frac{1}{\sqrt{3}}) & (\frac{1}{\sqrt{3}}) & (\frac{1}{\sqrt{3}}) \\ (\frac{1}{\sqrt{3}}) & (\frac{1}{\sqrt{3}})e^{i\frac{2\pi}{3}} & (\frac{1}{\sqrt{3}})e^{i\frac{4\pi}{3}} \\ (\frac{1}{\sqrt{3}}) & (\frac{1}{\sqrt{3}})e^{i\frac{4\pi}{3}} & (\frac{1}{\sqrt{3}})e^{i\frac{2\pi}{3}} \end{pmatrix}.$$

This transformation is a particular case of Fourier transform. If we are computing $f(0, 1, 2)$, $f(1, 2, 0)$ or $f(2, 0, 1)$ (these are all even 3-permutations) the amplitude of the state q_1 becomes, correspondingly, 1, $e^{i\frac{2\pi}{3}}$ or $e^{i\frac{4\pi}{3}}$. After measuring this state we get the probability 1. If we are computing $f(0, 2, 1)$ (which is an odd permutation) the amplitude of the state q_1 becomes 0 but the amplitude of the state q_2 becomes 1. If we are computing $f(1, 0, 2)$ or $f(2, 1, 0)$ (which are odd permutations) the amplitude of the state q_1 becomes 0 but the amplitude of the state q_3 becomes $e^{i\frac{4\pi}{3}}$ or $e^{i\frac{2\pi}{3}}$, correspondingly. □

3 Further Results

In this section we first prove that there is an exact quantum query algorithm deciding the parity of $2n$-permutations with n queries. Obviously we need $2n - 1$ deterministic queries.

Theorem 2. *For an arbitrary n, there is an exact quantum query algorithm deciding the parity of $2n$-permutations with n queries.*

Proof. Let $x_1 = a_1$, $x_2 = a_2$, ..., $x_n = a_n, x_{n+1} = a_{n+1}$, ..., $x_{2n} = a_{2n}$ be a permutation of $2n$ numbers, 0, 1, through $2n - 1$, namely $a_i \in \{0, ..., 2n - 1\}$ and $a_i \neq a_j$ if $i \neq j$. Then the parity of this permutation, say X, can be calculated as follows:

First we show an elementary (and well known) lemma for permutations. Let a sequence of transpositions (exchanging $x_i = a$ and $x_j = b$ into $x_i = b$ and $x_j = a$) $t_1, t_2, \cdots, t_m$ transforms X into the identical permutation. Then the parity of X does not depend on the efficiency of this transposition sequence. Namely,

Lemma 1. *If there is such a sequence of transpositions, then the parity of X is even if and only if m is even.*

We say that x_i is *outside* if for $i \in \{1, ..., n\}$ ($\in \{n + 1, \cdots, 2n\}$, respectively) $a_i \in \{n, ..., 2n - 1\}$, ($\in \{0, ..., n - 1\}$, respectively). Let $x_{i_1}, x_{i_2}, ..., x_{i_k}$ be outside variables in the first half (i.e., all $i_l \in \{1, ..., n\}$). Obviously we must have the same number of outside variables, $x_{j_1}, x_{j_2}, ..., x_{j_k}$ in the second half.

Now we define the new permutation Y, $x_1 = b_1$, $x_2 = b_2$, ..., $x_n = b_n$, $x_{n+1} = b_{n+1}$, ..., $x_{2n} = b_{2n}$, as follows: (i) If x_i is not an outside variable in X, then $b_i = a_i$. (ii) If x_i is an outside variable and a_i is the h-th smallest value in $\{a_{i_1}, a_{i_2}, ..., a_{i_k}\}$ (namely a_i is the h-th smallest value in the missing values $\geq n$ in $\{a_{n+1}, ..., a_{2n}\}$, then b_i is the h-th smallest value in $\{a_{j_1}, a_{j_2}, ..., a_{j_k}\}$. Let's say that x_i has the h-th smallest missing value. Here is a small example:

Let

$$(x_1, x_2, x_3, x_4, x_5, x_6, x_7, x_8) = (2, 1, 6, 7, 3, 0, 5, 4).$$

Then since $x_3 = 6$ is the first smallest missing value (i.e., the smallest one in the missing values that are 4 or larger in the second half (6 and 7 are missing)), $y_3 = 0$ (i.e., the first smallest missing value in the second half). Also, $x_4 = 7$ and $x_5 = 3$ are the second smallest missing values. As a result, the new permutation Y is

$$(x_1, x_2, x_3, x_4, x_5, x_6, x_7, x_8) = (2, 1, 0, 3, 7, 6, 5, 4).$$

We are ready to give our key lemma (recall that k is the number of outside variables in the first half of X):

Lemma 2. *The parity of X is equal to (the parity of Y) +k mod 2.*

Before the formal poof, let's look at the above example. Since $k = 2$, the parity of X should be equal to the parity of Y. Observe that the first half of the string Y, namely 2, 1, 0, 3 can be transformed into 0, 1, 2, 3 by one transposition (of 2 and 0). The second half of Y, i.e., 7, 6, 5, 4, is transformed into 4, 5, 6, 7 with two transpositions. Thus the parity of Y is 1 (odd). Note that the original permutation, X, can be transformed into the identical permutation with five transpositions (6 and 0 first, and 7 and 3 second, and the same as above after that) and its parity is also odd.

Proof of Lemma 2. It is not hard to see that the following algorithm transforms X into the identical permutation:

(1) Let x_i and x_j be the h-th missing values in the first half and in the second half, respectively. Then exchange x_i and x_j. Do this for $h = 1, ..., k$.

(2) Now the resulting permutation is obviously Y. So, we now transform Y into the identical permutation.

Note that we need k transpositions for (1) and therefore the lemma follows by Lemma 1.   □

Now we are entering the final part of the proof of the theorem. The basic idea is that we can construct the new permutation Y from the original X by looking at the first half and the second half *independently*. Furthermore, we can get the value k also from the first half only and calculate the parity of Y also by looking at the two parts independently. This allows us to design the following quantum algorithm:

The quantum query algorithm asks the first half of the input permutation with amplitude $\frac{1}{\sqrt{2}}$ in the state q_1 and the second half of the input permutation with amplitude $\frac{1}{\sqrt{2}}$ in the state q_2. In the case when the first half is asked the algorithm computes the value k mod 2 and whether the first half of the permutation of Y is even or odd. The state q_1 does not change the amplitude if those two parities are both even or both odd and it multiplies the amplitude to (-1) otherwise. In the case when the second half is asked the algorithm computes whether the second half of the permutation is even or odd. The state q_2 does not change the amplitude if that is even and it multiplies the amplitude to (-1) otherwise. Hadamard operation

$$\begin{pmatrix} (\frac{1}{\sqrt{2}}) & (\frac{1}{\sqrt{2}}) \\ (\frac{1}{\sqrt{2}}) & -(\frac{1}{\sqrt{2}}) \end{pmatrix}$$

is applied to the states q_1 and q_2 followed by measurements of the states q_1 and q_2. Lemma 2 provides the correctness of this exact quantum query algorithm.   □

Corollary 1. *For arbitrary n, there is an exact quantum query algorithm deciding the parity of $(2n + 1)$-permutations with $n + 1$ queries.*

Proof. $2n + 1$-permutations can be regarded as $(2n + 2)$-permutations with a fixed value $x_{2n+2} = 2n + 2$.   □

Theorem 2 and Corollary 1 produce our best results on advantages of exact quantum query algorithms over deterministic ones when deciding the parity problem for permutations.

Open problem 1. Does there exist a better quantum query algorithm for parity of permutations? The case for $n = 4$ might be particularly interesting; two queries are enough by Theorem 2 and a single one is enough for $n = 3$. More observation on this issue will be given in Section 4.

Note that a quantum lower bound of $n/2$ queries is known for determining the parity of n Boolean variables [6]. Hence it might be hard to improve Theorem 2 substantially. However, if we consider other permutation problems and more restrictive promises, it is possible to achieve much more advantages of exact quantum query algorithms over deterministic ones.

Theorem 3. *There is a 4m-permutation problem and a promise such that:*

1. *There is an exact quantum query algorithm deciding this problem with two queries.*
2. *There is no deterministic query algorithm deciding this problem with less than $2m + 2$ queries.*

Proof. Our problem is whether or not the given permutation is identical. However, we also impose the following promise which is always satisfied by the input: Consider the following $6m$ pairs:

$$(x_1, x_2), (x_5, x_6), ..., (x_{4m-3}, x_{4m-2}),$$
$$(x_1, x_3), (x_5, x_7), ..., (x_{4m-3}, x_{4m-1}),$$
$$(x_1, x_4), (x_5, x_8), ..., (x_{4m-3}, x_{4m}),$$
$$(x_2, x_3), (x_6, x_7), ..., (x_{4m-2}, x_{4m-1}),$$
$$(x_2, x_4), (x_6, x_8), ..., (x_{4m-2}, x_{4m}),$$
$$(x_3, x_4), (x_7, x_8), ..., (x_{4m-1}, x_{4m}).$$

Then the promise asserts that the input is an identical permutation (answer YES) or exactly half of the above-mentioned $6m$ pairs (x_i, x_j) are such that $x_i \neq i$ or $x_j \neq j$ (answer NO). A closer look at the $6m$ pairs shows that these pairs have a simple structure. There are m groups of the variables, namely,

$$(x_1, x_2, x_3, x_4)$$
$$(x_5, x_6, x_7, x_8)$$
$$\cdots \cdots$$
$$(x_{4m-3}, x_{4m-2}, x_{4m-1}, x_{4m})$$

such that all the variables of each group are pairwise related in some pair.

We first consider the deterministic query complexity. Let an instance be $x_1, x_2, ..., x_{4m}$. Namely, we have $n = 4m$ variables and m groups including four variables in each. Also let A be an arbitrary deterministic algorithm that solves the problem. A query to position x_i reveals whether that position is "identical," i.e., $x_i = i$ or "non-identical," i.e., $x_i \neq i$. Note that the number of non-identical positions must be zero when the answer is YES, but many different cases exist for NO, such as (i) x_1 to x_3, x_5 to x_7 and so on (3/4 positions in total) are identical, (ii)) x_1 to x_{2m} (1/2 positions in total) are identical, and many others.

We now prove that A needs at least $n/2+2$ queries. Notice that in the course of A's execution, if we have an answer of non-identical for any position, then we can output NO immediately. So the hard case is that all the answers are identical where we are supposed to answer YES. The idea for the proof is to consider "efficiency" of the queries to each single group. One can see that if we ask four queries to a group, then (if all the answers are identical) we can assure that six pairs are identical, or 1.5 pairs per query on average. However, if we ask three queries to a group, we can assure only three pairs are identical, or 1.0 pair per query on average. If we can spend at most $2m + 1$ queries, then since we need to assure at least $3m + 1$ pairs are identical to answer YES, we must use the most efficient queries for almost all groups.

We consider two (even m and odd m) cases. Suppose that A needs at most $n/2+1(= 2m + 1)$ queries.

Case 1. We first consider the case that m is even.

Lemma 3. A asks four queries (i.e., asks the values of all the four variables) against at least $m/2$ groups for at least one instance.

Proof. Suppose for contradiction that A (at most $2m+1$ queries for any instance) asks four queries against $m/2 - 1$ groups for any instance X. Then we already spent $2m - 4$ queries and so the number of remaining queries is five. There are several possibilities for how to use those five queries; let's consider, e.g., A asks three queries to one new group and two queries to another new group. Furthermore suppose also that all the answers are identical. Then it is assured that $6(m/2 - 1) + 3 + 1 = 3m - 2$ pairs are identical. However, this number of identical pairs still leaves the possibility of answer NO (and of course answer YES is also possible for exactly the same pattern of answers), a contradiction. Other ways of spending the five queries, two queries against two new groups and one query against another new group, for example, makes the situation even worse, or the number of assured identical pairs decreases. If A asks four queries against less than $m/2-1$ groups also makes the situation worse. Thus the lemma is proved.   □

By Lemma 3, A already spent $2m$ (four queries against $m/2$ groups) queries and it has only one remaining query. However, if we ask one query to a new group and the answer is identical, we cannot assure even one additional identical pair. So, if all the answers are identical against those $2m + 1$ queries, we cannot distinguish the two cases, one that there are 3m identical pairs (answer is NO) and the other that all pairs are identical (answer is YES).

Case 2. We next consider the case that m is odd.

Lemma 4. A asks four queries against at least $(m - 1)/2$ groups for at least one instance.

Proof. Similar to the proof of Lemma 3. This time, if we ask four queries against $(m-1)/2 - 1$ groups, then we already spent $2m - 6$ queries and have remaining seven queries. The most efficient way of using these seven queries is to use $3, 3$ and 2 queries to new three groups. Even so, we can assure $6(m-1)/2 - 6 + 3 + 3 + 1 = 3m - 2$ identical pairs, which is not sufficient for the same reason as before. □

Let's continue the proof for Case 2. After four queries against $(m-1)/2$ groups, we have three queries remaining. However, if all the answers are identical, then we can assure $3m$ identical pairs, which is again not sufficient as in Case 1. Thus the deterministic complexity has been proved.

The quantum query algorithm asks with an amplitude $\frac{1}{\sqrt{6m}}$ of the state $q_{i,j}$ the values of the variables x_i and x_j from any of the $6m$ pairs from the list above. If $x_i = i$ and $x_j = j$ then the amplitude is not changed. Otherwise, the amplitude is multiplied to (-1). After that we can use the standard Fourier transform to see whether all the amplitudes are positive or exactly one half of them negative. □

Note that the deterministic algorithm given above is optimal, namely we can obtain a correct answer (whether the input has all identical positions (YES) or exactly one half of the pairs are identical (NO)) with at most $n/2 + 2 (= 2m + 2)$ queries. Our algorithm is simple: if m is even, just make four queries to each of $m/2$ groups in an arbitrary order. If we get answer non-identical for any position, then answer NO. Otherwise, i.e., if all the answers are identical, then we make two queries to an arbitrary new group. If both answers are identical, then we now know that the number of identical pairs are strictly more than one half and therefore the answer must be YES by the promise. Otherwise, answer NO.

If m is odd, then we make four queries to each of $(m-1)/2$ groups. If all the answers are identical, then we ask two queries to a new group. If both answers are identical, then we now know that if the answer is NO, then this group must be three identical pairs and no identical pairs exist in any of the remaining group. (Notice that it is impossible for exactly two pairs to be identical in a group.) Thus we ask two queries to another new group and output NO if at least one answer is non-identical. Output YES otherwise.

4   Conclusion

Obviously there is a lot of interesting future work. As mentioned in Section 3, obtaining lower bounds seems most important. Suppose that n is even and our input X, given as $x_1, x_2, ..., x_n$, is restricted as follows: For $i = 1, 2, ..., n/2$, $x_i = i$ and $x_{(n/2)+i} = (n/2) + i$ (i.e., both are identical) or $x_i = (n/2) + i$ and $x_{(n/2)+i} = i$ (i.e., two positions are exchanged). Then one can easily see that X is even iff the identical positions in the first half is even. This means that we can derive a lower bound of $n/4$ for our problem from the lower bound for the Boolean parity function [6]. The real bound is probably more than that but we do not have any specific bound in the moment and that is why there is still a possibility that the case for $n = 4$ can be solved with a single quantum query, as mentioned in Section 3.

One can also notice that the pairs in Theorem 3 can be changed to triples and in general to k-tuples (and we also need to change the size of groups accordingly). Then the quantum query complexity is k as before, but we can probably prove several different deterministic complexities due to the different settings.

References

1. Ambainis, A.: Quantum lower bounds by quantum arguments. Journal of Computer and System Sciences 64(4), 750–767 (2002)
2. Ambainis, A.: Polynomial degree vs. quantum query complexity. In: Proceedings of FOCS 1998, pp. 230–240 (1998)
3. Ambainis, A., Freivalds, R.: 1-way quantum finite automata: strengths, weaknesses and generalizations. In: Proc. FOCS 1998, pp. 332–341 (1998); Also quant-ph/9802062
4. Ambainis, A., de Wolf, R.: Average-case quantum query complexity. In: Proceedings of STACS 2000, pp. 133–144 (2000)
5. Buhrman, H., de Wolf, R.: Complexity measures and decision tree complexity: a survey. Theoretical Computer Science 288(1), 21–43 (2002)
6. Beals, R., Buhrman, H., Cleve, R., Mosca, M., de Wolf, R.: Quantum lower bounds by polynomials. Journal of the ACM 48(4), 778–797 (2001)
7. Buhrman, H., Cleve, R., de Wolf, R., Zalka, C.: Bounds for small-error and zero-error quantum algorithms. In: Proceedings of FOCS 1999, pp. 358–368 (1999)
8. Cleve, R., Ekert, A., Macchiavello, C., Mosca, M.: Quantum algorithms revisited. Proceedings of the Royal Society of London A 454, 339–354 (1998)
9. Deutsch, D., Jozsa, R.: Rapid solutions of problems by quantum computation. Proceedings of the Royal Society of London A 439, 553 (1992)
10. Simon, I.: String matching algorithms and automata. In: Bundy, A. (ed.) CADE 1994. LNCS, vol. 814, pp. 386–395. Springer, Heidelberg (1994)

Time-Optimal Winning Strategies
for Poset Games

Martin Zimmermann*

Lehrstuhl Informatik 7, RWTH Aachen University, Germany
zimmermann@automata.rwth-aachen.de

Abstract. We introduce a novel winning condition for infinite two-player games on graphs which extends the request-response condition and better matches concrete applications in scheduling or project planning. In a poset game, a request has to be responded by multiple events in an ordering over time that is compatible with a given partial ordering of the events. Poset games are zero-sum, but there are plays that are more desirable than others, i.e., those in which the requests are served quickly. We show that optimal strategies (with respect to long term average accumulated waiting times) exist. These strategies are implementable with finite memory and are effectively computable.

1 Introduction

The use of two-player games of infinite duration has a long history in the synthesis of controllers for reactive systems (see [3] for an overview). Classically, the quality of a winning strategy is measured in the size of the memory needed to implement it. But often there are other natural quality measures: in many games (even if they are zero-sum) there are winning plays for Player 0 that are more desirable than others, often given by notions of waiting that reflect periods of waiting in the modeled system. In reachability games, this can be the number of steps before the play reaches one of the designated vertices, in Büchi games the number of steps between visits of the designated vertices, and in parity games the number of steps between visits of the minimal even color seen infinitely often.

Another winning condition with a natural notion of waiting is the request-response condition [6]. It is given by pairs (Q_j, P_j) of subsets of the graph's vertices. Player 0 wins a play if every visit of Q_j is eventually responded by a visit of P_j. The waiting time is given by the number of steps between a request and the next response. As there might be several request-response pairs, there is a trade-off between the pairs: it can be favorable to delay the response of a pair to answer another request more quickly. Wallmeier [5] defined the value of a play to be the long-term average accumulated waiting time and the value of a strategy to be the worst-case outcome. He then proved that optimal winning strategies exist and are effectively computable (see also [4,7]).

---

* This work was supported by the ESF project GASICS.

S. Maneth (Ed.): CIAA 2009, LNCS 5642, pp. 217–226, 2009.

However, request-response winning conditions are often too weak to express real-life requirements concisely, because a request is responded by a single event. Imagine an intersection with a level crossing: if a train approaches the crossing (a request), then all traffic lights have to be switched to red, then the boom barriers are lowered, the train gets an all-clear signal and crosses the intersection. Afterwards, the barriers are raised and the lights are switched to green. It would be rather cumbersome to model this requirement using request-response conditions with a single event as response. Another example is motivated by project planning: a project consists of several subtasks (and their durations) and a partial ordering of the subtasks, e.g., specifying that the roof of a house cannot be constructed before the walls are built. A plan is then a linearization of this partial ordering.

These examples motivate to replace a response by a partially ordered set of events and require Player 0 to answer every request by an embedding of these events in time. This generalization of request-response games retains the natural definition of waiting times. Hence, the framework for request-response games can be adapted to the new type of games, called poset games.

We prove that optimal winning strategies for poset games exist, which are again finite-state and effectively computable. To this end, we adapt the proof presented in [4] for request-response games. However, the increased expressiveness of poset games requires substantial changes. As a request is no longer responded by a single event, there can be different requests that are answered to a different degree at a given position, i.e., the embeddings can overlap. This requires additional bookkeeping of the events that still have to be embedded and changes to the definition of waiting times. Informally, in request-response games, there is a single clock for every pair (Q_j, P_j) that is started when Q_j is visited and stopped as soon as P_j is visited afterwards; requests that are encountered, while the clock is already active, are ignored. This is no longer possible in poset games: here, we need a clock for every request, due to the overlapping of embeddings. Hence, we do not only have to bound the waiting times to obtain our result, but also the number of open requests, i.e., the number of active clocks.

This paper is structured as follows: Section 2 fixes our notation and introduces poset games, which are solved by a reduction to Büchi games in Section 3. Finally, in Section 4 the existence of optimal strategies is proven. All proofs omitted due to space restrictions can be found in [8].

2   Definitions

Throughout this paper let P be a set of *events*. The power set of a set S is denoted by 2^S, $\mathbb{N}$ is the set of non-negative integers, and let $[n] := \{1, \ldots, n\}$. The prefix-ordering on words is denoted by $\sqsubseteq$, its strict version by $\sqsubset$. Given a sequence $(w_n)_{n \in \mathbb{N}}$ of finite words such that $w_n \sqsubset w_{n+1}$ for all n, $\lim_{n \to \infty} w_n$ denotes the unique ω-word induced by the w_n. Let $(f_n)_{n \in \mathbb{N}}$ be a sequence of functions $f_n : A \to B$ and $f : A \to B$. We say that $(f_n)_{n \in \mathbb{N}}$ *converges to* f, $\lim_{n \to \infty} f_n = f$, if $\forall a \in A \, \exists n_a \in \mathbb{N} \, \forall n \geq n_a : f_n(a) = f(a)$.

Infinite Games. An *(initialized and labeled) arena* $G = (V, V_0, V_1, E, s_0, l_G)$ consists of a finite directed graph (V, E), a partition $\{V_0, V_1\}$ of V denoting the positions of *Player* 0 and *Player* 1, an *initial vertex* $s_0 \in V$, and a *labeling function* $l_G : V \to 2^P$. It is assumed that every vertex has at least one outgoing edge. A *play* $\rho = \rho_0\rho_1\rho_2\ldots$ is an infinite path starting in s_0. A *strategy for Player i* is a (partial) mapping $\sigma : V^*V_i \to V$ such that $(s, \sigma(ws)) \in E$ for all $w \in V^*$ and all $s \in V_i$. A play ρ is *consistent with* σ if $\rho_{n+1} = \sigma(\rho_0, \ldots \rho_n)$ for all $\rho_n \in V_i$. The unique play consistent with the strategies σ for Player 0 and τ for Player 1 is denoted by $\rho(\sigma, \tau)$.

A *game* $\mathcal{G} = (G, \varphi)$ consists of an arena G and a *winning condition* φ specifying the set of *winning plays* for Player 0. All other plays are won by Player 1. A strategy σ is a *winning strategy for Player i* if every play consistent with σ is won by Player i. Player i *wins* $\mathcal{G}$ (and Player $1 - i$ loses $\mathcal{G}$) if she has a winning strategy for $\mathcal{G}$. A game is *determined* if one of the Players has a winning strategy.

Game Reductions. A *memory structure* $\mathfrak{M} = (M, m_0, \text{update})$ *for* G consists of a set M of *memory states*, an *initial memory state* $m_0 \in M$, and an *update function* update : $M \times V \to M$. The update function can be extended to a function $\text{update}^* : V^* \to M$ by defining $\text{update}^*(s_0) = m_0$ and $\text{update}^*(ws) = \text{update}(\text{update}^*(w), s)$. A *next-move function for Player i* next : $V_i \times M \to S$ has to satisfy $(s, \text{next}(s, m)) \in E$ for all $s \in V_i$ and all $m \in M$. It induces a *strategy σ with memory* $\mathfrak{M}$ via $\sigma(ws) = \text{next}(s, \text{update}^*(ws))$. A strategy is called *finite-state* if it can be implemented with finite memory, and *positional* if it can be implemented with a single memory state.

An arena G and a memory structure $\mathfrak{M}$ for G induce the *expanded arena* $G \times \mathfrak{M} = (V \times M, V_0 \times M, V_1 \times M, E', (s_0, m_0), l_{G \times \mathfrak{M}})$ where $((s, m), (s', m')) \in E'$ iff $(s, s') \in E$ and $\text{update}(m, s') = m'$, and $l_{G \times \mathfrak{M}}(s, m) = l_G(s)$. Every play $\rho' = (\rho_0, m_0)(\rho_1, m_1)(\rho_2, m_2)\ldots$ in $G \times \mathfrak{M}$ has a unique *projected play* $\rho = \rho_0\rho_1\rho_2\ldots$ in G. Conversely, every play $\rho = \rho_0\rho_1\rho_2\ldots$ in G has a unique *expanded play* $\rho' = (\rho_0, m_0)(\rho_1, m_1)(\rho_2, m_2)\ldots$ in $G \times \mathfrak{M}$ defined by $m_{n+1} = \text{update}(m_n, \rho_{n+1})$. A game $\mathcal{G} = (G, \varphi)$ is *reducible* to $\mathcal{G}' = (G', \varphi')$ via $\mathfrak{M}$, written $\mathcal{G} \leq_{\mathfrak{M}} \mathcal{G}'$, if $G' = G \times \mathfrak{M}$ and every play in $\mathcal{G}'$ is won by the player who wins the projected play in $\mathcal{G}$.

Remark 1. If $\mathcal{G} \leq_{\mathfrak{M}} \mathcal{G}'$ and Player i has a positional winning strategy for $\mathcal{G}'$, then she also has a finite-state winning strategy with memory $\mathfrak{M}$ for $\mathcal{G}$.

Poset Games. A *(labeled) partially ordered set (poset* for short) $\mathcal{P} = (D, \preceq, l_{\mathcal{P}})$ consists of a domain D, a reflexive, antisymmetric and transitive relation $\preceq$ over D, and a labeling function $l_{\mathcal{P}} : D \to P$. The set of non-empty upwards-closed subsets of $\mathcal{P}$ is denoted by $\text{Up}(\mathcal{P})$; its size can be bounded by $|D| \leq |\text{Up}(\mathcal{P})| \leq 2^{|D|} - 1$.

Let ρ be an infinite path in an arena G with labeling function l_G. An *embedding in time, embedding* for short, of $\mathcal{P}$ in ρ is a function $f : D \to \mathbb{N}$ such that $l_{\mathcal{P}}(d) \in l_G(\rho_{f(d)})$ and $d \preceq d'$ implies $f(d) \leq f(d')$. An embedding of $\mathcal{P}$ in a finite path w is defined analogously.

A *poset game* $\mathcal{G} = (G, (q_j, \mathcal{P}_j)_{j \in [k]})$ consists of an arena G as above and a finite collection of *(request-poset) conditions* $(q_j, \mathcal{P}_j)$ where $q_j \in P$ is a *request (of condition j)* and $\mathcal{P}_j = (D_j, \preceq_j, l_j)$ is a finite labeled poset. Player 0 wins a play ρ iff $q_j \in l_G(\rho_n)$ implies that $\mathcal{P}_j$ can be embedded in $\rho_n \rho_{n+1} \rho_{n+2} \cdots$ for all $j \in [k]$ and all $n \in \mathbb{N}$.

To define the waiting times we need to keep track of the unanswered requests. For $j \in [k]$, $D \subseteq D_j$ and $s \in V$ let $\mathrm{New}_j(s) = D_j$ if $q_j \in l_G(s)$ and $\mathrm{New}_j(s) = \emptyset$ otherwise, and $\mathrm{Emb}_j(D, s) = \{d \in D \mid \exists d' \in D : d' \preceq_j d \text{ and } l_j(d') \notin l_G(s)\}$. The set $\mathrm{Emb}_j(D, s)$ contains the elements of D that cannot be embedded into s since a smaller element $d' \in D$ cannot be mapped to s. The *set of open requests of condition j after the finite play w* is defined inductively by $\mathrm{Open}_j(\varepsilon) = \emptyset$ and

$$\mathrm{Open}_j(ws) = \{(\mathrm{Emb}_j(D, s), t+1) \mid (D, t) \in \mathrm{Open}_j(w) \cup \{(\mathrm{New}_j(s), 0)\}\} \setminus \{\emptyset\} \times \mathbb{N}.$$

That is, $\mathrm{Open}_j(ws)$ deletes all those elements from the open requests D in $\mathrm{Open}_j(w)$ that can be embedded into s, adds a tick to the clock t of every request that is not yet responded completely, checks for new requests, and deletes responded requests. If $(D, t+1) \in \mathrm{Open}_j(\rho_0 \cdots \rho_n)$, then there was a request of condition j at position $n - t$, the elements of $D_j \setminus D$ can be embedded into $\rho_{n-t} \cdots \rho_n$, and Player 0 has to embed all elements of D in the future to respond to this request.

Note that $\mathrm{Open}_j(w)$ contains only upwards-closed subsets of $\mathcal{P}_j$. The *number of open requests $D \in \mathrm{Up}(\mathcal{P}_j)$ of condition j after w* is $s_{j,D}(w) = |\{t \mid (D, t) \in \mathrm{Open}_j(w)\}|$. A set $D \in \mathrm{Up}(\mathcal{P}_j)$ is *open indefinitely* in $\rho_0 \rho_1 \rho_2 \cdots$, if there exists a position n such that $(D, t) \in \mathrm{Open}_j(\rho_0 \cdots \rho_{n+t})$ for all $t > 1$.

Lemma 1. *Let $\rho = \rho_0 \rho_1 \rho_2 \cdots$ be a play. For all $j \in [k]$:*

(i) If Player 0 wins ρ, then $(\mathrm{Open}_j(\rho_0 \cdots \rho_n))_{n \in \mathbb{N}}$ induces an embedding f_m of $\mathcal{P}_j$ in $\rho_m \rho_{m+1} \rho_{m+2} \cdots$ for every position m such that $q_j \in l_G(\rho_m)$.
(ii) ρ is won by Player 0 iff there is no $D \in \mathrm{Up}(\mathcal{P}_j)$ that is open indefinitely.

For the remainder of this paper, let $(G, (q_j, \mathcal{P}_j)_{j \in [k]})$ be a poset game, where $\mathcal{P}_j = (D_j, \preceq_j, l_j)$. Furthermore, let $c_j := |\mathrm{Up}(\mathcal{P}_j)|$ and $c := \sum_{j=1}^{k} c_j$.

3   Solving Poset Games

In this section, poset games are reduced to Büchi games. The memory stores the elements of the posets $\mathcal{P}_j$ that still have to be embedded. A cyclic counter ensures that all requests are responded by an embedding eventually.

Theorem 1. *Poset games are reducible to Büchi games and therefore determined with finite-state strategies.*

Proof. Let $h = \sum_{j=1}^{k} |D_j|$ and fix an enumeration $e : [h] \to \bigcup_{j=1}^{k} \{j\} \times D_j$. We assume $h > 1$ (without loss of generality) to obtain a nontrivial counter. The memory structure $\mathfrak{M} = (M, m_0, \mathrm{update})$ consists of $M = \prod_{j=1}^{k} \mathrm{Up}(\mathcal{P}_j) \times [h] \times \{0, 1\}$, $m_0 = (\mathrm{Emb}_1(\mathrm{New}_1(s_0), s_0), \ldots, \mathrm{Emb}_k(\mathrm{New}_k(s_0), s_0), 1, 0)$, and we define $\mathrm{update}((O_1, \ldots, O_k, m, f), s) = (O'_1, \ldots, O'_k, m', f')$ with

$$- O'_j = \begin{cases} \mathrm{Emb}_j(D_j, s) & \text{if } q_j \in l_G(s) \\ \mathrm{Emb}_j(O_j, s) & \text{if } q_j \notin l_G(s) \end{cases},$$

$$- m' = \begin{cases} (m \bmod h) + 1 & \text{if } e(m) = (j, d) \text{ and } d \notin O'_j \text{ or } l_j(d) \in l_G(s) \\ m & \text{if } e(m) = (j, d) \text{ and } d \in O'_j \text{ and } l_j(d) \notin l_G(s) \end{cases},$$

$$- f' = \begin{cases} 1 & \text{if } m \neq m' \\ 0 & \text{otherwise} \end{cases}.$$

Finally, let $F = V \times \prod_{j=1}^{k} \mathrm{Up}(\mathcal{P}_j) \times [h] \times \{1\}$ and let $\mathcal{G}' = (G \times \mathfrak{M}, F)$ be a Büchi game in the expanded arena. Verifying $\mathcal{G} \leq_{\mathfrak{M}} \mathcal{G}'$ is now straightforward. Positional determinacy of Büchi games [3] and Remark 1 finish the proof.

If e is defined such that the elements of each domain D_j are enumerated consecutively and such that $d \preceq_j d'$ implies $e^{-1}(j, d) \leq e^{-1}(j, d')$, then it takes at most $h + |D_j|$ visits to vertices in F after a request of condition j to complete an embedding of $\mathcal{P}_j$ in the projected play.

The size of $\mathfrak{M}$ can be bounded by $|M| \leq h \cdot 2^{h+1}$, which is asymptotically optimal. This can be shown by transforming the family of request-response games presented in Theorem 2 of [6] into poset games.

4   Time-Optimal Strategies for Poset Games

Waiting times for poset games are defined employing the information given by the open requests in $\mathrm{Open}_j(w)$. Define the

- *totalized waiting time for* $D \in \mathrm{Up}(\mathcal{P}_j)$ *after* w: $t_{j,D}(w) = \sum_{(D,t) \in \mathrm{Open}_j(w)} t$,
- *penalty after* w: $p(w) = \sum_{j=1}^{k} \sum_{D \in \mathrm{Up}(\mathcal{P}_j)} t_{j,D}(w)$,
- *value of a play* ρ: $v(\rho) = \limsup_{n \to \infty} \frac{1}{n} \sum_{i=0}^{n-1} p(\rho_0 \cdots \rho_i)$,
- *value of a strategy* σ: $v(\sigma) = \sup\{v(\rho(\sigma, \tau)) \mid \tau \text{ strategy for Player 1}\}$.

Hence, the influence of an open request on the value of a play grows quadratically in the waiting time, which penalizes longer waiting times more severely. A strategy σ for Player 0 is *optimal* if $v(\sigma) \leq v(\sigma')$ for all strategies σ' for Player 0. The following lemma is a simple consequence of Lemma 1.

Lemma 2. *Let ρ be a play and σ a strategy for Player 0.*

(i) If $v(\rho) < \infty$, then Player 0 wins ρ.
(ii) If $v(\sigma) < \infty$, then σ is a winning strategy for Player 0.

Note that the other directions of the statements are false: there are plays of infinite value that are won by Player 0.

Theorem 1 implies an upper bound on the value of an optimal strategy.

Corollary 1. *Let $h = \sum_{j=1}^{k} |D_j|$. If Player 0 wins $\mathcal{G}$, then she also has a winning strategy σ with*

$$v(\sigma) \leq \sum_{j=1}^{k} \left(c_j \cdot \frac{|G|(h + |D_j|)(|G|(h + |D_j|) + 1)}{2} \right) =: b_{\mathcal{G}} .$$

Let σ be a strategy for Player 0 and $D \in \text{Up}(\mathcal{P}_j)$ for some condition j. We say that σ *uniformly bounds the waiting time for D to b*, if for all finite plays w consistent with σ it holds that $t \leq b$ for all $(D, t) \in \text{Open}_j(w)$. Analogously, σ *uniformly bounds the totalized waiting time for D to b*, if $t_{j,D}(w) \leq b$ for all finite plays w consistent with σ. If the (totalized) waiting time for all $D \in \text{Up}(\mathcal{P}_j)$ is bounded, then the length of the embeddings that respond to a request is also bounded.

Remark 2. Let σ be a strategy for Player 0. If σ uniformly bounds the waiting time for D to b, then σ also uniformly bounds the totalized waiting time for D to $\frac{1}{2}b(b+1)$.

We are now able to state the main theorem of this paper, which will be proved in the remainder of this section.

Theorem 2. *If Player 0 wins a poset game $\mathcal{G}$, then she also has an optimal winning strategy which is finite-state and effectively computable. The value of an optimal strategy is effectively computable as well.*

4.1   Strategy Improvement for Poset Games

We begin by defining a *strategy improvement operator* $I_{j,D}$ for every $D \in \text{Up}(\mathcal{P}_j)$. It deletes loops of plays, consistent with the given strategy, that are spent waiting for a position into which an element from D has been embedded. Hence, the intervals in which D is an open request will be shorter if Player 0 plays according to the improved strategy. Doing this repeatedly will uniformly bound the waiting time $t_{j,D}$. However, the improved strategy has to ensure that no other responses get incomplete by deleting loops, i.e., the improved strategy is still winning for Player 0. Also, we do not want the value of the improved strategy to be greater than the value of the original strategy. We begin by defining the operator and then prove that it has the desired properties. Afterwards we show how to obtain uniform bounds on the waiting time by applying each $I_{j,D}$ infinitely often.

Let σ be a winning strategy (not necessarily finite-state) for Player 0 such that $v(\sigma) \leq b_{\mathcal{G}}$. The strategy $I_{j,D}(\sigma)$ is implemented with memory structure $\mathfrak{M} = (M, m_0, \text{update})$ where M is a subset of the finite plays consistent with σ and defined implicitly. The initial memory state is $m_0 = s_0$ and $\text{update}(w, s)$ is defined by a case distinction:

Player 0 only skips loops if the totalized waiting time for D is guaranteed to be higher than the value of the strategy, i.e., at least $b_{\mathcal{G}}$. Then, the value of the play does not increase from taking a shortcut. Thus, if $t_{j,D}(ws) \leq b_{\mathcal{G}}$, let $\text{update}(w, s) = ws$. Hence, if the totalized waiting time is small, then she copies the original play according to σ.

Otherwise, if $t_{j,D}(ws) > b_{\mathcal{G}}$ consider the tree $\mathfrak{T}^{\sigma}_{ws}$ containing all finite continuations of ws that are consistent with σ restricted to those paths wsx such that $\text{Open}_j(wsx') \cap (\{D\} \times \mathbb{N}) \neq \emptyset$ for all $x' \sqsubseteq x$. This tree contains all continuations of ws up to the point where the first element of the open request D can be embedded into. This tree is finite since σ is a winning strategy. The set of finite plays zs of $\mathfrak{T}^{\sigma}_{ws}$ such that $t_{j',D'}(zs) \geq t_{j',D'}(ws)$ and $s_{j',D'}(zs) \geq s_{j',D'}(ws)$ for all $j' \in [k]$ and all $D' \in \mathrm{Up}(\mathcal{P}_{j'})$ is non-empty as it contains ws. Let x be a play of maximal length in that set. Then, update$(ws) = x$. So, if the totalized waiting time for D is sufficiently high, then Player 0 looks ahead whether ws is the start of a loop such that the totalized waiting times and the number of open requests for all $j' \in [k]$ and all $D' \in \mathrm{Up}(\mathcal{P}_{j'})$ are higher at the end of the loop than they were at the beginning. Then, she jumps ahead (by updating the memory to x) and continues to play as if she had finished the loop already.

The condition on $t_{j',D'}$ ensures that she does not miss a vertex that she has to visit in order to embed an element of the posets. This ensures that the improved strategy is still winning for Player 0. The condition on $s_{j',D'}$ guarantees that the value of the play does not increase from taking a shortcut by jumping ahead to a position where more requests will be open than before.

Finally, define next$(s, ws) = \sigma(ws)$. Thus, Player 0's choice of the next move assumes that she has already finished the loops which were skipped by the memory update. The improved strategy $I_{j,D}(\sigma)$ is now given by $\mathfrak{M}$ and next.

Lemma 3. *Let σ be a winning strategy for Player 0, $j \in [k]$, and $D \in \mathrm{Up}(\mathcal{P}_j)$.*

(i) *If σ bounds the totalized waiting time for some $D' \in \mathrm{Up}(\mathcal{P}_{j'})$ to b, then so does $I_{j,D}(\sigma)$.*
(ii) $v(I_{j,D}(\sigma)) \le v(\sigma)$.
(iii) $I_{j,D}(\sigma)$ *is a winning strategy for Player 0.*

In order to obtain small bounds on the waiting times, each improvement operator $I_{j,D}$ is now applied infinitely often to a given initial winning strategy. The limit of the strategies improved with $I_{j,D}$ uniformly bounds the totalized waiting time for D. Furthermore, all properties stated in Lemma 3 can be lifted to the limit strategy as well.

The order of improvement is given by enumerations $e_j : [c_j] \to \mathrm{Up}(\mathcal{P}_j)$ such that $|D| > |D'|$ implies $e_j^{-1}(D) < e_j^{-1}(D')$. Thus, the subsets are enumerated in order of decreasing size. Given a winning strategy σ_0 for Player 0 such that $v(\sigma_0) \le b_{\mathcal{G}}$ (whose existence is guaranteed by Corollary 1), define

$$- \ \sigma_{j,l,0} = \begin{cases} \sigma_{j-1} & \text{if } l = 1 \\ \sigma_{j,l-1} & \text{otherwise} \end{cases} \quad \text{for } j \in [k] \text{ and } l \in [c_j],$$
$$- \ \sigma_{j,l,n+1} = I_{j,e_j(l)}(\sigma_{j,l,n}) \text{ for } j \in [k], \ l \in [c_j], \text{ and } n \in \mathbb{N},$$
$$- \ \sigma_{j,l} = \lim_{n \to \infty} \sigma_{j,l,n} \text{ for } j \in [k] \text{ and } l \in [c_j], \text{ and}$$
$$- \ \sigma_j = \sigma_{j,c_j} \text{ for } j \in [k].$$

For notational convenience, let $\sigma_{j,0} = \sigma_{j-1}$ for $j \in [k]$. Before we discuss the properties of the strategies defined above, we need to introduce some additional notation that is used to bound the waiting times.

The strategy improvement operator $I_{j,D}$ skips a loop if the vertices at the beginning and at the end coincide and the values $s_{j',D'}$ and $t_{j',D'}$ at the end are greater than or equal to the values at the beginning. Hence, we say that two finite plays $y_1 \sqsubset y_2$ form a *Dickson pair* [1] if their last vertices coincide and $s_{j',D'}(y_1) \le s_{j',D'}(y_2)$ and $t_{j',D'}(y_1) \le t_{j',D'}(y_2)$ for all $j' \in [k]$ and all $D' \in \mathrm{Up}(\mathcal{P}_{j'})$. Dickson pairs are candidates for deletion by $I_{j,D}$.

The set D is in Open_j throughout a loop skipped by $I_{j,D}$. Accordingly, an infix $\rho_m \ldots \rho_{m+n}$ of a play ρ is called *non-Dickson save D* if $t_{j,D}$ increases strictly monotonic throughout the infix and if there are no $m \leq g < h \leq m+n$ such that $\rho_0 \ldots \rho_g$ and $\rho_0 \ldots \rho_h$ are a Dickson pair. The length of such an infix can be bounded inductively by a function b in the size n of G and in $c = \sum_{j=1}^{k} |\text{Up}(\mathcal{P}_j)|$.

If $c = 1$, then the single set is D, whose values increase monotonically. Hence, there is a vertex repetition after at most $|G|$ steps. Therefore, $b(n, 1) = n$.

If $c + 1 > 1$, then $t_{j',D'}$ (and thereby also $s_{j',D'}$) has to be reset to 0 after at most $b(n, c)$ steps for every $D' \neq D$. If not, then the initial prefix of length $b(n, c)$ contains a Dickson pair by induction hypothesis. For the same reason, for every $c' \in [c]$ there are c' sets D' such that $t_{j',D'}$ (and also $s_{j',D'}$) was reset to 0 in the last $b(n, c')$ steps. If not, then this infix would again contain a Dickson pair by induction hypothesis. Accounting for all possible combinations, we obtain $b(n, c + 1) = b(n, c) + nc! \prod_{j=1}^{c} \frac{1}{2}(b(n, j))^2(b(n, j) + 1)$, as we have $t_{j',D'}(xy) \leq \frac{1}{2}|y|(|y| + 1)$ and $s_{j',D'}(xy) \leq |y|$ if $t_{j',D'}(x) = 0$.

Note that the same idea can be applied to request-response games, which lowers the bounds given in [4,5].

Now, we are able to lift the properties of the strategy improvement operator to the limit of the improved strategies and to bound the waiting times.

Lemma 4. *Let $j \in [k]$, $l \in [c_j]$, and $e_j(l) = D$. Then:*

(i) $\lim_{n \to \infty} \sigma_{j,l,n}$ *exists.*
(ii) If $\sigma_{j,l-1}$ uniformly bounds the totalized waiting time for some $D' \in \text{Up}(\mathcal{P}_{j'})$, then so does $\sigma_{j,l}$.
(iii) $v(\sigma_{j,l}) \leq v(\sigma_{j,l-1})$, *and therefore* $v(\sigma_j) \leq v(\sigma_{j-1})$.
(iv) $\sigma_{j,l}$ *uniformly bounds the waiting time for D to*

$$b_{j,D} := b_G + (|D_j \backslash D| + 1) \cdot b(|G|, c) .$$

These properties of the improved strategies can be combined to show that the waiting times can be bounded without increasing the value of a strategy.

Lemma 5. *For every winning strategy σ_0 for Player 0 with $v(\sigma_0) \leq b_G$, there is a winning strategy σ_k for Player 0 that bounds $s_{j,D}$ to $b_{j,D}$ and $t_{j,D}$ to $tb_{j,D} := \frac{1}{2}(b_{j,D}(b_{j,D} + 1))$ for all $j \in [k]$ and all $D \in \text{Up}(\mathcal{P}_j)$. Furthermore, $v(\sigma_k) \leq v(\sigma_0)$.*

4.2   Reducing Poset Games to Mean-Payoff Games

In this subsection, we reduce the poset game to a mean-payoff game [2], which we will introduce in the following.

A *mean-payoff game* $\mathcal{G} = (G, d, l)$ consists of an arena $G = (V, V_0, V_1, E, s_0)$, $d \in \mathbb{N}$ and a labeling function $l : E \to \{-d, \ldots, d\}$ (note that l labels the edges in this case). Let ρ be a play in G. The *gain* $v_0(\rho)$ for Player 0 is defined as $v_0(\rho) = \liminf_{n \to \infty} \frac{1}{n} \sum_{i=0}^{n-1} l(\rho_i, \rho_{i+1})$ and the *loss* $v_1(\rho)$ for Player 1 is $v_1(\rho) = \limsup_{n \to \infty} \frac{1}{n} \sum_{i=0}^{n-1} l(\rho_i, \rho_{i+1})$. Player 0's goal is to maximize $v_0(\rho)$

whereas Player 1 aims to minimize $v_1(\rho)$. A strategy σ for Player 0 guarantees a gain of v if $v_0(\rho) \geq v$ for every play ρ consistent with σ. Analogously, τ for Player 1 guarantees a loss of v if $v_1(\rho) \leq v$ for every play ρ consistent with τ.

Theorem 3 ([2,9]). *Let $\mathcal{G}$ be a mean-payoff game. There exists a value $\nu_\mathcal{G}$ and positional strategies σ and τ that guarantee $\nu_\mathcal{G}$ for Player 0 and Player 1, respectively. These strategies are optimal, i.e., there is no strategy for Player i that guarantees a better value for her. Furthermore, σ, τ and $\nu_\mathcal{G}$ are computable in pseudo-polynomial time.*

Now, we explain the reduction. The memory keeps track of the totalized waiting time $t_{j,D}(w)$ for every $j \in [k]$ and every $D \in \mathrm{Up}(\mathcal{P}_j)$. To be able to compute $t_{j,D}(ws)$ from $t_{j,D}(w)$ in every update of the memory state, $s_{j,D}(w)$ has to be stored as well. Due to Lemma 5 we can bound $t_{j,D}(w)$ by $tb_{j,D}$ and $s_{j,D}(w)$ by $b_{j,D}$. If these bounds are exceeded, then the memory is updated to a sink state $m_\uparrow$. Hence, we obtain a finite memory structure $\mathfrak{M}$. The formal definition is straightforward, but technical, and can be found in the long version of this paper [8].

The arena for the mean-payoff game $\mathcal{G}'$ is $G \times \mathfrak{M}$ where an edge is labeled by the sum of the totalized waiting times at the source of the edge. The value d is defined appropriately and is also the weight of all edges originating from a vertex with memory state $m_\uparrow$. As it is Player 1's goal to minimize the limit superior of the average edge labels, we have to exchange the positions of the players. This finishes the definition of $\mathcal{G}'$.

If the totalized waiting times in play ρ of the poset game $\mathcal{G}$ are bounded by $tb_{j,D}$, then the values $v(\rho)$ and $v_1(\rho')$ are equal, where ρ' is the expanded play of the mean-payoff game $\mathcal{G}'$. Dually, if a play ρ' of $\mathcal{G}'$ avoids the vertices with memory state $m_\uparrow$, then $v_1(\rho') = v(\rho)$, where ρ is the projected play of ρ'.

Now, we are able to prove Theorem 2: let Player 0 win $\mathcal{G}$. Corollary 1 and Lemma 5 imply that there is a strategy for Player 1 in $\mathcal{G}'$ that avoids the vertices with memory state $m_\uparrow$. Hence, the value $\nu_{\mathcal{G}'}$ is smaller than d and an optimal strategy for Player 1 for $\mathcal{G}'$ avoids the vertices with memory state $m_\uparrow$, too. It is now easy to show that an optimal positional strategy for Player 1 for $\mathcal{G}'$ induces an optimal finite-state strategy for Player 0 for $\mathcal{G}$. Furthermore, the values of both optimal strategies coincide.

5   Conclusion

We have introduced a novel winning condition for infinite two-player games that extends the request-response condition while retaining a natural definition of waiting times. These games are well-suited to add aspects of planning to the synthesis of finite-state controllers for reactive systems. We proved that optimal strategies (with respect to long-term average accumulated waiting times) exist and are effectively computable. The memory size of the optimal strategy computed here is super-exponential. However, this holds already for request-response games. Thus, the increased expressiveness of the poset condition does not add too much additional complexity.

In future research, the memory size should be analyzed: determining the computational complexity of finding optimal strategies and proving tight upper and lower bounds on the memory size of an optimal strategy. The size of the mean-payoff game (and thus the memory) can be reduced by finding better bounds on the length of non-Dickson infixes. Also, one should investigate, whether the (costly, in terms of time and space) reduction to mean-payoff games is necessary: can an optimal strategy be computed without a reduction?

Another direction of further research is to consider *discounted* waiting times and to establish a reduction to *discounted payoff games* [9]. Furthermore, the reduction to Büchi games induces a uniform upper bound on the waiting times in poset games, but the (efficient) computation of optimal bounds should be addressed as well.

Acknowledgments. This work presents results of the author's diploma thesis [7] prepared under the supervision of Wolfgang Thomas. I want to thank him for his advice and suggestions. Also, I want to thank the anonymous referees for their helpful remarks.

References

1. Dickson, L.E.: Finiteness of the odd perfect and primitive abundant numbers with n distinct prime factors. Amer. J. Math. 35(4), 413–422 (1913)
2. Ehrenfeucht, A., Mycielski, J.: Positional strategies for mean payoff games. International Journal of Game Theory 8(2), 109–113 (1979)
3. Grädel, E., Thomas, W., Wilke, T. (eds.): Automata, Logics, and Infinite Games. LNCS, vol. 2500. Springer, Heidelberg (2002)
4. Horn, F., Thomas, W., Wallmeier, N.: Optimal strategy synthesis in request-response games. In: Cha, S.D., Choi, J.-Y., Kim, M., Lee, I., Viswanathan, M. (eds.) ATVA 2008. LNCS, vol. 5311, pp. 361–373. Springer, Heidelberg (2008)
5. Wallmeier, N.: Strategien in unendlichen Spielen mit Liveness-Gewinnbedingungen: Syntheseverfahren, Optimierung und Implementierung. PhD thesis, RWTH Aachen University (2008)
6. Wallmeier, N., Hütten, P., Thomas, W.: Symbolic synthesis of finite-state controllers for request-response specifications. In: Ibarra, O.H., Dang, Z. (eds.) CIAA 2003. LNCS, vol. 2759, pp. 11–22. Springer, Heidelberg (2003)
7. Zimmermann, M.: Time-optimal Winning Strategies in Infinite Games. Diploma Thesis, RWTH Aachen University (2009), automata.rwth-aachen.de/~zimmermann
8. Zimmermann, M.: Time-optimal winning strategies for poset games. Technical Report AIB-2009-13, RWTH Aachen University (2009)
9. Zwick, U., Paterson, M.: The complexity of mean payoff games on graphs. Theoretical Computer Science 158(1,2), 343–359 (1996)

Amount of Nonconstructivity in Finite Automata*

Rūsiņš Freivalds

Institute of Mathematics and Computer Science, University of Latvia,
Raiņa bulv. 29, Rīga, Latvia
Rusins.Freivalds@mii.lu.lv

Abstract. When D. Hilbert used nonconstructive methods in his famous paper on invariants (1888), P.Gordan tried to prevent the publication of this paper considering these methods as non-mathematical. L. E. J. Brouwer in the early twentieth century initiated intuitionist movement in mathematics. His slogan was "nonconstructive arguments have no value for mathematics". However, P. Erdös got many exciting results in discrete mathematics by nonconstructive methods. It is widely believed that these results either cannot be proved by constructive methods or the proofs would have been prohibitively complicated. R.Freivalds [7] showed that nonconstructive methods in coding theory are related to the notion of Kolmogorov complexity.

We study the problem of the quantitative characterization of the amount of nonconstructiveness in nonconstructive arguments. We limit ourselves to computation by deterministic finite automata. The notion of nonconstructive computation by finite automata is introduced. Upper and lower bounds of nonconstructivity are proved.

1 Introduction

The use of nonconstructive methods of proof in mathematics has a long and dramatic history. In 1888 a young German mathematician David Hilbert presented to his colleagues three short papers on invariant theory. Invariant theory was the highly estimated achievement of Paul Gordan who had produced highly complicated constructive proofs but left several important open problems. The young David Hilbert had solved all these problems and had done much-much more. Paul Gordan was furious. He was not ready to accept the new solutions because they provided no explicit constructions. Hilbert merely proved that the solutions cannot fail to exist. Gordan refused to accept this as mathematics. He even used the term "theology" and categorically objected to publication of these papers. Nonetheless the papers were published first in *Götingen Nachrichten* and later, in final form, in [10].

Later Hilbert had one more highly publicized controversy. This time L. E. J. Brouwer was involved. Following H.Poincare ideas, Brouwer started a struggle

---

* Research supported by Grant No.09.1437 from the Latvian Council of Science.

S. Maneth (Ed.): CIAA 2009, LNCS 5642, pp. 227–236, 2009.

against nonconstructive proofs. The *intuitionist* movement was started in mathematics. This was part of the attempts to overcome the crisis in foundations of mathematics. Many possible ways out of the crisis were proposed in twenties of the 20th century. Hilbert axiomatized geometry and wished to axiomatize all mathematics. K.Gödel proved his famous incompleteness theorems and showed that the crisis cannot be overcome so easily. Brouwer reasonably turned everybody's attention to the fact that considering infinite sets as objectively existing objects is dangerous and it can bring us to unforeseen conclusions not related to our experience. Brouwer challenged the belief that the rules of the classical logic, which have come down to us essentially from Aristotle (384–322 B.C.) have an absolute validity, independent of the subject matter to which they are applied. Nonconstructive proofs were to be thrown out of mathematics.

In the forties the situation, however, changed. In spite of all philosophical battles the nonconstructive methods found their way even to discrete mathematics. This was particularly surprising because here all the objects were finite and it seemed that no kind of distinction between *actual infinity* and *potential infinity* could influence these proofs while most of the discussions between intuitionists and classicists were around these notions. Paul Erdős produced many nice nonconstructive proofs, the first paper of this kind being [5].

We try in this paper to go another step. We propose a quantitative approach to measure the amount of nonconstructivity in a proof. A notion of nonconstructive computation is introduced as a result of examination of three examples of nonconstructive proofs. This notion can easily be used for many types of automata and machines. In this paper we prove several upper and lower bounds for the amount of nonconstructivity in nonconstructive deterministic finite 2-way automata. This type of automata is sufficiently simple but it allows nontrivial constructions.

When this paper was submitted to the CIAA'2009 conference, an anonimous referee pointed to the author that a notion similar to our amount of nonconstructivity has already been studied. Indeed, R. Karp and R. Lipton have introduced in [11] a notion *Turing machine that takes advice* which is practically the same notion for Turing machines as our *nonconstructive computation by finite automata* below. Later C. Damm and M. Holzer have adapted the notion of advice for finite automata. Since there was no reference to intuitionism in [11], the adaptation was performed in the most straightforward way (what is quite natural). However the notion of *finite automata that take advice* in [4] differs from our notion very much. These notions are equivalent for large amounts of nonconstructivity (or large amounts of advice) but, for the notion introduced in [4] and later extensively used by T.Yamakami and his coauthors [18,14,17], languages recognizable with polynomial advice are the same languages which are recognizable with a constant advice. Our notion of the amount of nonconstructivity is such that our most interesting results concern the smallest possible amounts of nonconstructivity.

A similar situation was in sixties of the 20th century with space complexity of Turing machines. At first space complexity was considered for one-tape off-line

Turing machines and it turned out that space complexity is never less than linear. However, it is difficult to prove such lower bounds. Then the seminal paper by R.E.Stearns, J.Hartmanis and P.M.Lewis [16] was published and many-tape Turing machines became a standard tool to study sublinear space complexity.

2   Re-examining Nonconstructive Proofs

2.1   Codes and Kolmogorov Complexity

The textbook [9] contains

Theorem 1. *[9] For any integer $n \geq 4$ there is a $[2n, n]$ binary code with a minimum distance between the codewords at least $n/10$.*

However the proof of this theorem in [9] has an unusual property. It is nonconstructive. It means that we cannot find these codes or describe them in a useful manner. This is why P.Garrett calls them mirage codes.

The paper [7] was written to prove that the size (i.e. the number of the states) of a deterministic finite automaton and the size of a probabilistic finite automaton recognizing the same language can differ exponentially, thus concluding a long sequence of papers describing the gap between the size of deterministic and probabilistic finite automata recognizing the same language.

A counterpart of Theorem 1 for cyclic linear codes was needed, but an attempt to prove it failed. Instead of cyclic generating matrices a slightly different kind of generating matrices was considered. Let p be an odd prime number, and x be a binary word of length p. The generating matrix $G(p, x)$ has p rows and $2p$ columns. Let $x = x_1x_2x_3 \ldots x_p$. The first p columns (and all p rows) make a unit matrix with elements 1 on the main diagonal and 0 in all the other positions. The last p columns (and all p rows) make a cyclic matrix with $x = x_1x_2x_3 \ldots x_p$ as the first row, $x = x_px_1x_2x_3 \ldots x_{p-1}$ as the second row, and so on. We will refer below the generating matrices with this property as bi-cyclical.

The notion of Kolmogorov complexity was used to prove the counterpart of Theorem 1 for the codes with a bi-cyclical generating matrix.

Definition 1. *We say that the numbering $\Psi = \{\Psi_0(x), \Psi_1(x), \Psi_2(x), \ldots\}$ of 1-argument partial recursive functions is **computable** if the 2-argument function $U(n, x) = \Psi_n(x)$ is partial recursive.*

Definition 2. *We say that a numbering Ψ is reducible to the numbering η if there exists a total recursive function $f(n)$ such that, for all n and x, $\Psi_n(x) = \eta_{f(n)}(x)$.*

Definition 3. *We say that a computable numbering φ of all 1-argument partial recursive functions is a **Gödel numbering** if every computable numbering (of any class of 1-argument partial recursive functions) is reducible to φ.*

Theorem 2. *[6] There exists a Gödel numbering.*

Definition 4. *We say that a Gödel numbering ϑ is a* **Kolmogorov numbering** *if for arbitrary computable numbering Ψ (of any class of 1-argument partial recursive functions) there exist constants $c > 0, d > 0$, and a total recursive function $f(n)$ such that:*

1. *for all n and x, $\Psi_n(x) = \vartheta_{f(n)}(x)$,*
2. *for all n, $f(n) \leq c \cdot n + d$.*

Theorem 3. *[12] There exists a Kolmogorov numbering.*

Definition 5. *We say that a binary word w has Kolmogorov complexity s with respect to the Kolmogorov numbering ϑ if the least value of n such that $\vartheta(0) = \omega$ where ω is a natural number whose binary representation equals w.*

Unfortunately (or fortunately) there are infinitely many distinct Kolmogorov numberings. Nonetheless, the Kolmogorov complexities of the same word with respect to distinct Kolmogorov numberings differ at most by an additive constant. The Kolmogorov complexity is usually understood as the degree of the extent how much the word can be compressed without loss of information. For an individual word it may be difficult to implement this semantics but if we consider infinite sequences of words then this semantics is applicable to all sufficiently long words.

The crucial point in the proof of the main result of [7] was the following lemma.

Lemma 1. *[7] If p is a sufficiently large prime, and the word $x = x_1x_2x_3\ldots x_p$ in the definition of a bi-cyclical matrix has Kolmogorov complexity $p - o(p)$ then the Hamming distance between arbitrary two codewords is at least $\frac{4p}{19}$.*

Kolmogorov complexity brings in an element of nonconstructivity. Indeed, no algorithm can exist finding such a word $x = x_1x_2x_3\ldots x_p$ for a given p. Such words merely exist. Moreover, nearly all the words of the length p have this property. However, every algorithm producing the needed words inevitably fails. On the other hand, if somebody from outside could help us and provide us with a word $x = x_1x_2x_3\ldots x_p$ with the property "*Kolmogorov complexity of this word is maximal possible for the words of this length*", we would be able to construct the bi-cyclical generating matrix.

2.2 Kolmogorov Complexity of Recursively Enumerable Sets

J.Bārzdiņš in [2] studied Kolmogorov complexity of binary words of the length n expressing whether a natural number x (where $0 \leq x \leq n - 1$) belongs to a recursively enumerable set. Recursively enumerable sets are those for which an algorithm exists enumerating (not always in an increasing order) all the elements of the set.

The result was surprising. It turned out that Kolmogorov complexity of such words never exceed $\log n$. The main technical lemma from Bārzdiņš' paper can be reformulated as follows.

There is no algorithm uniform in n such that it would show which numbers belong to the recursively enumerable set and which ones do not belong. However, when we are trying to decide which natural numbers x (where $0 \leq x \leq n-1$) belong to the recursively enumerable set, somebody from outside would come and provide us with the number of the natural number y such that $0 \leq y \leq n-1$ and the enumerating algorithm lists this y as the last among the numbers x from the elements of the recursively enumerable set such that $0 \leq x \leq n-1$, then we would be able to construct the needed decision algorithm for the initial fragment $0 \leq x \leq n-1$ ourselves.

2.3 Learning Programs for Total Functions

K. Podnieks studied learning in the limit programs of total recursive functions by deterministic and probabilistic learning algorithms. Among other results he produced two theorems on deterministic learning in the limit of indices of total recursive functions in numberings defined by a total universal function of two arguments $U(n, x) = f_n(x)$.

Theorem 4. *[15] If the numbering U is such that the algorithmic problem of equivalence of indices is decidable, then there is a learning algorithm which makes on any function $f_i(x)$ (where $0 \leq i \leq n$) no more that $g(n)$ mindchanges where $g(n)$ is a total recursive function arbitrarily slowly monotonically growing to infinity.*

Theorem 5. *[3] There is a numbering U such that arbitrary learning algorithm for infinitely many values of n makes on some function $f_i(x)$ (where $0 \leq i \leq n$) no less than $\frac{n}{2}$ mindchanges.*

We can re-interpret K.Podnieks' results as follows. The learning of indices of total recursive functions in numberings defined by a total universal function of two arguments $U(n, x) = f_n(x)$ demands in general $\frac{n}{2}$ mindchanges for infinitely many functions $f_n(x)$. However, if somebody from outside would come and provide us with the information which indices are equivalent and which ones are not, then we would be able to construct the needed learning algorithm with many less mindchanges.

3 Definitions

In all 3 considered examples of nonconstructive methods there is something common. An algorithm is presented in a situation where (seemingly) no algorithm is possible. However, this algorithm has an additional input where a special help is fed in. If this help is correct, the algorithm works correctly. On the other hand, this help on the additional input does not just provide the answer. There still remains much work for the algorithm.

Is this nonconstructivism merely a version of nondeterminism? Not at all. The construction of bi-cyclical generating matrices for codes in subsection 2.1 had nothing to do with existence of certain inputs. If Kolmogorov complexity of the word is high, the Hamming distance is large.

The additional information about the recursively enumerable sets in subsection 2.2 always exists. No problem of existence again. If this information is provided correctly, the algorithm is correct. The answer YES or NO depends on x and the additional information is much more compact than a list of all the answers.

The additional information in the index learning problem in subsection 2.3 also does not provide the needed answers directly. Surely it is also not a version of nondeterminism.

All these examples naturally lead to a following notion of nonconstructive computation.

Definition 6. *We say that an automaton A recognizes the language L noncon-structively if the automaton A has an input tape where a word x is read and an additional input tape for nonconstructive help y with the following property. For arbitrary natural number n there is a word y such that for all words x whose length does not exceed n the automaton A on the pair (x, y) produces the result 1 if $x \in L$, and A produces the result 0 if $x \notin L$. Technically, the word y can be a tuple of several words and may be placed on separate additional input tapes.*

Definition 7. *We say that an automaton A recognizes the language L noncon-structively with nonconstructivity $d(n)$ if the automaton A has an input tape where a word x is read and an additional input tape for nonconstructive help y with the following property. For arbitrary natural number n there is a word y of the length not exceeding $d(n)$ such that for all words x whose length does not exceed n the automaton A on the pair $(x.y)$ produces the result 1 if $x \in L$, and A produces the result 0 if $x \notin L$. Technically, the word y can be a tuple of several words and may be placed on separate additional input tapes. In this case, $d(n)$ is the upper bound for the total of the lengths of these words.*

The automaton A in these definitions can be a finite automaton, a Turing machine or any other type of automata or machines. In this paper we restrict ourselves by considering only deterministic finite automata with 2-way behavior on each of the tapes.

This way, we can characterize the amount of nonconstructivity in the non-constructive algorithms considered in subsections 2.1, 2.2, 2.3. Freivalds' non-constructive algorithm for construction of bi-cyclical generating matrices of size $2n \times n$ has nonconstructivity n. Bārzdiņš' nonconstructive algorithm for construction of decision algorithm for initial fragments $[0, n-1]$ of characteristic functions of recursively enumerable languages has nonconstructivity $\log n$. Podnieks' nonconstructive algorithm for learning in the limit of indices of total recursive functions in numberings defined by a total universal function of two arguments $U(m, x) = f_m(x)$ with at most $g(n)$ mindchanges for all the functions in the set $f_0(x), ..., f_{n-1}(x)$ has nonconstructivity $const.n^2$. Of course, these are only up-per bounds. It is quite possible that for some of these problems nonconstructive algorithms with a lesser nonconstructivity are possible. (This is not the case for recursively enumerable languages since J.Bārzdiņš has also proven a tight lower bound for the Kolmogorov complexity of recursively enumerable languages.)

4   Results on Finite Automata

Theorem 6. *There exists a nonregular (and even a nonrecursive) language L such that it can be nonconstructively recognized with nonconstructivity n.*

Proof. Let $a_1, a_2, a_3, \cdots$ be an infinite sequence of zeros and ones. We define the language L as follows. A word x is in L iff it coincides with some initial fragment of the sequence $a_1, a_2, a_3, \cdots$.

If the sequence is not recursive then the language is also nonrecursive. On the other hand, the nonconstructive automaton with the nonconstructive help $a_1, a_2, a_3, \cdots, a_n$ is able to provide the results whether the given word w is in L for all binary words of the length not exceeding n.   □

Theorem 7. *For the language L from Theorem 6 , if $h(n)$ is a total function such that $\log_2 n = o(h(n))$ then no nonconstructive 2-way deterministic finite automaton can recognize L with nonconstructivity $(n - h(n))$.*

Proof. P.Martin-Löf in [13] proved that there exists an infinite sequence $a_1, a_2, a_3, \cdots$ such that infinitely many initial fragments of it have Kolmogorov complexity n and all the initial fragments of it have Kolmogorov complexity no less than $n - O(\log_2 n)$. (He also proved that there are no infinite binary sequences with a higher Kolmogorov complexity.) Take this sequence. Consider the corresponding language L. Assume from the contrary that there exists a nonconstructive deterministic finite automaton such that for infinitely many values of n the nonconstructivity is less than $(n - h(n))$. From the given program of the automaton and from the given nondeterministic help one can algorithmically reconstruct the values $a_1, a_2, a_3, \cdots, a_n$. Hence Kolmogorov complexity of the initial fragment $a_1, a_2, a_3, \cdots, a_n$ exceeds the length of the nonconstructive help no more than by a constant and the initial fragment has Kolmogorov complexity no higher than $(n - h(n))$. Contradiction.   □

Theorem 8. *For arbitrary natural number k there exists a nonregular language L such that it can be nonconstructively recognized with nonconstructivity not exceeding $n^{\frac{1}{k}}$.*

Proof. At first we consider the language L consisting of all the words

$$0_m 1 0_m 1 0_m 1 \cdots 1 0_m$$

where the number of arrays of zeros is the same as the length of these arrays.

May be the help-word can be 0_m? Indeed, this help-word helps for the word $0_m 1 0_m 1 0_m 1 \cdots 1 0_m$. However, our definition of nonconstructive computation demands that the help-word works for all the shorter input words as well. Unfortunately, 0_m does not help for shorter words. The help-word $0_1 1 0_2 1 0_3 1 \cdots 1 0_m$

works both for $0_m 10_m 10_m 1 \cdots 10_m$ and for all the shorter input words. Unfortunately, the length of this help-word is $O(n)$.

Now we consider the language consisting of all the words

$$0_m 10_m 10_m 1 \cdots 10_m 20_m 10_m 10_m 1 \cdots 10_m 2 \cdots 20_m 10_m 10_m 1 \cdots 10_m.$$

This language can be helped by the same help-word $0_1 10_2 10_3 1 \cdots 10_m$ and this help-word works for all input words the length of which does not exceed m^3. Hence the length of the help-word in terms of the length of the input word is $n^{\frac{2}{3}}$.

This idea can be extended even more, and the language can be considered which consists of all the words $w_2 3 w_2 3 \cdots 3 w_2$ where

$$w_2 = 0_m 10_m 10_m 1 \cdots 10_m 20_m 10_m 10_m 1 \cdots 10_m 2 \cdots 20_m 10_m 10_m 1 \cdots 10_m$$

This language can be helped by the same help-word $0_1 10_2 10_3 1 \cdots 10_m$. This reduces the length of help-word to $n^{\frac{2}{5}}$. Iterating this idea r times, we get the length of the help-word $n^{\frac{2}{r}}$ which can be made smaller than any $n^{\frac{1}{k}}$. □

Theorem 9. *There exists a nonregular language L and a function $g(n)$ such that L can be nonconstructively recognized with nonconstructivity $g(n)$ and $\log n \leq g(n) \leq (\log n)^2$.*

Proof. The language L consists of all binary words in the form $0^m 20^k$ such that k is a multiple of the product of the first m primes (where $p_1 = 2, p_2 = 3, p_3 = 5, \cdots$). The help-word is

$$0^{p_1} 10^{p_2} 10^{p_3} 1 \cdots 10^{p_m}.$$

The nonconstructive automaton has 2-way heads on the two tapes. This allows it to check whether the length k of the array 0^k is a multiple of p_1 being the length of the first array of zeros on the help-tape, whether the length k of the array 0^k is a multiple of p_2 being the length of the second array of zeros on the help-tape, etc.

If the input word w has a prefix $0^m 1$ and $w \in L$ then the length of w is at least the product of all first m primes. This product is called *primorial of m* and it is known that $Primorial(m) \approx e^{m \ln m}$ (see e.g. [1]) The length of the help-word that helps for all the input words with such a prefix is

$$\Sigma(m) = \Sigma_{s=1}^{m} p_s.$$

It is known that

$$\Sigma(n) \approx \frac{1}{2} n^2 \ln n.$$

However, it is not true that all the input words of such a length have the considered prefix. It may happen that the prefix contains more zeros before the first symbol 1. Nonetheless, the help-word described above works for such input words as well. Indeed, if the input word w has a prefix $0^r 1$ and $r > m$ and the length of w is less than $Primorial(m)$ then $w \notin L$. On the other hand, $|w| < Primorial\ (m)$ implies that there exists a natural number u such that $|w|$ does not divide p_u and the help-word described above provides the needed result NO.   □

Theorem 10. *If a language L can be nonconstructively recognized with a nonconstructivity bounded by a function $d(n) = o(\log n)$, then L is regular.*

Proof. Our proof is based on the following feature of the definition of nonconstructiveness. We have demanded that for arbitrary natural number n there is a word y such that for all words x whose length does not exceed n the automaton A on the pair $(x.y)$ produces a correct result. Let A be a deterministic finite automaton nonconstructively recognizing L, and $d(n)$ be the smallest possible length of the help-word for the words x of the length n. Assume from the contrary that $d(n)$ grows to infinity. It follows that there exists a word x such that A on x produces a wrong result on x with the help $y(n)$. By x_0 we denote the shortest word x with this property. Denote the length of x_0 by m. Let $y(m)$ be the shortest possible help-word for all words x of the length not exceeding m.

The automaton A is two-way on each of the tapes. For arbitrary k we consider the set of all possible configurations of the memory and the help-tape at moments when the head on the work-tape in on the distance k from the beginning of the input word. By $B(k)$ we denote such a set of configurations for A on x_0 with the help $y(n)$ and by $C(k)$ we denote such a set of configurations for A on x_0 with the help $y(m)$.

Since $d(n) = o(\log n)$, there exist two distinct k and l such that both $B(k) = B(l)$ and $C(k) = C(l)$. Cutting out the fragment between k and l from x_0 we get a shorter word x_1 with the same property. Contradiction.

We have proved that the nonconstructivity is bounded by a constant. Hence there is a help-word which fits for infinitely many n. We can conclude that this a help-word fits for all input words x. This universal help-word can be incorporated into the automaton, and we get a deterministic finite 2-way automaton recognizing the language without any help from outside. It follows that the language is regular.   □

Theorem 11. *There exists a nonrecursive language L and a function $g(n)$ such that L can be nonconstructively recognized by a DFA with a nonconstructivity $g(n) \in polylog(n)$.*

Proof. To define the language we need an infinite nonrecursive binary sequence $r_1, r_2, r_3, \cdots$. We define

$$s_i = \left\{ \begin{array}{l} p_{2i} \ \ if\ r(i) = 0, \\ p_{2i+1} \ if\ r(i) = 1. \end{array} \right\}$$

The language L consists of all binary words in the form $0^m 2 0^k$ such that k is a multiple of the product of the first m numbers in the sequence $s_1 = 2, s_2 = 3, s_3 = 5, \cdots$. The help-word is $0^{s_1} 1 0^{s_2} 1 0^{s_3} 1 \cdots 1 0^{s_m}$.   □

References

1. Bach, E., Shallit, J.: Algorithmic Number Theory, vol. 1. MIT Press, Cambridge (1996)
2. Bārzdiņš, J.: Complexity of programs to determine whether natural numbers not greater than n belong to a recursively enumerable set. Soviet Mathematics Doklady 9, 1251–1254 (1968)
3. Bārzdiņš, J., Podnieks, K.: Towards a theory of inductive inference. In: Proceedings of 2nd Symposium and Summer School on Mathematical Foundations of Computer Science, Štrbske Pleso, High Tatras, Czechoslovakia, pp. 9–15 (1973)
4. Damm, C., Holzer, M.: Automata that take advice. In: Hájek, P., Wiedermann, J. (eds.) MFCS 1995. LNCS, vol. 969, pp. 565–613. Springer, Heidelberg (1995)
5. Erdös, P.: Some remarks on the theory of graphs. Bulletin of the American Mathematical Society 53(4), 292–294 (1947)
6. Ershov, Y.L.: Theory of numberings. In: Griffor, E.R. (ed.) Handbook of computability theory, pp. 473–503. North-Holland, Amsterdam (1999)
7. Freivalds, R.: Non-Constructive Methods for Finite Probabilistic Automata. International Journal of Foundations of Computer Science 19(3), 565–580 (2008)
8. Freivalds, R., Bārzdiņš, J., Podnieks, K.: Inductive Inference of Recursive Functions: Complexity Bounds. In: Barzdins, J., Bjorner, D. (eds.) Baltic Computer Science. LNCS, vol. 502, pp. 111–155. Springer, Heidelberg (1991)
9. Garrett, P.: The Mathematics of Coding Theory. Pearson Prentice Hall, Upper Saddle River (2004)
10. Hilbert, D.: Uber die Theorie der algebraischen Formen. Mathematische Annalen 36, 473–534 (1890)
11. Karp, R.M., Lipton, R.: Turing machines that take advice. L' Enseignement Mathematique 28, 191–209 (1982)
12. Kolmogorov, A.N.: Three approaches to the quantitative definition of information. Problems in Information Transmission 1, 1–7 (1965)
13. Martin-Löf, P.: The definition of random sequences. Information and Control 9(6), 602–619 (1966)
14. Nishimura, H., Yamakami, T.: Polynomial time quantum computation with advice. Information Processing Letters 90(4), 195–204 (2004)
15. Podnieks, K.: Computational complexity of prediction strategies. Theory of Algorithms and Programs, Latvia State University 3, 89–102 (1977) (in Russian)
16. Stearns, R.E., Hartmanis, J., Lewis II, P.M.: Hierarchies of memory limited computations. In: Proceedings of FOCS, pp. 179–190 (1965)
17. Tadaki, K., Yamakami, T., Lin, J.C.H.: Theory of one tape linear time turing machines. In: Van Emde Boas, P., Pokorný, J., Bieliková, M., Štuller, J. (eds.) SOFSEM 2004. LNCS, vol. 2932, pp. 335–348. Springer, Heidelberg (2004)
18. Yamakami, T.: Swapping lemmas for regular and context-free languages with advice. The Computing Research Repository (CoRR), CoRR abs/0808.4122 (2008)

Multiflex: A Multilingual Finite-State Tool for Multi-Word Units

Agata Savary*

Université François Rabelais Tours, France
agata.savary@univ-tours.fr

Abstract. Multi-word units are linguistic objects whose idiosyncrasy calls for a lexicalized approach allowing to render their orthographic, inflectional and syntactic flexibility. *Multiflex* is a graph-based formalism answering this need by conflation of different surface realizations of the same underlying concept. Its implementation relies on a finite-state machinery with unification. It can be applied to the creation of linguistic resources for a high-quality natural language processing tasks.

Keywords: multi-word units, finite-state morphology, Multiflex.

Describing the variability of multi-word units. Multi-word units (MWUs) encompass a number of hard-to-define linguistic objects: compounds, complex terms, named entities, etc. They are composed of two or more words, and show an important degree of flexibility on different levels: orthographic (*head word* vs. *headword*), inflectional (*man servant* vs. *men servants*), syntactic (*birth date* vs. *date of birth*), and semantic (*hereditary disease* vs. *genetic disease*). This flexibility is hard to represent precisely and exhaustively within general grammar-based models due to idiosyncrasy (e.g. *chief justices* vs. *lords justice*).

Multiflex is a formalism and a tool that copes with flexibility and idiosyncrasy of MWUs by a fully lexicalized two-layer approach. Figure 1 shows the description of a German MWU whose inflection and variation paradigm is given in examples (1) and (1). The sequence is segmented into tokens (here $1 through $7) by the underlying module handling the morphology of single words. The possibly inflected tokens are annotated by their lemmas, morphological features, and any data needed to generate other inflected forms of the same unit.

Example 1. Organisation der Vereinten Nationen :neF:aeF:deF:geF
'United Nations Organisation' in singular (*e*) feminine (*F*) nominative (*n*), accusative (*a*), dative (*d*) and genitive (*g*)
  Vereinte Nationen :nmF:amF; *Vereinten Nationen* :nmF:amF:dmF:gmF
'United Nations' in plural (*m*) with a determined or undetermined adjective

A path in a graph starts with the leftmost edge and ends with the final encircled box. The morphological information contained in the boxes refers to

---

* The project is partially financed by the Polish Ministry of Science and Higher Education, decision number 567/6. PR UE/2008/7.

S. Maneth (Ed.): CIAA 2009, LNCS 5642, pp. 237–240, 2009.

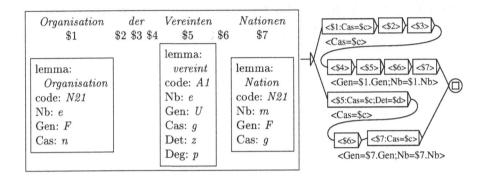

Fig. 1. Lemma annotation and inflection graph of a German MWU

the constituents of the MWU while the one placed under a box refers to the morphological description of the resulting MWU inflected form. Both types of information usually take the form of possibly uninstantiated and partial feature structures. Here, the upper path describes all forms in example (1). Constituents $2 through $7 are recopied as such from the MWU lemma, while constituent $1 (*Organisation*) is inflected for any case due to the unification variable $c which can take any value from the case domain in German. The lower path represents all elliptic variants in example (1). Constituents $1 through $4 are omitted while constituent $7 (*Nationen*) shifts to the head position and becomes case-inflected. The modifier $5 agrees with the new headword in case (same unification variable $c) and inflects for determinedness. In the full form (upper path) the morphological features of the whole MWU are inherited from the first constituent. The number and the gender are those that $1 takes in the MWU lemma ($\langle Gen = \$1.Gen; Nb = \$1.Nb\rangle$), here *eF*, while the case is as in the particular MWU inflected form ($\langle Cas = \$c\rangle$). In the elliptic form (lower path) the same kind of inheritance occurs with respect to the seventh constituent.

The use of unification variables allows for a compact description of unification paradigms. Here, the 10 forms would need 10 different paths if no unification variables were available. In highly inflected languages, such as Slavic languages, this facility is crucial: although many compounds may have several dozens of forms, a unique path is often enough to render them all.

Finite-State Machinery. *Multiflex* is inspired by the Paris school of finite-state morphology. It uses the graph editor of the *Unitex* system [9], and its generic finite-state library for binary representation and exploration of graphs (boxes and arrows in graphs correspond to transitions and states in finite-state transducers). However the semantics introduced in *Multiflex'* graphs is novel, although formally close to decorated RTNs in [3], regular expressions with feature structures in [4], and flag diacritics [2]. It represents a meta-grammar: (i) each compound with its tokenization and annotation is a rule, (ii) each inflectional graph is a meta-rule, i.e. the transformations that can be applied to a rule in order to produce new rules (compound inflected forms). This view is inspired from [5].

However in *Multiflex* all transformations (except in embedding) are gathered within the same metarule. Thus the dependencies between meta-rules are very scarce, which avoids the problem of a "card tower" in traditional grammars (the modification of a rule perishes the validity of other rules). This highly modular aspect of *Multiflex* rules makes their management and debugging easier.

At present, *Multiflex* operates in the generation mode. When applied to an annotated compound it performs the depth-first search exploration of the minimal finite-state transducer behind the graph. A transition is followed if its input and its output labels are sound. An input is sound in one of the two cases: (i) it is a constant string, (ii) it refers to an existing component (*$8* would be invalid in Fig. 1) and all the category-value equations (if any) can be fulfilled. The last condition means that: (i) categories are relevant to the component (unlike *Det* for $7 in Fig. 1), (ii) values belong to the domains of their categories (*Nb=masc* is incorrect), (iii) unification, if any, can be performed. If a unification variable has already been instantiated in a previous transition on the same path then its value must belong to the right category, and it must be accepted by the inflection paradigm of the current constituent. If however a unification variable has not yet been instantiated, it is instantiated to each value of its category's domain for each outgoing path. Thus, each path represents at least as many forms as there are allowed combinations of all unification variables it contains. An output label is sound if the category-value equations can be fulfilled: (i) the values belong to their categories' domains, (ii) if a value is fixed, its category has not yet been associated with a different value, (iii) if the value is inherited it refers to an existing component and a relevant category, (iv) unification can be performed.

While exploring a graph, *Multiflex* collaborates with an external morphological module for single words. This module must share the same morphological model (up to identifier replacement), must provide a clear-cut definition of a token boundary, and must generate on demand particular inflected forms for single tokens. Its implementation is not necessarily based on finite-state machines. *Multiflex* has been successfully interfaced with two underlying modules, one FSM-based ([9]), and one using a relational database ([14]).

Applications and Evaluation. Our first motivation for an inflection tool for MWUs came from the FSM-toolkit *Intex* [12], and led to a prototype which was applied to the creation of two DELA-type electronic lexicons of (general and terminological) English compounds (about 60,000 lemmas and 110,000 inflected forms each). The first one is distributed with *Intex* and *Unitex*, the second one was used in a translation aid software *LexProCD Databank* for term extraction.

Later our formalism was improved and re-implemented as *Multiflex*. It was released with *Unitex* (under the LGPL license), where it is used for an automatic generation of electronic lexicon of compound inflected forms (the so-called DELACF) which are matched against a corpus during the process of morphological analysis. It was tested on a 2000-entry sample of a Serbian MWU lexicon [8], and on examples of French, German, Polish, Portuguese and English. *Multiflex* is also a part of two encoding support tools: (i) *WS2LR* [7], which allows an automated controlled encoding of morphological dictionaries, aligned corpora and wordnets in Serbian, (ii) *Topostaw* [11], an outcome of the European LUNA project (http://ist-luna.eu) supporting controlled description of Polish toponyms in written and spoken corpora. Finally, *Multiflex* is incorporated into to the linguistic interface of the multilingual ontology of proper names *Prolex* [13].

In [10] a large contrastive study of 11 lexical approaches to the inflection and variation of MWUs in 7 languages was performed. It analyzes a dozen linguistic properties of MWUs (exocentricity, irregular agreement, defective paradigms, variability, etc.), and desirable descriptive and computational facilities (unification, non-redundancy, encoding interface, etc.). In the light of this study *Multiflex* belongs to the most expressive and effective tools along with *lexc* [6], *FASTR* [5], and *HABIL* [1]. Its drawbacks include the lack of modeling of derivational and semantic variants, abbreviations, and dependencies existing between a MWU and neighboring external elements. In the long run *Multiflex* needs to be enlarged to non-contiguous MWUs such as verbal expressions, admitting insertions of free external tokens. We also wish to integrate machine learning tools allowing both to acquire new data from the corpora and to predict inflection graphs for them.

References

1. Alegria, I., et al.: Representation and Treatment of Multiword Expressions in Basque. In: ACL Workshop on Multiword Expressions (2004)
2. Beesley, K.R., Karttunen, L.: Finite State Morphology. CSLI (2003)
3. Blanc, O., Constant, M.: Lexicalization of Grammars with Parameterized Graphs. In: Proceedings of RANLP 2005 (2005)
4. Drożyński, W., et al.: Shallow Processing with Unification and Typed Feature Structures - Foundations and Applications. Künstliche Intelligenz 1, 17–23 (2004)
5. Jacquemin, C.: Spotting and Discovering Terms through Natural Language Processing. MIT Press, Cambridge (2001)
6. Karttunen, L., Kaplan, R.M., Zaenen, A.: Two-Level Morphology with Composition. In: Proceedings of COLING 1992, Nantes, pp. 141–148 (1992)
7. Krstev, C., Stanković, R., Vitas, D., Obradović, I.: Workstation for Lexical Resources - WS4LR. In: Proceedings of LREC 2006, Genoa, Italy (2006)
8. Krstev, C., Vitas, D., Savary, A.: Prerequisites for a Comprehensive Dictionary of Serbian Compounds. In: Salakoski, T., Ginter, F., Pyysalo, S., Pahikkala, T. (eds.) FinTAL 2006. LNCS, vol. 4139, pp. 552–563. Springer, Heidelberg (2006)
9. Paumier, S.: Unitex 2.1 User Manual (2008), http://www-igm.univ-mlv.fr/~unitex
10. Savary, A.: Computational Inflection of Multi-Word Units. A contrastive study of lexical approaches. Linguistic Issues in Language Technology 1(2), 1–53 (2008)
11. Savary, A., Rabiega-Wiśniewska, J., Woliński, M.: Inflection of Polish Multi-Word Proper Names with Morfeusz and Multiflex. LNCS (LNAI), vol. 5070. Springer, Heidelberg (to appear)
12. Silberztein, M.: Dictionnaires électroniques et analyse automatique de textes: Le système INTEX. Masson, Paris (1993)
13. Tran, M., Maurel, D.: Prolexbase: Un dictionnaire relationnel multilingue de noms propres. Traitement Automatiques des Langues 47(3), 115–139 (2006)
14. Woliński, M.: Morfeusz – a Practical Tool for the Morphological Analysis of Polish. In: Proceedings of IIS:IIPWM 2006. LNCS, pp. 503–512. Springer, Heidelberg (2006)

Efficient Parsing Using Filtered-Popping Recursive Transition Networks

Javier M. Sastre-Martínez

Laboratoire d'Informatique de l'Institut Gaspard Monge,
Université Paris-Est, F-77454 Marne-la-Vallée Cedex 2, France
Grup Transducens,
Departament de Llenguatges i Sistemes Informàtics,
Universitat d'Alacant, E-03071 Alacant, Spain
javier.sastre@univ-mlv.fr

Abstract. We present here filtered-popping recursive transition networks (FPRTNs), a special breed of RTNs, and an efficient parsing algorithm based on recursive transition network with string output (RTNSO) which constructs the set of parses of a potentially ambiguous sentence as a FPRTN in polynomial time. By constructing a FPRTN rather than a parse enumeration, we avoid the exponential explosion due to cases where the number of parses increases exponentially w.r.t. the input length. The algorithm is compatible with the grammars that can be manually developed with the Intex and Unitex systems.

1 Introduction

This paper describes filtered-popping recursive transition networks (FPRTNs), an extension of recursive transition networks [1] (RTNs) which serves as a compressed representation of a potentially exponential set of sequences, and give the modifications to perform on the Earley-like algorithm for RTNs with string output (RTNSOs) given in [2] for building a FPRTN recognizing the language of translations of a given input sequence in polynomial time. If RTNSOs represent grammars where transition output labels are tags bounding sentence compounds, then the algorithm computes the set of parses of a given sentence. Extending Earley's algorithm [3] for output generation raises its asymptotic cost from polynomial to exponential due to cases where the number of outputs increases exponentially w.r.t. the input length; for instance, sentences with unresolved prepositional phrase (PP) attachments [4] produce an exponentially large number of parses w.r.t. the number of PPs (e.g.: the girl saw the monkey with the telescope under the tree). RTNs with output are used by both Intex [5] and Unitex [6] systems in order to represent natural language grammars.

2 Recursive Transition Networks

Given the definition of RTNSO in [2], we define a RTN $R = (Q, \Sigma, \delta, Q_I, F)$ by removing the output alphabet Γ and by removing the output labels of

S. Maneth (Ed.): CIAA 2009, LNCS 5642, pp. 241–244, 2009.

- translating and inserting transitions, which become consuming transitions $\delta(q_s, \sigma) \rightarrow q_t$, that is, just read input symbol σ, and
- deleting and ε^2-transitions, which become explicit ε-transitions $\delta(q_s, \varepsilon) \rightarrow q_t$, that is, do not read or write symbols.

Call, push and pop transition definitions are not modified since they define no output. We obtain RTN execution states (ESs) $x = (q, \pi) \in (Q \times Q^*)$ by suppresing outputs from RTNSO ESs, x representing the fact of reaching a state q after generating a stack π of return states. Δ, the extension of transition function δ for a set of execution states (SES) V and input symbol σ, becomes

$$\Delta(V, \sigma) = \{(q_t, \pi) : q_t \in \delta(q_s, \sigma) \wedge (q_s, \pi) \in V\}, \tag{1}$$

and ε-moves adding elements to the ε-closure are redefined as follows:

- **explicit ε-transitions:** add (q_t, π) for each (q_s, π) in the ε-closure and for each $q_t \in Q$ such that $q_t \in \delta(q_s, \varepsilon)$;
- **push transitions:** add $(q_c, \pi q_t)$ for each (q_s, π) in the ε-closure and for each $q_c, q_t \in Q$ such that $q_t \in \delta(q_s, q_c)$;
- **pop transitions:** add (q_r, π) for each $(q_f, \pi q_r)$ in the ε-closure such that $q_f \in F$;

The initial SES is redefined as $X_I = Q_I \times \{\lambda\}$, that is, recognition starts from an initial state without having started any call, and the acceptance SES as $X_F = F \times \{\lambda\}$, that is, recognition ends once an acceptance state is reached without uncompleted calls. Δ^*, the extension of Δ for input sequences, is not modified except for the use of the redefined Δ and ε-closure functions. We define the language of a RTN A instead of the language of translations as

$$\mathcal{L}(A) = \{w \in \Sigma^* : \Delta^*(X_I, w) \cap X_F \neq \emptyset\}. \tag{2}$$

3   Filtered-Popping Recursive Transition Networks

A FPRTN $(Q, K, \Sigma, \delta, \kappa, Q_I, F)$ is a RTN extended with a finite set of keys K and a $\kappa : Q \rightarrow K$ function that maps states to keys in K. FPRTNs behave as RTNs except for pop transitions: bringing the machine from an acceptance state q_s to a popped state q_r is only possible if $\kappa(q_s) = \kappa(q_r)$; we say pop transitions are *filtered*.

4   Language of a RTN via Earley-Like Processing

We define the Earley-like computation of the acceptance/rejection of an input sequence by a RTN by suppressing the outputs from the Earley-like processing for RTNSOs given in [2]. ESs become 4-tuples $(q_s, q_c, q_h, j) \in Q \times (Q \cup \{\lambda\}) \times Q \times \mathbb{N}$, the Δ function, analogous to Earley's "scanner", becomes

$$\Delta(V, \sigma) = \{(q_t, \lambda, q_h, j) : q_t \in \delta(q_s, \sigma) \wedge (q_s, \lambda, q_h, j) \in V\} \tag{3}$$

and the ε-moves adding ESs to the ε-closure are redefined as follows:

- **explicit ε-transitions:** add (q_t, λ, q_h, j) for each (q_s, λ, q_h, j) in the ε-closure of V_k and for each q_t such that $q_t \in \delta(q_s, \varepsilon)$;
- **push transitions:** analogously to Earley's "predictor", add (q_t, q_c, q_h, j) and (q_c, λ, q_c, k) for each (q_s, λ, q_h, j) in the ε-closure of V_k and for each q_c and q_t such that $q_t \in \delta(q_s, q_c)$; (q_t, q_c, q_h, j) is the paused ES waiting for q_c's call completion and (q_c, λ, q_c, k) is the active ES initiating the call;
- **pop transitions:** analogously to Earley's "completer", for each (q_f, λ, q_c, j) such that $q_f \in F$ (the ESs completing call to q_c) and for each $(q_r, q_c, q_h, i) \in V_j$ (the paused ESs depending on call to q_c), *retroactively* add (q_r, λ, q_h, i) to the ε-closure of V_k (we resume these paused ESs).

Retroactive call completion is explained in [2], which is based on the management of deletable non-terminals for CFGs explained in [7]. The initial SES is redefined as $X_I = \{(q_s, \lambda, q_s, 0) : q_s \in Q_I\}$, that is, the ESs initiating a call to each initial state, and the acceptance SES as $X_F = F \times \{\lambda\} \times Q_I \times \{0\}$, that is, the ESs triggering a pop from an initial call. Δ^* and $\mathcal{L}$ are not modified w.r.t. section 2 except for the use of the sets and functions redefined here.

5   Translating a String into a FPRTN

We give here the modifications to perform on the Earley-like algorithm in [2] for the generation of a FPRTN $A' = (Q', K, \Sigma', \delta', \kappa, Q'_I, F')$ from a RTNSO $A = (Q, \Sigma, \Gamma, \delta, Q_I, F)$ and input $\sigma_1 \ldots \sigma_l$, where $\Sigma' = \Gamma$, $K = \{0, \ldots, l\}$ and given a path p within A' having r and r' as start and end states, p consumes a possible translation of $\sigma_{\kappa(r)+1} \ldots \sigma_{\kappa(r')}$ (see Fig 1). First of all, we obtain a RTN Earley-like algorithm from the one for RTNSOs in [2] by suppressing outputs, as shown in the equations above. Then we insert the following instructions for the construction of the FPRTN:

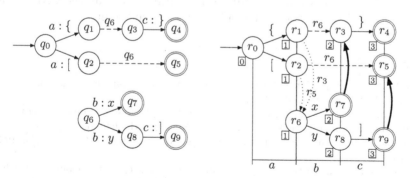

Fig. 1. At the left, an ambiguous RTNSO, and at the right, an FPRTN recognizing the language of translations of *abc* for this RTNSO. Boxes contain the key of the state they are attached to. FPRTN push and pop transitions are explicitly represented as dotted and thick arrows, respectively. Only pop transitions corresponding to connected input segments are allowed: pop transitions from r_7 to r_5 and from r_9 to r_3 are forbidden since the former skips the translation of *c* and the latter translates *c* twice.

- create states $r_I \in Q'_I$ with $\kappa(r_I) = 0$ and $r_F \in F'$ with $\kappa(r_F) = l$
- for each active ES x_t to be added to a SES V_k, create non-initial state $r_t \in Q'$ with $\kappa(r_t) = k$, create map $\zeta_s(k, x_t) \to r_t$ and add r_t to F' iif x_t represents to have reached an acceptance RTNSO state,
- for each $x_t \in X_I$ add transition $\delta'(r_I, \zeta_s(0, x_t)) \to r_F$,
- for each paused ESs $x_p \in V_k$ derived from an active source ES $x_s \in V_k$ due to a call transition with $x_c \in V_k$ as active ES initiating the call, create maps $\zeta_s(k, x_p) \to \zeta_s(k, x_s)$ and $\zeta_c(k, x_p) \to \zeta_s(k, x_c)$,
- let $x_s \in V_j$ be the active ES $x_t \in V_k$ is derived from, if the derivation is due to a non-call RTNSO transition generating $g \in \Gamma \cup \{\varepsilon\}$ then add transition $\delta'(\zeta_s(j, x_s), g) \to \zeta_s(k, x_t)$, otherwise
- if it is due to a call completion resuming paused ES $x_p \in V_i$, then add transition $\delta'(\zeta_s(i, x_p), \zeta_c(i, x_p)) \to \zeta_s(k, x_t)$.

6   Empirical Tests

The algorithm has been tested for the same exponential RTNSO translator and under the same conditions than the ones shown in [2], section 6. The meassured times are just twice the ones of the acceptor-only Earley algorithm (see Fig. 2 of [2]), hence keeping a linear cost instead of exponential for this case.

7   Future Work

We are currently studying probabilistic prunning methods for weighted FPRTNs in order to compute the highest-ranked outputs in polynomial time.

Acknowledgments. This work has been partially supported by the Spanish Government (grant number TIN2006–15071–C03–01), by the Universitat d'Alacant (grant number INV05–40), by the MENRT and by the CNRS. We thank Profs. E. Laporte and M. Forcada for their useful comments.

References

1. Woods, W.A.: Transition network grammars for natural language analysis. Commun. ACM 13(10), 591–606 (1970)
2. Sastre, J.M., Forcada, M.L.: Efficient parsing using recursive transition networks with string output. LNCS (LNAI), vol. 5603. Springer, Heidelberg (in press)
3. Earley, J.: An efficient context-free parsing algorithm. Commun. ACM 13(2), 94–102 (1970)
4. Ratnaparkhi, A.: Statistical models for unsupervised prepositional phrase attachment. In: COLING-ACL 1998, Morristown, NJ, USA, ACL, pp. 1079–1085 (1998)
5. Silberztein, M.D.: Dictionnaires électroniques et analyse automatique de textes. Le système INTEX. Masson, Paris (1993)
6. Paumier, S.: Unitex 1.2 User Manual. Université de Marne-la-Vallée (2006)
7. Aycock, J., Horspool, N.: Practical Earley Parsing. The Computer Journal 45(6), 620–630 (2002)

Forest FIRE: A Taxonomy-based Toolkit of Tree Automata and Regular Tree Algorithms*

Loek Cleophas[1] and Kees Hemerik[2]

[1] FASTAR Research Group, Department of Computer Science, University of
Pretoria, 0002 Pretoria, Republic of South Africa
http://www.fastar.org
[2] SET Group, Department of Mathematics and Computer Science, Eindhoven
University of Technology, P.O. Box 513, NL-5600 MB Eindhoven, The Netherlands
loek@loekcleophas.com, c.hemerik@tue.nl
http://www.win.tue.nl/set

Abstract. We report on a toolkit of tree automata and algorithms for
tree acceptance, pattern matching, and parsing. Despite many applications, no large toolkit of such algorithms existed, complicating choice
among them. Our toolkit's design was guided by our taxonomies of such
algorithms, and this is clearly reflected in its structure. We outline one
taxonomy and discuss how its hierarchy determines the toolkit's class and
interface hierarchies. The toolkit, available at http://www.fastar.org,
contains about 50 tree algorithms and automata constructions.

1 Introduction

We consider *regular tree languages* for *ordered, ranked trees*. These have a rich
theory, with many generalizations from regular string languages [1,2]. Parts of
the theory have broad applicability in areas ranging from logic to code generation
in compilers. We focus on algorithms for *tree acceptance, tree pattern matching*
and *tree parsing* ('tree algorithms'). Many of these appear in the literature, but
deficiencies existed, including: inaccessibility of theory and algorithms; difficulty
of comparing algorithms due to variations in presentation style and formality
level; and lack of reference to theory in many publications. To effectively order
the field, we constructed *taxonomies*—systematic classifications in an algorithmic problem domain—for tree acceptance and tree pattern matching [1].

Practical deficiencies also existed: no large, coherent collection of implementations existed; and for practical applications it was difficult to choose between
algorithms. We therefore designed, implemented, and benchmarked a highly coherent *toolkit* of these algorithms. Taxonomies are a good starting point for the
construction of such toolkits. High-level design choices are guided by the structure of the taxonomies (indicating commonalities and differences between the
algorithms), while their presentation of algorithms simplifies implementation.

---

* The research reported on was performed while the first author was at TU/e. We
thank Roger Strolenberg for his work on the toolkit and GUI, and Mark van den
Brand, Vreda Pieterse, and Derrick Kourie for remarks on earlier paper versions.

S. Maneth (Ed.): CIAA 2009, LNCS 5642, pp. 245–248, 2009.
© Springer-Verlag Berlin Heidelberg 2009

We report on FOREST FIRE, our taxonomy-based toolkit of tree algorithms and automata constructions, which is accompanied by the FIRE WOOD GUI [1,3,4]. Other 'tree toolkits' contain fewer algorithms and automata and focus on their use in a specific application area. We refer to [1,3] for references. In subject and style our work is close to Watson's [5], in which he applied taxonomy-based software construction to string pattern matching and finite automata construction and minimization.

FOREST FIRE—a Java package—contains: representations of trees, regular tree grammars, and pattern sets; algorithms for analysis and transformation of grammars e.g. to detect and remove chain rules; various kinds of finite (tree) automata and generators for them; and tree acceptance/parsing and pattern matching algorithms using such automata. Our focus in this paper is on the taxonomy-based design of the toolkit parts for the latter two categories.

2   Tree Automata for Acceptance and Pattern Matching

We refer to [1,2] for definitions of finite tree automata (TAs) and regular tree grammars (RTGs). The tree acceptance problem is to determine, given an RTG and a subject tree, whether the tree is an element of the language defined by the RTG. As in the string case, for every RTG G there is a TA M such that $\mathcal{L}(G) = \mathcal{L}(M)$. This justifies the use of TAs for tree acceptance. Similarly, a TA for tree pattern matching can be constructed from a *pattern set*.

3   Taxonomies

In our technical sense a taxonomy is a means of ordering algorithms. Each node of a taxonomy graph corresponds to an algorithm (which can be generic, allowing for different instantiations; the corresponding node then is a generic one representing multiple algorithms). The graph's root represents a high-level algorithm of which the correctness is easily shown. A branch corresponds to addition of a detail, i.e. a correctness preserving algorithm refinement. Hence, the correctness of each algorithm follows from the details on its root path and the correctness of the root. Considering new detail combinations may lead to new algorithms.

Our taxonomies and the details used in them are treated in detail in [1]. Figure 1 depicts the tree acceptance taxonomy. Three main subgraphs can be distinguished. The first part contains algorithms based on the RTG/TA correspondence. By adding detail, viz. a direction (detail FR: frontier-to-root or detail RF:

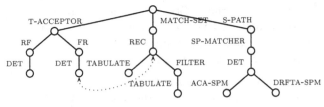

Fig. 1. Tree acceptance taxonomy

root-to-frontier) or determinacy (detail DET) more specific constructions are obtained. (The nodes are generic, since the algorithms depend on particular choices of TA state and transition set.) The middle part contains algorithms based on suitable generalizations of $S \overset{*}{\Rightarrow} t$ (for RTG start symbol S and subject tree t). For each subtree of t, they compute a *match set* of items from which the subtree is derivable. They differ in the kind of items used and in the way match sets are computed. (Certain algorithms in this and the first part are related, indicated by the dotted line in the figure.) The third part contains algorithms based on decomposing items into *stringpaths* and subsequent use of string matching techniques. Using matches found, item matches and hence match sets can be computed for t's subtrees.

4   Toolkit Design and Implementation

In the taxonomy graphs, nodes near leaves correspond to directly implementable algorithms, whereas nodes higher up serve as abstract intermediate forms. The toolkit reflects this structure: higher nodes result in abstract classes or interfaces, while leaves result in concrete classes and method implementations.

In total, the implemented acceptance algorithms cover seven algorithm nodes and about thirty different automata constructions. For tree pattern matching, a slightly smaller number from similar taxonomy branches has been implemented.

The tree algorithms and TA constructions from the taxonomies use TA types that differ in a number of aspects: their *(non)determinism* (indicated in their acronym by N and D respectively); the presence of *ε-transitions* (indicated in their acronym by ε); their *direction* (either frontier-to-root (FR) or root-to-frontier (RF)); the *item sets (and types)* used to construct their states; their use of a technique called *filtering*, in the case of DFRTAs; and their intended use for *tree acceptance/parsing* or *tree pattern matching*. For each of the two problems, the class inheritance hierarchy corresponding to the TA types is determined by—in order—the differences in direction, determinism, and the use of filtering.

A TA state corresponds to an item or a set of items, depending on the (non)determinism of the TA. The items are derived from patterns or grammars' productions. While most TAs use *subtrees* as items, *dotted trees/productions*—trees or productions with a specific node being indicated, providing for context information—may also be used. The toolkit uses a single class *AutomatonState* containing a set of items (a singleton set for a DFRTA state). A generic parameter for a descendant of *IItem* accommodates item type variability. By varying the items used to construct states and by adding details (e.g. direction, determinacy), over 30 TA constructions are obtained.

Most acceptance and pattern matching algorithms in the taxonomies and toolkit use TAs. Such tree acceptance (pattern matching) algorithms are implemented in Java classes implementing an interface, called *IAcceptor* (*IMatcher*). It specifies a constructor to set the TA to be used, and a method *accept* (*match*) running the acceptance (pattern matching) algorithm on a given tree. Tree acceptance algorithms using different TA types share this interface yet differ in algorithm, data structure and state. This lead to classes *DFRAcceptor*, *NFRAcceptor*, and *NRFAcceptor*. Similar classes exist for tree pattern matching.

Generator classes implement the standard imperative TA constructions [1, Ch. 5–6]. The construction of deterministic and nondeterministic automata is quite different, so two generator classes exist: *DFRTAGenerator* and *NTAGenerator*. Both work for pattern matchers and for acceptors/parsers, using function overloading to deal with different inputs and construction internals. Nevertheless the functions share a lot of code. The *NTAGenerator* can generate both FR and RF directed TAs, yet is not aware of the direction: its *generateAutomaton* method uses a particular TA's *addTransition* method to add transitions.

The abstract algorithms in the taxonomies form an excellent guideline for methods' implementation. The algorithm structure remains essentially the same but is rephrased in OO-style, and types and variables of the abstract version are systematically replaced by their Java counterparts.

5   Concluding Remarks

Our toolkit and GUI allow easy access to implementations. This was used for benchmarking experiments reported in [3,4]. Such experiments gave insight in the algorithms and constructions, and in their running times and memory use. Most interestingly, the experiments showed that in practical cases newly developed algorithms—using new so-called *filters* in DFRTAs—outperform algorithms using existing filters [3,4]. The toolkit and GUI can be extended with e.g. bitvector implementations of tree algorithms, and with support for e.g. instruction selection and tree/term rewriting. Earlier extension work leads us to expect that such extensions will not be highly time consuming to implement.

References

1. Cleophas, L.G.W.A.: Tree Algorithms: Two Taxonomies and a Toolkit. PhD thesis, Dept. of Mathematics and Computer Science, Eindhoven University of Technology (2008), http://alexandria.tue.nl/extra2/200810270.pdf
2. Comon, H., Dauchet, M., Gilleron, R., Jacquemard, F., Lugiez, D., Tison, S., Tommasi, M.: Tree automata: Techniques and applications (2007), http://www.grappa.univ-lille3.fr/tata/
3. Cleophas, L.: Forest FIRE and FIRE Wood: Tools for tree automata and tree algorithms. In: Post-proceedings of the 7th International Workshop on Finite-State Methods and Natural Language Processing (FSMNLP 2008). IOS Press, Amsterdam (2009)
4. Strolenberg, R.: ForestFIRE & FIREWood, A Toolkit & GUI for Tree Algorithms. Master's thesis, Dept. of Mathematics and Computer Science, Eindhoven University of Technology (2007), http://alexandria.tue.nl/extra1/afstversl/wsk-i/strolenberg2007.pdf
5. Watson, B.W.: Taxonomies and Toolkits of Regular Language Algorithms. PhD thesis, Dept. of Mathematics and Computing Science, Technische Universiteit Eindhoven (1995), http://www.fastar.org/publications/PhD_Watson.pdf

Formally Synthesising a Protocol Converter: A Case Study

Jing Cao and Albert Nymeyer

The University of New South Wales, Australia
{jcao,anymeyer}@cse.unsw.edu.au

Abstract. A formal method of synthesising a converter that translates signals between two heterogeneous, off-the-shelf protocol IPs is presented in the form of a case study. At the heart of the method is a model checker that guarantees the converter satisfies correctness conditions, as well as user-defined properties. In this approach, the issue of nondeterminism is explicitly addressed, and is used to synthesise an optimal converter.

1 Introduction

The increasing demands by society on smaller, more complex, reliable and powerful embedded systems has increased the need for component reuse and synthesis methods in chip design. We address this issue by presenting a formally-based synthesis method that generates a converter for 'reusable' component IPs.

In the figure on the right we illustrate the basic model of our converter. In this figure, protocols P_1 and P_2 interact via a converter. This interaction involves control signals c_s and c_r, and data d_s and d_r, being sent and received. Each data channel has its own buffer. A protocol IP is a 'black-box': it is 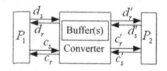 a component that has well-defined behaviour, and can be controlled only by (the converter) sending appropriate control signals to it. All control signals sent between a protocol and the converter must be handled by the converter in such a way that the data sent and received by the two components match. The converter must prevent a component from sending so-called 'invalid' control signals. Components may be nondeterministic, which means that different (deterministic) behaviours are possible. The converter that is synthesised is optimal insofar as the (deterministic) converter that has the best performance based on some criteria is selected. The criteria used in this work is the data transfer rate. The resulting optimal converter must also be guaranteed correct.

Nondeterminism is a fundamental issue and is directly addressed in our framework. We differentiate between nondeterminism that is under converter control, and nondeterminism that cannot be controlled by the converter. The former can be eliminated by actions of the converter. If multiple behaviours are possible in a protocol component, not all of which will satisfy the correctness conditions, the converter is able to *force* correctness by sending appropriate control signals

S. Maneth (Ed.): CIAA 2009, LNCS 5642, pp. 249–252, 2009.

to the component. As well, if a protocol includes behaviour that is *invalid* for a communicating protocol, the converter is able to control the communication in such a way as to avoid this behaviour.

Using FSMs to model a converter is well-known, and dates back to work by [1]. Recent work that provides the backdrop of our research includes [2] who also formally model control and data separately, use buffers, have correctness conditions and deal with data mismatch explicitly. But their formal model is completely different to ours, there is no verification phase in their approach, they do not handle nondeterminism, or treat invalid data in the same way. Other related work is [3], who also use the tableau method to verify the converter. However, our approach is more general and we (again) use a completely different formal framework. As well, buffers are defined explicitly in our formal model, and the issue of nondeterminism is formally addressed. Avoiding invalid states, and forcing correctness, and optimising for performance as part of the formal model are notions that are unique to our work.

Converter synthesis should not be confused with controller synthesis. In controller synthesis, an environment and a reactive machine called the controller are modelled as an interactive event system. The aim is to synthesise a controller that guarantees global performance constraints, independent of how the environment behaves [4]. Converter synthesis is a method of component reuse where well-defined, off-the-shelf components are connected through a so-called converter. The aim is to synthesise a converter (assuming one exists) that guarantees *correct communication* between the components. Converter synthesis is in essence therefore a 'language compatibility' problem, and is aimed at component reuse, in contrast to controller synthesis, where strategy is the focus.

2   The Formal Architecture

Our formal converter-synthesis architecture is shown in Fig. 1. The architecture consists of a front-end and a back-end, much like a compiler generator. In essence, the front-end analyses the input IPs, represented as FSMs, and synthesises (i.e. generates) an intermediate representation called the *raw converter* (RC in the figure), also represented as a FSM. The back-end refines the raw converter by resolving nondeterminism, and generates the final converter.

There are four main phases in the front-end: the two input protocols are first composed, buffers are then added to the states followed by the correctness conditions. The correctness conditions are defined by the system (e.g. there are no invalid states) and by the user as input (e.g. the converter cannot deadlock), generally in the form of temporal formulae. The finite-state model extended

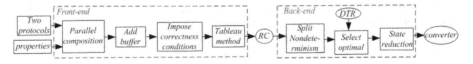

Fig. 1. A converter synthesis architecture

to include buffers and properties is then model checked by using the tableau method [5]. During tableau, states that violate correctness conditions may be removed, but in some cases they may also be 'forced' to satisfy properties. Particular invalid states are also avoided.

The resulting raw converter may contain nondeterministic states. These states are split, resulting in deterministic automata called *sub raw converters*. The sub raw converter with the best data transfer rate (DTR) is selected (Other criteria could also have been used). The final step is to reduce the number of states by removing buffers from the transitions, which results in states being merged.

3   Case Study

We have applied our converter-synthesis framework to two industrial protocols ASB and APB [6]. Here however, for the sake of brevity, we consider just simplified versions of these protocols ASB' and APB', depicted in Fig. 2 on the left. ASB' is a (slave) protocol that can handle write transfers, and APB' a protocol that only reads. Note that in state s_2 of ASB', 3 outgoing transitions have no input, only output, and send signals *bwait*, *blast* and *berror* with different values: $1, 0, 0$ (means 'wait'), $0, 0, 0$ ('done'), and $0, 1, 1$ ('retract'). Thus s_2 is a nondeterministic state and ASB' a nondeterministic protocol.

ASB' and APB' are inputs to the front-end. After parallel composition, a buffer is added. The correctness conditions that we impose are $\phi_1 \colon AG(s_{1,1,0} \rightarrow AXAF\, s_{1,1,0})$ and $\phi_2 \colon \forall s \in S^R, k = 0$, where $s_{1,1,0}$ is the initial and final state, and k is the buffer value in each state. The automaton is then model checked. States violating the correctness conditions are removed, and this results in a raw converter consisting of 6 states, shown in Fig. 2 on the very right.

In the raw converter, just state $s_{1,1,0}$ (which is non-deterministic) is split in the first phase of the back-end, resulting in 2 sub raw converters. In one of the sub raw converters, SRC_1, the self loop at $s_{1,1,0}$ is removed, and in the other, SRC_2, the transition from $s_{1,1,0}$ to $s_{2,1,0}$ is removed. In the second phase, we select SRC_1 because it has the better DTR. The DTR of SRC_1 is $\frac{1}{2x_1+3x_2+4}$, where x_1 is the number of times that $s_{5,1,0}$ is visited (remembering that this

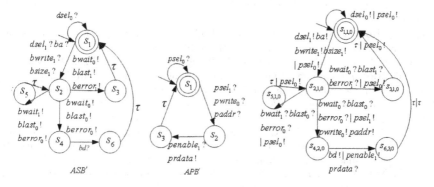

Fig. 2. Left: ASB' and APB'. Right: a raw converter that interfaces ASB' and APB'.

corresponds to a 'wait' in ASB'), before reaching $s_{4,2,0}$. Similarly, x_2 records visits to $s_{3,1,0}$. The DTR of SRC_2 is 0, because there is no data transferred in the self loop. No reduction will occur in the final phase in the back-end, since in this case the buffer size is 0, so no merging is possible.

Note that property ϕ_2 above restricts the buffer size to 0. If we increase the buffer to size 2 (say), then ϕ_2 will change to $\forall s \in S^R, 0 \leq k \leq 2$, and the resulting raw converter will have more states (in fact 28), which will reduce to 18 in the final converter. Note that the size of the buffer is a state variable.

We have not demonstrated above how the tableau method removes invalid states that are caused by non-determinism in the input protocol. An example is state s_2 in ASB' that leads to states s_3 and s_4. A fragment of the automaton that is input to the tableau method can be seen in the figure on the right. States $s_{3,1,0}$ and $s_{3,2,0}$ are generated 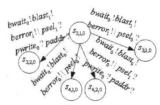 from the ASB' state s_3, and $s_{4,1,0}$ and $s_{4,2,0}$ from s_4. State $s_{4,1,0}$ is in fact invalid because it leads to buffer underflow (the details are not shown). If the converter removes $s_{4,1,0}$, then we have a potential problem because the converter cannot prevent ASB' choosing s_4. To avoid this, the raw converter generated by tableau will not send the signal $psel_0$ in that case. Tableau can also force states to satisfy properties. E.g. if we have a third property: $AG(s_{1,1,0} \rightarrow \neg penable_1 \ U \ dsel_1)$, then there is again a potential problem because in state $s_{1,1,0}$ $penable$ may be either 0 or 1. This could violate the property, so tableau forces the raw converter to send $penable_0$ to APB' in that case.

Full details of our formal framework can be found in [7,8], including results of experiments comparing our converter with those represented in the literature.

References

1. Akella, J., McMillan, K.L.: Synthesizing converters between finite state protocols. In: Computer Design on VLSI in Computer & Processors, pp. 410–413. IEEE, Los Alamitos (1991)
2. Avnit, K., D'Silva, V., Sowmya, A., Ramesh, S., Parameswaran, S.: A formal approach to the protocol converter problem. In: Proceedings of the conference on Design, automation and test in Europe (DATE 2008), pp. 294–299. ACM, New York (2008)
3. Sinha, R., Roop, P.S., Basu, S.: A model checking approach to protocol conversion. Electr. Notes Theor. Comput. Sci. 203(4), 81–94 (2008)
4. Passerone, R., de Alfaro, L., Henzinger, T., Sangiovanni-Vincentelli, A.: Convertibility verification and converter synthesis: two faces of the same coin. In: International Conference on Computer Aided Design, November 2002, pp. 132–139 (2002)
5. Clarke, E.M., Grumberg, O., Peled, D.A.: Model Checking. MIT Press, Cambridge (2000)
6. ARM: AMBA Specification (Rev. 2) (May 1999), www.gaisler.com/doc/amba.pdf
7. Cao, J., Nymeyer, A.: Formal model of a protocol converter. In: Fifteenth Computing: The Australasian Theory Symposium. CRPIT, vol. 94, pp. 107–117 (2009)
8. Cao, J., Nymeyer, A.: Formal, correct and optimal component reuse. In: United international systems conference (Uniscon 2009) (to be published, 2009)

Compiler Generator Based on Restarting Automata[*]

Jan Procházka

Charles University, Department of Computer Science,
Malostranské nám. 25, 118 00 PRAHA 1, Czech Republic
HProchy@gmail.com
http://hippies.matfyz.cz

Abstract. Restarting automata are a very strong theoretical model which can recognize much more than context-free languages in its most general variant. However, for its wider usage in real-world applications it is necessary to fill two gaps: to add semantics – instead of accepting we would like to get a meaning of the input – and to design a tool which for a given restarting automaton in human-readable format generates a program computing the meaning of an input text. The resulting tool is actually a compiler compiler.

Keywords: restarting automata, semantics, compiler-compiler.

In this publication we want to outline a new tool for generating compilers – CCRA. It uses the formal model called restarting automata. But it is necessary to modify them in order to allow working with semantics.

1 Restarting Automata

Out of many variants of restarting automata [1] we use one of the most powerful (accepting a superset of context-free languages) model called RRWW-automaton (we use its definition based on meta-instructions [2]):

A *shrinking restarting automaton* is a system $M = (\Sigma, \Gamma, w, I)$, where Σ is an input alphabet, Γ is a working alphabet ($\Sigma \subseteq \Gamma$), $w : \Gamma \to \mathbb{R}^+$ is a weight function and I is a finite set of meta-instructions of the following two types:

1. A *rewriting meta-instruction* is of the form $(E_l, x \to y, E_r)$, where $x, y \in \Gamma^*$ such that $\sum_{i \in x} w(i) > \sum_{j \in y} w(j)$, and $E_l, E_r \subseteq \Gamma^*$ are regular languages called left and right constraints.
2. An *accepting meta-instruction* is of the form (E, Accept), where $E \subseteq \Gamma^*$ is a regular language.

---

[*] This work was partially supported by the program 'Information Society' under project 1ET100300517.

S. Maneth (Ed.): CIAA 2009, LNCS 5642, pp. 253–257, 2009.

A word w can be reduced (rewritten) into a word w' if there exists a rewriting meta-instruction $(E_l, x \rightarrow y, E_r)$ such that w can be written as uxv, where $u \in E_l$, $v \in E_r$ and $w' = uyv$ – we write $uxv \vdash uyv$. Let $\vdash^*$ denote the reflexive and transitive closure of $\vdash$. An input word w is accepted by the automaton if there exists a word z such that $w \vdash^* z$ and $z \in E$ for some accepting meta-instruction (E, Accept).

Purpose of the weight function is only to ensure a finiteness of the computation. We even settle for its existence (we don't require its realization, so we can ignore it).

EXAMPLE:

Let's take a context-sensitive language $L = \{a^n b^n c, a^n b^{2n} d : n \in \mathbb{N}\}$.
We can describe it by a restarting automaton this way:

$\Sigma = \{a, b, c, d\}$
$\Gamma = \{a, b, c, d\}$
$I = \{(a^*, aab \rightarrow a, b^+ c), (a^*, aabb \rightarrow a, b^+ d), (abc, \mathsf{Accept}), (abbd, \mathsf{Accept})\}$

---

2   Regular Expressions

Regular languages E_l, E_r and E used in the above definition are usually written as regular expressions. Usual implementations of regular expressions do not allow a complement operation though they contain many extensions which we do not use. Hence we have implemented a small own library for regular expressions (based on nondeterministic finite state automata) with traditional syntax but including a prefix-tilde-operator which means complement of the following expression. But be careful with this operator. It needs the automaton (representing the complemented expression) to be deterministic, therefore this operation can be very time and space expensive. But typical usage is on nearly deterministic expressions.

3   Restarting Automata with Semantics

Restarting automata are a linguistically motivated model which can be used as a tool for analysis by reduction. Consider the following example: "Peter has blue eyes." is reduced to "Peter has eyes." We expect from the semantics that it makes a mark that the word "eyes" has the attribute "blue". So for each word (token) we have a set of flags which can be changed during each reduction.

Two modifications have been done because it is not easy to realize referring to flags of symbols in regular expressions. When a sequence of tokens B is rewriting a sequence A, then the flags of A can only be read and the flags of B can only be set. The second modification is the replacement of accepting meta-instructions by another formalism of the same power. A new symbol can be added to Γ and the computation is changed so that the input is accepted if there exists a reduction to a sequence containing this symbol.

The possibility of collecting all meanings of the input has been realized like in Prolog – at the end of the computation the user can artificially create a rejection and this way collect the results from all branches of the computation leading to acceptance.

4 Compiler Generator

The most universal (but but for the purposes of joining with sematics the most comfortable) way allowing the user to make data analysis by restarting automata has been chosen – creating of a compiler generator. Maybe the most known application of this type is called bison [3]. There are many reasons to make the new tool similar (e.g. interfaces or an automatic convertibility from the bison inputfile format). The chosen language is C++.

The general form of a grammar file has been maintained:

```
%{
Prologue          // user's code for the header file
%}
Declarations      // definitions of token sets (%DefSet),
                  // accepting tokens (%Accept), etc.
%%
Grammar rules     // definitions of meta-instructions
%%
Epilogue          // user's code for the main file
```

Some examples of the grammar rules:

meta-instruction $(E_l, x \rightarrow y, E_r)$	grammar rule $E_l \ / \ x \ \text{->} \ y \ / \ E_r \ @\{ \ sem \ \};$
$(.^*, x{\rightarrow}y, .^*)$	`/ x -> y / ;`
$(.^*a^+, x\ y{\rightarrow}k\ l\ m, .^*b)$	`a+ / x y -> k l m / .*b$ @{ sem };`
$(\hat{}[\hat{}abc]^+.^*, x \rightarrow, (a|cd)^*)$	`^[^abc]+.* / x -> / (a|cd)*$ @{ sem };`

The positions marked *sem* are the places where the semantic parts of the meta-instructions (if any) in C++ should be written. Refering to tokens is like in bison. The old ones are referred to by $n the new ones by $$n, where n is the index counted from left. If we, for example, want to set the val flag of token m as the sum of these flags in tokens x and y in the second meta-instruction, we can write $$3.val = $1.val + $2.val;.

Moreover if E_l does not begin with ˆ or E_r does not end with $ it is concatenated with .* in the given order.

The generated file is a C++ class. Its most important method is `parse()`. It loads all tokens by lexical analyser and then finds the acceptance sequence of applications of meta-instructions (the searching heuristic is selected or written by user). If the input is accepted then the accepted sequence (with its semantics) is returned.

EXAMPLE:

Let's take the automaton from the previous example. And let's say that we're interrested in the value of n. The inputfile for CCRA can be written this way:

```
%{
    struct param{   // semantics of tokens
        int n;
    };

    #define CCRA_PARAMS_TYPE param  // set type of tokens on param
%}

%Accept accept      // definition of accepting symbol
%ClassName "Sample" // name of generated class
%MainGen            // generate main function

%%

^a* / a a b -> a / b+ c $    @{ $$1.n = $2.n + 1; };
^a* / a a b b -> a / b+ d $  @{ $$1.n = $2.n + 1; };
^/ a b c -> accept / $       @{ $$1.n = $1.n + 1; };
^/ a b b d -> accept / $     @{ $$1.n = $1.n + 1; };

%%
```

---

5   Conclusion

We have implemented a tool that generates parsers based on restarting automata with semantics (which we have formulated). It seems to be a great tool for processing of seminatural languages. But it is a work in progress and we need more tests. Although it is used nearly the bison inputfile syntax we have much stronger tool so the time requirements are much bigger (after all the model is nondeterministic).

In the future we want to test the applicability on the Czech nomenclature of the organic chemistry which is very complicated and has some context rules [4]. Next it would be interesting to add tests of some features of the input language which could make the analysis faster.

References

1. Otto, F.: Restarting automata. In: Esik, Z., Martin-Vide, C., Mitrana, V. (eds.) Recent Advances in Formal Languages and Applications. Studies in Computational Intelligence, vol. 25, pp. 269–303. Springer, Berlin (2006)
2. Mráz, F., Otto, F., Plátek, M.: Learning analysis by reduction from positive data. In: Sakakibara, Y., Kobayashi, S., Sato, K., Nishino, T., Tomita, E. (eds.) ICGI 2006. LNCS, vol. 4201, pp. 125–136. Springer, Heidelberg (2006)
3. Donnely, C., Stallman, R.: Bison, `http://www.gnu.org/software/bison/manual/html_mono/bison.html`
4. Procházka, J.: Vizualizace molekul popsaných v ženevském názvosloví: Bakalářská práce. Univerzita Karlova, Matematicko-fyzikální fakulta, Praha (2007)

Are Statecharts Finite Automata?*

Hanlin Lu and Sheng Yu

Department of Computer Science
University of Western Ontario, London, Ontario, Canada
{hlu47,syu}@csd.uwo.ca

Abstract. Statecharts, which have been introduced by D. Harel in 1987, provide compact and expressive visual formalisms for reactive systems. They have been widely used as a modeling tool and adopted by Unified Modeling Language (UML) as an important technique to model the dynamic behaviour of objects. One of the fundamental questions concerning statecharts is what the computation power of statecharts is. Until now, most descriptions consider that the computing power of statecharts is the same as that of Finite State Machines or Finite Automata, though no accurate arguments or proofs have been provided.

In this paper, we show for the first time that the computation power of statecharts is far beyond that of finite automata. We compare statecharts with Interaction Machines introduced by P. Wegner more than ten years ago. We show that the Interaction Machines are the most accurate theoretical models for statecharts.

Keywords: statecharts, finite automata, interaction machines.

1   Introduction

Although statecharts have been introduced for more than twenty years [3] and used in many application areas, there has not been a thorough and careful study of them in comparison to other theoretical models. Until now, most descriptions in literature consider that the computation power of statecharts is the same as that of finite state machines (FSMs) or finite automata (FAs) although no accurate arguments or proofs have been provided. Since statecharts have been used in many application areas during the last twenty years, we consider that it is important to study accurately what statecharts can do, i.e., what the computation power of statecharts really is. There are at least the following two questions here: (1) Is the computation power of statecharts the same as that of FAs? (2) If the answer to the first question is negative, then what theoretical computation model would correspond to statecharts more accurately?

In this paper, we consider those fundamental questions concerning statecharts. After a comprehensive and comparative study of statecharts, we find that statecharts cannot be described by FAs in general. Thus, we make it clear for the first time that the statecharts of more than twenty years old are not variations of FAs.

---

* Work supported by the Natural Sciences and Engineering Research Council of Canada grant OGP0041630.

S. Maneth (Ed.): CIAA 2009, LNCS 5642, pp. 258–261, 2009.

Instead of FAs, we consider that the *Interaction Machines (IMs)*, introduced more than ten years ago by P. Wegner [5], are much more accurate theoretical models for statecharts. We will study the linkage between the statecharts and the interaction-based models.

2   Preliminaries

Although there have been various definitions of statecharts, the primary elements of statecharts are states, transitions, events, actions, conditions and variables. Note that variables are not explicitly described as elements of statecharts in a number of definitions [1,2,4]. However variables are actually an indispensable part of statecharts that constrains reactive behaviors. An example can be found in [3], where the original statecharts were introduced. The "wristwatch" is able to memorize an arbitrary alarm setting "T_1" and the watch will activate its alarm only when (the current time) "T hits T_1". The behavior of the alarm clock is depended on the setting history "T_1", which is modeled by a variable rather than several states. Although variables may imply infinite storage theoretically and this fact seems to imply that statecharts are not FAs automatically, we have to show that the unboundedness of variable values has been indeed used in the statechart model and that some statecharts do behave beyond the boundaries of FAs.

Formally, we define that a statechart S is a 9-tuple $(Q, E, A, C, V, \delta, \eta, s, T)$, where Q is the nonempty finite set of states; E is the nonempty finite set of events; C is the finite set of conditions; A is the finite set of actions; V is the finite set of variables; $\delta : Q \times E \times C^* \rightarrow Q$ is the transition function; $\eta : \delta \rightarrow A^*$ is the action function; s is the initial state; and $T \subseteq Q$ is the set of terminating states. Note that the variables of V are used in the actions of A and conditions of C.

Interaction Machines (IMs) were introduced more than ten years ago by P. Wegner [5], which are considered to be a further development of the Turing machine (TM) model. P. Wegner claims that TMs cannot model behaviors of interactive systems, such as operating systems and object-oriented systems. The computation of a TM is history-independent since it shuts out the world during its computation and stops after generating an output [5]. He introduced the IMs by extending TMs with dynamic streams to record interaction histories with the environment [6]. In [8] the Interactive Turing Machines (ITMs) are formally defined based on Wegner's IM model.

3   Statecharts Are Not Finite Automata

Clearly, many statecharts can be modeled by FAs. However, those facts do not imply that the computation power of statecharts is limited to that of FAs. In this section, we will show that there are statecharts that cannot be described by any FAs.

We look at a statechart M for an ATM model. The ATM can collect and dispense money to the identified clients and also maintain their information. The client can enter more than one request in each session before choosing "*Exit*".

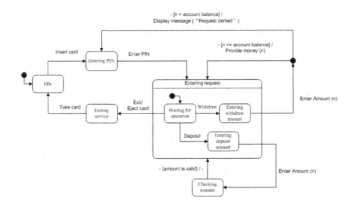

Fig. 1. A Statechart of an Automatic Teller Machine (ATM) model

However, withdrawing more money than the client's balance will never be accepted. The statechart M for the ATM model is shown in Figure 1.

Let M be $(Q, E, A, C, V, \delta, \eta, s, T)$. The event set E of M consists of *Insert card, Take card, Enter PIN, Withdraw, Deposit, Enter amount, Exit*, which are abbreviated to $E = \{i, t, p, w, d, a, e\}$. The state set Q of M consists of *Idle, Entering PIN, Waiting for operation, Entering withdraw amount, Entering deposit amount, Exiting service, Checking amount*, where the *Idle* state is the default starting state s as well as the terminating state, i.e., $s = Idle$ and $T = \{Idle\}$. In order to simplify the consideration, we assume that all *"withdraw"* and *"deposit"* requests process the same amount of money ($\$20$), and the subsequent "Enter amount" events are omitted. A larger amount of withdrawal or deposit is represented by the multiple copies of *withdraw* or *deposit*.

We consider the language of M in the following for simplicity. For each client, we consider the sequence of all events that the client has been involved from the very first session instead of only the current session. For example, the sequence of events of a client's first session is "ipddet" and that of the second session is "ipwet". Then we consider the word "ipddet" for the first and the word "ipddetipwet" for the second. Let L_M be the language of all such words that are acceptable by M. Each word in L_M may or may not be applied by a client. We can easily prove the following:

Theorem 1. L_M *is not a regular language.*

4   Statecharts and Interactive Turing Machines

In this section, we will discuss how the essential elements of statecharts and ITMs correspond to each other.

Let $S = (Q_S, E_S, A_S, C_S, V_S, \delta_S, \eta_S, s_S, T_S)$ be a statechart. Without loss of generality, we assume that S is a one-level statechart and interacts with only one source. We show that we can construct an equivalent multi-tape SITM as follows

$$M = (I_M, O_M, Q_M, \Gamma_M, \gamma_M, \omega_M, s_M, \#, \$, B, T_M).$$

The **state set** Q_S is represented by the state set Q_M of M. The set of **events** E_S is the set of inputs I_M of M. The set of **actions** A_S is divided into two categories: internal and external. The set of external action symbols correspond to the set of outputs, O_M, of M. The internal action symbols correspond to M's work tape symbols Γ. The performances of these two sets of actions of S correspond to the writing of M on the interaction tape and the work tapes, respectively. Note that an action in one transition of S may correspond to several steps of writing of M. New intermediate states may have to be introduced. The **variables** of V_S correspond to work tapes of M. The **conditions** in their original form are boolean-valued functions that can decide whether state transitions can take place. C_S is also divided into external and internal conditions. External conditions can be considered as events or combinations with events. The combinations with events can be considered as enlarged sets of events. They are all corresponding to the inputs of M. The internal conditions correspond to the values carried by M's work-tapes. The **transitions** in S are specified by source and target states, events, conditions and actions. Each transition in δ_S corresponds to one or more transitions in γ_M for the event and the conditions and also one or more transitions in ω_M for the actions. M may require more steps of transition because of the computation for conditions and actions. The **initial state** s_S and the set of **terminating states** T_S are just corresponding to s_M and T_M, respectively. Then, for any statechart, there is an equivalent ITM by the above descriptions.

The above descriptions give also the basic idea on how an SITM can be simulated by a statechart.

By the above arguments, we can conclude that the computation power of statecharts is the same as that of Interactive Turing machines.

References

1. Douglass, B.P.: UML statecharts. Tech. report, I - Logix (1999)
2. Drusinsky, D.: Modeling and Verification Using UML Statecharts. Elsevier Newnes, Oxford (2006)
3. Harel, D.: Statecharts: A visual formulation for complex systems. Sci. Comput. Program. 8(3), 231–274 (1987)
4. von der Beeck, M.: Formalization of UML-statecharts. In: Gogolla, M., Kobryn, C. (eds.) UML 2001. LNCS, vol. 2185, pp. 406–421. Springer, Heidelberg (2001)
5. Wegner, P.: Why interaction is more powerful than algorithms. CACM 40(5), 80–91 (1997)
6. Wegner, P.: Interactive foundations of computing. Theo. Comput. Sci. 192(2), 315–351 (1998)
7. Yu, S.: Regular Languages. In: Rozenberg, G., Salomaa, A. (eds.) Handbook of Formal Languages. LNCS, vol. 1. Springer, Heidelberg (1997)
8. Yu, S.: The time dimension of computation models. Where mathematics, computer science, linguistics and biology meet, 161–172 (2001)

Author Index